Principles and Practices of
TEACHING READING
Second Edition

Arthur W. Heilman
Pennsylvania State University

CHARLES E. MERRILL PUBLISHING COMPANY
A Bell & Howell Company
Columbus, Ohio

Library of Congress Catalog Card Number: 67-20192

Standard Book Number 675-09979-X

4 5 6 7 8 9 10/72 71 70 69 68

Printed in the United States of America

Preface

The rapidly advancing developments in the field of reading have, by necessity, brought about the second edition of *Principles and Practices of Teaching Reading.* New developments in the field of reading have been covered, including complete new chapters on Beginning Reading, Individualized Reading, Linguistics, and Study Skills. The principles of learning evolve rather slowly, and thus the chapter on principles, although expanded slightly, was not changed materially. Children as beginning readers also have not changed nearly as much as has beginning reading instruction; therefore, the chapter on beginning readers has not changed much while the material on beginning instruction has been expanded extensively. Other chapters have been revised and updated according to the trends brought about and supported by the most authoritative sources in the field of reading. Our criterion for revision has not been change for the sake of change, but change to support and expand the knowledge in theory and practice needed by the teacher.

Even as changes have taken place, the basic premises upon which the first edition of this book were written have not fundamentally altered:

This book is addressed to the teachers who are or will be trusted with the responsibility of teaching children to read. It is designed to assist the teacher in developing:

1. An understanding of child growth and behavior and the ability to relate this knowledge to the developmental process called reading.

2. An understanding of how children learn and an understanding of the factors which interfere with learning the complicated symbolic process of reading.
3. A wide array of techniques for teaching specific, immediate short-term goals in reading.
4. A set of principles to follow in teaching which will serve as a test for any method or technique employed.

The major objective of this book is to present a balanced combination of theory and suggested practices. Several portions of the book break new ground or at least extend discussion of particular problems beyond what is usually found in a book on teaching reading.

The first chapter presents principles which, it is advocated, should be followed in all teaching of reading. The point is stressed that violating sound principles of teaching leads to the production of reading problems, pupil problems, and teaching problems.

Emphasis is placed on the necessity of understanding the learner as a prerequisite of teaching him the complicated process called reading.

A chapter on sex differences in learning to read invites educators to see this as an educational problem and not just as a statistic.

The problem of teaching children who have experienced failure in learning to read is dealt with at some length. Although labeled *remedial reading,* the discussion in this book applies to any classroom in which such children are found. Concrete illustrations of procedures for dealing with specific reading problems are included.

The importance of a good start in beginning reading is stressed, but it is also emphasized that reading is a developmental process and that barriers to progress are found at all levels of instruction.

I wish to acknowledge members of the Editorial Production and Art staffs of Charles E. Merrill Publishing, particularly Miss Julia Estadt, Mrs. Madelon Aylwin, and Mr. Marc McIntosh, who worked with me on this second edition.

To the hundreds of instructors and thousands of students who read this book in its first edition, particularly to the many who offered valuable criticism and evaluation in their letters, comments, and reviews, I offer my sincere thanks. Their insight and knowledge are inevitably and gratefully reflected in this edition. Naturally, any errors of omission or commission are solely the responsibility of the author.

Arthur W. Heilman

April, 1967

Chapter opening photo credits

Chapter 1 — Courtesy H. Armstrong Roberts
Chapter 2 — Courtesy Northern Illinois University Regional Services, Joe Marsh, Photographer.
Chapter 3 — Courtesy H. Armstrong Roberts
Chapter 4 — Courtesy De Wys, Inc.
Chapter 5 — Courtesy De Wys, Inc.
Chapter 6 — Courtesy H. Armstrong Roberts
Chapter 7 — Courtesy Cincinnati Public Schools, Cincinnati, Ohio
Chapter 8 — Courtesy Cincinnati Public Schools, Cincinnati, Ohio
Chapter 9 — Courtesy De Wys, Inc.
Chapter 10 — Courtesy H. Armstrong Roberts
Chapter 11 — Courtesy H. Armstrong Roberts
Chapter 12 — Courtesy Los Angeles City School Districts
Chapter 13 — Courtesy H. Armstrong Roberts
Chapter 14 — Courtesy H. Armstrong Roberts
Chapter 15 — Courtesy H. Armstrong Roberts
Chapter 16 — Courtesy H. Armstrong Roberts
Chapter 17 — Courtesy H. Armstrong Roberts

Contents

To Rosemary

ANDY AND THE LION
OLA

Principles of Teaching Reading

1

During the past decade reading instruction in American schools has attracted the attention of a broad cross-section of citizens. While there were differences of opinion as to what should be done, there was general agreement that existing instruction was not adequate for the educational goals of our schools and our society. The importance of reading ability to the mastery of all subject matter areas was reaffirmed. Reading instruction ceased to be a matter of only local school and community concern and was viewed broadly as relating to the national welfare. The federal government, which had previously offered substantial support for science, mathematics, and foreign language education, began to channel support into research and teacher training in reading.*

*During the early 1960's only a limited number of reading research projects were supported by federal grants in the co-operative research program. In 1964 twenty-seven studies for first-grade reading instruction were supported and conducted simultaneously. The summer of 1965 marked the first support of teacher-training institutes devoted to reading.

In the wake of widespread interest in reading instruction, methodology and teaching materials received the bulk of attention. New "breakthroughs" were announced frequently. Allegedly new methods-materials were described superficially but enthusiastically in the popular press. Each new approach, the public was assured, was destined to revolutionize reading instruction in our schools while solving the problems which had plagued our schools for decades. This emphasis upon developing new materials represented a naive assumption that teaching materials represented the most important ingredient of effective reading instruction.

There is no question that materials are important. If materials could solve our reading problems, this would certainly be an easy and economical solution. But a more important factor than the materials themselves is what teachers do with them in the classroom. An affluent society such as ours should never permit the effects of good teaching to be diluted through the use of inadequate materials. On the other hand, pupil achievement which might accrue from the use of any materials is very much influenced by instruction; whether this be represented by a latter day Mark Hopkins, Louis Agassiz, or the latest computer-based instruction.

Unless teachers and educators can evaluate teaching materials and their impact on learning, reading instruction will likely be dominated by efficient advertising and public relations programs. Teachers must learn to ask pertinent questions which are relevant to sound educational goals, and evaluation of particular materials should determine how they propose to achieve these goals. To be meaningful, evaluation must be based on understanding of children as learners, reading as a learning process, and learning to read as a long-term developmental process. These concepts lead to a discussion of *principles* of reading instruction.

As the term is used here, "principles" of teaching reading are those basic rules which constitute the theoretical framework out of which all practices are evolved. The principles do not spell out the best procedures or practices for particular situations. However, when one accepts a set of principles, he will be inconsistent if he uses practices which violate the principles.

Principles are necessarily stated in broad and general terms, but if we are to understand their meaning, they should never be vague or nebulous. The principles of teaching reading evolve from the best knowledge available in the fields of psychology, educational psychology, and curriculum planning, from studies in child growth and development, and from child-guidance and psychological clinics. In formulating these principles, it is necessary to consider all facets of human growth and development, including the intellectual, physiological, and emotional.

Most teachers are familiar with the principles discussed in the following pages. Like scientific laws, the principles of teaching reading are subject to modification or repeal as new data are discovered and new theories erected on the basis of this data. Some readers will undoubtedly feel that one (or more) of the following principles is not absolutely valid. Such questioning is healthy, especially if it stimulates the formulation of rational alternatives. If the following principles are a sound basis for teaching reading at all levels of instruction, there are many practices in our schools which need to be re-examined.

PRINCIPLES

1. *Learning to read is a complicated process and is sensitive to a variety of pressures. Too much pressure or the wrong kind of pressure may result in non-learning.* A fact that attests to the complexity of the reading process is that authorities have never agreed on one definition of reading. There are, however, many statements about the complexity of reading on which experts would agree. One such statement is that reading involves more than the mechanical process of correctly pronouncing words—it involves the recognition of meaning. On the other hand, reading cannot be defined as getting the only correct meaning from written symbols. This definition cannot be reconciled with the variety of interpretations that good readers have given to the Constitution of the United States, laws on negligence, the Bible, or passages from Shakespeare. It is evident that such readers have brought something of themselves to the reading materials. Although reading cannot be defined as "what the reader brings to the reading situation," it is apparent that there must be interaction between the reader and the printed symbols. At the moment, "reading is thinking" has become a popular phrase, but the reading and thinking are not always synonymous. To modify this phrase to "critical reading is thinking while reading" will help to satisfy some readers and to frustrate others. Reading is not the simple sum of its parts, because in every case the reader must be considered in the process and each reader is unique. Reading always involves the simultaneous application of a great number of mechanical skills and comprehension skills, all of which are influenced by the reader's attitudes, knowledge, and past experience. Reading is a complicated process.

Reading is a language function. It is the manipulation of symbolic materials. Psychologists and other observers of human behavior tell us that the symbolic process is sensitive to pressures of any kind. It is axiomatic that language is the most sensitive indicator of personal or emotional maladjustment. Yet in no area of learning in our schools is greater pressure brought to bear on the pupil than in the area of reading. This is partly due to the high value which our society places on education and to the recognition that education is based on reading skill.

Often the school and the home present a united front in exerting overt and subtle pressures on the child. (6)* Reading is the first school task in which the child is deliberately or inadvertently compared with others in his peer group. It is the first task in which he must compete. How he fares in this competition has a tremendous impact on his ego, his concept of himself, and the attitudes of his peers toward him. But, most important, this is the first school activity in which his performance has a direct impact on his parents' egos. Parents may sense that their anxiety is not an intelligent or mature response. Insofar as the average parents can be coldly analytical of their motivation and involvement in their child's nonsuccess in reading, they know their feelings are never far below the surface. These feelings of disappointment are perceived by the child as a judgment that he does not measure up to parents' expectations.

Teachers are familiar with the sources of many of the pressures which converge on the child in a reading situation and which often become acute when a child experiences failure. Table I outlines some of these pressures along with possible psychological consequences.

A detailed discussion of the relationship between emotional problems and reading is found in Chapter 15. The examples cited here are intended to be illustrative rather than exhaustive.

2. *Learning to read is an individual process.* Although group activities associated with reading enhance the learning process and even though it is true that learning is partly a social process, each child in a group who learns how to read learns as an individual. The complicated stimuli confronting the child are mastered by an individual nervous system. Dividing a class into three or more smaller groups on the basis of reading ability may be a wise procedure, but this in itself will not teach the children how to read. Even though all children in the lowest group have the common characteristic that they are poor readers, grouping them physically

---

*Numbers in parentheses refer to numbered references at the end of the chapter.

TABLE 1

SOURCES OF PRESSURES ON CHILDREN EXPERIENCING DIFFICULTY IN READING

Pressure from home and parents	Parents are ego-involved in their child's success. They set "high goals" for him. They cannot hide their disappointment in their child's non-success.
Pressure from the child himself (stems from ego-needs and concept of self)	The child senses that he is not living up to parents' expectations. He feels that he is a failure. He has guilt feelings since he has let his parents down. He may develop a conscious or unconscious feeling that his parents have withdrawn affection. This becomes a further threat to the child's ego and security.
Pressure from school	Children's attitudes result from the competitive atmosphere fostered by adults (parents, school, teacher) and from the conformity pattern imposed by society. The child has a need to conform or measure up to norms set by the school or teacher and fears non-promotion. Non-readers are a threat to the teacher because they frustrate her ego need for success. Fortunately this is not true of all teachers.
Pressure from basal reading materials	Many basal reader series may pose a threat to some children since the home life of Dick, Jane, Sally, Billy, and Baby, etc., may not be at all like the environment of the child with home problems. Some children find it impossible to identify with these characters. Since they are rejected, they may unconsciously reject that which impinges on the "traumatic area." This idea is hypothetical. At present there are few experimental data to support it.

in the classroom and psychologically in the teacher's mind is of negligible value unless the teacher adjusts learning situations to each child's need for instruction.

3. *Pupil differences must be a primary consideration in reading instruction.* This implies that instruction cannot be dominated by the grade-level system, promotion practices, or graded instructional materials. It is hypothesized that any classroom will house pupils whose present achievement and instructional needs vary greatly. Identical educational experiences, particularly reading the same material, cannot be equally effective for all. Differentiation of both instruction and free-choice reading will inevitably result in larger pupil differences, which in turn will call for more differentiation.

4. *Reading instruction should be thought of as an organized, systematic growth-producing activity.* If any combination of strictly environmental factors will in the absence of systematic instruction produce optimum growth in reading, then instruction per se is superfluous. Sound instruction will start from the premise that the classroom environment is an integral part of instruction. The presence of adequate reading materials and the evolvement of a desirable classroom organization are prerequisites for good instruction. The absence of these precludes effective instruction, but their presence does not assure it.

5. *Proper reading instruction depends on the diagnosis of each child's weaknesses and needs.* This principle is applicable to ordinary classroom teaching, as well as to remedial reading. Individual diagnosis in reading has somehow become associated more with "retarded" readers and pupils with a clinical history of non-learning than with ordinary classroom procedure. Diagnosis has become associated too often with cure or remedy rather than with preventing the development of poor reading. In many cases, proper diagnosis will warn a teacher before bad habits or unhealthy emotional reactions cripple a potentially capable reader.

A survey test used as the basis for grouping children into poorest, average, and best categories is not in itself a diagnosis. To know that children A, B, and C are among the poorest in the class and that they are reading at least a year below their grade level tells us nothing about what it is that inhibits their reading progress. Nor does such a test tell us what aspect of reading should be attacked first in order to improve the child's reading. To establish the fact that a child is reading below what might be expected is not diagnosis. It is an invitation to diagnosis.

6. *The best diagnosis is useless unless it is used as a blueprint for instruction.* Diagnosis itself has no salutary effect on the per-

formance of the child tested. If diagnosis alone had salutary effects, it would be possible to raise a child's level of performance indefinitely by more and more diagnosis. It may be noted that extensive testing and metal filing cabinets full of individual folders do not necessarily make a better school. Testing in many American schools has become an end in itself. When test results are not used for instructional purposes, the educational objectives of the testing program are defeated.

There is no area of the curriculum in American schools more ideally suited to constant diagnosis than reading in the elementary and intermediate grades. The good teacher knows this and proceeds with continuous diagnosis of the children in her room. She knows that numerous factors inhibit progress in reading during this period. Any skill not mastered or only partially mastered may be instrumental in producing other reading problems. A teacher's manual or curriculum guide can point out a logical sequence for introducing skills and tasks, but it offers no help in determining what in the sequence has been learned. The manual or guide is like an artist's conception of the total edifice before it is constructed. Intelligent instruction must be based on accurate information regarding children's present accomplishments and weaknesses. In this sense, a thorough diagnosis is a blueprint for instruction.

7. *No child should be expected or forced to attempt to read material which at the moment he is incapable of reading.* Although applied here specifically to reading, this principle has a much wider application in our schools. All curriculum study and the placing of learning tasks at different points on the educational continuum are related to this principle. The principle should be followed in all areas of child growth and development—physical, social, emotional, intellectual. The principle amounts to a rejection of the myth that "the child is a miniature adult." We know that he is not. Today, informed teachers and parents expect the average child of six years to have developed social and emotional responses only to a level of maturity commensurate with his experience.

This principle is also related to the fact that different children develop at different rates and that the growth pattern of an individual child is not uniform. The data from which we derive norms or averages of physical, emotional, social, and intellectual growth warn us that there are differences in rates of development. The principle does not imply that children should avoid difficult tasks or that a child should be able to read a passage perfectly before he attempts to read it. It does imply that we cannot expect a child to perform up to a given standard when at the moment he is incapable of such performance. To do this is to expect the impossible.

The following episode, although it illustrates the point under discussion, is not advanced as being representative of teacher practice. Arrangements were made in an elementary school for thorough testing of a number of pupils who were not making expected academic progress. One fourth grade boy could read successfully no higher than primer level. The counselor inquired of the boy's teacher what reading program the boy was following. The teacher explained that for a while she had the boy attempt to read third grade materials. Failing in these, he was given second grade materials with no better success. Since the boy read these materials no better than he read the fourth grade texts, the teacher concluded that he might as well read the fourth grade books. Teachers who would not endorse this solution may occasionally expect a child to do what he cannot do at the moment. Untold numbers of pupils face such a situation, and probably more instances occur because of lack of reading ability than for all other reasons combined.

A given child may have average or superior ability but may be below grade norm today in his reading. With proper guidance, he may later master the reading process commensurate with his overall ability. Each child is entitled to the best guidance available. It is not conducive to social, emotional, or educational growth to subject a child to failure experiences because he is physically present in a classroom where arbitrary achievement goals have been set.

8. *Reading is a process of getting meaning from printed word symbols. It is not merely a process of making conventionalized noises associated with these symbols.* This principle means that reading is more than a mechanical process, even though mechanics are an essential part of the process. Mechanical word-calling is not reading any more than a parakeet making the noises "pretty-bird-sing-sing" can properly be said to be using language. Because of the limitations of children just beginning to read and the necessity for repetition of a relatively small number of words in beginning instruction, one might easily confuse beginning reading with the mechanics of reading.

The principle stated above has been phrased with a view to avoiding certain semantic quicksands. By not using the phrase "reading is the process of getting *the* meaning," an attempt has been made to avoid the implication that there is one and only one meaning which every reader gets from reading the same passage. This could not be achieved if it were a goal of teaching reading.

Creativity and versatility are basic requirements for successful teaching. Children enjoy depicting ideas and concepts through characterization. Personal experiences bring word symbols to life. (Photo courtesy H. Armstrong Roberts.)

9. *Any given technique, practice, or procedure is likely to work better with some children than with others. Hence, the teacher of reading must have a variety of approaches.* Virtually every method and procedure described in the vast literature on reading is reported to have been successful with some children and unsuccessful with others. Creativity and versatility are basic requirements for successful teaching. If a teacher begins to take sides in methodological squabbles or if she begins to crystalize her ideas on an either/or basis, she is likely to be less receptive to other points of view and approaches which may be helpful to her teaching.

Authorities in the field of reading are in general agreement that "There is no one best method of teaching." The evidence indicates that one method is not necessarily superior to another. Regardless of the efficiency of a given method of teaching reading, it will produce its share of problem cases and impaired readers if used exclusively. If there are significant individual differences in the way children learn to read, it follows that different approaches are advisable. Unfortunately, children do not have identifiable characteristics which make it possible to know at a glance which approach will yield the highest return in learning. It is for this reason that flexibility, ingenuity, and creativity are essential to successful teaching, and particularly for teaching reading.

When a teacher becomes enamored of one method to the exclusion of others, she shuts out the possibility of adjusting method to individual pupil needs. Although such a teacher may be highly successful in teaching some of her pupils, she will inevitably produce a number of frustrated, unhappy misfits in the educational arena. If she is authoritarian and presses hard, some of her pupils will develop behaviors which result in such labels as "bad," "dull," "dreamers," "lazy," and "anti-social." These behaviors, instead of being interpreted as the logical psychological outcome of failure, frustration, and tension evolving from the reading situation, become in turn the explanations of why the child failed in reading.

10. *Learning to read is a long-term developmental process extending over a period of years.* This principle rests on two premises. First, every aspect of the instructional program is related to the ultimate goal of producing efficient readers. This is particularly important in light of the many recent "newer approaches" to beginning reading instruction. What is done during this period influences the child's concept as to what constitutes reading. In other words, beginning reading instruction can inculcate any one of a number of pupil "sets."

The second premise is that the child's early attitude toward reading is important from the educational standpoint. It can influence a student's reading habits for life. Nothing should be permitted to happen in beginning instruction which impairs later development of efficient reading.

There are several approaches to beginning reading which may result in a "fast start" or relatively high achievement at the end of a year of intensive instruction. The materials used stress analysis of letter sounds and, in the opinion of some observers, fail to achieve a balanced program. The overemphasis on analysis permits rapid initial growth, but carries with it the potential of producing readers who over learn this specific technique. Some pupils will tend to overrely on analysis to the detriment of smooth facile reading.

The question which teachers must answer is, "Do higher reading achievement scores at the end of grade one establish the procedures and materials used as the best approach to *beginning reading instruction?*" If principle 10 is accepted as valid, the question cannot be answered on the basis of the short-term achievement.

11. *The concept of readiness should be extended upward to all grades.* Few teachers maintain that readiness applies more to one level of education than to another. Nevertheless, in the area of reading, there seems to be a predilection for associating readiness with beginning or first grade reading. This is the level at which we have "readiness tests," and much of the literature on readiness is concerned with the beginning reader. Even though readiness has been achieved at one level of experience, it does not necessarily follow that readiness is retained at a higher level of experience. There should be as much concern with readiness at the third-, fourth-, or sixth-grade levels as there is at the first-grade level.

A good start is an important factor in the learning process. But a good start is not always half the race because reading is a continuous developmental process. What is learned today is the foundation for what is learned tomorrow. A smooth, unfaltering first step is not a guarantee that succeeding steps will be equally smooth. For example, some children display no complications in the learning process until they are asked to sound out a number of words not known at sight. At this point they encounter difficulties, the degree of which could not have been predicted on the basis of readiness tests administered in the first grade. Even so, some of these failures stem from non-readiness for the experience.

12. *Early in the learning process the child must acquire ways of gaining independence in identifying words whose meanings are known to him but which are unknown to him as sight words.* Pronouncing words is not reading, but sounding out words not known as sight words is essential in independent reading. The more widely a child reads, the less likely it is that he will know every word he meets as a sight word. Hence, developing independence in reading depends on acquiring methods of unlocking the pronunciation of words. The clues used in identifying words are discussed in later chapters. These include unique configuration of words, structural

analysis (prefixes, suffixes), context clues, and phonic analysis. Phonics is undoubtedly the most important of the word analysis skills.

The recently completed co-operative First Grade Reading Studies* reported data on a number of methodological issues. In many instances the data failed to reveal any clear cut superiority for particular instructional procedures and materials. However, in regard to the efficacy of teaching letter-sound relationships, the findings were remarkably uniform. Programs of instruction which featured systematic phonics instruction resulted in consistently superior pupil reading achievement when compared with programs which did not.

The principle just discussed is not in conflict with number eight above which states that the child must see reading as a meaning-making process. To read for meaning, one must be able to recognize printed word forms. Those words which are not instantly recognized must be analyzed by associating printed letters with speech sounds.

13. *Children should not be in the classroom if they have emotional problems sufficiently serious to make them uneducable at the moment or if they interfere with or disrupt the learning process.* Physical disturbances such as a slight temperature, an inflamed throat, an abscessed tooth, or a skin blemish are cause for removing a child from the classroom. Many schools require that children not come to school until inoculated against certain diseases; other schools strongly urge these precautions. These measures seem natural and logical today. The suggestion that children with serious emotional problems get their maladies corrected as a condition for attending school will probably be scoffed at—today. Tomorrow the concept of emotional health will be as readily accepted as the concept of physical health. Just as the practice of "beating the devil" out of the "obsessed" came to an end, so we will stop trying to beat learning into a child who is at the moment uneducable.

The reason for emphasizing emotional health in a book on reading is that our entire educational structure is based on the ability to read. One of the principles stated earlier was that a child should not be expected to do something he cannot do. When a child is uneducable because of serious emotional involvements and we persist in drilling him on sight words when he cannot learn at the moment, we are violating this earlier principle. Unless the class-

*See Chapter 4 for further discussion of these studies.

room teacher can overcome the barrier to learning, the uneducable child should be removed for treatment and returned when he is educable. The vast majority of youngsters with emotional problems can be helped with personal and environmental therapy. If the emotional problem is not severe, it is possible for some children to continue in school while receiving outside treatment; in some cases the treatment can take place in the classroom, concurrently with the regular learning situation. In the latter type of case, the teacher is a key factor.

14. *Emphasis should be on prevention rather than cure. Reading problems should be detected early and corrected before they deteriorate into failure-frustration-reaction cases.* However excellent the instruction in our schools, some children will not profit as much as others. The early detection of impairments and immediate attention to them are cornerstones of effective reading instruction. Although this is obvious, the emphasis in our schools is still on cure, not prevention. The following discussion of school practices explains in part how this came about.

Recently reading instruction in American schools has been under heavy criticism. Parallel with the criticism emerged many new materials, suggested modifications in practice, and suggested shifts in philosophy. A few of the methodological emphases include i/t/a, language-experience materials, individualized reading, words in color, and integration of writing with beginning reading instruction. Questions raised include: "Is readiness training essential? Should the content of instructional materials parallel children's language usage? Should initial reading instruction consist primarily of teaching letter-sound relationships?"

Reading instruction seems particularly susceptible to overenthusiasm for whatever bears the label "new." Too often, highly publicized "new approaches" capture the attention of the general public and of a number of educators. Based on the publicity the method-materials receive, one might surmise they would soon be in universal use. Generally, interest wanes, and approaches heralded as breakthroughs are deserted for some other new approach in which interest builds to a peak and then recedes. (14)

During periods of ferment, such as the present, it is easy to lose sight of fundamental principles of instruction. Much time and energy can be spent in climbing on and off so-called "instructional bandwagons." Occasionally a "new emphasis" in instruction emerges which has some excellent features but which may neglect certain essentials while overemphasizing others. To illustrate, assume one agrees with the principles discussed above. It is still possible to overemphasize one or more to such a degree that others are either ignored or actually violated.

Sound principles of reading instruction should apply with equal validity to any instructional approach; and by definition such principles cannot reflect what might be called an either-or bias as to particular methodologies. If a set of principles are valid criteria for instructional practices, a sound reading program cannot be built by paying lip service to several valid assumptions while making only one the cornerstone of instruction.

SCHOOL PRACTICES WHICH INTERFERE WITH TEACHERS' FOLLOWING SOUND PRINCIPLES

It is logical that a book on teaching reading should open with a statement of the principles upon which good teaching is based. For principles should evolve ahead of practices so that teacher and school practices can be evaluated in light of these principles. The view accepted here is that the principles formulated above are sound and that teachers who find them so should follow them in teaching reading. Some of the techniques used by teachers in their daily practice may inadvertently or unconsciously inhibit them from applying the principles which they have accepted as sound and desirable.

With a particular principle in mind, a teacher may use practices which violate another principle because she fails to recognize that both impinge on the case at hand. According to one principle, proper instruction depends on individual diagnosis of each child's weaknesses and needs. According to another, diagnosis is useless unless used as a blueprint for instruction. It has been pointed out that the act of administering a diagnostic instrument has no salutary effect on poor readers. A series of standardized tests which disclose a number of weaknesses in the mechanics of reading may lead to instruction aimed at specific weaknesses and still be ineffective because some other principle has been overlooked.

For example, assume an impaired reader is given a series of standardized reading tests and an intelligence test. Frank W., age 9 years, 6 months; I.Q. 112; reading level 2-0. Specific weaknesses include inadequate sight vocabulary, inability to sound unknown words, mispronouncing small service words, omitting words, and substitutions. The boy appears cooperative, but his attention span is short. He states that he wishes to learn to read. With these data in hand the teacher may feel that the logical procedure is to launch into work aimed at mastering sight words and phonic analysis. A factor not taken into consideration was Frank's attitude toward reading and his attitude toward his ability to learn to read. These were such that, even though Frank seemed passive, cooperative, and compliant, he was so emotionally upset by being confronted with reading tasks that no amount of individual help that embraced help only in reading would have the desired results. The lack of overt behavior symptoms may have been a factor in the teacher's failure to perceive Frank's serious emotional involvement in reading. At the moment he was incapable of harnessing energy for the task. What the teacher interpreted as individual help was to Frank undue pressure. Reading materials threatened him, as did his teacher's knowledge of his weaknesses. He adjusted better while lost in the class than he did to individual work in reading. Thus principles three and four above, though sound in themselves, were not an adequate basis for procedure until other principles were made a part of the total picture.

As a matter of habit a teacher may follow sound principles even though she does not verbalize them. She grades carefully all lessons in the reading workbook and works individually with children as they correct errors. She explains and re-explains the basic idea of the lesson. She works with different children on different aspects of the reading process. When asked what she is doing, she may reply: "I am providing drill for the children who need it. John needs drill on hearing the long sound of vowels. Mike is confused by figurative language. He always tries to get a concrete meaning from these sentences. 'The man pulled the horses to the side of the road.' Mike said that the man got down from the seat and dragged the horses off the road. He was confused also by 'the bird ate on the wing.' I have had some materials dittoed that are not found in the workbook he is using. He is working on these now. On the other hand, Mary breezes through the pages of examples on figurative language, so I had her write five other examples. She came up with some pretty high-level examples. She certainly doesn't need any more drill on this phase of reading."

While this activity might be construed as drill, it happens that it follows logically from some of the principles of reading we have just reviewed, namely:

1. Proper instruction is dependent on individual diagnosis.
2. Diagnosis is useless unless used as a blueprint for instruction.

3. Reading is a process of getting meaning.
4. Any given practice is likely to work better with some children than with others. (Mike could not have done what Mary did because he missed the point of the exercise. Therefore, to ask him to write new illustrations of figurative language would have violated other principles we have discussed.)

School Practices Affecting Instruction

Most defections from sound principles of teaching reading probably stem from undesirable classroom conditions. For the most part, these conditions are institutionalized practices that have become part of American education. The practices have often evolved from economic pressures or community pressures, sometimes advocated as emergency measures. It is doubtful if any of these practices have been accepted because someone thought that they would enhance the quality of American education.

Schools do not deliberately produce non-readers or impaired readers, but educators often sacrifice sound principles and practices in the face of pressure. Emergencies produce compromises which tend to become permanent. These compromises often become standard procedure to such an extent that after a while they are defended on the basis that "we've been doing this for years." Some of the more obvious school practices which prevent teachers from doing as well as they know how are listed below.

Class Size. Classes containing thirty-five to forty students are, unfortunately, numerous.* Teachers of reading in these classrooms complain that they cannot do the job. They mean that they cannot find time for thorough, ongoing diagnosis and individual programs for the children who need individual help. If this is true, large classes prevent teachers from following some of the principles we have discussed.

When conditions force one sound principle to be ignored, it is likely that other principles will also be violated. Some children will be expected to read materials which are too difficult. When a

---

*Some data relative to class size are misleading. Some school systems may report class size or pupil-teacher ratio as somewhat smaller than is actually the case. This can occur when supervising personnel, school counselors, nurses, psychologists, speech therapists, etc., are included as instructional staff. Class size, as used in this discussion, refers to the actual mean number of children present in one teacher's classroom during the school year.

teacher lacks an accurate picture of a child's ability and specific reading weaknesses, she will have a tendency to expect him to read at grade level. When this happens, another danger is that pressures both overt and subtle will be brought on the child experiencing failure. These pressures are not conducive to reading facility, at least not for all children.

Too often teachers are not aware that they work under conditions which prevent them from applying sound reading principles. But if teaching is a profession, the violation of sound principles of teaching is unprofessional. There is a tendency to absolve teachers of responsibility for teaching practices resulting from over-crowded classrooms with the statement that the community desires large classes or that teachers have no recourse since class size is an administrative decision. Teachers who feel responsible for making professional decisions will perceive that these arguments are rationalizations. (7)

Promotion Versus Concept of Mastery of Skills. The problems arising from large classes are compounded by the widespread school practice of universal or almost universal promotion. We are not concerned here with the merits of promotion versus retention, but rather with pointing up the inevitable results of our present-day practices.

Our schools are set up on a grade-level basis in which the curricula of the various grades are progressively more difficult. Everyone agrees that the learning tasks in the second grade are more difficult than those in the first. This is inherent in the grade-level system. This arrangement is obviously logical, but the logic implies that children in the second grade have mastered the skills taught in the first grade, because the second grade curriculum is based on the assumption of mastery of first grade skills. In similar manner, the third grade curriculum is based on skills presumably mastered in the second grade.

As school systems adopted the practice of social promotion, one might expect that the grade-level concept would be abandoned or drastically revised. In the majority of our schools neither of these things happened. The result is that today we find children moving from grade to grade mainly because they have been physically present in a particular grade for an academic year. True, many children master the skills required for the next year's curriculum, but many do not. And when many do not, the grade-level concept is unsound because it was not designed to function under these conditions. The higher the grade level under consideration, the more apparent becomes the inadequacy of our efforts to impose automatic promotion on a graded system. When we attempt to justify automatic promotion on the grounds that it is psychologically sound because promotion prevents failure, we are being unrealistic in our concept of failure. Children who progress through the grades without adequate skills to deal with the tasks expected of them experience failure every day they attend school.

The foregoing is not intended to imply that non-promotion is desirable. Such data as we have on retaining students in the same grade for another year indicate that this is also an ineffective practice. A truly ungraded primary school will accept various levels of competency. As students master certain skills, they move on to the next level of tasks. The emphasis on promotion abates and each child moves at his own pace.*

Non-Teaching Activities In and Out of the Classroom. In addition to the increase in class size, there have been many other encroachments on the teacher's time and energy which leave less time for teaching. It is disturbing, especially during a time of acknowledged teacher shortages and increased class size, that teachers are compelled to fill out complicated daily attendance forms, collect lunch money, supervise playgrounds before school and during recess periods, supervise the cafeteria, collect tickets at athletic events, sponsor and advise student organizations, attend frequent staff meetings on their own time, and serve as members of school committees and P.T.A. These activities are closely related to children's failure to learn. A tired, harassed teacher can hardly be expected to be an effective teacher. A teacher responsible for a host of administrative duties will have less time and energy for creative teaching activities. It is unfortunate when teachers accept these encroachments which reduce teacher effectiveness and contribute to the failure and maladjustment of students.

Teacher morale and effectiveness of instruction would be greatly increased if teachers could have short periods of time, morning and afternoon, when they are completely free of all school activities and pressures—free from children, grading workbooks, preparing records, and filling out forms. Teachers now enjoying such free periods may be surprised to learn that many teachers do not.

Disinclination to Base Instruction on Readiness. As noted earlier, reading readiness is a factor in reading at all levels. At the moment,

---

*See Chapter 5 for a discussion of the ungraded primary plan.

however, let us concern ourselves with beginning reading. According to prevailing theory, reading readiness activities blend almost imperceptibly into formal instruction. In practice, most first grade teachers follow a schedule of a given number of weeks of readiness activities, including tests of readiness, followed by instruction in reading materials. Some teachers are quick to point out that all students do not start on the same day with the latter materials. Others point out that while they start their pupils together, they do not insist that all progress at the same rate. They point out that these practices are followed because of differing degrees of readiness among pupils.

Rarely does the teacher withhold reading materials from the least ready for more than a few weeks after the rest of the class has started to use them. As a rule, teachers readily admit that some of their pupils are not ready for formal instruction, but the instruction is begun. Ironically, teachers frequently rationalize these practices on the grounds that "parents insist that their child start reading" or that "the school administration expects it." This is another example of teacher knowledge being far ahead of practice. If teachers are professionally qualified, it is essential that they work toward achieving conditions in which it will not be necessary for them to sacrifice their professional integrity and their pupils' psychological well-being because of pressures from the community.

School Entrance Based on Chronological Age. Another school practice that tends to produce problems in the teaching of reading is the use of chronological age as the criterion for admitting children to school. Educators generally agree that instruction should be based on readiness for attempting the tasks to be performed. Once the school and community accept the chronological-age criterion for entering school, however, it is a simple step for parents and communities to reason: "Johnny is six years old. Therefore, he is ready for school."

Systematic Reading Instruction Not Found in Upper Grades. Reading is taught systematically in the elementary grades. Reading instruction is part of the curriculum. As we go upward in the grades, more reading is required, but instruction in reading is not as systematic as in the lower grades. In practice, reading seems to be regarded as a skill to be acquired in the elementary and intermediate grades and used in all areas of the curriculum from that point on. Although most schools and teachers know that many children need thorough, planned, deliberate instruction above the sixth grade, they are also aware that systematic instruction at these levels is lacking.

At the junior high and high school levels we tend to rely more on slogans than planned instruction. "Every teacher is a teacher of reading" is such a slogan. The slogan does not fit the facts because some teachers are not qualified to teach reading. The job calls for specific training, knowledge, and skills, just as it does at lower grade levels. It is wrong to assume that poor readers will outgrow poor reading habits when they reach these grades, and it is wrong to assume that poor readers will read widely and better because they have more reading assigned in these grades. If children entering seventh and eighth grades had mastered the fundamental reading skills required for the reading tasks in these grades, present practices in our schools would be justified. Research data for these upper grades tell a different story. It has been found that in these grades about one in four students functions at a level one grade below actual placement; more than 10 per cent function at a level two grades below, and 5 per cent at three grades below placement. (15)

More and more we hear criticism that students are not proficient readers and that they cannot meet the demands of the curriculum. There is a growing consensus that one of the major ills of our educational system is that the systematic teaching of reading is terminated too early.

These are a few of the school practices which have led observant teachers to the conclusion that we do not live in the best of all educational worlds. In our schools we have the ready and the non-ready; we have increased class size to the point that the teacher finds it impossible to deal adequately with the problems of the individual child; we have adopted the practice of almost universal promotion while clinging to a grade-level concept based on mastery of skills taught in preceding grades. There are few schools which teach reading systematically beyond the sixth grade. If one examines these practices separately, he might conclude that they are exclusively administrative in nature. But when one looks at the effect of the whole group of practices on what happens in the classroom, he cannot escape the conclusion that they have a considerable impact on instruction.

Although this book has been designed as a guide for teaching reading, *how to teach* cannot be divorced from the environment in which teaching must take place. Specific methods for dealing with some of these problems are discussed later, but it is beyond the scope of this book to attempt a prescription for bringing about needed changes in the structure of American education. Certainly the school practices just discussed cannot be modified by individual teachers. Thus, the teacher who is a trained professional in the classroom finds that she has little control over a number of school practices which determine the degree to which she can apply what she knows about teaching reading. These practices, which have prevented or militated against teachers' assuming the role of competent professionals, have also been contributing factors in the production of reading problems as well as teaching problems.

YOUR POINT OF VIEW?

The problems following each chapter are not intended primarily to test recall of material presented. The problems may serve as a basis for class discussion or, in some instances, library research papers.

YOUR POINT OF VIEW?

Defend or attack the following statements.

1. Chronological age is the most practical and most justifiable criterion for having children enter school.

2. Parents' ego-involvement in their child's learning to read is a causal factor in many reading failures and is a major problem for the schools and first grade teachers.

3. Teachers have erred in accepting non-teaching activities as part of their occupational obligation.

4. There is little basis for assuming that the school can prevent a substantial number of reading failures among pupils.

5. "Individual differences in achievement increase as we move upward through the grades." Which one of the following factors would you prefer to defend as being most important in effecting these differences in achievement? Why?
    A. Pupil ability
    B. School promotion policies
    C. Competency of instruction
    D. Factors outside the school

6. Assume that the use of standardized reading tests in the elementary grades was prohibited for the next five years. Suggest logical hypotheses as to what would happen in reading instruction if this unlikely event occurred.

7. Assume that you are assigned the task of improving the teaching of reading in your state and that you can eliminate or modify *one* school practice which is now prevalent. What would be your recommendation? Why?

BIBLIOGRAPHY*

1. Cutts, Warren G. (ed.), *Teaching Young Children to Read,* Washington: U.S. Office of Education, Bulletin No. 19, 1964.

*Bibliographies contain references cited in the text and other selected reference works.

2. Dewey, John, "The Primary Education Fetish," *Forum,* XXV (May 1898), 315-28.

3. Dodson, Dan W., "Factors Influencing Curriculum Development," *Review of Educational Research,* XXVII (June 1957), 262-69.

4. Gray, William S., and Nancy Larrick (eds.), *Better Readers for Our Times,* International Reading Association Conference Proceedings, 1, 1956. New York: Scholastic Magazines, Part 4.

5. Greene, Harry A., and Walter T. Petty, *Developing Language Skills in the Elementary School.* Boston: Allyn and Bacon, Inc., 1959, Chapter 1.

6. Ilg, Frances L., and Louise Bates Ames, *School Readiness.* New York: Harper and Row Publishers, 1965.

7. Lieberman, Myron, *Teaching as a Profession.* Englewood Cliffs, New Jersey: Prentice-Hall, Inc., 1956.

8. McKee, Paul, *The Teaching of Reading.* Boston: Houghton Mifflin Co., 1948.

9. McKim, Margaret G., Carl W. Hansen, and William L. Carter, *Learning to Teach in the Elementary School.* New York: The Macmillan Company, 1959, Chapter 2.

10. Morrison, Coleman (ed.), *Children Can Learn to Read . . . But How?* Rhode Island College Reading Conference Proceedings. Providence, Rhode Island: Oxford Press, 1964.

11. Oliver, W. A., "Teachers' Educational Beliefs versus Their Classroom Practices." *Journal of Educational Research,* XLVII (September 1953), 47-55.

12. Rowland, Thomas D., and Calvin C. Nelson, "Off to School—At What Age?" *Elementary School Journal,* LX (October 1959).

13. Slagle, Allen T., "What Is the Tack of Our Schools?" *Elementary School Journal,* LX (December 1959), 140-45.

14. Smith, Nila Banton, *Reading Instruction for Today's Children.* Englewood Cliffs, New Jersey: Prentice-Hall, Inc., 1963.

15. Stroud, J. B., *Psychology in Education* (rev. ed.). New York: Longmans, Green and Co., 375-77.

16. Thorndike, Edward L., "Reading as Reasoning: A Study of Mistakes in Paragraph Reading," *Journal of Educational Psychology,* VIII (June 1917), 323-32.

5
5
Happy Birthday
to

Preparing for Reading

2

THE TASK OF THE SCHOOL

Every generation has questioned its educational system, its school's curriculum, and the school's current methodology in teaching basic subjects. Questions such as education for whom and education for what have apparently never been answered satisfactorily, because these questions continue to be asked again and again. At the present time, debate on the question of what courses of study will sharpen the mind and prepare children for living in tomorrow's world is particularly intense. Past technological advances may have caused each generation to believe that the educational problems facing it were greater than at any other time in the nation's history. Nevertheless, it is doubtful whether we have ever been further away from understanding our environment and our major problems than we are today. This dilemma raises the question of how a people who do not understand the world in which they now live can devise a curriculum that will prepare their children for *tomorrow*—a tomorrow which will undoubtedly make today's science fiction appear workaday and unimaginative.

This "cultural lag" in education has made the job of the school so complicated and involved that frustration is inevitable. Yet there is one element in yesterday's curriculum which is equally germane to today's world and also the best hope for preparing today's children for tomorrow. This is the mastery of communication skills. Without knowing what will be important and worthwhile tomorrow, we know that what will be essential and worthwhile in science, the arts, and the humanities will belong to those who can read. Keeping its eye on the future, the school cannot be content with teaching a number of interesting facts about the remarkable world in which the pupils live. It must teach skills as rapidly as possible so that these pupils can mine the vast mountain of knowledge available to them.

The first step in teaching the developmental process called reading is to provide guidance aimed at getting the learner ready for the various tasks involved in the process.

CONCEPT OF READING READINESS

Children begin school on the basis of chronological age. While this practice has some virtue from the standpoint of administration, it has little relationship to learning the complicated process of reading. Many children are absorbed into a school environment that resembles an assembly line approach to education. Each child is expected to move x distance along an instructional continuum in a specified time. Much of this depersonalized atmosphere in education can be traced to the grade-level structure which has dominated American education for some time.

Some children are not ready to move at a predetermined rate, and others are handicapped because they are ready to move faster than this prescribed pace. One of the major misconceptions with respect to the readiness period is that it consists of a more or less fixed program in which every child participates in the same activities for the same length of time. Such a program would negate the known facts relative to individual differences among pupils.

A good readiness program will be characterized by flexibility. Briefly, the purpose of this period is to lay the foundation upon which later maximum success in reading can be built. The readiness period is not a waiting period but a highly structured, deliberately teacher-planned program. It is not aimed at removing individual differences among pupils, but at seeing that each child has experiences which will remove blocks to learning. It can be thought of as a filling in and smoothing out process. There must be no gaps in the foundation upon which reading skill is to be built. (20)

The readiness period attempts to synthesize new experiences with the previous experiences that children have had. These previous experiences, or the lack of them, are extremely important, since they determine to a large degree the kind and the amount of experience that is still needed and which the school must provide prior to formal instruction in reading. How accurately the teacher discerns what is still needed and how successful she is in filling these needs may well be the most important factor in determining each child's later success or failure in reading.

Assessment of Readiness

Differences between pupils when they enter school have a considerable influence on achievement in school. This fact has given rise to efforts to determine "which differences" have the most significant impact on learning to read. Do certain experiences—previous learnings, or acquired skills—tend to make some children preferred risks and others poor risks in a beginning reading program? If this question could be answered unequivocally, the school would have the information necessary for beginning or withholding formal instruction until essential criteria were met by each pupil. Even though precise measurement is lacking, most schools attempt to measure pupils' readiness for reading through the use of methods presently available.

Reading Readiness Tests

These tests are standardized instruments designed to assess the child's ability to profit from formal instruction in reading. They fulfill their purpose insofar as they predict success in learning to read. That is, the score made on the test itself must be indicative of what can be expected in achievement in reading during the first year or two of formal reading instruction.

The term *readiness* applies to all facets of development as well as to subject-matter achievement at all grade levels. Nevertheless, the term *reading readiness test* applied for many years exclusively to the first grade, and to a large extent still refers to instruments devised to measure skills related to success in *beginning* reading. The discussion here is concerned with the general topic of reading readiness tests and not with an attempt to compare the values of different tests.

Readiness tests are, as a rule, administered as group tests. Some tests are primarily group tests but may contain one or more subtests which must be given individually. Examples of such subtests include appraisal of the child's ability to recognize letters of the alphabet or tell whether words rhyme. In general, readiness tests contain items which attempt to measure physiological maturity, comprehension of spoken language, ability to perceive similarities and differences, ability to follow directions, and ability to draw simple figures. Representative test items include:

1. *Associating pictured objects with the spoken word for that object.* The child has before him a series of four or five pictures in a line running across the page. The pictures might be of a frog, a boat, a shoe, and a turkey. He is asked to "underline (or circle) the shoe."
2. *Visual discrimination.* Four or five similar objects are shown. One is already circled or checked. One other picture in the row is exactly like this one. The child is to mark the identical picture. Variations of this test include the recognition of one or more digits or letters which are identical to the stimulus at the beginning of the line.
3. *Sentence comprehension.* The child must grasp the meaning of an entire sentence. Before him are pictures of a calendar, clock, lawnmower, and thermometer. "Mark the one which tells us the time."
4. *Drawing a human figure.* In a space provided on the test booklet, the child is asked to draw a man or a woman.
5. *Ability to count and to write numbers.* A series of identical objects are shown, and the child is told to mark the second, fourth, or fifth object from the left.

   To test his ability to recognize digits, he is told to underline or put an "X" on one digit in a series.
6. *Word recognition.* A common object (doll, house, barn, cow, man, etc.) is pictured. Three or four words, including the symbol for the picture, are shown, and the child is to mark the word represented by the picture.
7. *Copying a model.* A series of geometric figures and capital letters serve as models. The child is to duplicate the stimulus.

8. *Auditory discrimination.* On a group test this might consist of a series of pictures placed horizontally across the page. At the left of each series is a stimulus picture. The child marks each object in the series whose name begins with the same initial sound as the name of the stimulus. If the first picture is that of a dog, for example, it might be followed by illustrations of a doll, a cow, a door, and a ball. Another test situation would be marking each picture whose name rhymes with the name of the stimulus picture.

Readiness tests vary as to the types of skills tested. Some of the earlier tests lack provision for measuring auditory discrimination, but most of the more recently published tests include such a subtest. In general, norms are based on total scores which determine pupil placement in categories such as superior, above average, average, or poor. Since the chief objective of readiness tests is prediction of success in learning to read, it is hoped that the test will separate the ready from the non-ready and that when first grade pupils are thus identified, the school will adjust the curriculum accordingly. This brings us to the question of how accurately reading readiness tests predict success in beginning reading.

Predictive Value of Readiness Tests

In general, the experimental data indicate a positive relationship between scores on readiness tests and success in beginning reading, although readiness scores alone cannot be used as predictors of success in reading. Bremer (8) tested over 2,000 first graders with a reading readiness test and later with a test of reading achievement. He reported only a moderate relationship between the scores on the two tests. Studies also report that teacher estimates of pupil success in reading, made without a knowledge of readiness test scores, correlate as high with achievement as do the actual test scores. (22) Karlin (28) studied over one hundred first grade children, all of whom had an I.Q. of 90 or above, had attended kindergarten, and had no serious visual, hearing, or emotional problem. He found a correlation of .36 between scores on the Metropolitan Reading Readiness Test administered in September and achievement on the Gates Primary Reading Test (paragraph) administered at the end of the school year. In this study, prediction of reading achievement based on readiness test scores was only about 4 per cent superior to teacher prediction made in the absence of the readiness data. Karlin concluded, "The confidence which teachers place in the concept of reading-readiness is well merited, but the desirability of using existing reading-readiness tests almost exclusively to measure extent of readiness should be re-examined."

Lee et al., (30) testing 164 first grade children, found a correlation of .49 between scores on the Lee-Clark Readiness Test and the Lee-Clark Primary Reading Test and a correlation of .54 between the former and the Gates Silent Reading Test. In the same study a group of teachers predicted the reading achievement of the pupils in their respective classes. The correlation between individual teachers' predictions and actual achievement ranged from .10 to .88. Only about half of the teachers were as effective in predicting pupil achievement as was the readiness test. Mitchell, (34) testing over a thousand first grade children, reported a correlation of .57 between scores on the Metropolitan Readiness Tests and end of year achievement as measured by the Metropolitan Achievement Test.

Long-term prediction of reading achievement, based on readiness tests administered in first grade, is also hazardous. Moreau (35) reports a correlation of .46 between readiness scores made in first grade and reading achievement in sixth grade. Baker (2) reports data for over 200 children in grades four, five, and six who read below grade norm, many of them showing severe retardation. Readiness scores achieved on tests administered during first grade showed that an extremely high percentage of these reading failures had exceeded the national norm on the readiness tests (63 per cent of the fourth-grade pupils, 71 per cent of fifth, and 83 per cent of sixth grade). Baker hypothesized that these findings stem from two factors: standardized readiness tests rate children too high; and the elementary classrooms from which these pupils came were characterized by drab, stereotyped instruction with emphasis on workbooks, intensive reading of a few books, and oral reading.

Thus, experimental data suggest that readiness tests, intelligence tests, and teacher evaluations appear to be about equally effective in predicting success in beginning reading. This does not imply that readiness tests have little value to teachers. It does suggest that educators should not project into these tests a degree of predictive infallibility which they do not possess. It appears that some readiness tests "overrate" children in regard to their readiness to deal with reading. It is possible that some of the tasks on the test are more closely related to the child's previous experiences than to what he will actually encounter in beginning reading.

It must be kept in mind that readiness tests measure only selected factors which are believed to be related to reading. There are many other factors which affect learning to read, such as the instruction the child receives, his attitude toward his teacher and toward reading, his reaction to varying degrees of success and failure, his home stability, and the like. This points up the need for intelligent use of readiness test results. The purpose of administering such tests is not to get a score for each child or to rank or compare children in the group, but rather to secure data for planning experiences.

In fact, unless the teacher is alert, actual scores may divert attention from child behavior which merits close scrutiny. This tendency is particularly marked where the administration of tests has become an end in itself. When this occurs, the inevitable result is that many trees become obscured by the forest. If teachers would analyze readiness test results and if they could adjust their teaching to each child's needs, numerous reading problems might be averted.

Factors Associated with Readiness for Reading

Both investigators and theorists have attempted to determine the relationship between a great number of factors and success in reading. It is very difficult to measure such a relationship because no factor is ever found operating in isolation. On the other hand, it is not easy to rule out a given factor completely as having no relationship to reading, except on an a priori basis. Thus, precise knowledge about readiness for reading and what should be included in a reading readiness program are still a matter of controversy.

RELATIONSHIP BETWEEN MENTAL AGE AND SUCCESS IN BEGINNING READING

Of all the factors assumed to be related to success in beginning reading, mental age has received the lion's share of attention in the literature on reading. Research data appear to be in agreement that mental age is more closely related to success in reading than is chronological age or I.Q.

Authorities do not agree as to the minimum mental age which should be attained before beginning reading. The most often repeated figure is six years and six months. In fact, this figure is so often quoted in the literature that one would assume that a vast array of evidence must be available to substantiate this position. However, very little experimental data is to be found. A great deal of generalization from one or a few studies is apparent in the literature on reading. The study which initiated most of the discussion was published by Morphett and Washburne (36) in 1931. They report data for 141 first-grade children who were given an intelligence test at the beginning of the school year and tested on reading achievement in February. The subjects were then divided into nine groups on the basis of mental age. The lowest range was 4-5 to 4-11, the highest 8-6 to 9-0 (these figures represent years and months of mental age). Of approximately 100 children who had attained an M.A. of 6-6 or higher, 78 per cent made satisfactory progress in general reading and 87 per cent made satisfactory progress in sight words. Of a group of twenty children whose M.A. ranged from 6-0 to 6-5, 52 per cent made satisfactory progress in reading and 41 per cent in sight words. Children below this range in M.A. showed little success in reading achievement.

In a follow-up study Washburne (51) reports on a group of twenty-five pupils who were delayed in beginning reading instruction until the middle of second grade. Their reading achievement was compared with a number of control pupils who began reading at the usual time in first grade. By the end of the third grade the experimental group had caught up with the controls; by the end of the fourth grade they had surpassed them; and at the end of seventh grade they were approximately one year ahead of the controls in reading. Unfortunately, the original experimental group of twenty-five had been reduced to approximately half that number by the end of the experiment and drawing conclusions on such a small sample is precarious. In addition there were, according to the author, important variables which could not be controlled.

Gates (18) unequivocally challenges the contention that research data have established a "critical point" on the M.A. continuum below which reading cannot be mastered. He states, "The fact remains . . . that it has by no means been proved as yet that a mental age of six and a half years is a proper minimum to prescribe for learning to read by all school methods or organizations or *all* types of teaching skills and procedures." In a study of four different first grade classes, Gates reports the correlation between M.A. and reading achievement as .62, .55, .44, and .34. He postulated that much of the discrepancy between these figures was actually accounted for by the instructional procedures found in the classrooms and that good instruction results in a higher correlation between pupil M.A. and success in reading.

The aim of the preceding discussion is not to minimize the importance of mental capacity in learning to read, but rather to see it in its proper perspective. The data available attest to the importance of

M.A., but at the same time do not establish a particular point on the mental-age continuum as the point below which children will not achieve success in reading. To posit that 6-6 mental age is such a point implies that all children with this M.A. are alike and ignores the fact that teachers, teaching methods, and programs are not everywhere comparable.

Other investigations attest to the importance of factors such as pre-reading activities, methodology, and readiness programs in determining how well children learn to read. One such study, carried on in first grade, reports that some children with an M.A. of 5-6 who had had no specific readiness program did not achieve up to grade norms in reading, while a group with M.A.'s of 5-0 who had had an extensive twelve-week readiness program did achieve up to national norms. Furthermore, a number of children who did poorly on readiness tests, and for whom prognosis in reading achievement was poor, achieved up to grade norm following specific readiness instruction. (16)

PRE-SCHOOL EXPERIENCE AND INFORMATIONAL BACKGROUND

Pre-school experience and informational background have been studied to determine their relationship to reading readiness. In one study, scores made by first-grade children on a readiness test correlated .49 with later achievement in reading. However, when only the scores of those children who had attended kindergarten were treated separately, the correlation between the two measures was .68. (30) After studying a group of children who had kindergarten experience and a group which had no such experience, Pratt (39) questioned the validity of using the same reading readiness tests and applying the same assumptions to both groups.

In a study designed to show the relationship between children's informational background and progress in reading, first-grade children were tested on vocabulary, picture completion, and previous experience. On the basis of data secured, children were divided into "rich background" and "meager background" groups. Reading readiness tests were administered to all children at the beginning of first grade. Reading achievement tests were administered to first graders in January and again in December of their second year. The rich background group was superior on both readiness tests and later reading achievement although there was no significant difference between the groups in mental age. (26)

VISUAL FACTORS

Here the teacher must be concerned with two developmental factors: the child's vision as it relates to reading and the task of developing skill in visual discrimination. Steps in acquiring visual discrimination include the visual readiness program, learning to recognize words, mastering a left-to-right sequence, and the like.

Vision. The bulk of all visual work in reading is at close range. The stimulus is about fourteen inches from the eyes. The retinas of both eyes reflect the image seen, in this case word symbols. For proper vision, the tiny images on both retinas must be perfectly synchronized or "fused." If fusion does not take place, the image will be blurred, or, in extreme cases, two distinct images will appear. When the stimulus is near the eyes, as in reading a book, the eyes must converge slightly. This convergence is accomplished by muscles in each eye. Any muscular imbalance between the eyes can result in the lack of fusion described above.

Other muscles operate to put pressure on the lens of the eye, which is capable of changing its shape (degree of convexity). This adjustment is essential in order to compensate for differences in the reflected light rays striking the two eyes. The muscular action determining the degree of convexity of the lens is called *accommodation.**

Ruling out the more serious visual defects which prevent the child from seeing printed word symbols, it is difficult, on the basis of published research, to come to a conclusion regarding the precise relationship between visual problems and reading deficiency. (7) However, many educators have warned that the school may be expecting too much physiologically of some children as they begin school and attempt to cope with the tasks the school has prescribed. Around 1898 John Dewey cautioned that children six years of age were physiologically immature "for more than incidental attention to visual and written language forms." Stone (48) quotes a number of authorities who have suggested deferring the teaching of reading long past the age at which it is currently begun. In discussing the relationship between poor vision and reading problems among children between six and eight, Broom et al. (9) conclude from research that the problem stems from a lack of maturation, or slow development, of good binocular vision, rather than from actual visual defects. This point of view finds support among investigators

*For further discussion and illustrations of the structure of the eye, see: William Kottmeyer, *Teachers Guide for Remedial Reading* (Manchester, Mo.: Webster Publishing 1959), pp. 49-64.

in the area of child development who are not primarily concerned with reading behavior.

More recently, Eames (15) has conducted research which he interprets as refuting the "claims that children's eyes are too immature for them to start reading safely at the usual ages of school entrance. Children five years of age were found to have *more* accommodative power than at any subsequent age." Poor visual acuity (near vision) was not found to be a significant factor which would interfere with the child's reading of the usual textbook material.

One of the most common visual problems found among children beginning school is farsightedness (hyperopia). A child with this problem may see quite adequately and pass a far vision test such as the Snellen or be able to read an experience chart at the front of the room, and still be poorly equipped visually to deal with material in a book twelve to fourteen inches from his eyes. Any test of vision which purports to have a relationship to actual reading must include a test of near vision. The farsighted child may be able to compensate by straining eye muscles for short periods of time to correct some refractional problem, but he cannot do this for any great period of time without causing strain and fatigue. If the teacher can detect the visually immature child, she may be able to protect him from too much close work.

Teachers Are Not Optometrists. Since it is so obvious that adequate vision is important in reading, it is often suggested that teachers of reading should thoroughly understand the anatomy of the eye and the nature of problems such as myopia, hyperopia, astigmatism, fusion, and strabismus, as well as be proficient in administering tests such as the Snellen, Eames, and Keystone telebinocular.* It might be well for teachers to resist such responsibilities, or at least to question seriously whether they should take the time to become proficient in the use of eye charts, audiometers, or the telebinocular. If these devices are available in the school system, a trained person should use them. Elementary school teachers have more than enough to do in today's classrooms without getting involved in these procedures. Furthermore, if the teacher is not expert in the use of these instruments, she may create the illusion that her pupils have been adequately examined, an illusion which could be a serious matter for the child whose diagnosis is faulty. The less the classroom teacher gets involved in this type of diagnosis, the better. The less she gets

---

**The Snellen Chart,* American Optical Co., Southbridge, Mass.; *The Eames Eye Test* (Tarrytown-On-Hudson, N. Y.: World Book Co.); *Keystone Visual Survey Test Telebinocular* (Meadville, Pa.: Keystone View Co.).

involved in these matters, the more time she will have for the teaching of reading. The issue here is not whether such a diagnosis should be made, but rather who should make it.

Goins (19) reports a study of first-grade children designed to determine (1) the relationship between visual perception and reading ability and (2) whether training in rapid recognition of digits and geometric and abstract figures would aid children in beginning reading achievement. A visual perception test consisting of fourteen subtests was designed. It included no verbal or reading content such as letters or words, but did include numerous items of matching pictures and geometrical figures, completion of geometric designs which had a part missing, finding a reversed picture in a series otherwise identical, and a test of closure in which incomplete pictures were the stimulus and the child identified what was represented by the incomplete drawing.

The total scores of first-grade pupils on the visual discrimination test showed a correlation of .49 with reading achievement at the end of grade one. Certain of the visual discrimination subtests showed considerable value in predicting first-grade reading achievement. Further, certain of the subtests indicated that among first-grade children, poor and good readers appear to be "different types of perceivers." This was particularly true of the ability to achieve "closure" and to keep in mind a particular configuration. The hypothesis was advanced that children who are widely different in these skills possibly should be taught reading by different methods in grade one.

It was found that the training with the tachistoscope (flashing digits and figures on a screen for extremely brief exposures) was helpful with good readers in improving *their visual perception of such forms* but that this type of training resulted in no appreciable improvement in reading achievement. (19) Barrett (3) found that visual discrimination factors, namely, the ability to name letters and numbers was the best single predictor of reading achievement at the end of grade one. However, he cautions that the predictive precision of these factors does not warrant their being used exclusively to predict first-grade achievement.

AUDITORY DISCRIMINATION

The child of six years who has had normal development in understanding and using speech will have acquired one type of proficiency in auditory discrimination. He can distinguish between the pronunciations of words which sound very much alike such as *bath-path*, *drink-drank*, *feed-feet*. Although the differences in each pair of examples is caused by interchanging one phoneme (front-middle-last), the child hears each of the words globally.

Discrimination of speech sounds in words is highly important in determining a child's success in learning to read. Many types of mechanical devices aid in auditory analyses.

The fact that a child can make these whole word distinctions is not prima facie evidence that he will have equal success in noting the speech-sound representations of letters in printed words. Neither is it assurance that he will be able to blend a number of speech sounds in words which he is able to pronounce but which he does not recognize in their printed form.

For instance, assume a child recognizes the printed word *bath* and a number of words which begin with *p* and *l*. He should be able to solve the printed words *p*ath and *l*ath. Some children have trouble making this type of transfer or substitution of speech sounds. After learning the above words, they may fail to note the *ath* combination in *path, bath, lath* is the same sound represented by the *ath* in *athletic*. Fortunately, most children learn these letter sound relationships step by step. If they fail to acquire this skill, they *inevitably* experience difficulty in becoming independent readers.

There are studies which indicate that impaired readers lack skill in the discrimination of speech sounds. Robinson (41) points out that this skill is linked to success in reading on two counts: its relation to language and speech, and its role in phonic analysis. Durrell and Murphy (14) state, "Although there are many factors which combine to determine the child's success in learning to read, it is apparent that his ability to notice the separate sounds in spoken words is a highly important one." The authors indicate that most children who come to the Boston University Reading Clinic with reading ability below first-grade level are unable to discriminate between speech sounds in words. Tests usually reveal that the problem of these children is not a hearing loss but an inability to discriminate between minute differences in speech sounds.

An illustration is provided by a third-grade boy who read the word *wish* as *woush*. When asked, "What did you call this word?" he responded "woush." The teacher said, "You mean *wish*, don't you?" He replied, "Sure, that's right, *woush*." The child who repeatedly says *tauk* for *talk*, *with* for *width*, *mus* for *must*, and *except* for *accept* is laying the foundations for trouble in later work in phonetic analysis as well as in spelling. After a child has said *artic* or *Febuary* fifty to a hundred times, he does not hear *arc tic* or *Feb ru ary* even if enunciated clearly by another person. When children approximate the sound of words, they reinforce these imprecise sounds each time they say them.

Hildreth (24) asserts that the rapid noting of auditory clues results in more efficient reading. Betts (4) stresses a substantial relationship between a child's inability to name the letters and impaired reading. He adds that this does not imply that rote memorization of the alphabet is desirable. Walter B. Barbe and others compiled the types of reading difficulties found among eighty remedial readers receiving help at a reading clinic. More than forty different problems were noted and tabulated. The weakness showing the highest incidence was sound of letters not known (found in 95 per cent of cases at the primary and 62 per cent at the intermediate age levels).

Other studies suggest the importance of the ability to synthesize or fuse phonetic elements of words. (37) Hester, (23) reporting data gathered on approximately 200 children admitted to a reading laboratory, states that blending of consonant sounds was particularly difficult for these children. Another study of over one hundred remedial readers (retarded two years or more on the basis of M.A.) indicated that these impaired readers were below average on auditory memory span as measured by specific subtests on the Stanford Binet. (42)

A series of studies conducted at Boston University which tested over 1500 first grade children led Durrell to conclude that "most reading difficulties can be prevented by an instructional program which provides early instruction in letter names and sounds, followed by applied phonics and accompanied by suitable practice in meaningful sight vocabulary and aids to attentive silent reading."*

Rudisell (43) reports data from a study which compared achievement of children who participated in a planned program emphasizing letter-sound relationships, with the achievement of a matched group which did not receive this instruction. At the end of eight months the experimental group had mean reading achievement and spelling scores which were superior to the mean scores of the control group at the end of sixteen months.

LANGUAGE DEVELOPMENT

Reading readiness is not confined specifically to experiences found on readiness tests. As a child grows and matures in all phases of human growth — intellectual, social, emotional, and physiological — he is growing into reading. Children can "grow" without a professionally planned curriculum. However, the school's function is to provide guidance and direction, to structure learning situations so that certain experiences are likely to result. A program aimed at preparing children for beginning reading is limited only by the facili-

*Donald D. Durrell, ed., "Success in First Grade Reading," Boston University *Journal of Education, CLX* (February 1958).

ties and resources of the school and the understanding and creativeness of the teacher. A great majority of pre-reading activities can be encompassed under the heading *language*.

The role of the school in preparing children for reading begins the first day of school and continues for varying lengths of time for different children. Whatever the school does in the reading readiness period will be done in order to guide each child into being a "good risk" as a beginning reader. The school attempts to structure the situation so that each child will acquire the right combination of abilities, skills, and attitudes. The study of how children acquire language is both interesting and rewarding. The understanding of this process is a prerequisite to planning a curriculum for children or putting it into practice.

The child first develops oral language, acquiring the ability to make sounds in isolation and then in combination. As sounds are combined into words, they become associated with meanings. The range of meaningful language one uses is referred to as his *speaking vocabulary*. The child beginning school has a speaking vocabulary of several thousand words. He can say, and has concepts for, a great variety of speech sounds, such as *horse, train, jet, farm, elephant, river*. In addition, he will have some concept for the relationship of *up* to *down, over* to *under, high* to *low, hot* to *cold, dry* to *wet, large* to *small, dark* to *light*. Speech sounds, coupled with the mysteries of meaning, fascinate the child. Some first graders will tend to "talk over their heads," to use speech sounds for which they have not learned meanings. Every child at this age has been exposed to more language than he has absorbed.

It is inevitable that the child will harbor many misconceptions. He will probably be vague about *good* and *bad, right* and *wrong, justice, government, God, Heaven,* and *death*. Children come to school with varying degrees of insight into concepts such as these. Many decades later, even if he has earned the title of Philosopher, one may still be attempting to develop, extend, and clarify some of these concepts.

Language cuts across every goal and function of the school. Everything that is taught in the school must pass through a communication process before it is learned by a pupil. Excellent books have been written about the school curriculum. These books discuss objectives, the impact of the school's curriculum on our culture, and the factors in our culture which in turn shape the school curriculum. The merits of various curricular philosophies such as the "traditional," "progressive," "integrated," and "core" are often debated. In these debates the point is sometimes overlooked that the real function of the school is to provide children with guidance in developing concepts. Our schools at all levels rely heavily on reading as the means of building and extending concepts in all subject areas.

No matter how one organizes the curriculum or the debate on the curriculum, the school can do no more than guide and direct the development of concepts. Therefore, the debate must center on *what* concepts, *when* to teach them, and *how* best to teach them. As Ragan (40) points out: "The curriculum does not exist in the content to be learned. The selection of useful, accurate content is a very important responsibility of the teacher, *but content does not constitute the curriculum until it becomes a part of the experience of the child.*" (Italics added.) The effectiveness of any curriculum cannot be judged by the statements in the curriculum guide, but rather by the learning which takes place in the classroom.

Individuals learn and use language skills in social and cultural and emotional settings. The teacher is expected, and to some degree is trained, to become cognizant of, and concerned with, all facets of human growth and development — physical, social, emotional, and intellectual. The one reason why the school *must* be concerned is that these factors influence learning.

Language and Socialization

The school is very much involved in guiding the social growth of its pupils. In the case of normal children, socialization is almost exclusively built around communication. Up to the time children reach school age, spoken language is the chief means of communication. There is no better tool than language facility for gauging the social needs or social maturity of children. Among the first experiences provided in the modern school's curriculum are those which have to do with social growth. The logic of this is apparent. Many children have had little or no experience in a group as large as that in which they will find themselves upon beginning school. There will be many learning situations which will call for group coherence. Each member of the group will have to follow certain social patterns in order not to disrupt the learning situation for the others in the group.

Gradually, step by step, the teacher moves in the direction of establishing social control within the class so that learning can take place. Whether the teacher structures this control on an authoritarian basis or has the group control evolve out of the group itself, the medium for establishing control will be language. Many group activities in the classroom, if they are to end successfully, will call for co-operation and sharing among pupils. Language is the most important basis for co-operation. Co-operation and sharing help the child grow and develop from a very self-centered organism into a social being. If the process breaks down and the individual, for any reason, does not learn the social rules, or does not within certain limits follow them, his behavior sets him apart from the group. When this behavior is reacted to by those in the peer group, he and the group are out of adjustment.

These maladjustments among children beginning school are almost inevitable because some children have further to go in order to live up to the group standards, some learn slowly, and some have learned to use anti-social responses when attempting to satisfy their needs. A teacher who does not perceive the symptoms of maladjustment fairly early may soon have cases of non-affiliation in her class. These can develop very rapidly into isolates, or children rejected by the group. The teacher may be the best teacher of reading in the district, but if she lets the security of some children become seriously threatened in the school situation, the odds are that she will not teach them reading. In their unskilled efforts to strike back at threats they do not understand, these pupils may disrupt the learning for others in the group.

Language and Emotional Adjustment

Language usage is a most important factor in the study of emotional maladjustment and the revelation of psychological needs. Clinicians state that language is the most sensitive indicator of maladjustment. The classroom, the playground, in fact the total environment, is one never-ending projective technique if one but heeds the language of children. Both as adults and as teachers, we sometimes learn very little about children from children. This happens when we consciously or unconsciously feel that what children say is not important. The truth of the matter is that their language mirrors their needs, feelings, aspirations, and fears; and if one's job is to help children grow, knowledge of these is essential.

A child's need for ego satisfaction seems to increase by a geometric ratio in the face of frustration. That is, a little denial of love, attention, and acceptance, or a little threat to self worth and integrity, is reacted to by an increased drive for these goals. If rebuffed again, the child seems to redouble his efforts to maintain his prestige and self-worth. It is apparent that when children are trying to fulfill ego needs, they invariably use behavior which by adult logic seems ill-conceived and not likely to achieve the child's goal. The child who wants and needs friendship and is rebuffed may resort to the use of aggressive, hostile, or abusive language, perhaps feeling that he can force acceptance or that his language will reduce the stature of those persons to whom it is addressed. Another child, after each failure, may withdraw more and more and make very few language overtures to others in his peer group. This non-use of language is itself a clue which should have diagnostic value for the teacher. Here is a child who has elected to withdraw from the arena, but the fight to salvage his ego will go on within himself. This child, at the moment, poses no problem to the teacher or society, but his response is potentially more dangerous than overt aggression.

Language and Mental Growth

Psychologists agree that the most valuable insights into the child's mental growth are gained from a study of the development of language facility. A brief though acceptable definition of intelligence is that it is "the ability to do abstract thinking." Stated another way, it is the ability to manipulate in a meaningful manner symbolic materials of which language is our best example. Intelligence itself cannot be measured but is inferred from behavior which can be measured. We measure certain behavior which by agreement is said to be representative of intelligence. The one kind of behavior most universally measured on intelligence tests is language behavior. Our society puts a high value on the ability to use and understand language. The degree of the child's mastery of communication skills determines to a large extent his readiness to do school tasks and to profit from instruction. Although he cannot read, spell, or write when he starts school, he has had years of experience with language. His language proficiency is used as an index of his mental growth, just as it provides data for appraisal of social and emotional growth and adjustment.

Furthermore, when we wish to assess what the student has learned at any grade level, we rely on language usage. In other words, a change in language behavior is often the sole criterion of learning. Language reveals the number and breadth of concepts acquired. All concepts exist within the framework of some symbolic process and all are arrived at, and refined through, thought processes which in turn depend on the manipulation of language symbols.

It is a truism that a society such as we have today could not have evolved without language. It is equally obvious that education would not have developed along the lines it has without language. Language provides a bridge which permits ideas, information, and data to pass between parent and child, teacher and pupil, and child and peer. As an individual masters new forms of language usage, he is developing "mind tools" which he can use from that time forward in the pursuit of knowledge. Reading is our best example of such a tool.

Language Development and Reading

Over and above what the child's language usage can tell the teacher about intellectual, social, and emotional development is the relationship of previous language experiences to the specific learning task called *reading*. Skillful, effective teaching of beginning reading is based on the teacher's understanding:

1. That reading is related to all language functions found in the curriculum.
2. That learning to read is related to, and built upon, past language experiences.
3. That learning to read should be a natural outgrowth of these past language experiences.
4. That learning to read is a developmental process that involves years of guided study.
5. That different methods of teaching reading may be justified, but the one criterion a method should meet is that it builds logically and systematically.

It is important for teachers who are preparing children for reading to be aware of the experiences and growth which have taken place during the pre-school years. Some children will have had many pleasant experiences with books, parents having read to them frequently. They will be able to recognize and point out the duck, the owl, the moose, the pony, the baby bear, or the tug boat and tell what each is doing in the picture, having learned to find meaning in pictures. Some children will be able to recite almost word for word certain of their favorite stories. Others will have a surprisingly large stock of concepts derived from viewing television, from travel, or from contact with adults. On the other hand, some children will have been read to rarely if at all. A depressing home environment will undoubtedly be reflected in a child's language usage and stock of concepts. The range of previous experiences among first-grade children is tremendous.

The curriculum of the first grade cannot be unrelated to the child's previous development since what is done in the classroom must of necessity be built on previous experience. Even before the child begins to read, the numerous activities included in the curriculum are related to reading. This relationship is easy to see in such activities as hikes, visits, excursions, field trips, bulletin boards, stories read by teachers, and the like. But other activities, such as drawing, painting, rhythm, sharing periods, planning periods, play, and problem-solving, are also related. All are bound together with language and communication; all involve developing and extending concepts. Each of these in turn is fixed by word symbols. Reading is an extension of the communicative process which involves learning the printed equivalent for the known spoken symbols.

There are certain differences between the language experiences which children have before coming to school and those they encounter early in the school situation. The first new adjustment will be using speech in groups larger than those in which the child has thus far participated. More speech responses will have to be inhibited, since the child will have to share talking time with so many others. His pre-school language was probably more ego-involved than will be acceptable in the school situation. Here the speaker must consider his listeners or lose them. The pre-schooler can flit from topic to topic; his response need not dovetail with what has just been said by another. However, in the group discussion in the classroom there is usually a central topic, and the children must gradually learn to follow a discussion and to build logically on what has been said previously. (27)

Learning to read is probably one of the most important accomplishments that the child will achieve during his formal schooling. This is not to imply that learning to read will be his most difficult or dramatic academic achievement, for if he gets off to a good start the whole process may be so uneventful that he will not recall how this particular learning took place. On the other hand, if he fails in reading, the frustrations and defeats which can beset him in the future are so numerous and varied that they have never been tabulated in one source. Thus, the experiences which the school arranges for children prior to launching into the formal teaching of reading are extremely important.

Programs of instruction designed to develop reading readiness should differ considerably from classroom to classroom. Activities which are suitable for some children will be unnecessary for others. If one were to recommend that a particular program be adopted for all children, this would negate what is known about individual differences. The following discussion suggests a limited number of activities which are illustrative of approaches which might have merit in certain situations.

DEVELOPING VISUAL DISCRIMINATION

This is one of the major objectives of beginning instruction in reading. The child's need to make fine visual discriminations is self-evident since the symbols which must be read are visual stimuli. Even a cursory examination of words is sufficient to establish that many of them look very much alike. A child who cannot differentiate between the various words in a passage cannot possibly get meaning from that passage. The widely accepted definition that "reading is getting meaning from printed symbols" does, to some degree, slight the sensory skills which are absolutely essential before reading can become "getting the meaning."

By the time he comes to school, a child has had thousands of experiences in seeing and noting likenesses and differences. He has developed the ability to make fairly high-order visual discriminations, in many cases based on relatively small clues. At the age of three years he was able to identify and claim his tricycle from a group of three-wheelers, even though he was not able to tell us the exact criteria he used in this identification. All we do know is that it was a visual discrimination. Later, two coins much the same size but bearing different symbols will not confuse him. The pictured head of a man or woman no larger than a postage stamp will contain enough visual clues for correct identification. Common trademarks are correctly identified on the basis of size, color, and configuration. A pack of playing cards can be sorted correctly as to suit on the basis of visual perception.

Maturation cannot be hastened, but visual discrimination can be sharpened through experience and practice. The school must provide as much of this experience as is needed, and different children will need different amounts. Fortunately, there are many ready-made exercises which the teacher can use. Reading readiness books provide excellent practice in developing the ability to make finer and finer discriminations. Both reading readiness tests and workbooks can aid the teacher in evaluating the child's progress, provided they are used with diagnosis in mind. For the child who needs more practice than is provided in these activities, a number of teacher-made exercises can be developed. Such exercises take time to build; therefore, they should be duplicated in quantities and used from year to year. They never become outdated with one class use. One thorough preparation will provide for many pupils who need this particular type of experience.

A few examples of visual discrimination exercises follow. Each example could be developed by the teacher into a full page of work. In every case the child is to underline the object, figure, part of a word, or word which is identical to the stimulus in the box at the beginning of each row. See Figures 1-9. These exercises are designed to help develop the following skills:

1. Identifying similar geometric figures
2. Identifying geometric figures with finer discriminations
3. Finding identical elements at the beginning of words
4. Finding identical elements at the end of words
5. Identifying letters and small words
6. Finding a given letter in words of a sentence
7. Identifying common objects with slight differences
8. Recognizing similar digits
9. Recognizing "word families"

FIGURE 1

Underline the figure that is exactly like the sample at the left.

FIGURE 2

Underline the figure that is exactly like the sample at the left.

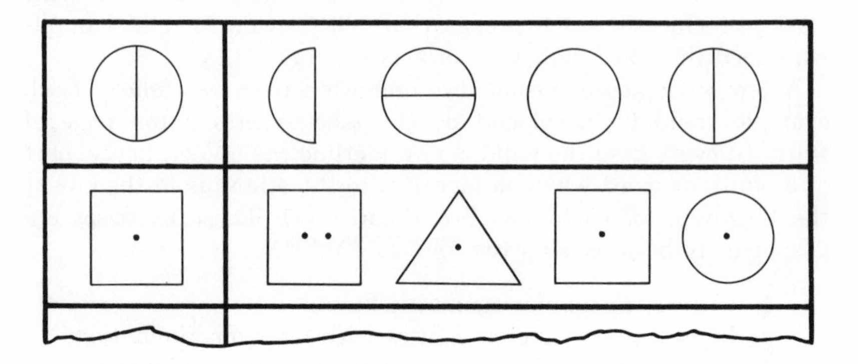

FIGURE 3

Underline the beginning of each word that is exactly like the sample.

shall	Sally	shot	hall	shut
from	frog	flap	fry	free

FIGURE 4

Underline the ending of words which are exactly like the sample.

hat	hit	hot	cat	has
home	come	cane	love	same

FIGURE 5

Underline the letter or word that is exactly like the one at the left.

M	N	W	M	Z	U
WHO	HOW	WON	WHO	WAH	

FIGURE 6

Underline each letter in the sentence which is like the sample at the left.

a	a small black ant ate it all.
l	a small lady led the lads.

FIGURE 7

Underline the object that is exactly like the one at the left.

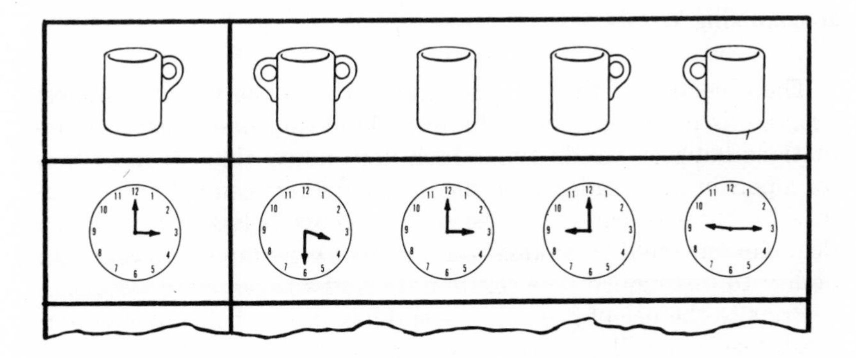

FIGURE 8

Underline the number that is exactly like the sample on the left.

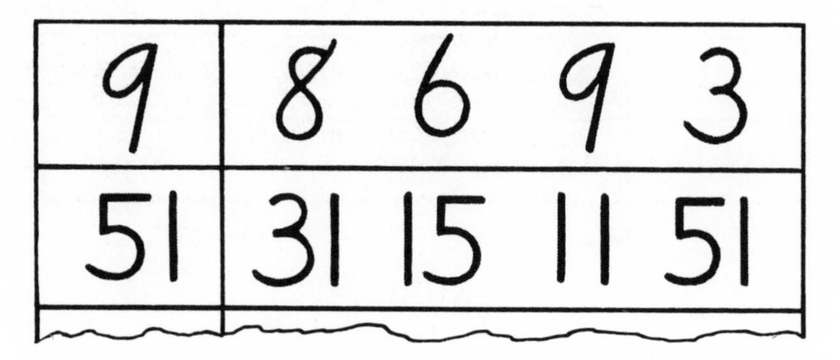

FIGURE 9

Underline the ending of words which are exactly like the sample.

hi<u>ll</u>	bell	mill	fill	call
b<u>all</u>	fall	pill	call	halt

Recognizing Words

The objective of the various experiences in the visual readiness program is to prepare the child for making very fine visual discriminations between words which look very much alike. It is as easy for a person who reads to see the difference between *cat* and *dog* as it is for the six-year-old to see the difference between *a* cat and *a* dog. Yet the child beginning to read must very rapidly develop the ability to distinguish between hundreds of written word symbols.

Prior to the use of pre-primers and long after their introduction, most teachers will provide classroom activities aimed at helping children to learn to recognize words. Teachers will employ different methods, but most prefer to teach words related to the child's actual experience. Discussion of the experience method and the use of experience charts is found in Chapter 4, "Beginning Reading." Examples of readiness experiences commonly used to help children in word recognition are briefly described here.

1. *Child's name.* Probably the easiest word to teach a child is his own name. He sees his name on his readiness book and on his pictures and drawings which the teacher displays. In addition, there will be many occasions when the teacher will write pupils' names on the board for birthdays, committees, special assignments, and the like. The child will notice similarities between his own name and other pupils' names and will learn a few words in this manner.

2. *Color names.* To teach color names, large circles cut from solid-color construction paper can be placed on the blackboard or a table. Names of colors are printed on white cards. The pupil selects a card, says the word, and places the color name on the proper colored circle.

3. *Matching words with pictures.* All children in the readiness group are capable of identifying a great number of objects and pictures of objects. Familiar pictures are found and word names are printed on separate cards: *car, swing, duck, cow, house.* Each child selects a word and places it beneath the proper picture.

4. *Objects in classroom.* A word card is made for familiar objects in the classroom such as door, table, window, book, chair. A child selects a word card, shows it to the group, and touches the object.

5. *Following directions.* Words previously studied can be used in "direction sentences" printed on heavy paper or oaktag. A child selects a sentence, reads it aloud, and does what it suggests: *walk to the door; clap your hands; ask John to stand.*

In any exercise that uses single words as stimuli, the teacher can ask that the word be used in a sentence. As she writes on the board, she pronounces each word and then the whole sentence. Emphasis can be placed on visual clues found in words, on the sentence as a meaning unit, and on left-to-right progression in reading.

Left-to-Right Sequence

It is important that during the readiness period and beginning reading stages children learn that the eyes move from left to right across the page while reading. There is apparently only one reason why teachers would neglect this skill: they might think that all children have mastered it. It is easy to project this ability onto children because, to adults who have learned to read, the technique appears to be one of the most simple of the procedures which make up reading. It is also true that the majority of children learn the proper sequence without trouble. A child may identify words without realizing that the conventional way to interpret words and sentences is left to right. However, embarking on the next steps in learning to read without having mastered this response can develop other serious and harmful reading habits including reversals, omissions, losing the place, and pointing with the finger. This skill should never be taken for granted by the teacher, and "overlearning" it would certainly be justified.

There are a number of ways in which left-to-right sequence can be emphasized. Readiness workbooks contain training exercises calling for a line to be drawn from left to right over a series of dots. Sometimes the point of such an exercise is not grasped if the child fails to relate it to reading. A large square can be drawn on the blackboard with short horizontal lines representing words. The teacher states, "Let's play that this is a page from a book. The heavy little lines are words. Where should I start reading?" Children can draw a line through the "words" moving from left to right. In using experience charts the teacher can demonstrate left-to-right reading with hand or pointer.

Rearranging the Pictures

This exercise consists of two or more picture cards which tell a story when arranged properly from left to right. The cards are laid out in improper arrangement, and after a child corrects the sequence, he relates the story the cards tell. Telling the story forces him to progress from left to right, note details, see relationships, and organize the material in a logical manner. Figure 10 illustrates two teacher-made series. A pupil's story for each example is given here:

> *Story A.* "The tallest candle should be in the first picture — then it burns down a little and the third picture shows it real small."

> *Story B.* "Mother is baking pies. In the first picture she puts one on the table, then two on the table. In the third picture there are three pies."

FIGURE 10

A. "The candle is burning."

B. "Mother is baking pies."

DEVELOPING AUDITORY DISCRIMINATION

The ability to discriminate between speech sounds heard in words, and the ability to blend speech sounds represented by different graphemes in words is an absolute prerequisite for independent reading. The readiness and beginning reading program should provide sufficient experience and drill to assure that every child develops a good foundation in auditory discrimination. Some children will need much more instruction in this area than will others. A few suggestions follow.

Drill on Initial Letter Sounds. The teacher: "Listen carefully. I am going to say a word, and I want you to think of any word that begins with the same sound." She then gives several examples such as *lady, lake, line, look,* emphasizing but not distorting the sound of *l*. Next, other initial consonants are used—*m, c, b,* etc. The particular order of introducing initial sounds is not crucial. In all hearing-sounding exercises the teacher should make sure all children have an opportunity to participate. In this way, children who need further help in this skill can be identified.

Use children's names. "Listen to the sound that begins Mike's name — *M*ike. Can you think of any other children's first names which begin with this sound?" (*M*ary, *M*ark, *M*arcia.) The beginning sound should be emphasized but not distorted.

Use pictures. Cut small pictures from magazines or catalogues and paste a number of them on a blank sheet of paper. Children select and name those which begin with the same letter sound (*b*icycle, *b*aby, *b*all; *c*ap, *c*ane, *c*ow; *t*iger, *t*elevision, *t*able).

Similar Sounds at the Ends of Words

The same procedure that is used with initial letter sounds is followed here, using words that rhyme. If the teacher selects the word *tall,* she stresses the likeness of the sound in words like *ball, call, fall.* These words can be printed on the chalkboard to emphasize the visual likeness. It should be kept in mind that such workbook and teacher-made exercises can result in visual training only if they are done individually as seatwork. To incorporate auditory training, the children must say and hear the sounds being dealt with.

Different Final Sounds in Words

Three or four words are pronounced by the teacher, all but one of which end like the first word pronounced (pen, been, plan, peach; car, tall, tar, far). The child repeats the one that is different. Exercises such as this can help develop auditory discrimination and auditory memory.

Similar Sounding Picture Names

This technique calls for the teacher to secure a number of pictured objects whose naming words contain some identical phonemes. Show each picture and pronounce its correct identifying name such as *clown* and *cloud.* This will prevent children from guessing other words such as *funny man* or *sky.* Place a pair of pictures on the chalk tray and pronounce only one of the naming words. A child, or the class, then pronounces the other word. Examples of usable pictures include:

clown	cloud	stairs	stars
swing	swan	frog	flag
bread	red	king	ring
crib	bib	lamp	lamb

Eye and Ear Training

Combination eye and ear training usually comes after children have learned to recognize letters and some words. A series of work sheets can be prepared using single letters, letter blends, or words. This type of exercise may be viewed as moving beyond readiness activities, since the child must be able to recognize printed words.

A. *The teacher says one of the letter symbols in each box and the child circles what he hears (N—P—B—D).*

(N) M R	B (P) D	S C (B)	T B (D)

B. *The teacher pronounces one word in each series (flap, cap, tap, went) and the child underlines that word.*

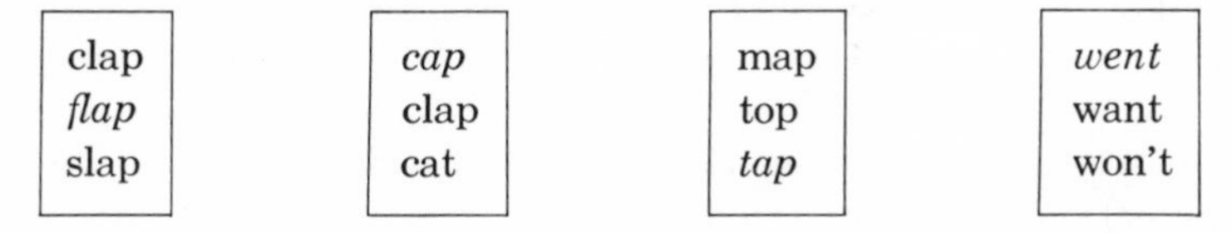

clap	*cap*	map	*went*
flap	clap	top	want
slap	cat	*tap*	won't

C. *The child marks the word in each box which rhymes with the stimulus word the teacher pronounces (am, land, jump, day).*

hand	lamp	Jane	said
any	*sand*	came	sail
ham	fan	*dump*	*say*

Interdependence of Visual and Auditory Discrimination

Although visual and auditory discrimination may be discussed separately and lessons may be devised which emphasize one or the other, the two skills invariably work together in the reading situation. The child who learns to rely exclusively on visual clues will experience extreme difficulty as he meets hundreds of new printed words which have only minimal differences in letter configuration (*thumb, thump*). On the other hand, one cannot profit from learning letter-sound relationships if he cannot visually distinguish letters.

Attempting to teach the characteristic sound of *b* and *d* in such words as *big-dig, day-bay, dump-bump, bread-dread* cannot help the child "sound out" words unless he can instantly recognize the *b* and *d* configurations. First graders have learned to make hundreds of minute auditory discriminations required for understanding oral language. They can build upon this previous learning only if they learn to:

1. Focus on sounds (phonemes) which are blended into whole words.
2. Associate these speech sounds with the proper graphic representations (letters).

DEVELOPING LISTENING SKILLS

Listening is closely related to many other facets of reading such as expansion of concepts, reading with proper intonation patterns, participating in oral reading situations and developing sound work habits. Children differ appreciably in listening ability. Some children come to school with poor listening habits, and others develop inadequate habits early in their school career. This naturally has an impact on classroom activities.

If we judge educators' interest in, and respect for, listening by their statements about its importance, we might conclude that there is a high degree of respect for listening as a means of learning. However, until very recently the research on listening has been meagre, despite the fact that during the past decade there has been more research on listening and more writing about listening than in the previous half century. Much of this work is at the college level and has little relationship to children beginning school.

Teacher training programs and actual classroom practices suggest that listening ability is taken for granted. Children come to school with the ability to listen, and it is sometimes assumed that they are listening whenever they are not involved in some overt ego-involved behavior. Studies indicate that the school does relatively little to help improve the listening abilities of pupils. (54) A recent review of a number of curriculum guides or bulletins used at the elementary level indicates a high degree of respect for listening. However, the amount of space devoted to this topic was extremely limited, and suggestions to teachers were very general. Listening situations found in the school were cited, but there were practically no concrete suggestions on how to *teach* children to become better listeners. (21)

Listening involves more than being physically present and immobile while the teacher is speaking. "It is just as important to provide experience-listening if we want learning to take place as it is to provide experience-*reading*." (50) It is inevitable that there will be a great number of learning activities in the school which depend on listening. These include listening to recordings of stories, poetry, and songs; listening to music and acting out what the music suggests; listening to the teacher read stories; participating in speaking-listener situations; and many other experiences which need little explanation. A few exercises which can be used in pre-reading as well as at higher levels are briefly described below.

Critical listening from which to draw conclusions. Here the teacher reads short descriptive passages, and the children are asked to identify or draw a picture of what is described. This technique can be tied in with motor co-ordination and imagination.

1. I grow outdoors.
   I grow tall.
   In summer I am full
   of leaves. Birds sit
   on my branches and sing.
   What am I?
   Draw a picture of me.
2. People live in me.
   I have windows and doors.
   I come in many different
   sizes and colors.
   Draw a picture of me.

The descriptions the teacher reads can vary in length and complexity, depending on the maturity or age level of the group. These exercises can help teachers discover many things about their pupils such as:

1. Which children can listen effectively and which cannot.
2. Which children are self-sufficient and able to work on their own initiative.

3. Which children are dependent and receive clues from others.
4. Information relative to the degree of maturity of each child.
5. Unusual responses which may suggest other problems needing attention.

Story periods. Practically all children can be held spellbound by a good story well told. When the teacher tells or reads stories, she plants the idea in the children's minds that good listening is the key to the enjoyment associated with the story. Equally important is the fact that she can stress a purpose for listening, whether for enjoyment, for information, for answers to specific questions, or for practice in social living.

Following directions can be used either as a class exercise, with small groups within a class, or with individual pupils. Several short commands are stated and the child, or the group, is to execute them in the order given. The performance will reveal ability to attend to oral directions and the ability to hold these in memory.

Finish the story provides practice in developing language skills such as training in listening, use of imagination, practice in using language, and expecting logic and meaning from reading. The teacher, while reading a story, interrupts it at a point of high interest and asks the children, "What happens next?"

"Once upon a time Jack went to visit his grandfather and grandmother. They lived on a farm. He went with his father and mother in their car. When they drove up to grandfather's house a big dog rushed out to the car and barked and barked. The boy and his parents had never seen this dog before. Father said '______.' " (Child finishes story.)

"Jane and Henry were tired of running and playing. They sat down on the porch to rest and talk. Jane said, 'Henry, let's ask mother to make us some lemonade.'

" 'Good,' said Henry, 'cold lemonade; I'm so thirsty I could drink three glasses.' They started into the house and Henry said: 'Jane, do you think your mother would make enough lemonade so we could have a lemonade stand and sell lemonade in paper cups?'

"Jane said, '______.' "

Complete the sentence is a variation of the above in which the child supplies a word which has been omitted. "A big dog came up to the car and ______ at them." "Jim was tired of running. He sat down to ______." This exercise gives practice in listening and in getting meanings from context.

What word disagrees with the picture? While looking at a picture, pupils listen to the teacher as she says a series of four words, one of which could not be logically associated with the picture. Children are then asked to identify the word which does not belong. This can be a challenging game, because children must observe closely, listen carefully, and remember the word while other stimuli are presented.

Retell a story. The teacher reads a story or passage to one group who then tell the story to children who have not heard it. This experience motivates children to be good listeners since they must pay attention and comprehend if they are to retell the story successfully.

Emphasizing expression. The teacher reads a sentence or short passage word by word, without inflection, then reads it with good expression. Pupils are lead to see that how a passage is read affects its interpretation.

LANGUAGE EXPERIENCES

There are many types of experiences which the school arranges so that skill in language and communication will be developed as rapidly as possible. Some of these tasks may at first seem unrelated to teaching reading. However, they involve skills used in reading, such as perception in noting details and making comparisons, extending the span of attention, learning to see relationships between events, and drawing inferences. What follows is a representative but not exhaustive list of such experiences:

1. Coloring, cutting, pasting
2. Working a jigsaw puzzle
3. An excursion to observe animals:
   a) at a farm
   b) at a zoo
4. Listening to musical records—"Do what the music tells you."
5. Listening to the teacher read a story
6. Celebrating birthdays
7. Bringing pets to the classroom—parakeet, puppy, duck, rabbit
8. Gathering leaves
9. Discussing the seasons

10. Growing a sweet potato in a glass of water
11. Using a medicine dropper—How can it pick up water?
12. Imitating sounds of animals—rooster, horse, dog, cat, frog
13. Learning what objects float—wide-mouthed gallon jar and numerous objects
14. Discussing the eating habits of different animals—cow, chicken, fish, frog
15. Taking an excursion to observe different occupations—to a bakery, a dairy, a farm
16. Planning a party (experience chart)
17. Flying a kite—Why does it fly?
18. Using a balance (scale)
19. Observing animals that can swim—fish, frog, duck
20. Using an electric fan with a home-made weather vane
21. Going on a nature hike. Turn over a fair-sized rock—Why is it damp underneath? Why do we find worms here?
22. Pouring water from quart jar into funnel—Why does the funnel run over?
23. Watching plants grow (outside garden or inside window box)
24. Planning an excursion and making an experience chart
25. Using clay, fingerpaints, colored paper, pictures, objects to express ideas

All of these experiences involve sensory experiences. It should be remembered that as the child matures, sensory impressions are automatically translated into language equivalents and are the basis for all learning. When the child feels the turtle's shell, he translates the sensation into language symbols. A duck is how a duck looks, how it swims, how it quacks, how it waddles, and how it eats. A concept of the wind grows out of sensory perceptions of paper blowing across a yard, sand or grit against one's face, a hat blown off, and trees and bushes bending. This process, like reading, is developmental in nature and illustrates how concepts evolve and develop.

"Show and Tell"

A technique used frequently to help children develop language facility and extend concepts is "show and tell," or sharing periods. The child brings something to school or makes something in school which he thinks may be of interest to the group. Since he is familiar with the object, even the shy child can tell something about it. Attention is focused on the object rather than the child and his speaking. This has psychological value for those children who fear speaking to the group. It is a situation that can be kept concrete. "I brought a box full of my rocks. I want to show you some of the ones I like. I collect these when we go on trips. This one is quartz. This one has iron in it. It's heavy. You can see the iron in it. These rocks are very smooth. They came from Lake Michigan. The waves rub the rocks with sand. They get smooth and round."

By telling about some interesting object, a child sees that language is the vehicle for his thoughts as well as the bridge for communication with others. (Courtesy of Bexley Schools, Bexley, Ohio; photographer: Arthur Burt, Inc.)

Precise descriptions with full explanations of processes and smooth transitions may be lacking, but communication has taken place, self-confidence has been strengthened, status has been enhanced. The speaker is asked some questions, and he answers with considerable poise. The teacher compliments him on his fine talk. He senses that when he has something interesting to tell, others will listen. "Show and tell" can be a very ego-satisfying experience for children.

Not all children will be successful. Some will have a difficult time even stating what they are showing the group. The teacher is the only hope of salvaging something from such a situation. A question at the right moment may possibly evoke a response. The tone of voice in which the question is asked will condition the group's reaction to the speaker. A child who cannot speak successfully to the entire class may be able to speak to a smaller group, but this can come about only if the teacher perceives the child's problem and structures the situation so that he participates.

"Show and tell" experiences can contribute much to the child's social and language development, but there are some pitfalls which must be avoided if this practice is to contribute its maximum to children's growth. Some teachers use the "show and tell" period as a means of obtaining a little time for their daily administrative chores. They call on youngsters and try to give the impression that they are avidly interested, but they actually are filling out attendance reports, checking lunch money, tabulating returns from a P.T.A. questionnaire which the children brought from home, setting up schedules for parents' conferences, and so forth.

Another factor which can detract from the effectiveness of this practice is the unequal distribution of experiences. Unless the teacher keeps some record, certain children will monopolize the "show and tell" periods while others will rarely have an opportunity to contribute. This may result in a neglect of those who need the experience most. The shy, unsure child is not likely to volunteer, although he may have come to class with some object in his pocket about which he had hoped to talk.

An illustration of this tendency is provided by an experienced teacher who checked back on the past week's activity in the sharing period and found that she had inadvertently been calling on the most persistent volunteers and more or less ignoring some of the other children. Figure 11 sets down her data for the most-called-on five children and the least-called-on in the "show and tell" period. Even if we assume some inaccuracy due to faulty memory, the data are suggestive of how easy it is to let some children develop habits of non-participation.

Conversation Groups

Dividing the class into conversation groups is another method of helping children acquire facility in using language. The advantage in this device is that more children can participate in a given period of time and the teacher can spend more time with the group that most needs her guidance. However, the children must have developed the ability to co-operate with and respect others.

FIGURE 11

A TEACHER'S RETROSPECTIVE RECORD OF THE FIVE STUDENTS WHO PARTICIPATED MOST AND THE FIVE WHO PARTICIPATED LEAST IN ONE WEEK'S "SHOW AND TELL" ACTIVITIES. THE SYMBOL *P* INDICATES PARTICIPATION.

Pupil	1	2	3	4	5	26	27	28	29	30
Mon.	P		P	P						
Tues.	P	P		P	P		P			
Wed.	P	P	P			P				
Thurs.	P	P		P	P			P		
Fri.	P	P	P		P					

Other means of practicing language usage that are more or less self-explanatory include:

Telling a story (not about self)
"My pet . . . ."
"We took a trip to . . . ." (Either a group experience or an individual child's experience)
"I have a riddle"
"My three wishes are . . . ."
"Who am I describing?" (A child in class or a well-known person)

Discussing Trips and Excursions

Discussion of class trips or excursions to a farm, the zoo, a dairy, or the airport will result in some learning for all of the children who participate. Children differ in the amount they learn and in the degree of thoroughness with which they form certain concepts. This occurs because children differ in previous experience and sensory perceptions. They cannot all have the same experiences when they are visiting the same farm, zoo, market, or TV station. Therefore, visiting these interesting places is not the only important phase of the total experience. Equally important is the planning which tells the child what to look for and the discussion which follows the excursion. This discussion can extend partial concepts or clear up hazy concepts. Here again, the teacher can structure these sharing experiences so that all children become involved. The shy child or the one who will have only a limited contribution can often be called on early in the discussion. This precaution assures that their ideas will not have been advanced before they have an opportunity to speak.

Contact with Books, Stories, and Pictures

A child may come to school with an interest in learning to read, and this interest may grow or it may be inhibited by school experience. Most children particularly enjoy a well-told story in school. After hearing the story, a picture of some dramatic incident in the story can be used to focus discussion and comment or to enhance understanding. One important way to arouse interest in reading is to instill the feeling that the reading itself is a key to the resulting pleasure.

It is very important that the child have access to numerous books. The actual handling of books, turning pages, studying pictures, and the like, are an important part of readiness for reading. Most basal reader series contain good art work, are colorful, emphasize the story approach, and hold the student's interest until he moves on to the next higher level. However, in the case of a poor reader, the continued, uninterrupted diet of one or two books can color attitudes toward reading. The teacher and the school must assume responsibility for having available numerous good supplementary books at various reading levels.

Using Pictures

The use of pictures is an excellent method of drawing children to books. A picture illustrating a familiar story may give the child a sense of security. On the other hand, a picture illustrating a story new to the child may be so exciting that he will want to hear the story. If the teacher has made it clear that she will, on occasion, read stories selected by pupils, the child will have an added incentive to seek and find a "good story." If the class enjoys "his story," he will experience keen satisfaction that will be associated with the reading process; at the same time, he will reinforce the knowledge that he can get "meaning" from pictures. After selecting a picture illustrating an unknown story, the child can be invited to tell what he thinks the story will be. Using this technique, the teacher can get some measure of the child's creative ability and his language facility. The use of pictures can help develop various other needed skills such as visual discrimination, attention to detail, and extension of concepts.

SUMMARY

Learning to read is an extension of language skills which the child has already developed. Yet reading calls for several skills which are very much different from those previously learned. Specific examples include visual discrimination of letters and word forms, auditory discrimination of speech sounds within words, association of printed letters with the sounds they represent, and the blending of a number of letter sounds to arrive at the pronunciation of words in one's oral usage vocabulary, but which are not known as sight words. Failure to make adequate progress in these skills will inevitably slow or derail the entire developmental process of reading. Despite the importance of these factors, preparing for reading involves many other skills and capacities. Growing into reading is part of the child's total growth pattern. Certainly social-emotional factors are the key to success or failure in beginning reading for some children. These factors are not measured on reading readiness tests, and possibly this may be one reason why the predictive value of these tests is not higher.

The readiness period should not be thought of as ending with a calendar date or dealing with a limited number of specific skills measured by readiness tests. The length of the readiness period should vary for different children, since no pre-determined school schedule could possibly fit all children's development. The readiness program does not attempt to remove individual differences among pupils. It does give the school the opportunity to work with children who have deficiencies in skills which are believed to be important to progress in reading. No part of the readiness period should be thought of as a waiting period. Preparing for reading implies activity on the part of the child and a deliberate structuring of experiences on the part of the school.

Concern for a child's readiness to read is highly justifiable. Expecting a child to read before he is ready violates an important principle of teaching reading. The chief aim of the readiness period is to assure that children get off to a good start in learning to read. Experiencing failure in the early stages of learning to read can lead to attitudes which have far-reaching influence on later development.

YOUR POINT OF VIEW?

What is the basis for your agreement or disagreement with each of the following propositions?

1. When readiness tests administered to a class of first-graders reveal a wide range of scores, all pupils may receive "reading instruction" providing it is highly differentiated.
2. The school provides readiness activities in order to assure that all pupils have a common experience background on which to build future instruction.
3. Reading readiness tests could also be defined as intelligence tests.
4. The extent to which pictures are used in beginning reading materials is unsound since some children form the habit of depending on the picture clues rather than mastering words as sight words.
5. Language usage is the best single indicator of a child's mental ability.
6. Readiness scores of pupils from culturally/economically depressed backgrounds can be expected to be low. The readiness experiences which the school traditionally provides are inappropriate for this group of children.
7. Teaching children to listen is, in general, neglected in the American elementary school.
8. "Context clues" are of little importance in first grade when instruction centers around a basic reader series because of "controlled vocabulary." (Be sure to use a representative basic reader series to illustrate your point of view.)

BIBLIOGRAPHY

1. Anglin, Eleanor M., and Edra Lipscomb, "Sixes Can Take a Giant Stride," *Elementary English,* XXXX (February 1963), 174-83.
2. Baker, Emily V., "Reading Readiness Is Still Important," *Elementary English,* XXXII (January 1955), 17-23.
3. Barrett, Thomas C., "Visual Discrimination Tasks as Predictors of First Grade Reading Achievement," *Reading Teacher,* 18 (January 1965), 276-83.

4. Betts, E. A., "Practical Considerations Based on Research," *Elementary English,* XXXIII (October 1956), 357-71.

5. Bing, Lois B., "Vision and Reading," *Reading Teacher,* 14 (March 1961), 241-44.

6. Blakely, W. Paul, and Erma M. Shadle, "A Study of Two Readiness-for-Reading Programs in Kindergarten," *Elementary English,* XXXVIII (November 1961), 502-6.

7. Bond, Guy L., and Miles A. Tinker, *Reading Difficulties: Their Diagnosis and Correction.* New York: Appleton-Century-Crofts, 1957, pp. 84-92.

8. Bremer, Neville, "Do Readiness Tests Predict Success in Reading?" *Elementary School Journal,* LIX (January 1959), 222-24.

9. Broom, M. E., M. A. Duncan, J. Stueber, and D. Emig, *Effective Reading Instruction* (2nd ed.). New York: McGraw-Hill Book Company, 1951.

10. Cappa, Dan, "Kindergarten Children's Spontaneous Responses to Storybooks Read by Teachers," *Journal of Educational Research,* LII (October 1959), 75.

11. Dechant, Emerald V., *Improving the Teaching of Reading.* Englewood Cliffs, N. J.: Prentice-Hall, Inc., 1964, Chapters 6 and 7.

12. Dixon, Norman R., "Listening: Most Neglected of the Language Arts," *Elementary English,* XXXXI (March 1964), 285-89.

13. Duker, Sam, "Listening and Reading," *Elementary School Journal,* 65 (March 1965), 321-30.

14. Durrell, Donald D., and Helen A. Murphy, "The Auditory Discrimination Factor in Reading Readiness and Reading Disability," *Education,* LXXIII (May 1953), 556-60.

15. Eames, Thomas H., "Physical Factors in Reading," *Reading Teacher,* 15 (May 1962), 427-32.

16. Edmiston, R. W., and Bessie Peyton, "Improving First Grade Achievement by Readiness Instruction," *School and Society,* LXXI (April 1950).

17. Fawcett, Annabel E., "Training In Listening," *Elementary English,* XLIII (May 1966), 473-76.

18. Gates, A. I., "The Necessary Mental Age for Beginning Reading," *Elementary School Journal,* XXXVII (March 1937), 497-508.

19. Goins, Jean Turner, *Visual Perceptual Abilities and Early Reading Progress.* Chicago: University of Chicago Press, Supplementary Educational Monographs Number 78, 1958.

20. Gray, Lillian, *Teaching Children to Read* (3rd ed.). New York: The Ronald Press Company, 1963, Chapters 5 and 6.

21. Heilman, Arthur, "Listening and the Curriculum," *Education,* LXXV (January 1955), 283-87.

22. Henig, Max S., "Predictive Value of a Reading Readiness Test and of Teacher Forecasts," *Elementary School Journal,* L (September 1949), 41-46.

23. Hester, Kathleen B., "A Study of Phonetic Difficulties in Reading," *Elementary School Journal,* XLIII (November 1942), 171-73.

24. Hildreth, Gertrude H., "The Role of Pronouncing and Sounding in Learning to Read," *Elementary School Journal,* LV (November 1954), 141-47.

25. Hillerich, Robert L., "Kindergartners Are Ready! Are We?" *Elementary English,* XXXXII (May 1965), 569-74.

26. Hilliard, G. H., and Eleanor Troxell, "Informational Background as a Factor in the Reading Readiness Program," *Elementary School Journal,* XXXVIII (December 1937), 255-63.

27. Johnson, Lois V., "Group Discussion and the Development of Oral Language," *Elementary English* XXXIII (1956), 496-99.

28. Karlin, Robert, "The Prediction of Reading Success and Reading Readiness Tests," *Elementary English,* XXX (May 1957), 320-22.

29. King, Ethel M., and Siegmar Muehl, "Different Sensory Cues as Aids in Beginning Reading," *Reading Teacher,* 19 (December 1966), 163-68.

30. Lee, J. M., W. W. Clark and D. M. Lee, "Measuring Reading Readiness," *Elementary School Journal,* XXXIV (May 1934), 656-66.

31. Lundsteen, Sara W., "Critical Listening: An Experiment," *Elementary School Journal,* 66 (March 1966), 311-16.

32. McKee, Paul, *Reading: A Program of Instruction for The Elementary School.* Boston: Houghton Mifflin Company, 1966, Chapters 1 and 3.

33. McKim, Margaret G., and Helen Caskey, *Guiding Growth in Reading* (2nd ed.). New York: The Macmillan Company, 1963, Chapters 3-5.

34. Mitchell, Blythe C., "The Metropolitan Readiness Tests as Predictors of First Grade Achievement," *Educational and Psychological Measurement,* 22 (Winter 1962), 765-72.

35. Moreau, Margaret, "Long Term Prediction of Reading Success," *California Journal of Educational Research* (September 1950), 173-76.

36. Morphett, Mabel V., and Carleton Washburne, "When Should Children Begin to Read?" *Elementary School Journal,* XXXI (March 1931), 496-503.

37. Mulder, Robert L., and James Curtin, "Vocal Phonic Ability and Silent Reading Achievement: A First Report," *Elementary School Journal,* LVI (November 1955), 121-23.

38. Newman, Robert E., "The Kindergarten Reading Controversy," *Elementary English,* XLIII (March 1966), 235-40.

39. Pratt, Willis E., "A Study of the Differences in the Prediction of Reading Success of Kindergarten and Non-Kindergarten Children," *Journal of Educational Research,* XLII (March 1949), 525-33.

40. Ragan, William B., *Modern Elementary Curriculum* (rev. ed.). New York: Holt, Rinehart & Winston, Inc., 1960, p. 4.

41. Robinson, Helen M., "Factors which Affect Success in Reading," *Elementary School Journal,* LV (January 1955), 263-69.

42. Rose, Florence C., "The Occurrence of Short Auditory Memory Span among School Children Referred for Diagnosis of Reading Difficulties," *Journal of Educational Research,* LI (February 1958), 459-64.

43. Rudisill, Mabel, "Sight, Sound, and Meaning in Learning to Read," *Elementary English,* XXXXI (October 1964), 622-30.

44. Russell, David H., *Children Learn to Read* (2nd ed.). Boston: Ginn and Company, 1961, Chapter 6.

45. Sister M. Edith C.S.F.N., "Developing Listening Skills," *Catholic School Journal,* 64 (February 1964), 72.

46. Spache, George D., *Reading in the Elementary School.* Boston: Allyn & Bacon, Inc., 1964, Chapter 2.

47. ———, C. Micalla, H. A. Curtis, Minnie Lee Rowland, Minnie Hall Fields, *A Study of a Longitudinal First Grade Reading Readiness Program.* Cooperative Research Project No. 2742. USOE 1965. (Note: this study is summarized in the *Reading Teacher* 19 [May 1956], 580-84.)

48. Stone, Clarence R., *Progress in Primary Reading.* St. Louis: Webster Publishing Co., 1950, Chapter 7.

49. Tinker, Miles A., and Constance M. McCullough, *Teaching Elementary Reading* (2nd ed.). New York: Appleton-Century-Crofts, 1962, Chapters 3-5.

50. Wachner, Clarence, "Listening in an Integrated Language Arts Program," *Elementary English,* XXXIII (December 1956), 491-96.

51. Washburne, Carleton, "Individualized Plan of Instruction in Winnetka," *Adjusting Reading Programs to Individuals,* Wm. S. Gray, (ed.). Chicago: University of Chicago Press, 1941, pp. 90-95.

52. Wepman, Joseph M., "Auditory Discrimination, Speech, and Reading," *Elementary School Journal,* LX (March 1960), 325-33.

53. ———, "The Interrelationship of Hearing, Speech and Reading," *Reading Teacher,* 14 (March 1961), 245-47.

54. Wilt, Miriam E., "A Study of Teacher Awareness of Listening as a Factor in Elementary Education," *Journal of Educational Research,* XLIII (April 1950), 626-36.

55. Witty, Paul A., and Robert A. Sizemore, "Studies in Listening I," *Elementary English,* XXXV (December 1958), 538-52.
II, *Elementary English,* XXXXI (January 1959), 58-70.
III, *Elementary English,* XXXXI (February 1959), 130-40.

Beginning Readers

3

The following discussion deals with the relationship between the cultural and educational environment of beginning readers and the formation of attitudes toward self and reading. The environment in which beginning reading takes place has a vital influence on potential learners. This educational and cultural environment should never result in standardized instruction. Pupils are not interchangeable parts within a classroom; each learner is a separate psychological component.

There are critics of American education who believe our schools have a laissez-faire attitude toward learning the three R's. The fallacy of this premise is nowhere so strongly apparent as in the case of beginning reading. Children become eligible for reading instruction on the questionable basis of chronological age. During their first year of formal instruction, whether ready or not, they are expected to achieve an arbitrary level of competence in reading. If a child shows no interest or ability, the home and school either consciously or unconsciously use coercive means of social control and pressures to motivate the child to achieve. This cultural behavior grows out of the extremely high value our society places on reading ability. This high value, in turn, determines to some degree the attitudes of both parents and school. The following is an illustration.

A group of teachers and administrators were discussing the problem of how to deal with retarded readers when it was established that low intelligence was not the causative factor. Various proposals for remedial teaching were discussed. Suddenly the tenor of the meeting was changed when a speaker made the following statement:

"We all know that there are tremendous individual differences among pupils in every type of skill performance—music, athletics, composition, creativity, oral expression, computation, reasoning, and achievement in all subject matter courses. We accept individual difference in these areas, but not in reading. Although we find great differences in reading skill in every classroom, we insist that all children should be reading at an arbitrary level which we refer to as grade level. The inferior reader must 'be taught' to read at this arbitrary level whether or not we can teach him, whether or not he can learn, and whether or not he is interested. Do we really believe that we never meet a child, even though he is not below average in intelligence, who is just not going to learn to read?"

The idea was promptly rejected with practically no discussion. Discussion of other ideas followed, but after a period of time the moderator asked the group to consider the question expressed above—"Do we have a tendency to reject the idea of individual differences in reading ability and accept those differences in every other facet of human growth and development?" In the discussion it was finally suggested that the community will not entertain the idea that children may lack the maturity to deal with the reading process once they have been accepted by the school for instruction.

Books on psychology and the teaching of reading stress the large range of individual differences among children in reading achievement. Educators, bolstered by additional evidence from classrooms, have nevertheless been unable to convince the community at large that differences among learners are instrumental in producing differences in learning. The pressure from the community and the fact that the curriculum is based on reading skill may partially explain certain school practices. The curriculum of the school rests on the premise that children in a given classroom read at or near a particular level. Once the curriculum and graded reading materials have been determined, the tendency is to try to fit the learner to the materials. It is much easier to cling to an original false premise than it is to revise the curriculum and the grade level system to fit the facts of learner variability.

EARLY READERS

Some children become readers at a much earlier age than do others. Durkin, (7) reporting test data for a population of 5,103 children entering first grade, shows that 49 (or roughly one per cent) met the criteria of having some ability in reading prior to school instruction. In his early studies of genius (upper one per cent of population based on intelligence scores), Lewis M. Terman reported a high incidence of early readers. There are many case studies which report on individual children as early readers. One factor noted frequently in the various reports of early readers is that they received no formal instruction, but learned to read as a result of incidental help provided by adults or siblings in the home.

The Debate on Early Instruction

In our culture, early readers are viewed with fascination and awe. Conversely, children who make less than average progress during the initial instruction period are often subjected to undue pressures in the hope that they will measure up to some arbitrarily predetermined achievement level.

Paralleling the recent emphasis on moving the teaching of subject matter downward in the grade level structure, there has been considerable discussion relative to providing formal reading instruction in kindergarten. Each highly publicized account of a child, or small group of children, who acquire some reading ability before entering school is interpreted in some quarters as evidence supporting earlier formal reading instruction.

Questions relative to the teaching of reading in the kindergarten are often posed in such a way as to lead protagonists into defending an either/or position. Polar positions preclude the possibility of arriving at a meaningful consensus. The question "Should reading be taught in the kindergarten?" is not the same as "Should some children be taught reading in the kindergarten?" The former can lead to logical analyses under such diverse titles as *Let's* Not *Teach Reading In Kindergarten,* (17) and *Kindergartners Are Ready! Are We?* (11)

The early reading controversy is rooted in an important educational principle, to which lip service is paid by practically all educators. This principle is that "the school is to educate each child up to his maximum ability, taking each child where he is and moving him at his own pace." Speaking of learning the reading process, Newman (20) states, ". . . no child should be denied entré to probably the most important of our school-learned forms of expression if he is at the point in his development when it is opportune for him to take part in this expression himself . . ."

When relatively few children attended kindergarten, the issue of reading could be safely ignored. With the rapid increase in kindergarten (and even earlier pre-school experiences) the problem of "What is the proper curriculum for kindergarten?" becomes a significant educational issue. To attempt to resolve this question by recourse to personal predilections results in a meaningless debate.

It is probable that one's concept of the role of the kindergarten will influence his attitude toward early reading instruction. If the kindergarten is seen as a *pre school* experience, the principle referred to above may be waived. On the other hand, if kindergarten is seen as an integral part of the planned educational sequence, rather than as play time or an educational holding action, growth in significant educational processes would be expected.

In much of the discussion of reading instruction in the kindergarten there is either a tacit or openly expressed fear that if reading is taught, the situation can, and likely will, somehow get out of hand. Past practices in our schools would seem to indicate that such fears are well-founded. Newman (20) presents a rationale which favors reading instruction in the kindergarten, adding the reservation, " . . . but only if the reading activities are taught in such a way as to build enthusiasm for books and reading and the foundation for a lifelong interest in reading for pleasure and inquiry. This is a big 'if'. . . ."

In addition to the problem of what type of reading instruction might be appropriate for kindergarten, there is the question of "instruction for whom?" There is no experimentally established chronological or mental age at which children should begin receiving reading instruction. It is well-established that large numbers of children admitted to first grade on the basis of chronological age, rather than readiness for reading, do experience difficulty in learning. Many of these non-reading pupils react adversely to the pressures which accompany instruction under such conditions. The fear of many educators is expressed in the question "What is to prevent more of this type of pressure, administered even earlier in the child's educational career, if formal reading instruction is moved into the kindergarten?"

By a process of careful selection of research data one can build a fairly strong case for earlier reading instruction for *some* children. No manipulation of data will result in a mandate for extending earlier instruction to *all* children.

There is good reason for raising the question of how well the school is equipped for making the proper differentiation of instruction. If we have failed to achieve a workable differentiation at the level we now introduce reading instruction, by what educational alchemy can we expect to achieve this goal by making the task much more complicated?

There is a related problem which should be considered. It is unrealistic to devise a new role for the kindergarten without revamping the curriculum and teaching practices of later grades. One of the saddest things that could happen to a community would be to develop an outstanding kindergarten program in which reading is taught to those children who are ready to read and in which the primary grades continued their present traditional grade-level-dominated teaching. Any gains made in reading would be lost if succeeding grades did not provide a flexible program built on on-going diagnosis of children's present achievement. A breakthrough achieved at any particular level must be accompanied by breakthroughs all along the educational continuum.

It might be argued that the above rationale is extraneous to the question of whether or not reading should be taught in the kindergarten. It should be kept in mind that the points raised are not advanced as arguments *against* the proposition, but rather as an effort to view it in a larger educational context.

"Should reading be taught in the kindergarten?" is the type of question heard too often in education. In essence, this is an abstraction, or even an isolated fragment of a much more complex question. The larger question should focus on "What are the experiences one would find in an ideal kindergarten?" As a first step in answering this question, one would have to determine the *purpose* of kindergarten.

It would take years of evaluation and re-evaluation to cut through the shibboleths developed in the past. Purpose could hardly be divorced from learning and learners. Is kindergarten to be characterized by an informal relaxed approach to growth? Growth in what areas? Is its purpose to take advantage of one of the "golden years" of great potential growth in formal learning? Or is it to "school break" the child and prepare him for the institutionalized environment of the school? Is kindergarten a last fling before institutionalism? Is it to be child-centered? If so, what does this mean? Does the kindergarten have a curriculum? Should much of the present first grade curriculum be moved down into kindergarten? Should kindergarten be renamed first grade?

ATTITUDES TOWARD SELF AND ADJUSTMENT

The reaction of the school and the home to reading skill has a very pronounced effect on the beginning reader. Children cannot help seeing the importance which is attached to learning to read. Many beginning readers must fail because success is measured by an arbitrary criterion, grade level achievement. We will look briefly at the way in which attitudes and later behavior are influenced during the beginning reading period.

Among educators, parents, or psychologists there would be few dissenters to the proposition that "getting the right start" in learning to read is of the greatest importance. For some children who experience difficulty, a poor start is often the key to later reading difficulty as well as a factor in maladjustment. The fact that some children can fail in the beginning stages of reading and still develop into adequate readers and well-adjusted individuals does not in the least militate against the fact that the beginning stage in reading is extremely important. It is during this period that the child develops attitudes toward self, toward reading, and toward competition. These attitudes, in turn, are related to the motivations which may arouse anti-social behavior.

The child's attitude toward self is influenced by the attitudes of others toward him. There are parental reactions toward him as their child and as a learner, possibly complicated by an unconscious comparison of him with siblings. The teacher in turn reacts to the child as a learner, to his home and parents, and to the child as a problem if he develops behavior not condoned by the school. The child senses that his parents and teacher feel that learning to read is extremely urgent. Pressures from home, school, and self do not always result in learning. There are many activities which may call for intense competition, but in most cases it is optional with the individual whether he elects to compete. In the elementary schools there is not a choice of curriculums, one including reading and the other not. The curriculum is *based* on reading. The non-reader has no place to hide except behind the defenses he can devise. Unfortunately, the defenses he develops are not honored by the society in which he lives as substitutes for reading. Examples of these defenses are:

I'm too dumb to read.
Don't-care attitude.
Aggression.
Withdrawal, daydreaming.
Compensation.

Self-confidence is very important for the beginning reader. The child who lacks confidence in his own ability is likely to over-react when he encounters difficulty in learning reading. It is true that the type of home the child comes from and the relations he has had with parents or adults will have already affected his confidence before he gets to school. It is the teacher's task to structure school experiences in such a way that the classroom will be an area of safety rather than a threat. This is one of the most difficult tasks confronting the teacher; it is also one of the most important. The task is difficult because the school is only one of several institutions which parcel out failure and success, ego-satisfaction, and frustration. It has no control over the home, neighborhood, or community. Children entering school have patterns of behavior which reflect experiences of rejection, overprotection, success, personal inadequacy, and the like. (37)

Today there are few educators who question that these experiences relate to learning. It is true that the school cannot undo the past of each child, nor can it control the present in the community and home. A child may come to school with feelings of inadequacy so strong and so reinforced by the home that the school cannot satisfy his need for attention and acceptance. But the school can, in many cases, compensate to some degree for the unfulfilled needs of children. Chapter 1 deals with practices found in many schools which tend to limit effective education. Even if teachers take the position that their only job is to teach an agreed upon curriculum, they must still understand that they teach the subject matter to potential learners. Factors which diminish this potential among learners are teaching problems.

An alert and observant teacher can see many clues which suggest how a particular child fits in with, or is accepted by, the peer group.

Four children are playing in the sand box. Eddie approaches with the intention of joining the group, but is met with: "Get away from here!" "You can't play with us." "There's no more room—let us alone." These responses in themselves are not atypical of six-year-olds. What the teacher has to discover is whether this is just a group of "haves" protecting their domain, the sandbox, from a "have not," or whether this is an illustration of the group's rejection of Eddie.

There are two types of behavior, over-shyness and aggression, which pose special problems for the teacher and special threats to the learning situation. These behaviors are vastly different, yet it is safe to conclude that the same drives are often behind these apparent opposites in behavior. The shy and the aggressive child both desire responses from others. Each has learned the behavior patterns which he uses in an attempt to cope with his environment. Each will also need some help in learning to use behavior that will be likely to lead to group acceptance rather than group rejection.

ATTITUDES TOWARD READING

Most first-grade teachers would agree that one of the most important aims of the beginning reading period is to help the child develop a positive attitude toward reading. Failure in reading is likely to produce the opposite attitude. When the school sets an arbitrary goal or level of achievement, namely, the reading of first grade material, the child feels that non-success in achieving this arbitrary standard is failure regardless of promotion policies.

A number of experienced teachers were given a conventional checklist of reading difficulties. This was a one-page list of difficulties which appear frequently among retarded readers. The teachers were asked to select the two problems which they thought would:

a) Be present in most remedial reading cases
b) Be the most serious problems noted

The majority of teachers gave as their first choice "aversion to reading." If one thought only in terms of the actual mechanics of reading, he might not include aversion as a reading problem. However, it *is* a problem in working with most reading failures. Once a child has developed a dislike for reading, stemming from failure, he is not likely to give up his aversion as a result of persuasion based on the authoritarian statements that reading is fun, pleasant, and important. The child's dislike of reading is a most logical reaction.

The fact that the child will be told it is an unfortunate response will have little influence on its removal.

LATER DEVELOPMENT IN READING

Attitudes and habits acquired by children during the beginning reading period influence later reading behavior. According to the experience of persons working with impaired readers in the upper elementary and intermediate grades, it is not safe to assume that children will outgrow ineffective reading habits. Poor reading habits seem to feed on themselves and multiply. Common but serious pitfalls which threaten the beginning reader include:

1. Word-calling without comprehension; the mere mechanics of reading is equated with reading.
2. Failure to use punctuation properly. Unless the weakness is overcome, the child can never enjoy reading because he will continually distort or destroy meaning.
3. Failure to develop and use methods of attacking unknown words, i.e., structural analysis, phonic analysis, and context clues.
4. Development of crutches which become substitutes for actual sight recognition of words when the sight-word method is used. An inadequate stock of sight words accompanied by pressure to read beyond one's present ability can lead to numerous bad reading habits such as:

    a. Guessing at unknown words
    b. Miscalling words
    c. Substituting words
    d. Inserting or omitting words
    e. Slow reading

These habits tend to be reinforced with practice rather than to disappear with time.

DEVELOPING INDEPENDENT WORK HABITS

This topic is of considerable importance in beginning reading and is related to attitudes toward reading, later development in reading, and emotional maturity. At the present time there is some concern with whether children are developing independence in work habits and self-responsibility. (5) Despite this concern, it is quite possible that the importance of the relationship between independent work habits (or self-responsibility) and success or failure in reading is underestimated. The data on emotions and reading strongly suggest that learning to read cannot be reduced to a perceptual or associative process, even though reading cannot take place without these functions. Reading is more than a sum of skills. There are also psychological factors which are much more difficult to analyze. This supports the hypothesis that reading is a part of the total development of the child.

Primary children need to develop self-confidence through independent work habits. These promote emotional maturity and, in turn, reading readiness. (Courtesy Cincinnati Public Schools.)

In any discussion of reading readiness one invariably meets the term *immaturity*. An immature child has not attained a specific level of behavior associated with his chronological age. Lack of responsibility or self-dependence is universally cited as evidence of immaturity. The child of six who has avoided or who has been prevented from developing independence and self-reliance is not likely to become self-reliant and independent in school unless he receives some specific guidance. The point is that immaturity, in the psychological sense, has been learned. The child's behavior may have developed out of the parents' needs to keep the child dependent. It should be kept in mind that one of the easiest things to learn in early life is a pattern of abdicating responsibility. The child who learns this pattern has become accustomed to social controls from without. He will naturally find it difficult to develop self-discipline or controls from within. In this connection, Staiger (30) suggests that some children fail to learn to read because they have never had to do anything and therefore feel that they do not have to learn to read. Delays, procrastination, and lack of self-responsibility can only increase the difficulty of learning to read. In other situations where this behavior was learned, the parents can eventually make a response which resolves the problem. They can hang up the clothes, pick up the toys, write an excuse for the child when he is tardy, and take him to school in the car if he misses the bus. But learning to read is a task which no parent can perform for the child.

The aim of instruction in beginning reading is to make the child an independent reader. It is here that the child will develop habits of reading and study which will help or hinder him throughout his academic career. Independent work habits and self-responsibility are essential for children in today's schools because of group instruction in which children have to work out their own problems. Grouping practices create a problem since the teacher must divide her time among several different groups, thus leaving the child on his own during a good part of the time devoted to reading instruction. A recent summary of the literature on the development of responsibility in children suggests a number of principles, some of which are abstracted and presented below. (19)

1. Training for responsibility begins early.
2. The child needs guidance from adults.
3. Children can learn responsibility only by practicing it.
4. Intelligent training for responsibility should be different for different children.
5. The child needs to know what is expected of him. This need demands consistency from adults.
6. No child should be expected to achieve perfection.
7. Adult attitudes toward responsibility influence its development in children.
8. Too much as well as too little responsibility can be harmful.

The child who develops independence and self-direction in his work habits early in the process of learning to read is not likely to become a severely retarded reader. The child who loses, or never gains, confidence in himself, the child who cannot work alone, complete tasks, and in general assume some responsibility for learning, is not well-prepared to weather a learning crisis. There are a number of ways in which a teacher can help pupils get off to a proper start in developing good work habits.

Give responsibility to all children and not just those who are already confident and at ease. Collecting workbooks or readers, stacking them neatly, cleaning up after art work, arranging chairs after group work, and stopping or beginning a task when requested to do so help develop self-discipline. It should be remembered that children learn best through experience. (22)

Do not give a child tasks that he does not understand or cannot do. He will lose interest, procrastinate, daydream, and soon conclude that this is what one does in school.

Set short-term goals which can be readily achieved. The teacher should never tell her students that she will look at their work when it is finished and then fail to do so. The child wants a reward, and the teacher's approval of the completed task is interpreted as a reward. The child will then have many experiences of success which he associates with the reading situation.

It is stated above that children should learn to begin and stop activities when requested to do so. If a child is engrossed in a task, such as coloring, printing, or working a page in a readiness book, permitting him to complete it might be better than interrupting and insisting that he join a group to do something else. When grouping is flexible and a good learning climate exists, he will be able to join the group in a few minutes without disrupting the activity. Furthermore, children have a relatively short attention span and become tired even of tasks they enjoy.

If a child works slowly on an activity that the teacher feels should be completed, she can give a moment's help and then praise the child for completing the task, thus instilling the idea that this is the standard of performance which she expects from him. Children's reading behavior should be observed very closely so that no child experiences too much failure and frustration with reading. Children should be praised when they try, even if their accomplishment falls short of arbitrary standards.

EXAMPLES OF BEGINNING READERS

We have discussed the social-educational environment in which beginning readers operate; we will now look briefly at the beginning readers themselves. Experienced teachers understand that the children who constitute any first grade class are tremendously different from each other, and few teachers would subscribe to the notion that a brief period of readiness experience in first grade appreciably narrows the range of individual differences. It is not an objective of the first year of formal schooling to remove individual differences. All children cannot be moved up to the level of the more advanced pupils, and it is educationally indefensible to attempt to hold the advanced pupils on a learning plateau until the slower ones have advanced. Although it is impossible to remove these individual differences, the teacher and school should be aware of them and concerned with them. (14)

The fact that children are so different when they come to school makes it imperative that the teacher discover those differences which are important factors in learning to read. Then she must develop a program of teaching which at its maximum effectiveness will help each child to grow at a rate commensurate with his ability. The teacher must guard against practices and classroom experiences which may damage the child psychologically and inhibit learning in the future. The discussion which follows attempts to show how differences among pupils are related to instruction. The cases used as illustrations were found in one first-grade class.

Scott was a boy of average intelligence who gave the appearance of being shy. He was reluctant to respond in class or to join in the playground activities for fear that he would fail. He would give up easily, make no effort to get help from the teacher when it was needed, and was showing no progress in reading. He was socially immature and inadequate in the group. Within three or four months he had been generally rejected by the group. On the surface, he seemed to accept this, yet he harbored intense hostility.

He did not manifest this hostility through overt attacks on other children but through such immature behavior as scribbling on another pupil's drawing, breaking another child's pencil, and putting his own coat on a hallway hook in place of another, which he would then drop on the floor. He displayed a tendency to tattle and call the teacher's attention to other pupils' shortcomings. Whatever form his aggression took, he always seemed to get caught.

Jerry was a boy of above average intelligence and, according to the teacher, just the opposite of Scott. She characterized him as being "pushy" in class, attempting to be the center of everything that went on. He was able to achieve leadership status among the class but still had an insatiable need to be the center of attention and to dominate others. Physically he was more mature than the other boys and extremely well-co-ordinated. He was not a problem in the sense of being a bully, simply because his superiority in things physical was never questioned.

Despite high ability he made a poor adjustment in class. He was unable to work alone or carry any project through to its conclusion. Instead of doing assigned seat work, he would wander around the room in an attempt to get an audience. He got off to a very poor start in reading, as did Scott.

Doris, a girl of high average intelligence, was one of the most mature children in the class. Her language facility was above average and, while not the brightest child in the class, she was as well-informed as any. She was accepted by both boys and girls as a leader and yet did not insist on the leadership role. Her social adjustment was excellent both in and out of class. She enjoyed reading from the start. Making better than expected progress in beginning reading, she continued this same level of performance in the following years.

What were the real differences between these pupils? On the basis of C.A., I.Q., and M.A. they were fairly well-equated. All came from homes of higher than average socio-economic status. Each child had been read to a great deal prior to school and since early infancy. Each had many books at home and each had rich and varied experiences prior to entering school, which included family picnics, rides on trains, long trips by car, eating out with their families, and visits to large cities, farms, zoos, and parks. How did they differ?

Scott was the older of two boys. Both parents set very high standards for him. His parents were perfectionists, and he could never quite measure up to their expectations. He became very aware of this. It was impossible to do anything exactly right. He was always nagged at when he attempted anything, and withdrawal was a most logical response. This response he soon learned and eventually over-learned. His ego was threatened by this inability to please his parents. When he really did wrong he was not rejected or severely punished. In fact, he was treated as an individual, for his parents tried to discover "Why did Scott do this?" The closest his psychological needs ever came to being fulfilled was when he was caught in some misbehavior which was a threat to his parents. School simply became a new and different arena, and he used the same weapons and approach, even though, from an adult standpoint, his responses were not the most logical ones available.

Reading became a threat to him very early in school. Like most parents, his were concerned about reading. They wanted him to get a good start. His confidence in himself and in his ability was already undermined, and he started from the premise that he would fail in reading. It is not surprising that with this emotional conflict he was unable to bring his energies to bear on the reading task. As tension from failure mounted, he used responses which further alienated him from people — his parents, peer group, and teacher. Needing acceptance more than anything else, and being denied it, he withdrew from any situation which in his mind might further jeopardize his status.

Jerry was the only child of parents who had both finished college, done graduate work, and acquired professional standing. They were quite concerned with status, but unconsciously so. They never verbalized comparisons between Jerry and members of his peer group. In their own minds such invidious comparisons were a sign of immaturity. Yet their need for Jerry to succeed, to be the best participant in all types of endeavor, while not perceived by them, was so close to the surface that it was somehow not lost on him. His security became tied up with excelling, with dominating others. Success was the safety region for him. Through it, he could dominate the home; it was the price paid for love, affection, and acceptance. As he grew to school age, most of his endeavors were rewarded by success. He was "superior."

Reading was a different story. He did not start school with a superiority in this skill. He found himself in a group where, in one particular skill, he was only average. He seemed never to be interested in reading. As other pupils' superiority in reading became marked, reading became a threat to him. A frontal attack on the problem was not the solution he chose. He elected to compensate. He withdrew from reading, disrupted class activities, interfered with others' learning, and tried to capture attention and maintain his status in numerous ways, none of which seemed logical to adults.

The needs and motives of the two boys were strikingly similar, as were their attitudes toward the reading situation. Yet their overt reactions to a frustrating situation were quite different, so much so that the teacher identified the boys as being "just the opposite." Would knowing the background of each boy, as related here, help the teacher in dealing with their reading problems?

Our third case, Doris, was not a reading problem. This girl was a well-adjusted, thoroughly accepted child. She was the youngest of several siblings, adored by her family, but not spoiled. She did not have to compete for affection. An outward appearance of the home lives of all three children appeared to be similar. Yet only one of the three had found security at home. Could this factor have had an important relationship to reading?

The three children just described were members of the same first grade class. This class contained over twenty other children, some of whom would merit an equally extensive individual analysis if they were to be understood as beginning readers. Here, only an important fact or two concerning these twenty children will be mentioned; teachers' knowledge or experience will show why these facts are important in beginning reading.

Some of the children were barely old enough to enter school. Others were eight or nine months older. Some had attended kindergarten the previous year, others had not. Three children had attended nursery school since they were three years old. Two of the mothers worked outside the home during those years.

The I.Q.'s of children in this group ranged from 76 to 130. Three children measured 85 or below. Mental age varied as much as 24 months within the group. Education of parents ranged from one year in high school to graduate work in college. Occupation of the parents ranged from manual laborer to physician. Two children had medical records showing excessive illness during childhood. One child wore glasses. There were emotional problems other than Scott and Jerry, mentioned above.

These and many other factors are definitely related to learning to read and to the differences in reading ability which will inevitably emerge in any first-grade class. Being able to detect differences and understand their significance is an invaluable aid to the teacher as she plans experiences and sets goals for individuals in her group. From the potential learner's position, having a teacher with this ability to detect subtle but important differences is a form of insurance against being pushed too fast, losing self-confidence, and forming an aversion to school and to reading.

EGO-INVOLVED BEHAVIOR IN THE CLASSROOM

Understanding the term ego-involvement, as used here, does not call for an extensive background in psychology. Teachers, like pupils and parents, have egos and know what it is like to have one's ego crushed. They also know the satisfaction felt when one's abilities and accomplishments are recognized by others.

Pupils like to do those things which are ego-satisfying and tend to dislike and resist doing those things which threaten the ego or the self. Previous discussion has centered around the interaction between the learner and instruction. To posit that this interaction is important is to recognize the importance of the learner's ego. The first-grade teacher starts with one advantage that should be exploited to the fullest: *The child is potentially ego-involved in learning to read.* At this stage of his career the child has usually been conditioned to enjoy books and stories. The sense of accomplishment felt when he reads a pre-primer for the first time is probably as great as for any subsequent academic accomplishment. When the child becomes engrossed in the process of learning to read, the effect is to minimize many of the interferences to learning found in the average classroom.

Ego-involvement, if it is not centered on the learning task, can work against the teacher. The following examples of behavior observed in classroom situations will call to mind parallel incidents which teachers have observed. Each incident occurred in a classroom where the teaching was excellent, preparation of pupils for class discussion was thorough, and motivation of the group was above average.

In a first-grade class the children had been divided into several groups, each of which practiced reading a story in a supplementary primer not being used by the class. Each group was to read its story to the class. In order that every pupil could make a contribution, one of the poorer readers was to show the pictures accompanying the story. In one group, a pupil other than the duly appointed one usurped this privilege and was slyly showing the picture from *his* book. The victim of this duplicity promptly and loudly called attention to the infringement. The disruption of the learning activity resulted from the importance the child attached to the ego-satisfying activity of showing the pictures.

A similar situation occurred in another class where five pupils had practiced reading a story in which they each read a predetermined number of lines. When they read this story to the class, one child paused a moment in his reading and the next pupil started to read his remaining lines. The injured party interrupted and loudly asserted, "No, it isn't your turn yet." This behavior interfered with the learning process for the entire class and shows that no child likes to be deprived of his "performance time" with its attendant ego-satisfaction.

In another first-grade class a film strip was being shown. The teacher selected children, one at a time, to walk up to the screen and indicate certain words by using a pointer. A motivational peak was reached each time a pupil was to be selected, followed by a lapse in interest until a new selection was to be made. Achieving the role of "demonstrator" was such a strong status-building activity that it worked against the intended learning situation of mastering the content of the film.

In a second-grade discussion of pioneers and how they cleared the land to plant crops, one pupil seemed extremely eager to make a contribution and pumped his hand up and down quite vigorously. When called on, his contribution to the topic was nil, but he produced a lengthy story which cast him in the central role: "I looked at some seed yesterday at home, and I remember I said to myself: 'this looks just like the cotton seed we had yesterday in school.' I said it looks just like it and I wondered if it was cotton seed. I was going to bring it to school today. . . ."

One third-grade class had studied a particular unit and was now ready to discuss it in class. Prior to the actual discussion, the teacher and pupils had worked out an outline of major points to be discussed, and the teacher had listed these points on the board. The outline was to serve both as a stimulus and as a means of keeping the discussion from wandering. One boy near the rear of the room held up his hand to make a contribution on item one, but since the entire class was prepared and responsive, all could not be called on. The discussion moved on through item two and was well into item three when this boy was finally called on. He gave an immediate answer which was in no way related to the question under discussion, but his response was logical and correct for item one.

The response was too spontaneous to support the hypothesis that he was caught without an answer for the question and simply talked to cover up. It was quite apparent that he had a contribution to make during the discussion of item one, and became so emotionally involved in this situation that he failed to make the shift to items two and three. His ego-involvement became a barrier to his own learning and interfered with the group learning situation.

No teacher, regardless of her skill and experience, can prevent such incidents from occurring in her classroom. From such incidents, however, the wise teacher will learn much about the needs of various pupils in her class. She will attempt to harness the children's egos to the reading tasks so that they will work for her instead of against her. She will realize that the more closely the beginning reading materials are related to the child and his interests, the easier it will be for him to become ego-involved in the reading situation. Illustrations of this point were observed in the same classrooms which provided the examples cited above.

John, a bright boy but a poor reader, could not read from the basal readers being used by the class. The teacher had John tell her a story involving one of his recent experiences. The teacher typed this story, using the easiest vocabulary possible. After reading it several times for him, she had John practice reading it. A flash card was made of each word be had difficulty in learning. John's progress in mastering the sight words was slow, but he did make progress. The last step was to fold a page of construction paper and fasten the typed story inside. On the front of this booklet John printed the words *John's Book*. He clutched his book tightly as he rushed out at the close of school. He would now earn praise and acceptance and restore some measure of self-esteem. Reading was less of a threat at that moment than it had been for many weeks.

Another teacher, whose practice it was to secure many different books for her second grade class, was able to help a very poor reader by finding for him a large colorful book with exciting, full-page pictures and very little reading text. Many pupils in the class showed interest in this book and asked if they might have it when Fred finished reading it. Fred was credited with reading a book and this experience attracted him, at least for the present, to books and reading. Every teacher knows how important these experiences are to the child involved. In the previous chapter it was noted that in the pre-reading stage the child's name is probably the first word he learns. In addition *his* birthday is announced on the board, and he learns the words used to designate *his* school, *his* street, *his* town. These relatively difficult words are learned after fewer exposures than are most words he learns during this period and illustrate the importance of ego-involvement in learning.

CONCLUSION

There are large and significant differences among children as they begin learning to read. Teachers are generally aware of this fact, but classroom practices and habits of thought prevailing in the school and community sometimes tend to slight the significance of these pupil differences. Our society places a high value on reading ability, and as a result all children in the group are expected to progress at a somewhat uniform rate. Failure to do so is a very noticeable failure. When some children in the group do not meet fixed arbitrary standards of achievement, pressures from both school and home increase. Reading is particularly sensitive to pressure because it involves learning a complicated symbol system.

Children as beginning readers are quite pliable, yet there are many who cannot adjust to, or profit from, a lock-step educational philosophy which treats pupils as interchangeable parts in the classroom. These children may have an initial desire to learn to read, but the type of experience they have can affect their goals and behavior. Reading and other learning tasks prescribed by the school can be interpreted as threatening rather than as rewarding.

Ego-involvement is extremely important in learning. A child who fails to meet arbitrary group standards will not experience satisfaction from reading. Even when failure is not present, ego-involvement in learning tasks may lead the child away from the structured activity and thus disrupt learning for himself or others. Too much uniformity of instructional method used with a group that includes a wide range of interests and abilities will not be equally motivating or equally appropriate for each member of the group. This is the sole reason why instruction must be concerned with individual differences.

YOUR POINT OF VIEW?

Would you prefer to defend or to attack the following statements?

1. The teacher, the school environment, and the curriculum inescapably function as barriers to, or means of, fulfilling the psychological needs of children.
2. Inadequate reading ability, or failure to learn to read well enough to meet the demands of the school curriculum, is a factor in producing anti-social behavior.
3. Recently, reading instruction has tended to focus more on materials and methodology than on "the child as a learner."
4. If every child in the class were ego-involved in the learning tasks, there would be practically no discipline problems in the classrooms.
5. Early experiences in learning to read have a considerable influence on pupils' later work habits and attitudes toward the school.
6. Despite grouping practices and educators' expressed concern for individual differences among pupils, the grade-level system inevitably results in "teaching to the mean of the group."
7. American schools' emphasis on reading readiness is more apparent than real. The concept of readiness is verbally embraced, but a large number of pupils are subjected to reading instruction before they are ready.

BIBLIOGRAPHY

1. Ames, Wilbur S., "The Understanding Vocabulary of First-Grade Pupils," *Elementary English,* XXXXI (January 1964), 64-8.
2. Anglin, Eleanor, and Edra Lipscomb, "Sixes Can Take a Giant Stride," *Elementary English,* XXXX (February 1963), 174-82.
3. Blair, Glenn M., *Diagnostic and Remedial Teaching.* New York: The Macmillan Co., 1956, Chapter 13.
4. Chall, Jeanne, "How They Learn and Why They Fail," *Improvement of Reading Through Classroom Practice,* International Reading Association Proceedings, 9, 1964, 147-8.
5. *Childhood Education,* XXXII (March 1956). Theme of Issue: "Children Learn Responsibility."

6. Denny, Terry P., and Samuel Weintraub, "Exploring First Graders' Concepts of Reading," *Reading Teacher,* 16 (March 1963), 363-5.

7. Durkin, Dolores, "Children Who Read Before Grade One," *Reading Teacher,* 14 (January 1961), 163-6.

8. Estvan, Frank J., "The Social Perception of Nursery-School Children," *Elementary School Journal,* 66 (April 1966), 377-85.

9. Hester, Kathleen B., *Teaching Every Child to Read* (2nd ed.). New York: Harper & Row, Publishers, 1964, Chapters 3-7.

10. Hillerich, Robert L., "Pre-Reading Skills in Kindergarten: A Second Report," *Elementary School Journal,* 65 (March 1965), 312-18.

11. ———, "Kindergartners Are Ready! Are We?" *Elementary English,* XXXXII (May 1965), 569-73.

12. ———, "An Interpretation of Research In Reading Readiness," *Elementary English,* XLIII (April 1966), 359-64.

13. Hymes, James L., Jr., *Behavior and Misbehavior*. Englewood Cliffs, N. J.: Prentice-Hall, Inc., 1955.

14. McKim, Margaret G., and Helen Caskey, *Guiding Growth In Reading* (2nd ed.). New York: The Macmillan Company, 1963, Chapter 3.

15. Marksberry, Mary Lee, "Kindergartners Are Not Too Young . . . .," *Elementary School Journal,* 66 (October 1965), 13-18.

16. Mason, George E., and Norma Jean Prater, "Early Reading and Reading Instruction," *Elementary English,* XLIII (May 1966), 483-8.

17. Micucci, Pat, "Let's *Not* Teach Reading in Kindergarten!" *Elementary English,* XXXXI (March 1964), 246-51.

18. Milner, Ester, "A Study of the Relationship Between Reading Readiness in Grade One School Children and Patterns of Parent-Child Interaction," *Child Development,* XXII (June 1951), 95-112.

19. Minton, Betty L., and Dale B. Harris, "The Development of Responsibility in Children," *Elementary School Journal,* LIV (January 1954), 268-77.

20. Newman, Robert E., "The Kindergarten Reading Controversy," *Elementary English,* XLIII (March 1966), 235-9.

21. Ponder, Eddie G., "Understanding the Language of the Culturally Disadvantaged Child," *Elementary English,* XXXXII (November 1965), 769-74.

22. Reed, Calvin, "A Sense of Responsibility: Are Classroom Activities Nourishing It?" *Elementary School Journal,* LVIII (April 1958), 394-7.

23. Rogers, Helen, and H. Alan Robinson, "Reading Interests of First Graders," *Elementary English,* XXXX (November 1963), 707-11.

24. Russell, David H., "Reading and the Healthy Personality," *Elementary English,* XXIX (April 1952), 195-200.

25. Schoephoerster, Hugh, et al., "The Teaching of Prereading Skills in Kindergarten," *Reading Teacher,* XIX (February 1966), 352-7.

26. Sears, Pauline Snedden, "Reading and the Sense of Competence," Twenty-ninth Yearbook, *Claremont Reading Conference,* Claremont, California, 1965, 20-34.

27. Sheldon, William D., "Teaching the Very Young to Read," *Reading Teacher,* XVI (December 1962), 163-9.

28. Smith, Nila Banton, *Reading Instruction for Today's Children.* Englewood Cliffs, N. J.: Prentice-Hall, Inc., 1963, Chapter 3.

29. Spache, George D., "Personality Characteristics of Retarded Readers as Measured by the Picture-Frustration Study," *Educational and Psychological Measurement,* XIV, 1954, 186-92.

30. Staiger, Ralph C., "Self Responsibility and Reading," *Education,* LXXVII (May 1957), 561-5.

31. Sutton, Marjorie Hunt, "First Grade Children Who Learned to Read in Kindergarten," *Reading Teacher,* XIX (December 1966), 192-6.

32. Veatch, Jeannette, *Reading in the Elementary School.* New York: The Ronald Press Company, 1966, Chapter 5.

33. Webster, Jane, "Using Books to Reduce the Fears of First Grade Children," *Reading Teacher,* XIV (January 1961), 159-62.

34. Witty, P. A., "Reading Success and Emotional Adjustment," *Elementary English,* XXVII (May 1950), 281-96.

35. Woolf, Maurice D., and Jeanne A. Woolf, *Remedial Reading Teaching and Treatment.* New York: McGraw-Hill Book Company, 1957, Chapter 2.

36. Wright, Benjamin, "Postscript on Permissiveness," *Elementary School Journal,* LXV (April 1965), 393-4.

37. ———, and Shirley Tuska, "The Price of Permissiveness," *Elementary School Journal,* LXV (January 1965), 179-83.

CRAYOLA

Beginning Reading

4

In order to understand the problems and pressures facing the school in regard to beginning reading instruction, one has to understand the educational milieu in which this instruction takes place. Post-Sputnik education in America has been characterized by several trends, which include:

1. Criticism of method-materials in the content areas which has resulted in sweeping changes in the curriculum of most subject fields.
2. A movement to force subject content downward in the grades.
3. Criticism of reading instruction and materials which for some reason tended to focus on beginning reading instruction.

Each of the above have had considerable impact both on the role of reading in the schools and on the question of how reading should be taught.

CURRICULUM REVISION

The designers of various "new curriculums" in content areas have, in general, been experts in a given subject area such as mathematics, the sciences, or social studies. Curricular materials in these areas have usually been developed with primary concern for content and sequence — *what* to include and *where* to teach it. There has been less than adequate consideration of the learner and his readiness for the prescribed experiences. Since there is a consensus that the content of the new curriculums is "good," the question is not raised as to "good for whom."

The grade placement of materials in the subject areas is based on an a priori assumption that the would-be learners will have mastered a certain level of reading ability which is commensurate with the demands of the materials. It would be relatively simple to design textbooks and related materials if this assumption held, but it does not hold. The question we face today is whether we can have a "good" program in science, mathematics, and the social sciences if we base our judgment only on the content of these courses and do not consider the learners' ability to absorb it.

The point has been raised that the upgrading of subject curriculums has resulted in the inclusion of many reading activities which are beyond the present capabilities of numerous students found in the various grades. Our quest for excellence has resulted in a curriculum which is better suited to the more capable students. The student with average or less than average reading ability is pressured more than taught. Yet, the school continues to embrace the philosophy that every child should be taught at his level; and our schools continue to enroll all youth.

NEW CURRICULUMS PUT PRESSURE ON READING

With subject matter being forced downward within the framework of the grade level system, the reading ability of pupils has become even more crucial today than it has been in the past. However, once the new programs of study in the content fields were accepted, the school was faced with the problem of developing pupil competency for handling the reading tasks involved.

Two suggestions as to how this goal might be achieved are to start reading instruction earlier and move beginning readers faster. A number of new materials for teaching beginning reading have been developed, each of which focuses on the latter method. Characteristics common to most of these materials are that they:

1. Do not offer a broad teaching program which deals with all essential skills.
2. Single out one or another essential skill and concentrate on this facet of instruction.
3. Focus only on beginning reading and offer little or nothing beyond this developmental stage.*

Achieving a fast start in beginning reading may be desirable, but it would not be desirable if it were achieved at the expense of later reading efficiency. It would not be desirable if it inculcated habits which inhibited later growth in facile reading.

READINESS FOR READING

Since beginning reading is the logical extension of a readiness program, there is no break between the two, no point where one ends and the other begins. In a well-organized first grade, the transition is so gradual that the children hardly perceive it. The use of pre-primers and experience charts and stories is seen simply as an extension of work done yesterday and last week. The period of beginning reading should provide intelligent, systematic guidance in activities which make learning to read a meaningful and natural growth process.

OBJECTIVES OF THIS PERIOD

Beginning reading instruction consists, in part, of efforts to teach a number of specific skills, all of which are related to the larger long-term goal of producing facile and critical readers. It is understandable that any process as complicated as beginning reading must have many objectives. Some of these objectives have been dealt with in previous discussions: to structure experiences so that the child feels accepted and develops desirable attitudes toward reading and toward self; to provide for group participation, development of verbal facility, listening ability, and auditory and visual

*A number of these materials are discussed later in this chapter along with data from studies which compare their relative effectiveness in beginning instruction.

discrimination; to teach left-to-right sequence; and to encourage contact with books, stories, and pictures. Despite the fact that these activities are very appropriate in the reading readiness program, it is apparent that the teacher must not neglect any of these goals when instruction in reading becomes more formal. In addition, the teacher will concern herself with other specific objectives:

1. Arousing and sustaining interest in reading.
2. Expanding sight-recognition vocabulary simultaneously with helping the child develop a means of working out unknown words, using all clues available — pictures, configuration of words, context, and structural and phonic analysis.
3. Providing practice in both silent and oral reading.
4. Stressing that reading is comprehension.
5. Providing experiences for developing and extending concepts.
6. Helping the child develop smoothness in the mechanics of reading, such as heeding punctuation, reducing the number of regressions, reading with expression, and using correct pronunciation.
7. Encouraging the development of independent work habits.
8. Providing individual instruction when needed, based on continuous diagnosis.
9. Keeping goals and procedures flexible for individual children.

BEGINNING READING MATERIALS

The process of learning to read is not dependent upon moving through a particular body of content. It consists of mastering a derived language process which is a long-term developmental endeavor. The child can learn needed reading skills through the use of any of a number of printed passages. These materials may be children's books, stories dictated by the child himself, basal texts, experience charts, myths, biographies, riddles, children's newspapers, programmed work books, or subject matter content in any area. The one criterion that any material would have to meet is that of appropriateness to the reader's present level of development.

The major question in reading instruction is not what printed material to teach from, but rather to determine what skills to teach and when and how to teach them. However, when an individual addresses himself to these questions, he usually develops a set of materials which reflect previous decisions relative to the questions of what to teach and where on the educational continuum to teach particular skills. Materials also reflect *how* to teach particular facets of reading.

The school's failure to teach all children to read up to arbitrary grade-level standards resulted in widespread criticism of reading instruction during the past decade. Much criticism was aimed at basal readers, the chief instructional vehicle in a vast majority of American schools. Some of these criticisms will be examined later in this chapter.

Paralleling the concern with materials and methodology was a phenomenal increase in the number and types of materials developed for teaching beginning reading. Materials were designed to emphasize certain premises which promised to be the best approach to reading instruction. Representative examples are augmented English alphabet, diacritical markings, basals following various philosophies, trade books, concomitant stress on reading and writing, use of projected materials (films, filmstrips, etc.), programmed reading workbooks, boxed materials, and reading kits stressing particular facets of reading ranging from phonics to appreciation of literature.

The proliferation of teaching materials undoubtedly held some promise for the teaching of reading since teachers and schools would have many different materials available. However, there developed a tendency to place unwarranted faith in "new" materials and approaches. This false hope was undoubtedly nourished by the producers of some of the new materials. Advertisements and brochures attributed qualities to these materials which had not yet been established in the classroom. "Breakthroughs in reading instruction" were announced with startling frequency, and the popular press joined in building shaky hypotheses into specious proofs for many of the newer materials.

After a decade or more of disillusioned search for a reading instruction panacea, the concensus is that none will be found. There is less of a tendency today to become a partisan for or against particular materials. Many observers feel that the more rigid the teaching, the more likely one is to find reliance on one set of materials; conversely, creative teachers are less bound by loyalties to specific materials and methodology.

The following discussion attempts to point up some of the potential strengths and weaknesses of various materials available for teaching beginning reading.

LANGUAGE-EXPERIENCE MATERIALS

Regardless of what other materials may have been adopted by schools or used by teachers, most teachers of beginning reading include teacher-written charts and stories in their reading programs. The use of pupil experience as the content for writing charts and stories is a practice of long standing. Throughout the years, modifications and extensions have resulted in renewed emphasis on this procedure. For a comprehensive history of the language experience approach, the reader might consult Smith (32) and Hildreth (17). In addition to these sources, two early publications devoted to descriptions of experience-based materials are Gans' (12) *Guiding Children's Reading Through Experience* and Lamoreaux and Lee's (20) *Learning to Read Through Experience.*

The latter work (1943) describes the rationale, as well as concrete procedures, for using teacher-written experience charts. These materials, written by teachers, were envisioned as the basic instructional program. A revision (1963) by Lee and Allen (22) deals not only with experience charts for use with the class as a whole, but stresses the advantages of teachers' writing individual stories for individual students.

The Experience Chart

The experience chart is a means of capturing the interest of children by tying their personal experiences to reading activities. The chart, which tells about a shared activity, is a story produced cooperatively by the teacher and the class. This is a natural extension of earlier and less difficult experiences wherein the teacher wrote single words or short sentences on the chalkboard. Examples, cited in a previous chapter, included days of the week, names of months, the seasons, children's birthdays, holidays, captions for pictures, and objects in the room. The experience chart provides practice in a number of developmental skills which are closely related to reading. For example:

1. Oral language usage in the group-planning prior to a trip and in recounting the experience, for chart building, after a trip
2. The give-and-take of ideas as the experience is discussed
3. Sharpening sensory acuity, particularly visual and auditory, while on excursions
4. Expanding concepts and vocabulary

5. Reinforcing the habit of reading from left to right
6. Experience in learning words as wholes, thus building sight vocabulary
7. Reading the sentence as a unit
8. Reading about one's own experiences, emphasizing that reading is getting meaning from printed words

All of the points cited above are appropriate both to readiness and to beginning reading, and the experience chart should not be thought of as belonging exclusively to one stage of development. The experience chart has merit in proportion to the degree to which certain logical practices are followed. For instance, vocabulary must be simple, and sentences short; a minimum of sentences must be used, and each sentence must contribute to the story. There should be deliberate repetition of common sight words.

Preparing a Group Experience Story

The teacher and children plan for a visit to the zoo, a nearby farm, or the library. Let us assume that the teacher has been able to make all of the necessary arrangements for a trip to the community library. She has arranged for the use of the school bus and has spoken to the librarian, who has volunteered to read the class a story and set up a display of children's books. When she has the attention of the entire class, the teacher might say, "I talked to Mrs. Winters, the librarian, the other day and she invited all of you to come to the library and look at the new books — maybe some of you would want to take a book home with you. I wonder if it would be fun if we took a trip to the library?"

CHILDREN: "Let's go!"
"I'd like that."
TEACHER: "If we go, we'll have to make plans first — what are some things we should decide first?"
BILLY: "Can we go today?"
TEACHER: "Billy asks when can we go? We can't go today, we have to make our plans first."
CHILD: "Let's go tomorrow."
TEACHER: "How many would like to go tomorrow?"
(General agreement)
TEACHER: "How shall we get to the library?"
MIKE: "Let's walk."
MARY: "Can we go in a car?"

TEACHER: "Mike suggests we walk, but it's quite a long way from here; Mary suggested we go in a car, but it would take a lot of cars for all of us. Maybe we could go in the school bus."

(Excitement heightens in the class.)

The class and the teacher talk about what they should do and what they should not do at the library. Following each discussion, the teacher writes the decision on the board; from this activity an experience chart emerges. The chart itself may not be the most important outcome of this educational endeavor. The children have experienced how the group process works; co-operative planning and individual contributions have resulted in identifying and structuring a goal. The children are now ego-involved in a trip to the library. Their experience chart follows:

PLANS FOR OUR TRIP

We will go to the library.
We will go tomorrow.
We will go in the school bus.
This will be fun.
We can look at books.
We will sit in our chairs.
We will hear a story.

The children enjoyed the trip to the library. Mrs. Winters, the librarian, had three tables of children's books available; she showed where the children's books were kept on the shelves and on a book rack. She talked about how to treat books — not to fold pages or tear the paper cover. The children were permitted to look at the books and the pictures. Finally, Mrs. Winters read them the story *Stone Soup.** The children clapped their hands when Mrs. Winters finished the story. They thanked her and then returned to their classroom on the school bus.

That same day they discussed their trip and the things they saw and did and heard. The natural outcome was to "write a story" about their experience. The teacher asked questions and occasionally substituted words to keep the vocabulary reasonable. The following discussion developed the title for the story.

---

*Marcia Brown (New York: Charles Scribner's Sons, 1947).

TEACHER: "What shall we call our story?"
BOB: "What we did at the library."
TEACHER: "That's a good suggestion; does anyone else have a name for our story?"
MARY: "I think it should be called 'We have a nice time at the library.' "
TEACHER: "Fine — anyone else?"
RUTH: "Things we did on our trip to the library."
TEACHER: "Those are all fine — we did have a very nice visit, we did learn many things and we did enjoy the story Mrs. Winters read us. Would it be all right to call our story 'Our Trip to the Library'?"

Since the children agreed to the title, she printed it on the chalkboard, saying each word as she wrote it and then reading the entire line, being careful to move her hand slowly from left to right as she read. Next, she inquired what incidents should be related in the story and accepted the various suggestions while attempting to keep the vocabulary as simple as possible. Each line of the story was developed in much the same way as the title was. The teacher was careful to see that all of the students participated. The following chart is the result:

OUR TRIP TO THE LIBRARY

We rode in the school bus.
The bus took us to the library.
We looked at many books.
We sat at tables.
We looked at books and pictures.
Mrs. Winters read us a story.
The story was *Stone Soup*.
We thanked Mrs. Winters.
Our trip was fun.

The teacher read each line as soon as she printed it on the board, again being careful to move her hand under the line from left to right as she read. The teacher and children then read the complete story. Next, a child was asked to point out the line that told how they had traveled to the library, the line that told the name of the story they had heard, the line that told where the children sat in the library, and so forth. In each case the child pointed out the desired line and attempted to read it.

The same chart may be used in other ways. Each line in the chart may be duplicated on a strip of heavy paper: *We thanked Mrs. Winters.* A child is handed a sentence and is asked to find this line on the chart. Individual words may also be placed on oaktag or cardboard and held up by the teacher and a child selected to point out that particular word on the chart: *books, us, bus.* Word cards may be prepared for each word in a particular line. These are handed to a child in mixed order, and he is to arrange them in proper order to correspond with the line on the chart. These tasks can be either seatwork or boardwork. The experience chart can be used with the class as a whole and also with various reading groups. After its main use with a unit, it may be referred to incidentally when certain words used on the chart come up in other contexts and in other activities.

Individual Experience Stories

Children enjoy talking about their experiences, particularly about incidents which involve them, their families, their pets, and the like. One of the best ways to take advantage of such motivation is to write individual experience stories. These language productions are usually brief, ranging from one to several sentences which deal with one incident. In the early stages of reading, the stories are usually dictated by the pupils and written by the teacher.

Some of the major principles which provide the rationale for language experience stories have been outlined by Lee and Allen (22) and include:

1. What a child thinks about, he can talk about.
2. What one talks about can be expressed in writing.
3. Anything the child or teacher writes can be read.
4. One can read what he writes and what other people write.
5. What a child has to say is as important to him as what other people have written for him to read.

Since these brief stories relate the child's own experiences, they tie his ego to the reading situation. The stories are always meaningful and are written in complete sentences which closely parallel the child's own language usage. In some cases the teacher can write brief stories based on her observation of children and events which occur in class. An excellent description of how one teacher introduced the writing of experience stories is provided by Lindberg:

"I have something to share with you, too," the teacher says to the first graders. "I like to write books for boys and girls. Here are the ones I wrote last night. Let me read them to you."

She holds up a gay booklet, "This one is called *Susan's Red Shoes*." Susan looks up. Can it be! She does have new red shoes. The other children look at Susan. They are very aware of her bright new sandals because she talked of nothing else yesterday.

The teacher opens the cover and reads the first page, "Susan has new red shoes." She turns to the next page. "Her father bought them for her at Smith's Shoe Store. They cost $3.98." Now the children know for certain that it is their Susan, and Susan is beaming.

The teacher continues to read. "See me stand on one foot," says Susan. "Now see me stand on the other. Now watch me jump."

"I have written the story," says the teacher to Susan, "but there are no pictures in the book. Perhaps you can make some."

The other children lean forward. What is in the other books?

"Read some more. Read one about me," are the cries from the first graders. So they are read. *Terry's Tooth, Jane's Trip to the Farm, Harry and His Big Brother, Roy's Birthday Cake, Cowboy Joe, Here Comes Josephine* are the titles.

"But there wasn't one about me!" is the refrain when all of the books have been read.

"See that pile of books on my desk? There isn't anything written in them. Why don't you tell me what to write — then you will have a book, too."

During their work period, several children dictate stories. These will be read to the others the next morning.(23)

The Experience Approach as Method

Experience charts and stories can be used in any method of teaching reading. When a program limits instructional materials to this one type, the resulting instruction might be referred to as the *experience method*. Any procedure may have both merits and limitations, and this seems particularly true of the experience approach to teaching reading. The major strengths of experience stories and charts have been discussed previously, some potential weaknesses which may result from *overreliance* on teacher-written materials are:

1. It is difficult to control vocabulary. Too many words may be introduced at one time.

2. Basic sight words may not be repeated often enough to insure mastery.
3. When used exclusively as a *method,* it puts too much of a burden on the teacher, demands much time and a high level of training.
4. It is difficult to adapt this type of instruction to the needs and abilities of *all* children.
5. It encourages memorization rather than mastery of sight words.

The strengths and weaknesses of the experience method are relative and not inherent in the method itself. Under certain conditions, all of the advantages of the method might be lost through overemphasis, misuse, or lack of understanding. In other situations the effects of certain of the cited disadvantages could be held to a minimum through a teacher's skill, experience, and clear understanding of objectives. In the writer's opinion, the experience approach is most vulnerable when advocated as a complete method in itself. Most teachers prefer to use the experience chart as a supplement to basals and other materials. This permits certain of the weaknesses to be minimized. The basic readers provide drill on sight vocabulary and control over the introduction of new words. The use of experience charts adds flexibility and interest to the program.

THE BASAL READER APPROACH TO TEACHING READING

For decades, basal reader series have served as one of the chief instructional materials used in the elementary grades for teaching reading. These materials are widely used today despite the fact that in recent years basals have been widely criticized. Critics have alleged that:

1. The materials are dull, insipid, and too repetitive.
2. The language used is somewhat removed from the child's own language usage.
3. Story material often lacks literary merit.
4. Too little emphasis was placed on teaching letter-sound relationships in grade one.
5. Content dealt almost exclusively with characters and incidents drawn from middle class strata; and conversely minority groups were practically ignored. (29)

Throughout the 1950's and early 1960's all basals series tended to be very much alike. Significant innovations were held to a minimum; and the above criticisms, as they related to many materials, were justified. (21) On the other hand, there were a number of indefensible teaching practices found in the schools which were not suggested or condoned by any basal program. However, certain critics of basals contended that these practices were inevitable outcomes of using basals. For instance, when using basals, teachers will:

1. Have a group of children "read round-robin" every story they read. Each child will be asked to focus his attention on the same line at a given time.
2. Without exception resort to "three groups" within a classroom, and these groups will remain static throughout the year.
3. Make no provision for individual differences beyond this "three-group" pattern.
4. Hold the more facile reader to the basal material only, forcing him to move through this material at a pace far below his capacity.
5. Prohibit children from selecting and reading other books in which they may be interested.

Unfortunately, the above practices could be found in certain classrooms. Removing basals from these classrooms, however, would not get at the basic problem which essentially is poor teaching. The following is a description of the materials usually found in any basal reading series. These materials are arranged to parallel the grade-level system. They range in difficulty from a work-type readiness book (containing pictures, geometrical forms and letter-matching exercises) to rather massive anthologies at seventh- and eighth-grade levels.

Readiness Books

At the readiness level one might find picture books in which a picture or series of pictures suggests a child-centered story. From the pictures the teacher and the pupils develop a story. The more skillful the teacher is in providing background and involving the pupils in participation and interpretation, the more successful the use of these materials will be. Other readiness books may call for children to identify and mark similar objects, letters, or words, to facilitate the development of visual perception. To strengthen auditory discrimination, the child will identify two pictures in a group which will rhyme when named. Identifying other pairs of pictures which start with the same sound gives practice in the discrimination of initial sounds.

Pre-Primers

The readiness books are followed by a series of pre-primers, two or three in number, in which the characters are the same ones the children met and talked about in the readiness books. The pre-primers introduce pupils to printed words *along with pictures*. The first few pages may have single words which are "naming words" to go with the picture. Gradually more words and sentences per page are used.

Primers

The primer is the first hard-back book in the series. It carefully builds on what has gone before, using the same characters the children are familiar with and reviewing the words already met, while it introduces 100 to 150 new words.

First Readers

Some series contain a single first reader; others have two (1^1 level and 1^2 level). Different series vary as to vocabulary load introduced, but a range between 315 and 400 words for first grade is representative.

Graded Readers

Each subsequent grade level introduces one or more basal reading books. Many series provide two books at each of the grade levels, second through fourth, and one book at grades five and on. These are usually designated by grade number plus a subscript which indicates first or second half of the year (2^1-2^2, 3^1-3^2, 4-5-6-7-8).

Workbooks

Separate workbooks which parallel each level (pre-primers, primers, first readers 2^1-2^2, etc.) are available. The workbooks present material arranged as teaching exercises. These are usually designed so that one concept or skill is dealt with on each page. The exercises reinforce the teaching of skills which are being dealt with in the readers. In some cases, workbook pages are tied to specific stories in the reader. In others, skill-building exercises are independent of story content and could be used whether or not a particular basal reader were available.

Supplementary Materials

It is becoming more common at all grade levels for basic reader series to include some supplementary books to be used in conjunction with the regular graded series. There has always been an abundant supply of these supplementary materials available at the intermediate level. Recently, good supplementary books have appeared at the early primary level, where they are sorely needed. Some of these are easy reading, introducing very few words other than those already met in the regular basal texts. Others are designed for the more advanced readers and are more difficult and more challenging than the regular graded series.

Other supplementary materials include large poster-size wall charts or spiral-book charts which exactly duplicate a pre-primer. The large picture and large print have obvious advantages for classroom use. There has been considerable emphasis on film strips designed for use with basic reader series. The reading gains reported as resulting from the systematic use of film strips and other visual aids are encouraging. (24, 25)

Teacher Manuals

Teacher manuals, or guide books, containing suggestions for effective use of materials, accompany each reading level. That is, a separate manual is available for the pre-primer, primer, and first reader stages as well as for each subsequent level (2^1-2^2-3^1-3^2, etc.). These manuals are discussed in more detail in the following section.

USING A BASAL READER SERIES

The purpose here is to deal with the framework of basal programs as designed for the first year of instruction. The major advantages of using a good series include:

1. Modern reader series are characterized by excellent use of pictures and art work.
2. A number of the first books used deal with the same characters, giving children a feeling of familiarity with the material and adding to their confidence in reading.
3. The books are graded to provide systematic instruction from the pre-readiness level through the upper elementary grades.
4. These graded materials permit teachers a great deal of flexibility in dealing with individual differences and in working with children grouped according to attained reading skill.
5. Excellent teacher guides are provided for each book or level. These provide suggestions for a step-by-step teaching program.
6. If used properly, the basic reader series deals with all phases of the reading program, guarding against overemphasis on some aspects and neglect of others.
7. Practice of new skills is introduced in a logical sequence.
8. A great deal of review is provided in deliberate, well-thought-out procedures.
9. To prevent frustration in beginning reading, the vocabulary is rigidly controlled.
10. Use of prepared materials saves teachers considerable time.

A Well-Balanced Program

Providing a well-balanced program is a virtue of basal series, particularly in the beginning reading stage. Provision is made for silent and oral reading, and by means of grouping and through individual work, the teacher can vary the emphasis for different pupils. The preparation of pupils for tasks is thoroughly outlined in the teacher's manual. During the readiness period the children have used a pre-reading book which included a number of pictures. Through these pictures the children were introduced to the characters that they will meet again in the pre-primer, primer, and first reader. The teacher acquaints the children with the names of these characters and prints their names on the chalkboard, thus preparing them for the first words they will encounter in the pre-primer. The pictures are specific in that they represent *particular* persons, but they are general in that the characters in them are doing things that most children understand. Out of these picture situations, discussion can grow and provide an introduction to formal reading in basal materials.

The first few pages of the pre-primer may be only pictures, but very soon words are introduced. These will probably be the names of the boy and girl who have been met previously in pictures—Jane, Sally, Ted, or Jack. The teacher will probably use the chalkboard and flash cards for both teaching and reviewing words. During seatwork, the children will draw a line from the word (*Sally*, *father*, *Ted*, etc.) to a picture the word represents. They might be asked to underline one of three sentences which describe a picture:

> Sally rides in the wagon.
> Sally plays with Spot.
> Sally plays with Father.

Such exercises help children learn words in the first pre-primer. Soon, more than one familiar word will appear on each page but rarely more than one *new* word.

The repetition of words in beginning reading can dull the child's appetite for reading. The teacher must guide the pupils into both imaginative and reminiscent "building of ideas and stories." The book may contain the words "Look, Mother" under the picture. These words, with the help of the picture, can serve as the basis for a great number of interesting and logical questions and conjectures. Perhaps from the following one might easily visualize the picture that accompanies "Look, Mother."

> "Who is in the picture?"
> "Yes, what is Tom doing?"
> "Does Spot like to wear Tom's hat?"
> "What is Tom's mother doing?"
> "Is she watching Tom?"
> "Would he like for her to see Spot?"
> "Does Spot look funny?"
> "What does Tom say to his mother—who will read what he says?"

Many other points could have been discussed—pets in general, kindness to pets (Tom was not hurting Spot, but playing). Why wasn't mother watching? (Sometimes mothers are busy.) Why was she picking flowers? (Innumerable good responses.) What season of the year was this? As the child learns more words, he has less need for pictures which suggest the context or hold attention. As the pupils move through the basal series and master sight words, they need less story analysis by the teacher.

Comprehension and meaning are emphasized as children select the best titles for paragraphs or short stories or as they recall sequences of events. Concepts of time, number, size, and direction are developed through seatwork which calls for children to follow directions, to perceive relationships, to grasp main ideas, and to anticipate events. Auditory discrimination exercises are provided in the form of rhyming exercises and an emphasis on the initial sounds of words. Motor co-ordination of small muscles is developed in exercises such as tracing, coloring outlined forms, drawing connecting lines between matching words, and copying words from a model.

Teacher Manuals

One of the greatest advantages in using a good series is the availability of excellent teacher guides. These guides are carefully worked out by the authors with the total reading program in mind. Sound laws of learning are followed, specific techniques are suggested, lesson plans are given in great detail, and the reasons for using certain approaches are explained. The beginning teacher would be remiss in not following the teacher guides and in not becoming very familiar with the rationale and concrete suggestions they contain. Experienced teachers might find the detail of these manuals a bit tedious, but they know that they can take what is offered and adapt it in light of their own experience.

The thorough extensive treatment typical of teacher guides is exemplified in the manual for the readiness book, *Getting Ready To Read.** This teacher guide contains over one hundred pages of suggestions and directions for use with a pre-reading program. In the Robinson, et al., series, a teachers' guide consisting of over 250 pages is available for use with two pre-primers.** Considering that these pre-primers contain 75 different words, it is obvious that the guide is thorough and goes beyond the mechanical aspects of instruction at this level. Separate manuals for the primer and

---

*Paul McKee and M. Lucile Harrison (4th ed.; Boston: Houghton Mifflin Company, 1966).

**Helen M. Robinson, et al., "The New Basic Readers" Guidebook, Second and Third Pre-Primers (Chicago: Scott, Foresman and Company, 1965).

first reader each contain approximately 250 pages of material addressed to the teacher.

With this type of meticulous concern for every facet of the reading program, the various guides can be excused for sometimes stressing the inevitable as if it were a deliberately planned virtue of the basic readers. It is common practice to find teacher guides making much of the fact that pre-primers, primers, and first readers "do not require children to deal with concepts beyond their experience level." Considering the small number of words found in these materials, it would be a challenge, using only this vocabulary, to confront the child with concepts beyond his experience level. He uses twenty to thirty times this number of words and understands many more.

The foregoing discussion has touched on the alleged major weakness of the basic reader series. The concern for controlling the introduction of new words puts a limit on the variety of reading material which can be accommodated within the framework of the controlled vocabulary. The teacher must motivate children to identify themselves with the characters and the situations depicted, even though these may be somewhat alien to children of certain socio-economic groups. Without identification, the vicarious experiences gained from reading about a set of middle-class siblings, their parents, and their dog, may not seem half as fascinating as television. If one reads the guides carefully, it will be obvious that a major portion of their content is devoted to suggesting ways and means of bringing in background and of extending the concepts and the meanings actually found in the reading materials. This is important because the child's interest must not be permitted to lag.

Use of Workbooks

As pointed out previously, workbooks constitute one of the important supplementary features of basal reader series. The educational value of using workbooks has been debated for years. It is true that seatwork in the form of workbook exercises can deteriorate into nothing more than "busy work" if teachers permit this to occur. However, this is only a potential danger not an inevitable outcome. A child may "learn" to daydream or doodle in workbook sessions. But with the right type of guidance, he can develop self-reliance and independence in work habits.

Workbooks properly used can have considerable educational value. Since a wide variety of skills are dealt with, it is likely that some exercises can be found that provide needed and meaningful practice in mastering essential skills. Workbooks can serve as diagnostic instruments since they will identify those children who do not understand a particular step in the reading process. A study of errors made by children will suggest to the alert teacher where further instruction is needed.

For some children, workbook exercises have value in that they are brief—usually one page. This factor is especially appealing to the child with a short attention span. A given workbook or developmental series deals with a wide variety of tasks. This provides work on new skills as well as review of skills partially mastered. Workbooks, like all other instructional media, are neither inherently good or bad. The way they are used can result in either of these outcomes.

Economy of Time

Economy of teachers' time is a major factor in the widespread use of basal series. This is closely related to the previous point of a balanced reading program. No teacher would ever have the time to match the meticulous planning that is reflected in the total program of a good basal series. When a teacher has materials available for teaching and drill on every facet of reading, she will have more time to prepare supplementary exercises as needed. It will still be necessary to prepare these for certain pupils, since the basal program cannot possibly meet all individual needs. However, it is easier to prepare supplementary lessons for a few than it is to build the entire program for all pupils.

Individual Differences

Individual differences are provided for in basal series even though the program will not be adequate for some pupils who have special problems. A number of levels of reading skill are encompassed in these materials. The teacher who understands her pupils, who understands the basal reading materials, and who is not compulsive in her teaching, will be able to use these materials to great advantage. Figure 12 attempts to illustrate the different levels one is likely to find among children in a given first grade and the correlative materials available in a basal reader series.

FIGURE 12

A GRAPHIC REPRESENTATION OF THE READING LEVELS WHICH COULD BE EXPECTED FOR A GIVEN CLASS NEAR THE END OF GRADE ONE.

1. Readiness work, auditory discrimination, beginning sound in words, rhymes, etc., visual discriminations, has not learned enough sight words to read pre-primer
2. Making progress in PP^{2-3}
3. Successful reading of primer
4. Successful first readers
5. Can read in 2^1 readers
6. Can read in 2^2 readers
7. Third readers or above

From the standpoint of the busy teacher, one of the major contributions of any good basal series is the well-thought-out seatwork which is provided in workbooks. A separate workbook is available at every level—readiness, pre-primer, primer, and first reader. Many exercises are tied to particular stories in the reading text; others are independent of actual stories but closely parallel or supplement the new tasks. This varied nature of the workbooks in the basal series allows for flexibility in assignments, which is an aid to the teacher searching for ways to accommodate individual differences.

Review

Adequate review is systematically provided in basal series. Children do not learn sight words, the sound of letters, initial blends, inflectional endings, and the like, as a result of one or two experiences. The introduction of new words is carefully controlled, and once a word or concept is introduced, it will be repeated many times. Tests, designed to show pupils' mastery of all skills previously introduced, are provided in workbooks. These workbooks, when used properly, can serve as diagnostic tools to indicate where more teaching or review is needed.

The previous discussion is not meant to imply that basal reader series *are* the reading program. A teacher may rely quite heavily on these materials and still teach reading through the use of bulletin boards, labeling objects, drawings and pictures, experience charts, and reading stories and poetry. These reading experiences are not incidental but are deliberately planned.

TRADE BOOKS

In addition to materials designed specifically for teaching children how to read, there are a number of "trade" or story books published every year. These materials are often referred to as "library books," but in any sound reading program such books will be present in abundance in every classroom. Until recently the number of such books which children with first-grade reading ability might read were quite limited. Today, hundreds of titles are available. Representative series include: *Beginner Books, Easy to Read Books, Early I Can Read Books, I Can Read Books.* Both the number of books and publishers producing such books are constantly being augmented.

Trade, or story, books for beginning readers follow the principle of controlled vocabulary. The easier books contain as few as 75 different words. At a somewhat higher difficulty level, children may participate vicariously in a space flight while reading a book containing no more than 300 different words. This vocabulary, abetted by excellent illustrations, manages to deal with some fairly high-level concepts. Thus, in addition to story-type materials, there are also many books available in such areas as science, travel, biography and exploration.

The extensive use of self-selected trade books as an integral part of the reading program is one of the basic trends of the individualized teaching movement. This approach is discussed in more detail in Chapter 11.

NEWER METHODS-MATERIALS

In addition to the materials described above, there are a number of other instructional approaches to beginning reading. They are discussed here because each of them includes special materials which, in essence, become part of the methodology of teaching. Although each of these materials represent efforts of early teaching of letter-sound equivalents, the first two involve modifications of standard English printing or orthography.

English writing is based upon 26 letter symbols and follows the alphabetic principle of graphic signs representing speech sounds. While approximately half of the letters are quite consistent with the sound they represent, other letters and letter combinations represent several sounds. There is little room to doubt that the degree of inconsistency of letter-sound relationships adds to the difficulty of learning to read English. There have been numerous attempts to devise modifications of the English printing so as to mitigate this inconsistency.*

All attempts thus far to resolve inconsistent letter-sound relationships have centered on two approaches (or a combination of the two): (1) The use of additional printed signs to represent particular sounds; (2) respelling of English words so that the orthography parallels speech sounds heard. The first of these might be illustrated by Fry's (10) *Diacritical Marking System:* a bar over vowels representing long vowel sounds; a slant line through silent letters; underlining of digraphs; a dot over vowels indicating the *schwa* sound; and a bar under letters representing irregular sounds for that letter. A sample sentence follows:

"Once upon a time Little Red Hen lived in a barn with her five chicks." This system preserves the traditional spelling of words but adds clues to pronunciation.

Learn English the New Way by Frank C. Laubach utilizes a slant line following any vowel which has its long sound, and in addition respells many words: *smile*—smi/l; *quite*—qui/t; *snake*—sna/k; *told* — to/ld; *woman* — wuumun; *Asia* — A/zhaa; *cease* — seass; *deceive*—de/seev; *pronounced*—pro/nounsst.

*See: Edward Fry, "New Alphabet Approaches," *First Grade Reading Programs,* Newark: International Reading Association Perspectives in Reading, No. 5 (1965), 72-85.

i/t/a (Initial Teaching Alphabet)

Sir James Pitman of England devised a new orthography which consists of a 44 character alphabet. This alphabet dropped the letters Q and X and added 18 new characters to the traditional

Among the number of instructional approaches to beginning reading is i/t/a. Here youngsters investigate the 44-character alphabet which approximates a one-to-one relationship between letters seen and speech sounds heard. (Courtesy Cincinnati Public Schools.)

English alphabet. Materials printed in this initial teaching alphabet (i/t/a) were used experimentally in certain English schools beginning in 1960. Since that time a number of American schools have used beginning reading materials printed in this augmented alphabet.

The purpose behind the development of this orthographic system was to permit a one-letter character to represent only one English sound or phoneme. Allowing for some irregularities in phoneme-grapheme relationships, the augmented alphabet does approximate a one-to-one relationship between letters seen and speech sounds heard. Use of the augmented alphabet was proposed only for teaching beginning reading. In general, this was envisioned to be the first year of formal instruction for the average child, and possibly less for the accelerated learner.

Issues

1. *Transfer to traditional English writing.* The questions most frequently raised regarding this approach to beginning reading focus on the issue of "what will the reader do when he transfers from the one-to-one relationship of letter-sound found in i/t/a materials and meets the frequently inconsistent graphic representations (i.e., spellings) of traditional English writing?" In some quarters this problem was somewhat summarily dismissed with the response that "there appears to be no problem of transfer." This opinion was often tied to "early reports from experimentation carried out in England" which conceivably lost something in translation.

Discussion by John A. Downing (8) of the early English experiments reveals caution on this point. He writes:

> If teachers *opinions* are supported by the results of the objective tests conducted last month [March 1963], we may feel encouraged in our *hopes* that all children will pass through the transfer stage with success, but *we must urge the greatest caution in drawing final conclusion or taking action on the basis of this preliminary trial* . . . . the full effects of the transfer cannot be judged until the majority of these children have been put on to books in conventional print for their everyday reading. *Even then the final assessment cannot be made until some years have elapsed* and we can determine the extent to which (i/t/a) pupils, at various ability levels, are able to maintain the advantage made possible through their early (i/t/a) experience. [Emphasis added.]

Some evidence as to the ease with which pupils transfer from i/t/a to regular print is supplied by several studies of American pupils. Mazurkiewicz, (27) reporting on a population of 451 i/t/a taught pupils (1963-64 school year), indicates that only 26% made the transition. In a second study covering the academic year 1964-65 and involving 417 i/t/a taught pupils, "almost half the i/t/a population had not made transition to the T.O. standard in instruction." Hayes and Nemeth (16) report a lower figure, 26% having not made the transfer.

2. *Amount of Phonics Instruction Involved in i/t/a.* There are numerous studies which indicate that emphasis on phonics instruction in grade one have a salutory effect on reading achievement, as measured by first-grade achievement tests, when such programs are compared with others which include significantly less phonics. The i/t/a program does include intensive systematic teaching of letter-sound analysis. The child's first learnings center on the sound associated with each graphic symbol. This stress is logical because the underlying principle of the system is uniformity of letter-sound relationships.

This discussion is not concerned with judging the value of such early phonics emphasis. The issue is that the intensive phonics emphasis found in i/t/a is an important factor which is ignored if reading achievement is attributed exclusively to the variable of the i/t/a orthography.

3. *Emphasis on Children's Writing in i/t/a Programs.* In i/t/a instructional programs there is considerable stress on children's writing, using the i/t/a symbols. This is also a feature of the language-experience approach and other integrated language arts programs. Although available data are inconclusive, it is generally hypothesized that such integration of reading and writing enhances the learning of the reading process. If this hypothesis proves tenable, the heavy emphasis on children's writing is a second variable which clouds the efficacy of the initial teaching alphabet.

A second and more immediate question is, if the child is to transfer from the initial teaching medium to traditional orthography within the first year of instruction, why should he learn and reinforce the augmented alphabet in his own writing? The question does not relate to the value of children's writing in grade one, but upon the medium in which that writing will be done. It is true that many letters are exactly the same in both systems, and in these particular cases transfer should be 100 per cent. On the other hand, there is no question that using i/t/a symbols in writing is more difficult than writing using traditional orthography, because one meets such letter characters as æ, ϵϵ, œ, ȼh, ŧh, ŋ, ω, ɷ, and the like.

4. *Respelling of Irregularly Spelled English Words.* In the promotional materials for i/t/a, it is claimed that there is a high degree of compatibility between spellings in i/t/a and traditional orthography. The question is asked, "Are the traditional alphabet and spelling of English important causes of failure in beginning read-

ing?" The answer is that problems in learning to read English do not stem from the traditional alphabet but from the spellings of words. A fact that is often overlooked is that in addition to the changed alphabet in i/t/a, a great number of words are changed to phonetic spellings. The following examples come from one small first grade book of less than primer difficulty.*

was — woz	watched — wotcht	walked — waukt
excited — eksieted	enough — enuf	thought — thaut
called — cauld	once — wunz	next — nekst
large — larj	find — fiend	boxes — boksez
busy — bizy	some — sum	George — Jorj
come — cum	one — wun	six — siks

i/t/a actually attempts to follow the traditional "rules" found in most phonic approaches, particularly with regard to the "two vowel" and "final e" rules. When words do not follow the rules, they are spelled phonetically:

one — wun	said — sed
some — sum	board — bord
once — wunz	couple — cupl
more — mor	head — hed
have — hav	laugh — laf

In such instances, i/t/a ceases to be a method for "cracking the code" (which is English writing) and becomes a substitute code. The respellings are logical; but the issue is that children will soon be exposed to the irrational spellings, and they will have to learn these word symbols as sight words whether or not they begin reading with i/t/a or regular orthography. Since all words met in i/t/a writing can be sounded out by heeding the individual letters, the learner will inevitably develop a set to utilize this approach. This habit will not serve him well when he meets hundreds of irregularly spelled words following the transition.

5. *Results of i/t/a Instruction.* Data from various studies have failed to indicate any significant superiority in reading achievement at the end of grade one which accrues from the use of i/t/a. Hahn (15) compared the reading achievement of three groups of children

---

*"A Seesied Holidae for Jaen and Toeby," Ann Thwaite (Cunstabl and Company, Limited, Lundon). [*sic*]

taught respectively by i/t/a, basal programs, and a Language Arts Approach. His conclusion was that no one approach was consistently superior to the others although significant differences favoring each approach were found on some particular reading subtests. Fry (11) found no significant differences in silent or oral reading achievement of first-grade children taught by i/t/a, the Fry Diacritical Marking System or the Sheldon Basal Readers (Allyn-Bacon).

Tanyzer and Alpert (34) compared the efficacy of i/t/a, the Lippincott basal program, and the Scott Foresman basal program. Reading achievement of pupils taught by both the Lippincott materials and i/t/a were significantly superior to that of pupils taught by the Scott Foresman basals on each of the subtests of the Stanford Achievement Test. The group taught by the Lippincott materials was significantly superior to the group taught with i/t/a on vocabulary and spelling. No significant differences were found between these groups on Word Reading, Paragraph Meaning and Word Study Skills.

Mazurkiewicz (28) found no significant differences in reading achievement between children taught by i/t/a and traditional orthography as measured by the subtests Word Reading, Paragraph Meaning, Vocabulary and Word-Study Skills, on the Stanford Achievement Test. Pupils taught in traditional orthography were significantly superior in spelling.

Hayes and Nemeth (16) compared four instructional approaches: i/t/a, Lippincott basal series, Scott Foresman basals plus the use of *Phonics and Word Power* * and Scott Foresman basals alone. It should be noted that the first three include a considerable amount of phonics while the Scott Foresman basals introduce a relatively small amount of letter-analysis in grade one materials. On the word reading subtest, no significant differences were found between i/t/a and Lippincott approaches but both were superior to the Scott Foresman basal program alone. There was no significant difference between i/t/a and Scott Foresman materials supplemented by the Phonics and Word Power Program. On paragraph meaning, no significant differences were found between i/t/a and any of the other approaches. On Word Study Skills, no significant differences were found between i/t/a, Lippincott and Scott Foresman supplemented by *Phonics and Word Power,* while each of these was significantly superior to Scott Foresman basals alone.

---

*American Education Publications, Columbus, Ohio, 1964.

One important finding which emerges from a number of these studies is that when programs which utilize extensive phonics instruction are compared, no significant differences in reading achievement appear at the end of grade one. However, phonics-emphasis programs appear to result in higher reading achievement (as measured by existing standardized tests) than do programs which include a significantly lesser amount of letter-sound analysis.

This tends to support the contention that studies which have purported to be dealing with the efficacy of i/t/a orthography as compared with traditional orthography have failed to control an important variable—the amount of phonics instruction in the programs being compared. The contribution of the augmented alphabet in learning to read can be evaluated only if the stress on phonics instruction is equated in comparative studies.

Words in Color

This is a system for teaching beginning reading, developed by Caleb Gattengo. Initial instruction involves the use of visual stimuli which provide two visual clues: (1) the traditional letter configurations, and (2) color. In this approach, 39 colors are used, each of which represents a speech sound in English. Any letter or combination of letters which represent a given speech sound will be presented as a visual stimulus in the particular color assigned to that speech sound. For instance, the long vowel sound of Ā is represented by the following combinations:

a........ (able)	*eigh*........ (weigh)
ey........ (they)	*aigh*........ (straight)
ay........ (they)	*ei*........ (their)
ai........ (mail)	*ea*........ (great)

Each group of italicized letters above would be one color (green). The sound of ă, regardless of letters which represent it, is shown in white; the sound of ē is represented by vermillion, etc.

The actual teaching of this color code is done through the use of a number of large wall charts. Twenty-one charts contain words, and eight phonic-code charts contain letters and letter combinations which represent given sounds. The only other learning experiences which utilize color are those in which the teacher may write on the chalk board using different colored chalk. *ALL other printed material which the child uses is printed black on white.*

Thus the wall charts are nothing more than "keys" to which the child may turn to see the color of particular letters. The following are some pertinent facts about *Words in Color*.

1. This approach places considerable emphasis on phonics instruction. Children learn "sounds" of letters rather than letter names. Instruction starts with short vowel sounds and then moves into consonant sounds. These are taught systematically and with a good deal of repetition.
2. At the time of this writing, there has been no research which suggests that the addition of color to *letter forms* has any positive effects on learning either letter configurations or sounds associated with letters.
3. The use of thirty-nine colors can make the learning process quite confusing. In the absence of letter configuration clues, many adults have difficulty in determining whether certain color samples are actually the "same" or "different." It is likely that some six-year-olds also have trouble in discriminating between colors which are very much alike. One series of color shades includes: dark green, olive green, cadmium green, yellow green no. 15, yellow green no. 47, light green, deep green, emerald green no. 45, emerald green no. 26, leaf green, yellow ochre, and brown ochre.
4. It is difficult to justify the emphasis on colored letters considering the fact that the child never reads any material printed in colors. His contact with words in color is limited to classroom charts composed of individual words, but no sustained reading matter.
5. Children who learn to *rely* on *color cues* could not read outside of class since the charts they depend on are large, bulky and expensive. It is highly improbable that these "aids" would ever become household fixtures.

Programmed Reading

Programmed reading materials fall into two categories: (1) those the purpose of which is to teach facts and understandings in any one of the numerous subject areas; (2) those whose chief aim is to teach the child *how* to read, i.e., dealing with various skills which make up the reading process. This discussion will deal only with the latter in the form of workbook-type programmed materials.

There are a number of such materials available. One example which may be considered fairly representative is *Programmed Reading* (Webster Division, McGraw-Hill Book Company). The materials in this program, which are designed for grade one, consist of seven conventional-sized workbooks. The pupil writes a letter or word or circles a response in each frame. There is considerable emphasis on "phonics," or associating printed letters with speech sounds. Initial teaching involves short vowel sounds and consonant sounds in words which enjoy "regular spellings." This term implies that the sound represented by individual letters is the most common or characteristic sound of those particular letters (cat, rat, fat, mat, etc.).

Before beginning to work with the programmed materials, the child must have mastered a sizable number of phonic skills including the following:

1. The names of the letters of the alphabet (capital and small)
2. How to print all the capital and small letters
3. That letters stand for sounds
4. What sounds to associate with the letters *a, f, m, n, p, t, th,* and *i,* which are used as the points of departure for the programmed readers.
5. That letters are read from left to right
6. That groups of letters form words
7. The words *yes* and *no* by sight, how to discriminate the words *ant, man,* and *mat* from each other, and how to read the sentences, *I am an ant, I am a man, I am a mat, I am a pin, I am a pan, I am tan, I am thin, I am fat*

These skills are taught in a stage called *programmed pre-reading* which, by the nature of what is taught, represents a rather heavy saturation of phonic analysis early in beginning reading.

One strength of programmed reading is that it makes possible individualized instruction. While every child would be using the same material, each may progress through it at his own rate. A second virtue is that even though programmed materials deal primarily with mechanical aspects of the reading process, many of these skills have to be practiced until they become automatic responses on the part of the learner. Thus, a well-planned program can relieve a teacher from a certain amount of repetitive drill and leave her more time for other important aspects of instruction. This assumes, of course, that programmed materials represent only one part of the instructional program.

DATA FROM FIRST-GRADE COMPARATIVE STUDIES

During the school year 1964-65, the Cooperative Research Branch of the Office of Education supported twenty-seven first grade reading research projects. A large majority of these studies compared the efficacy of various methodological approaches such as i/t/a, basal materials, basals supplemented with phonic programs, extended individualized approaches, diacritical marking, language experience, readiness programs, and linguistic approaches. primer While each of the studies was independent, they were also cooperative in that the same pre- and post-test measures were used in all studies. Further, a coordinating center was established at the University of Minnesota for the purpose of evaluating data from all of the individual studies. A description of this cooperative project and an analysis of the data from the studies has been provided by Guy L. Bond, (3) the director of the Coordinating Center.

Some of the conclusions listed by Bond include:

1. There is no one method that is so outstanding that it should be used to the exclusion of the others.
2. The effectiveness of any one approach appears to be increased when it is broadened by addition of other instructional components.
3. Specific approaches to first grade reading instruction appeared to increase children's achievement in certain instructional outcomes but proved to be weak in other outcomes.
4. As would be expected, there was greater variation between the teachers within methods than there was between the methods. This again points up the importance of the teacher's role in learning situations.

In addition to the above, more intensive analysis of the data resulted in the conclusion that basal readers supplemented by a phonics program were superior to the use of basals alone; that word study skills need to be emphasized and taught systematically; that classroom procedures can reduce the gap between reading achievement of boys and girls; and that the most successful teachers emphasized classroom diagnosis for locating individual instructional needs of children.*

---

*Data provided in a communication from Dr. Guy L. Bond, Abstracted from a paper presented at the Eighteenth Annual New England Reading Conference, Boston, October 1966.

CONCLUSION

Despite the unprecedented development of new materials for teaching beginning reading, there is a growing conviction that materials alone will not solve the myriad of instructional problems we face. This is a healthy trend. Undue loyalty to one instructional approach actually limits a teacher's effectiveness. The creative teacher does not view key practices from different approaches as being exclusive of each other, and she incorporates the best techniques and materials from many approaches.

There is a reawakening of interest in the concept that the single most important factor in the classroom is the teacher. A reading program, regardless of philosophy and materials used, can never rise above the level of instruction found in the classroom. Teachers are beginning to *believe* that teaching is the key to future developments in reading instruction. This too is healthy, because teachers who have this conviction will see the logic in the point of view that they must assume much of the responsibility for their own professional growth.

YOUR POINT OF VIEW?

Would you prefer to defend or attack the following premises? Why?

1. Normal developmental growth in reading reduces the efficacy of writing individual stories for pupils who are beyond the stage of beginning reading.

2. Programmed reading materials permit different pupils to be working on different skills and to work at different rates. This statement applies with equal validity to any workbook or series of workbooks.

3. Many "trade books" for children deliberately limit the use of different words (i.e., follow the practice of "controlled vocabulary"). This is inevitably bad, as it curtails story content.

4. Any given experience-chart-story will not be equally motivating for all pupils in a class.

5. There is little evidence that the reading material found in basal readers is inappropriate for children who come from depressed socioeconomic backgrounds.

6. Since children use thousands of words in oral language, stories which they dictate will depart from the practice of controlled vocabulary and repetition.

SUPPLEMENTARY READING

(Summaries of U.S.O.E. First Grade Reading Studies conducted 1964-65)

All of the following are found in *The Reading Teacher* Volume 19, May 1966.

1. Chall, Jeanne, "First Grade Reading: An Analysis of the Interactions of Professed Methods, Teacher Implementation and Child Background," 569-75.

2. Fry, Edward Bernard, "First Grade Reading Instruction Using Diacritical Marking System, Initial Teaching Alphabet and Basal Reading System," 666-69.

3. Hahn, Harry T., "Three Approaches To Beginning Reading Instruction — ITA, Language Arts and Basic Readers," 590-94.

4. Harris, Albert J., and Serwer, Blanche L., "Comparing Reading Approaches in First Grade Teaching with Disadvantaged Children," 631-36.

5. Hayes, Robert A., "ITA and Three Other Approaches to Reading in First Grade," 627-31.

6. Heilman, Arthur W., "Effects of an Intensive In-Service Program on Teacher Classroom Behavior and Pupil Reading Achievement," 622-27.

7. Macdonald, James B., Theodore L. Harris, and John S. Mann, "Individual Versus Group Instruction in First Grade reading," 643-47.

8. Manning, John C., "Evaluation of Levels-Designed Visual-Auditory and Related Writing Methods of Reading Instruction in First Grade," 611-17.

9. Mazurkiewicz, Albert J., "ITA and TO Reading Achievement When Methodology is Controlled," 606-11.

10. McCanne, Roy, "Approaches to First Grade English Reading Instruction for Children from Spanish-speaking Homes," 670-77.

11. Morrill, Katherine A., "A Comparison of Two Methods of Reading Supervision," 617-22.

12. Murphy, Helen A., "Growth in Perception of Word Elements in Three Types of Beginning Reading Instruction," 585-90.

13. Reid, Hale C., and Louise Beltramo, "Teaching Reading to the Low Group In The First Grade," 601-06.

14. Ruddell, Robert B., "Reading Instruction in First Grade with Varying Emphasis on the Regularity of Grapheme-Phoneme Correspondence and The Relation of Language Structure To Meaning," 653-61.

15. Schneyer, J. Wesley, "Reading Achievement of First Grade Children Taught by a Linguistic Approach and a Basal Reader Approach," 647-53.

16. Sheldon, William D., and Donald R. Lashinger, "Effect of First Grade Instruction Using Basal Readers, Modified Linguistic Materials and Linguistic Readers," 576-80.

17. Spache, George D., et al., "A Longitudinal First Grade Reading Readiness Program," 580-85.

18. Spencer, Doris U., "Individualized First Grade Reading Versus a Basal Reader Program in Rural Communities," 595-601.
19. Tanyzer, Harold J., and Harvey Alpert, "Three Different Basal Reading Systems and First Grade Reading Achievement," 636-43.
20. Wyatt, Nita M., "The Reading Achievement of First Grade Boys Versus First Grade Girls," 661-66.

The following summaries are found in *The Reading Teacher* Volume 19 (October 1966).

1. Bordeaux, Elizabeth Ann and N. H. Shope, "An Evaluation of Three Approaches to Teaching Reading in First Grade," 6-11.
2. Horn, Thomas D., "Three Methods of Developing Reading Readiness in Spanish-Speaking Children in First Grade," 38-42.
3. Kendrick, W. M., "A Comparative Study of Two First Grade Language Arts Programs," 25-30.
4. Marita, Sister M., "Beginning Reading Achievement in Three Classroom Organizational Patterns," 12-17.
5. Stauffer, Russell G., "The Effectiveness of Language Arts and Basic Reader Approaches to First Grade Reading Instruction," 18-24.
6. Vilscek, Elaine, Lorraine Morgan, and Donald Cleland, "Coordinating and Integrating Language Arts Instruction in First Grade," 31-37.

BIBLIOGRAPHY

1. Aaron, I. E., "Using Basal Materials Effectively," *Improvement of Reading Through Classroom Practice*. International Reading Association Proceedings, 9, 1964, 73-4.
2. Bloomer, Richard H., "Reading Methodology: Some Alternative Organizational Principles," *Reading Teacher,* 14 (January 1961), 167-71.
3. Bond, Guy L., "First-Grade Reading Studies: An Overview," *Elementary English,* XLIII (May 1966), 464-70.
4. Brown, Charles M., "Whither Basal Reading," *Education,* 82 (September 1961), 3-5.

5. Chall, Jeanne, "Different Approaches to Beginning Reading," *Reading as an Intellectual Activity*. International Reading Association Proceedings, 8, 1963, 250-54.

6. Cutts, Warren G., "New Approaches to Reading for Young Children," *Reading as an Intellectual Activity*. International Reading Association Proceedings, 8, 1963, 39-43.

7. Doctor, Robert L., "A Comparison of the Effectiveness of Workbook and Non-workbook Types of Follow-up Materials," *Challenge and Experiment in Reading*. International Reading Association Proceedings, 7, 1962, 156-58.

8. Downing, John A., *Experiments with Pitman's Initial Teaching Alphabet In British Schools*. New York: Initial Teaching Alphabet Publications, Inc., 1963, p. 25.

9. ______, "The Augmented Roman Alphabet for Learning to Read," *Reading Teacher,* 16 (March 1963), 325-36.

10. Fry, Edward, "A Diacritical Marking System to Aid Beginning Reading Instruction," *Elementary English,* XXXXI (May 1964), 526-29.

11. Fry, Edward Bernard, *First Grade Reading Instruction Using a Diacritical Marking System, The Initial Teaching Alphabet and a Basal Reading System*. USOE Cooperative Research Project No. 2745, 1965.

12. Gans, Roma, *Guiding Children's Reading Through Experiences*. New York: Bureau of Publications, Teachers College, Columbia University, 1941.

13. Gattengo, Caleb, *Words In Color*. Chicago: Learning Materials, Inc., 1962.

14. Gray, Lillian, *Teaching Children to Read* (3rd ed.). New York: The Ronald Press Company, 1963, Chapters 7 and 8.

15. Hahn, Harry T., *A Study of The Relative Effectiveness of Three Methods of Teaching Reading in Grade One*. USOE. Cooperative Research Project No. 2687, 1965.

16. Hayes, Robert B., and Joseph S. Nemeth, *An Attempt To Secure Additional Evidence Concerning Factors Affecting Learning to Read*. USOE. Cooperative Research Project No. 2697. 1965, 34.

17. Hildreth, Gertrude H., "Experience — Related Reading for School Beginners," *Elementary English,* XXXXII (March 1965), 280-97.

18. Kerfoot, James F. (ed.), *First Grade Reading Programs.* Perspectives in Reading No. 5. Newark, Del.: International Reading Association, Inc., 1965.

19. King, Ethel M. and Siegmar Muehl, "Different Sensory Cues as Aids in Beginning Reading," *Reading Teacher,* 19 (December 1965), 163-68.

20. Lamoreaux, L. A. and Dorris M. Lee, *Learning to Read Through Experience.* New York: Appleton-Century-Crofts, 1943.

21. Landau, Elliott D., "After They Learn to Read — What?" *Elementary English,* XXXXI (December 1964), 877-78.

22. Lee, Dorris M., and R. V. Allen, *Learning To Read Through Experience* (2nd ed.). New York: Appleton-Century-Crofts, 1963.

23. Lindberg, Lucile, "This Is Reading," *Improving Reading Instruction.* Joint Proceedings of the Twenty-fifth Reading Conference and First Intensive Summer Workshop, Volume I, University Park, Pa., 1963, 15.

24. McCracken, Glenn, "The Newcastle Reading Experiment: A Terminal Report," *Elementary English,* XXX (January 1953), 13-21.

25. ———, "The Value of the Correlated Visual Image," *Reading Teacher,* XIII (October 1959), 29-33.

26. McKim, Margaret G. and Helen Caskey, *Guiding Growth In Reading* (2nd ed.). New York: The Macmillan Company, 1963, Chapter 5.

27. Mazurkiewicz, Albert J., "Lehigh-Bethlehem — I/T/A Study Interim Report Six," *Journal of the Reading Specialist,* 4 (September 1964), 3.

28. ———, First Grade Reading Using Modified Co-Basal Versus The Initial Teaching Alphabet. USOE. Cooperative Research Project No. 2676, 1965.

29. Niemeyer, John H., "The Bank Street Readers: Support for Movement Toward an Integrated Society," *Reading Teacher,* 18 (April 1965), 542-45.

30. Ohanian, Vera, "Control Populations In I/T/A Experiments," *Elementary English,* XLIII (April 1966), 373-80.

31. Schonell, Fred J., *The Psychology and Teaching of Reading* (4th ed.). New York: Philosophical Library, Inc., 1961, Chapters 4 and 5.

32. Smith, Nila Banton, *American Reading Instruction*. Newark, Del.: International Reading Association, 1965.

33. Stone, Clarence R., "Questionable Trends in Beginning Reading," *Elementary School Journal,* 66 (January 1966), 214-23.

34. Tanyzer, Harold J. and Harvey Alpert, *Effectiveness of Three Different Basal Reading Systems on First Grade Reading Achievement*. USOE. Cooperative Research Project No. 2720, 1965.

35. Veatch, Jeannette, *Reading In The Elementary School*. New York: The Ronald Press Company, 1966, Chapter 9.

Beginning Reading—The Instructional Program

5

Chapter 4 provided an overview of various types of materials widely used in beginning reading instruction. It was noted that the transition from the readiness period into formal reading instruction is almost imperceptible. The goals of the readiness period extend into beginning instruction; and to these goals are added a number of other short-term objectives, each of which should build toward the ultimate objective of producing independent, facile readers.

LEARNING A SYMBOL SYSTEM

In order that we may partially recapture the challenge of learning a symbolic process like reading, let us look at a number of familiar symbols and a number which are new. In the following list, on the left are pairs of short word-symbols which are very much alike. For an adult it is extremely simple to distinguish between them. On the right are the same word symbols built from a different alphabet which at this point is unknown to the reader. The new word symbols are no more alike than the words on the left, but it is much more difficult to distinguish between them.

thin	than		
play	plan		
some	same		

The unknown symbols on the right are actually easier to learn than the ones on the left, for these reasons:

1. All letters are composed of three or fewer straight lines.
2. The lines are always horizontal or vertical (no slanting lines like *A, X, K, M;* no curved lines like *S, C, U;* no combinations of straight and curved lines like *D, B, P,* etc.).
3. The first thirteen letters of this alphabet are composed of long horizontal lines and short vertical lines and the last thirteen letters are composed of long vertical and shorter horizontal lines.

This new alphabet, with its equivalent in English, is found in Figure 13 on the next page.

Two short reading passages using this new symbol system are presented below Figure 13. The purpose is not to present a situation precisely analogous to beginning reading, since the reader will have to study the new alphabet in Figure 13 prior to reading. Attempting to read the passages will illustrate the difficulty of mastering a symbolic task in which the symbols are unknown. In this respect, the task is similar to beginning reading.

There are eleven different letter symbols and twelve word symbols in Passage A. Among the twelve words there are only six different words. Thus the vocabulary was carefully controlled. All of these words are found in the first few pages of pre-primers and have been used thousands of times by the reader. These factors might suggest that this reading exercise will be quite easy. Passage B should be extremely easy to read since, in this sixteen-word passage, only four new letters and four new words are introduced. Seventy-five per cent of the words are repeated from the first lesson.

FIGURE 13

Symbol	Letter	Symbol	Letter
	A		N
	B		O
	C		P
	D		Q
	E		R
	F		S
	G		T
	H		U
	I		V
	J		W
	K		X
	L		Y
	M		Z

PASSAGE A

PASSAGE B

If you had a little trouble reading these simple passages (translations below*), the experiment was worth the effort. The objective was to demonstrate that any symbolic process is potentially difficult and that when the symbols appear very much alike, it becomes doubly so. Before the child is confronted with a task as exacting as reading passages A or B (above), he will have had many hours

---

*Passage A: look oh look
see baby play
look at baby
play baby play

Passage B: baby likes to play
look at baby play
oh oh see baby
play with me baby

of practice aimed at helping him make finer and finer visual discriminations. He will also have had many experiences with the printed form of words in readiness books, in experience charts, and on bulletin boards.

BUILDING ON WHAT THE CHILD KNOWS

In teaching reading, as well as in other learning situations, the wise teacher builds on what the child has learned previously. The typical child comes to school with a remarkably well-developed ability to use and understand his language. Here we use the linguistic definition of language — language is oral — thus referring exclusively to speech. In teaching reading, the child must be taught that the printed marks he sees as visual stimuli represent speech patterns he already knows.

Reading is, in essence, a process of converting graphic symbols into their oral counterparts. One must decode the graphic representations, and in so doing he arrives at the known, or familiar, which is his speech. Teaching this fundamental relationship has always been one of the tasks of the first-grade teacher. When a child reads in a monotone or emphasizes each word as a separate utterance (word-by-word reading), teachers characteristically say, "John, let's read that again. This time read it with *expression.* Read it like you would say it. How did Billy feel when it appeared he could not make the trip to Grandfather's farm? How do you think Billy said, 'Oh, no! This can't be. We just have to go.' "

Whether such instruction is as thorough and as effective as it needs to be is debatable. Perhaps this particular learning was treated more as a "skill" than as an absolutely necessary prerequisite upon which all meaningful reading is built. This facet of instruction is presently receiving more attention as a result of the widely published views of certain linguists that learning to read depends upon the reader's re-creating the melody of the language.* In the following discussion, which deals with the definition of reading, the technique of building on the pupil's oral background will be met again.

DEFINING READING

It is difficult to understand why, with all the available written material on *reading* and all the efforts expended in teaching it,

*A further discussion of this technique is found in Chapter 8, *Linguistics and Reading.*

that there is no universally accepted definition of reading. Everyone who reads is sure he knows what reading is. It is only when he attempts to put his understanding into a definition that his ambiguity becomes apparent. The question of "what is reading" is of little consequence to the man in the street, bookstore proprietor, editor of the local paper, or the community's most successful professional writer.

However, one's concept of what reading is would seem to be of considerable importance to the person whose primary task is to teach reading. With this as justification, the following is included in this book on teaching reading. A brief restatement of a few premises is necessary.

1. Language is oral, and to use language one must string together a number of speech sounds in a limited number of "patterns." The structure of a given language dictates what patterns are acceptable.
2. A graphic representation of English has been worked out so that anything spoken in English can be "written" using 26 letter characters.
3. In any alphabetic language, of which English is one example, the graphic letter symbols stand for the same speech sound in thousands of different words. In English this correspondence between letter seen and sound represented is rather imperfect for certain letters and letter combinations.

Ab se bo sem fleebat is a series of speech sounds frequently heard in English, but to speak the above with *any* of several intonation patterns would not meet the requirement of language usage. One important criterion of language is missing. There has been no agreement as to the meaning of those speech sounds in the order found here.

1. Anyone who speaks English can "say" the sounds represented in the opening line of this paragraph.
2. Anyone who can read English can ____________ that material.

What word belongs in the blank space? After considerable deliberation, the word you decide upon can well provide insight into *your* definition of reading.

If *ab se bo sem fleebat* happened to be the graphic representation of an utterance found in the English language, one could not "read" it unless he knew or could discover what spoken words were represented by the graphic symbols. The potential reader might:

1. Know each printed word symbol as a sight word.
2. Recognize some words at sight and analyze letter sounds in others until he "hits" upon the pronunciation of each of the printed word symbols.
3. Assign intonation patterns which at least approximate those which would be acceptable in oral English usage.

Would he also, in order to qualify as a reader, have to ascribe particular meanings to each word symbol as well as to the "total word combination?"

A third grader had just been asked to interpret this sentence, " 'I will sample your wares,' said the traveler." Following his response the teacher said in a kindly voice, "John, I believe you read that wrong — the traveler was going to *buy* something from the peddler, not *sell* him something." The point of this illustration is that the teacher had not heard John read the sentence in question, yet she said, "I believe you read it wrong."

A further insight might be gained by reference to another sentence in English. "As face answerth face in water so the heart of man speaketh to man." Many primary-level readers could read aloud (i.e., pronounce) each word in this passage, but many of these same children could not arrive at an understanding of its meaning. (In essence, no further context is needed.) A school curriculum committee examining a science or social science text which contained many concepts at the difficulty level of this example would agree that, "This book is too difficult for third graders to read." Few, if any, critics of this position would counter with "most third graders can recognize the words in this book. I recommend it be adopted."

The following are English sentences. Anyone who reads English will have no trouble with word recognition or intonation:

1. "No square has four sides."
2. "Thomas Jefferson was a friend of tyranny."

These sentences, like all reading situations, demand reader interaction. The person reading "No square has four sides" might react in any of a number of ways: "This is a misprint — it should say, *all* squares have four sides. No, maybe that's not the kind of square it means; Michael Philbutt is a square and he doesn't have four sides. No, that's not what it means. Now a square is a plane figure, but it has a front and back, or does it have a back side? That's either five or six sides. What is the author talking about? Well, no matter what he means, I don't see how he can say that no square has four sides. Maybe this is one of those trick statements.

I better read another paragraph or two. If that doesn't help, I'll ask someone."

In sentence 2, a reader with no background knowledge about Jefferson might reason, "Well, it's good to be apprised of this man's character. I'll be suspicious of everything he says or writes, particularly about government and people's rights." With any degree of historical background, however, one immediately says, "How ridiculous! Who is writing this stuff; where was this book published? I better read a little more, this might be a misprint. Didn't Jefferson say, 'I have sworn eternal hostility to every form of tyranny over the mind of man?' This statement is weird."

While the above discussion has not provided a specific definition of reading, it has attempted to put the two essentials, decoding and arriving at meaning, in proper perspective. Recognizing, or distinguishing between, printed word symbols is an absolutely necessary prerequisite for reading. But the mere pronunciation of words is not reading until this act of recognition evokes meaning(s) which the written words-in-combination carry in oral language usage.

There are simpler concepts as to what the reading process involves. A number of these concepts, however, fail to take into consideration the interdependent relationship between word recognition and word meaning. Teachers of reading, as well as of other school subjects, must understand the complex nature of reading. Accepting a definition which is too simple can easily result in overemphasis on one facet of the learning process.

THREE MAJOR INSTRUCTIONAL TASKS

Insofar as mastering the reading process is concerned, there are three instructional tasks which represent the major thrust of beginning reading instruction. Their importance diminishes little, if any, throughout the entire process of learning to read. These instructional tasks are: Helping the child

1. Develop and expand a sight vocabulary.
2. Learn to associate visual symbols with speech sounds.
3. See that reading is always a meaning-making process, and that printed word symbols represent speech.

Some instructional materials tend to treat the first two of these facets of instruction as independent skills which should be taught in sequence, either 1. first or 2. first, over an extended period of time. Children can learn much of what is taught in such an instructional approach, but in doing so they run the risk of developing attitudes and habits which "color" their concept of the reading process. When beginning reading instruction overemphasizes letter analysis, learning sight words, or reliance on context, children tend to become overdependent on the particular skill emphasized.

It is easy to inculcate pupils with a "set" which may neglect one or more of these important clues. This is uneconomical and may result in habits which handicap the reader in his later development. For instance, a child may develop a set to sound out every word he meets. This means he will be sounding out the same word the tenth, twentieth, or even the fiftieth time it is met in reading situations. He has learned that reading is "sounding out words," and this becomes his goal in all reading situations.

On the other hand, overemphasis on learning sight words in the absence of letter-sounding techniques overburdens the child with the task of making minute visual discriminations, where minimal sounding techniques would have made his task much easier. Sight words, plus context, plus the use of the minimal sounding clues necessary to solve unknown printed words, is more efficient than overreliance on one technique alone.

The premise underlying this discussion is that the major instructional tasks identified above are inseparable parts of one total instructional process. Each of these skills — expanding sight vocabulary, learning letter-sound relationships, and using context — are essential at each point on the learning continuum. They interact and complement each other in every reading situation. Thus, the major task of reading instruction is to arrive at the proper blending of those three instructional components.

What makes reading instruction complicated is that there is no blueprint which spells out precisely where and how much instructional time and effort should be devoted to each of these skills. And second, there is no blueprint which tells us what particular instructional techniques will have the most efficacy with particular learners. Understanding individual differences among learners becomes the key to these questions.

SYNCHRONIZING THE TEACHING OF THE ESSENTIAL SKILLS

There is little basis for questioning the fact that children can learn to recognize "words as wholes." However, if this is seen as the exclusive approach to teaching beginning reading, the time quickly comes when distinguishing words becomes extremely confusing. The learning process is slowed or even halted. The child needs to apply the knowledge that a given letter in different words represents the same speech sound. For example, he must learn that an unknown printed word which begins with *M* must start with the same sound as any other *known* word which begins with *M*.

No matter how much letter-sound analysis a child learns, it is essential that he also continuously increase the number of words that he can recognize instantly. Letter analysis and contextual setting has helped him arrive at the speech equivalent of a number of printed word symbols. Repetition of a given response to particular printed word patterns has reinforced that response to the point where further clues are not needed. On the same page which contains dozens of known sight words, there will be found words which the reader is still solving through the help of letter analysis. When these words have been met and solved many times, they too become sight words; but analysis is still used with other less frequently met words.

This process is never-ending for the person who continues to read and who reads widely. No individual has ever mastered all of the approximately 600,000 words in the English language, but his sight vocabulary grows as he reads. The average reader in a third-grade class will have mastered hundreds of frequently met words as "sight words." If he has not done so, he does not meet the criterion of being an average third-grade reader.

Context clues can be useful aids in solving unknown words if the reader demands meaning from what he reads. Context plus a minimal amount of letter analysis focused on the beginning of the words is much superior to context alone. This combination of clues is also much superior to intensive analysis on a word-by-word basis which ignores the contextual setting of the unknown word.

In the following illustrations a blank line is used to represent an unknown word.

"The boy waved goodbye as the train left the ______." Even when the sentence has a blank line substituted for the word, most readers have no problem in supplying the correct word. One would have to strain in order to miscall the unknown word if he heeded the first letter supplied below:

"The boy waved goodbye as the train left the s______."

Other reading situations will present more difficult problems. For example:

"The girl waved goodbye to her ______."

Here quite a number of possible word choices would make meaning: friend, mother, sister, teacher, brother, parents, family, playmate, aunt, cousin, uncle, etc. Select *any* word that makes meaning and insert only its first letter in the blank space. Note how many of the words that were possibilities are now eliminated when the reader heeds the sound associated with that initial letter.

The efficacy of combining skills is often more dramatically illustrated in larger contexts. In the first version of a story provided below, it is possible to get the sense of the story even if one is not sure of the identity of a number of the missing words. The second version provides only the initial letter of each missing word.

> John and his Cousin ______ started on their fishing trip. John said, "I have my trusty ______ pole, a ______ full of lunch, and a can of ______." After walking a long time, John said, "Not far from here there is a ______ across the stream. We can sit on the ______ and fish." When they started fishing, John said, "I'm not going to ______ from this ______ until I catch a ______ ______." Finally ______ said, "I am tired of sitting on the ______. I am going to take a walk along the ______." ______ had walked only a short way when he lost his ______ and fell into the stream. The water was not very deep and he waded out. "Hey," said John, "you're lucky. You won't have to take a ______ when we get home."

The version below inserts the initial letter in each unknown word, which in all cases happens to be the letter *b*.

> John and his Cousin B _ _ started out on their fishing trip. John said, "I have my trusty b _ _ _ _ _ pole, a b _ _ full of lunch, and a can of b _ _ _." After walking a long time, John said, "Not far from here there is a b _ _ _ _ _ across the stream. We can sit on the b _ _ _ _ _ and fish." When they started fishing, John said, "I'm not going to b _ _ _ _ from this b _ _ _ _ _ until I catch a b _ _ b _ _ _." Finally B _ _ said, "I am tired of sitting on the b _ _ _ _ _. I am going to take a walk along the b _ _ _." B _ _ had walked only a short way when he lost his b _ _ _ _ _ _ and fell into the stream. The water was not very deep and he waded out. "Hey," said John, "you're lucky. You won't have to take a b _ _ _ when we get home."*

---

*Words in the order of their omission are: Bob, bamboo, bag, bait, bridge, bridge, budge, bridge, big bass, Bob, bridge, bank, Bob, balance, bath.

Mistakes in reading can be made even in situations where one has the ability to recognize all the words in a passage.

Mary had a little lamp
Its base was white as snow.

The child who knows the verse about Mary and her lamb may well be trapped into miscalling *lamb* for *lamp* and *face* for *base*, but as he reads further his mistake should become obvious.

Mary had a little lamp
Its base was white as snow,
She turned it on when she came in
And off, when out she'd go.

Since the reader has been taught to read for meaning, the mistakes on the first two lines do not permit a good fit with the concluding two lines. The reader would likely reason somewhat as follows: "Slow down — look again; that doesn't make sense; this is not about a lamb in school."

Advocating the simultaneous teaching of sight words, letter analysis, and context clues does not mean that occasional instructional periods cannot be devoted primarily to one or another of these teachings. What it does mean is that the teacher need not feel compelled to teach 50-70 sight words before teaching any letter-sound analysis. Or conversely, she will not devote the first 8-10 weeks of instruction to letter-sound analysis to the total exclusion of building sight vocabulary. Furthermore, she will not withhold insights about the role of context clues for fear a child may become a "word guesser." To do this is to negate the one important learning which the child brings to reading — language is meaning bearing.

DEVELOPING AND EXPANDING SIGHT VOCABULARY

The normal child's experience with reading will result in his acquiring a constantly enlarging stock of sight words. He will have established automatic stimulus-response patterns for dozens of frequently used words such as: *that, with, will, be, come, are, and, some, was, it, an, the, in, which, to, than, no, what, stop, you, they, now, us, said, when, him, go, little, can,* and the like. A number of these structure words and other frequently used words must be "overlearned" to the point where recognizing them is automatic.

There is a difference between overlearning certain frequently used words and learning to over-rely on one approach to beginning reading whether that approach be whole words, letter analysis, or context. The normal pattern of learning dictates that the child develop a sight vocabulary or learn some words "as wholes." The purpose of the following discussion is to briefly illustrate a limited number of approaches which may help to facilitate learning.

A. *Learning to read children's names*

1. Probably the first printed word a child learns is his name. Many first-grade teachers tape each child's first name on the front of his desk.

Children learn the names of other children, and many learn very quickly to recognize a number of names in printed form. The practice of learning names in printed form provides the basis for teaching letter-sound analysis, discussed later.

2. Use of blackboard announcements involving pupils' names.

<u>*Hand out books*</u>	<u>*Water the plants*</u>
John	Jean
Helen	Billy

B. *Labeling objects in the room*

The teacher prints a naming word on separate oak tag cards.

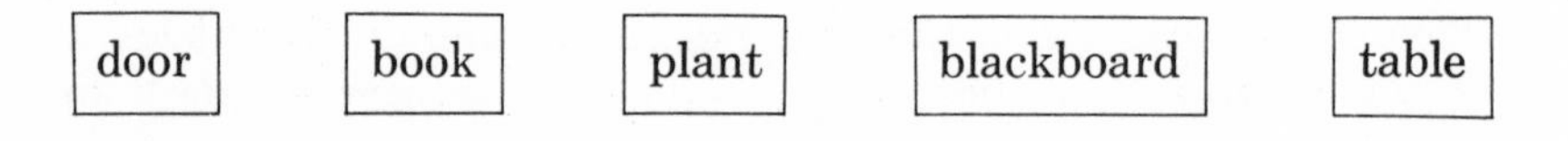

Each card is held up and a volunteer is selected to say the word and place the card on the object it names.

C. *Association of printed word with a picture it names*

1. Secure a number of pictures which depict objects or animals within the children's range of experience. Paste the picture on cardboard and print the naming word beneath it.

2. To add the kinesthetic sensory mode to the words, duplicate a page of outline drawings and leave space for the children to write (copy) the names from models displayed on the chalk tray. In the first experience the printed words may be outlined with dots. The child then marks over the dots writing the words.

3. A later exercise may be one which omits the dotted outlines and the child copies from the printed models on the chalk tray, blackboard, or bulletin board.

D. *Reading teacher-printed sentences*

1. Today is Tuesday.
   Today we have our music lesson.
   Miss Rogers comes to our room at 10:00 o'clock.

The teacher reads each sentence, then asks the class to read with her. Following this, she may ask different pupils to go to the board and underline particular words such as *have, our, today, room.*

2. Assembling scrambled sentences.

Individual words, from sentences used previously on the blackboard, are printed on separate cards. These are presented in scrambled order, and volunteers are chosen to arrange the words in proper order to be followed by a card bearing the proper punctuation mark.

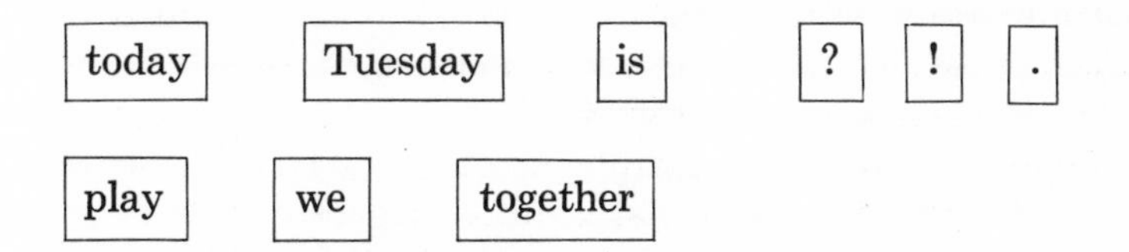

This is one of the many ways to provide repetition with particular frequently used words.

E. *Joint teacher-pupil planning and reading of experience charts* (Teacher prints on large easel or blackboard)
   1. Daily happenings in classroom or school
   2. Trips or visits
   3. Special events charts (Valentines Day, Halloween, Thanksgiving Day, National Elections, Lincoln's or Washington's birthday, etc.)

F. *Sentence completion exercises*

The child selects the correct word from a pair of "look alike" words which completes the meaning of a sentence.
   1. Child circles the correct word.
      a. "Let's play ______. ball, tall
      b. In winter it is ______. hold, cold
   2. At the next level of difficulty, the child may *write* the correct word in the blank space

G. *Use of "classify games" to teach common words*

animals	clothing	food
dog	hat	milk
cat	shoes	cookies
cow	dress	pie

1. Place the underlined classification words on the board. The teacher points to and reads each word. Pupils say each word after the teacher's pronunciation of it. Each of the other words to be used in the exercise is printed on oak tag or cardboard. The teacher holds up one word at a time and selects a volunteer to *pronounce* the word and to tell under which heading it belongs.

2. Variations include duplicated seat work pages with headings such as *Toys,* *Plants,* *Months,* *Days.* A number of appropriate words are placed in a box at the bottom of the page and pupils copy the words under the correct heading.

Sight words are learned in myriad ways; from television, road signs, bulletin boards, labels on cartons, and the like. Obviously the most important source of learning is from meaningful reading situations as provided by charts, individual teacher-written stories, pre-primers, and easy to read trade books.

Thus far, the rationale for reading sight words has stressed only that to be a facile reader one must acquire an ever-increasing stock of "instant recognition words." The degree to which printed words are mastered as sight words is one of the most meaningful ways of differentiating between poor and accomplished readers at all grade levels. A skill of such significance to the total reading process should be taught effectively. A number of justifications for learning words as-wholes are briefly summarized below:

1. If a child knows a number of words as sight words (instant recognition), he can be taught to see and to hear similarities between these known words and the new words he meets. Having a sight vocabulary is an invaluable tool in helping him "unlock" other words.
2. Learning words and reading them in logical combinations makes reading meaning-centered.
3. Early in the child's career as a reader, it is easier for him to learn a limited number of sight words than it is to learn a set of complicated rules of sounding and the numerous exceptions to each rule.
4. Many words in English violate one or more rules of sounding. These are often the so-called service words which comprise a large per cent of the words found in all reading material, from primers through college textbooks.
5. Teaching the child to analyze each word slows the reader and detracts from the pleasure of reading. This procedure can result in the habit of word-by-word reading or word analyzing if the child develops the idea that "this is reading."
6. Learning words as wholes should condition children to look at all of the word, beginning with the first letter and glancing on through.

WORD IDENTIFICATION SKILLS

As noted earlier, simultaneouly with developing a sight vocabulary, children must also acquire skills which will permit them to unlock or identify words which they do not instantly recognize as sight words. Since various English words are very much alike in their visual patterns, the child must learn that letters and letter combinations represent speech sounds. If English writing followed the alphabetic principle 100 per cent, we could say that particular letters always represent the same sound in all words. However, this is true only of some letters, all of which are consonants.

Instruction which emphasizes associating letter forms with speech sounds has been labeled phonics instruction. The application of phonic analysis is undoubtedly the chief means used by readers to identify unknown words. It is only one of several approaches, most of which are identified in the following discussion.

Word analysis is an inclusive term which covers all methods of solving the pronunciation of printed word forms. These skills are not concerned with teaching the child how to pronounce words since he has already mastered this in learning oral language. Word analysis deals with helping the child discover what known oral language unit is *represented* by an unknown printed word symbol. The skills under discussion fall in the following categories:

1. Noting the unique appearance of words or distinctive parts of words
2. Utilizing structural analysis
   a. Prefixes and suffixes
   b. Inflectional endings *s, ed, ing,* etc.
   c. Compound words
3. Profiting from context clues
4. Applying phonic analysis
5. Using picture clues
6. Using various methods in combination

Unique Letter Configurations

In the early stages of reading, some children undoubtedly learn to distinguish between words on the basis of configuration or particular distinct visual features found in words. For example, the words *like* and *different* suggest the configurational patterns [configuration] and [configuration] . A child may develop the habit of paying special heed to the length of words, to position of tall and short letters, the dotted *i* or double letters such as *ee, tt, oo,* or *ff.*

This discussion does not advocate that such clues be pointed out or taught, but rather that children may stumble on such clues on their own. If written English consisted of word-writing (ideographic writing in which graphic symbols are not related to speech sounds), rather than being based on the alphabetic principle, this type of clue would be of paramount importance. However, the task of learning to read would be much more difficult and time-consuming.

As a matter of fact, *all* printed English words *can* be distinguished by the unique visual clues provided by letter arrangements. The only exception would be several dozen homographs, live, live; record, record; etc., whose identification depends entirely on context. But to rely solely on these minute visual clues will preclude the reader's ever becoming an independent facile reader. The task of distinguishing between twenty or thirty thousand word symbols on the basis of such minimal visual clues would be practically impossible. This approach would break down for practically all would-be readers during the primary stage of reading instruction.

The child may learn to recognize the word *look* because he notes "it has two eyes (oo) in the middle." Soon he meets a great number of other words which contain this letter combination (f*oo*t, t*oo*k, w*oo*d, fl*oo*r, p*oo*l, s*oo*n, f*oo*d, r*oo*m, g*oo*d, b*oo*k, st*oo*d, d*oo*r, m*oo*n, b*oo*t, t*oo*th, etc.). The double *o* ceases to be a unique identifying characteristic, and the letters which precede and follow become more important as aids in word identification.

Teaching Analysis

Formal instruction in associating printed letters with speech sounds heard in words has been preceded by years of experience with related learnings. The child can discriminate rather minute differences in spoken words (*T*ed, *b*ed, *f*ed, *l*ed, *r*ed) (sa*t*, sa*d*, Sa*m*, sa*ck*). He hears and learns these words globally rather than perceiving that each consists of three sounds (phonemes). Nevertheless, the six year old does distinguish thousands of words on the basis of minimal phoneme differences.

He understands that *cat, rat, sat* and *call, tall, ball* rhyme. He notes that the words *cat, bet, cot* do not have this quality even though they have a common concluding sound. Children cannot "explain" what is being pointed out here, but they have mastered the auditory discriminations involved.

The reading readiness program has extended the child's knowledge of language sounds by providing much practice in this area. A fairly large per cent of children entering grade one have learned to make visual discriminations between some letter forms and all other letter forms. That is, they can name the letters *B, O, M, S, L, T*, etc., whenever they see these symbols. Most readiness programs now include formal instruction in letter recognition. The next step after learning to discriminate letter forms is to associate speech sounds with known letter forms. To achieve independence in reading, a child must master a good number of these letter-sound associations and be able to apply them in reading situations when he meets unknown printed words.

Phonics instruction in the schools today starts in the readiness period and extends through all stages of reading instruction. The teacher works with the children to make sure that they hear the similar beginnings or similar endings of these words. The next step is instruction on seeing that letter combinations correspond to the similar sounds in the beginnings or endings of words.

If the child recognizes *m*ine and *m*any, he is then led to perceive that *m*ilk and *m*ud begin with the same symbol and thus the same sound. While he is learning sight words, he is also learning the sounds that initial letters contribute to words. If he knows the words *tell* and *sell*, he may be able to work out the word *bell*, since he also knows the words *be*, *by*, *boat*, and *boy*. Gray (14) calls this process "initial consonant substitution" and points out that this process can work only in relation to other *known* words. In addition to the clues just mentioned, if the child knows all of the words in the sentence except the one new word *bell*, the context in which the new word is found will also aid him in arriving at the correct choice.

The question is sometimes heard, "When should phonics instruction be introduced?" The question seems to imply that this instruction is not seen as an on-going integral part of the total reading program, but rather as a block of skills which might be plugged in at one or another point on the learning continuum. A further implication suggested by certain instructional materials is that when one decides to plug in phonics, this is done with a degree of emphasis which neglects related teachings. Evidence that balance can be achieved is provided by one teacher who describes her first phonics lesson as follows:

> I usually have a phonics lesson the first day of school. Prior to the opening of school, I print on oak tag the first name of every child assigned to my room. As the children enter, each is given his name tag. I introduce the children on a first name basis, "Class, this is Mary. Does anyone else have a name that begins the same way as Mary?" If I get a correct response, I build on it. If not, I say, "Now I want to introduce Mike, I think Mike's name begins like Mary's. Listen, children, as I say these two names; *Mike, Mary*. I hear the same sound at the beginning of both names." I then have these two children stand at the front of the room and hold their name cards so everyone can see them. I point out that if the children look closely they will *see* that each name begins with the same letter and that this letter is called *M*. I then print both names on the board; we pronounce the names and look carefully at the initial letter. We then move to other names such as *Bobby, Billy;* or *Henry, Harry, Helen.*

Observing in this teacher's classroom, one is impressed with the variety of approaches she uses to teach reading. All of them include some emphasis on word analysis. Every day she writes the day of the week, the month, and date, both in numbers and spelled out in words. These writings often contain words which begin with the same sounds: *Today is Tuesday, September sixth, November ninth.* In response to her questions, the children note that *Today* and *Tuesday* begin with a *T* that represents the same sound in both. They add other words which begin with the sound heard in *Today* and *Tuesday*, and the teacher writes these in a column on the blackboard. They see the letter and say the words *t*omorrow, *t*ime, *t*ake, *t*ooth.

The teacher introduces the children to a game which involves participation, language usage, listening, observation of the environment, and word analysis. "I'm thinking of something in the room — its name begins like *d*og — what is it?" The children look around and respond *door, desk, David, dominos;* as well as *duck* and *dolphins,* which are seen in pictures on the bulletin board.

Every day the teacher lets three or four children come to the front of the room and dictate a "sentence story." If the child's story is a "run-on account" and becomes lengthy, the teacher and child abstract it to a sentence. This is placed on the board and read by the teacher. Then the child who dictated the story reads it to the class and chooses a pupil to underline a particular word in the sentence. This work on sight vocabulary is usually followed by some work on letter sounds. "Which two words begin with the same sound?" "There are two words that rhyme, what are they?" "Who can give a word that rhymes with *hand?*"

Techniques for teaching phonic skills are practically unlimited. A few examples follow:

1. Match two or more pictures of objects whose names begin with the same sound. The teacher secures pictures and pastes each one on cardboard. One picture from each letter series is placed on the chalk tray. As the children select a picture from the remaining pile, it is placed beside the picture whose name begins with the same sound:

fish	lamp	cake	tent	bus	horn
fence	lake	comb	turtle	book	horse

2. The final sounds in words may be stressed by using a different set of pictures:

hat	lamp	frog	book	bell	bus
boat	cup	flag	desk	towel	grapes

3. Duplicate a number of three-word series of rhyming words:

look	book	took
pick	sick	kick
name	game	fame

The teacher identifies the line and pronounces one of the words: "line a: *b*ook; line b: *p*ick; line c: *n*ame." The children circle that word. In addition to providing practice in auditory and visual discrimination, such sheets have diagnostic value for the teacher. At a glance, she can see which children are experiencing difficulty on particular letter-sound combinations.

4. The same type of exercise can be devised to teach and test consonant blends and digraphs as well as short and long vowel sounds.

*tr*ip	*dr*ip	*gr*ip
*ch*eat	*wh*eat	*sh*eet
b*a*t	bet	b*i*t
b*ee*t	b*oa*t	b*i*te

5. Substitute initial letters to make new words. There are many frequently used words which end with the same two or three letters. These common elements are referred to as phonograms and words containing them were once referred to as "word families." Substituting initial letters in such words often helps children see and hear the letter-sound relationships.

Make a new word by placing a letter in the blank space in front of each word.

______at	______all	______and
______at	______all	______and
______at	______all	______and

The exercise can be made easier by providing letters which can be used (b, f, h, s).

Variations:

a. "Add a '*b*' in front of each word and listen carefully as you pronounce the new word."

__and __it __old __eat __end

"Add an '*s*' in front of the same words and listen carefully as you pronounce the new word."

__and __it __old __eat __end

b. (Vowels) "Make a new word by adding the vowel '*e*' to each word in column B. Pronounce the old word under A and the new word under B. What happens to the vowel sounds you hear?"

A	*B*	*A*	*B*
at	at__	pin	pin__
past	past__	dim	dim__
cut	cut__	plan	plan__
rid	rid__	tub	tub__

Structural Analysis

Structural analysis refers to the recognition of new words by noting known roots and

1. Inflectional endings to root words (s, ed, ing).
2. Words combined to produce a different word (compound word).
3. Prefixes or suffixes added to root words (derivatives).

Some inflectional endings are taught in first grade along with a few compound words. Prefixes and suffixes are usually introduced at a later period.

Structural and phonic analysis go hand-in-hand. The structural changes caused by adding inflectional endings also result in added phonemes. In most cases prefixes and suffixes are separate syllables. Thus, they function as visual, auditory and meaning bearing units.

Teacher-made exercises can be developed that help the child see the structural changes which take place in words. Examples of simple inflectional endings and compound words are found in Figure 14.

FIGURE 14

A. Teaching endings: *s, ed, ing*

Notice how new words are formed when we add s, ed, *or* ing *to words.*

Word we know	Add *s*	Add *ed*	Add *ing*
walk	walks	walked	walking
ask	asks	asked	asking
call	calls	called	calling
look	looks	looked	looking
jump	jumps	jumped	jumping
show	shows	showed	showing
cover	covers	covered	covering

B. Teaching sight recognition of compound words

Notice how words under A *and* B *are put together to make a new word. Say each word and notice the word under* C *very carefully.*

A	B	C
any	one	anyone
up	on	upon
some	thing	something
in	to	into
when	ever	whenever
him	self	himself
snow	man	snowman
her	self	herself

In the following sentence the word in parentheses is unknown to the child. "The boy was (looking) for the kitten." If no attention is paid to the word itself, the context would permit several logical guesses, such as *reaching, looking, waiting, hoping*. However, the child has had experience with the root word *look*. The recognition of this familiar root word permits no other choice except the correct one. Structural analysis helps the child eliminate all incorrect responses which are plausible in this particular context.

In the next example the first word is unknown. It is also one of the longest words the child has met in his reading. " '*Somebody* must get the ball,' said Billy." The sentence does not stand in isolation as it does here. In the story the children have been playing ball. The ball has rolled under the fence into Mrs. Brown's yard and the game has momentarily come to a halt. Something logical must be done and Billy suggests something. Previously the children had learned the word *some*, and, prior to today's reading lesson, they had had a workbook exercise dealing with compound words, such as *sidewalk, playground, anyone, into*, and *anything*. If the child recognizes *some*, this much analysis plus the context should assure him of getting the word correct.

CLASSROOM MANAGEMENT

The need for classroom organization stems from pupil differences within the classroom. As they relate to learning, the most significant of these differences are: previous learnings, present instructional needs, the rate at which learning can take place, and attitudes toward self as a learner. Taken together, these factors provide the basis for the truism that whatever instructional approach a teacher may use, it will not be equally appropriate for all pupils in her class.

Good teachers attempt to organize the total learning environment so as to permit differentation of instruction. This is the most difficult task facing educators. It was noted in chapter II that any history of education that dealt with instructional practices would be primarily a catalogue of attempts to deal with individual differences of pupils being taught in a group situation. The search for a solution to this problem still continues. The chapter on *Individualizing Instruction* deals, in part, with this topic.

Administrative Procedures for Dealing with Individual Differences

Classroom organization involves many factors, such as providing for pupils an adequate supply of materials at various difficulty levels; selecting concepts and skills to be taught; devising a sequence for teaching these; evaluating the teaching-learning situation to determine what has been accomplished; assigning blocks of time for particular teachings; providing for class, group, and individual instruction. These considerations deal primarily with differentiation of instruction, but there remains the problem of how the teacher manages the actual teacher-pupil interaction necessary for learning. Two approaches to this problem are briefly discussed.

In-Class Grouping. Grouping pupils on the basis of previous learnings and present instructional needs is a practice of long standing in our schools.*

In recent years, grouping based on pupil ability has received considerable criticism. (16) Indefensible practices such as Round-Robin Reading and infrequent shifting of pupils within groups were far too commonplace in our schools. The central issue is whether such practices could be identified and rectified without proscribing all grouping procedures.

---

*For an historical account of the development and rationale of grouping practices found in schools since 1900, see: Kathleen B. Hester, *Teaching Every Child to Read,* 2nd ed. (New York: Harper & Row, Publishers, 1964), Chap. 18.

Further discussion of grouping practice may be found in *The Reading Teacher,* II (1957). This entire issue is devoted to the theme "Classroom Organization: Differing Viewpoints."

It is realistic to assume that grouping per se is neither inherently good nor bad. Practices carried out under any plan of grouping may enhance pupil growth or become a meaningless and even harmful educational ritual. Grouping pupils on the basis of instructional needs can provide the framework within which an alert teacher can develop meaningful differentiated instruction. Grouping can narrow the range of differences and reading problems with which a teacher has to cope during a given instructional period. As a result, she can focus on particular short-term goals for specific pupils.

There are always practical considerations which limit the degree and type of grouping. Many authorities in the past suggested that the class be divided into three groups. Five or six groups might well overtax the teacher, dividing her time with pupils in blocks too small to be effective. Two groups would undoubtedly leave her with too heterogeneous a collection of pupils in both groups.

Grouping practices should be extremely flexible. Good teachers are always more conscious of the goals of grouping than they are of the mechanics of the practice. They do not think of equal numbers of pupils in each group or of groups being rigid and final or that every pupil can be accommodated equally well within a three-group structure. They know from experience that one or more pupils may not fit logically into any of three groups. This point is best illustrated by the extreme cases found in every classroom — the very poor reader and the very accelerated reader.

Different classrooms at a given grade level will differ to such a degree that it is impracticable to outline any particular plan of grouping with the expectation that it will be equally appropriate for all. Factors other than the abilities of the pupils also influence grouping practices. These include class size; space for activities; and the availability of supplementary books, film strips, recordings, and the like. The teacher's method is also a factor. Relying heavily on basal readers may call for a structure different from the widespread use of the unit or project approach.

The Psychological Impact of Grouping. Grouping is sometimes discussed as being potentially threatening to pupils. There are various points of view as to how the grouping within a classroom is to take place so as not to introduce comparisons between children. Suggestions include calling the groups group one, group two, and group three; giving the groups some irrelevant titles such as bluebirds, redbirds, robins — the teacher knowing which is the superior group; referring to the groups by the names of children in the group. The latter has the merit of being a straightforward approach. No one is being humiliated on the basis of reading ability, and it is not made to appear that the teacher thinks every pupil should have a certain ability in reading. Psychologically, it is inadvisable for a teacher to attempt to hide differences among beginning readers. It is impossible to fool the children about their reading, and when the poorer readers see through the bluebirds versus the blackbirds, they too start attaching a stigma to poor reading ability. This of course is what the teacher has done, but she did not do it openly.

A wise teacher has had different groups of children doing different things at the same time throughout the year, and no significance was attached to this by either the teacher or the pupils. This teacher probably did not start all children reading from the pre-primer on the same day. She observed children closely and identified those who were ready. When she started this group on a pre-primer, other groups worked on reading also. Some children worked in a readiness workbook, some worked on teacher-prepared readiness materials, and some did preparation for making an experience chart. The teacher, in a natural way, had planted the idea that groups of pupils would be reading from different books and would be working on different pages of workbooks. The teacher who is successful in doing this helps her pupils in many ways.

1. She helps children build a foundation for independent work habits.
2. Competition and feelings of failure are reduced, since children are not arrayed against each other on the same reading tasks.
3. Tension and bad attitudes toward reading are held to a minimum.
4. Each child is permitted to progress at his own rate, and intergroup rivalry is minimized.
5. The teacher is prevented from embracing, consciously or unconsciously, a grouping system that is too rigid.
6. The teacher is granted flexibility in reducing the size of a group she works with by having some children work independently while she works intensively with others.

The Ungraded Primary. The concept of the ungraded primary represents another approach to dealing with the problem of pupil differences. The ungraded primary usually embraces the first three years of formal schooling; the children are designated as being in the primary school or at the primary level. They are not promoted or non-promoted at the end of years one and two. A recent study indicates that neither promotion or non-promotion is in itself a very satisfactory solution to low achievement in reading. It is suggested that more flexible curriculums, methods, and materials are needed "in a type of school organization which encourages continuous pupil progress." (27)

While instruction in the conventional grade-level system is geared to the mean, experience tells us that pupils do not cluster closely around an achievement mean. Differences in achievement are marked, and they increase with instruction. The ungraded primary starts from the premise that each child should progress at his own rate, and the instructional program centers on each child's need at the moment. This is accomplished by breaking the primary years into a number of units of accomplishment or levels of competency. As each child develops competency at one level, he is moved on into work at the next level. The number of levels and the skills to be mastered at each level are worked out co-operatively by teachers in the program.

Austin (2) describes an ungraded primary school that was eminently successful from the standpoint of both teachers and parents. No official reference is made to grade level; all primary grades, which cover the first three years of school, are simply designated primary rooms. Parents are always kept informed of their children's progress. Teachers are encouraged to work with the same group of children for more than one year, and new teachers are initiated into the program with a workshop held before the opening of school.

No single learning curve fits first graders' achievement, and pupil variability in achievement increases in succeeding grades. There is evidence that if the children are allowed three years of instruction to achieve the third-grade level, there will be fewer failures than there would be if all of the children had had to meet arbitrary standards at the end of grades one and two. Maturity and growth cannot be forced, and growth is characterized by both spurts and plateaus. The ungraded primary encourages continuous pupil progress without specifying precise amounts of growth which are to take place in a given year. Such a plan has particular merit for the child who starts slowly but later shows rapid progress. (12, 13)

Some of the educational advantages believed to be inherent in the ungraded primary plan are summarized below.

1. It is easier to provide for the child's reading growth *early* in his reading career if one is not thinking of "grade level norms" the first year.

2. There is likely to be less failure and frustration in the reading situation if there is less emphasis on comparison and promotion.
3. A teacher often stays with the same group of students two years or longer. This gives her an opportunity to know pupils better. She is less likely to push a student beyond his ability during the first year, since she expects to work with him the next year.
4. Students always work at the level on which they need instruction; i.e., they are not likely to miss some facet of instruction because they were absent several weeks.
5. The slower learner will not repeat the first or second grade, but he may take four years to move up from the primary level.
6. The ungraded plan is flexible in allowing pupils to cover some phases of learning quite rapidly when they are capable of doing so and in giving them more time when it is needed.
7. Bright pupils would not "skip a grade" and possibly be deficient in some skill taught there. They would simply go through the entire primary curriculum at a faster rate.

No method of grouping will automatically solve all instructional problems, and the ungraded primary plan is certainly not a panacea. If a shift to the ungraded plan is not accompanied by an understanding of the goals to be achieved, none of the potential benefits are likely to be realized. If teachers or parents continue to think in terms of a grade-level system, the plan is doomed from the start. On the other hand, if the philosophy of the plan is believed sound and the chief reason for adopting it is to help children grow in reading, problems which do arise will not be insurmountable.

CONCLUSION

During the past few years beginning reading instruction has received more attention than any other facet of the school curriculum. Practically all of the "newer approaches to reading" (discussed in Chapter 4) were, in essence, materials and methodology focusing primarily on the beginning reading period.

The fact that so many of the new materials emphasized the early and systematic teaching of letter-sound relationships has made this the foremost issue in reading instruction. Data from recent studies have reaffirmed the position that instructional programs which include considerable emphasis on phonics result in higher achievement at the end of grade one than do programs which include significantly less phonics instruction. Nevertheless, there are still a number of unanswered questions relative to beginning reading instruction, if one views learning to read as a long-term developmental process.

The 1964-65 USOE co-operative first-grade studies support the above statements relative to early letter-sound analysis. They failed to establish any one method of instruction as being superior to all other approaches. In general, there was more variability in achievement among pupils taught by teachers using a given method than there was between groups of pupils taught by different methods. This adds further proof to the bank of data which attests to the fact that the teacher is the most important variable in any learning situation.

Topics for Later Discussion

Since learning to read is a long-term developmental process, there are numerous facets of instruction which could justifiably be treated at each instructional level. To avoid repetition, certain topics which cut across grade levels have been omitted at the beginning reading level. Examples include oral reading, use of standardized and informal tests, recreational reading and comprehension skills which are discussed in the following two chapters.

YOUR POINT OF VIEW?

Would you prefer to defend or attack the following premises? Why?

1. If you want a child to hear the speech sounds in words, it would be more logical to teach these sounds in each word before teaching the word as a sight word.
2. One's definition of reading would in the final analysis have little impact on practices followed in teaching the reading process.
3. Teaching both sight words and letter-sound analysis as parallel or concommitant learnings will inevitably lead to confusion.
4. A justifiable criterion for judging good teaching in beginning reading is the extent to which a teacher uses different methods in her classroom. (Basic readers, experience method, individualized reading, etc.)
5. "In-class grouping" has not helped teachers in dealing effectively with individual differences.
6. The ungraded primary is in essence an attempt to break away from grade-level standards of achievement.
7. Deliberately teaching children to note and use context clues for solving unknown words is self-defeating since the possibility for "wrong guesses" is always present.

BIBLIOGRAPHY

1. Artley, A. Sterl., "Classroom Help for Children With Beginning Reading Problems," *Reading Teacher,* 15 (May 1962), 439-42.
2. Austin, Kent C., "The Ungraded Primary School," *Childhood Education,* XXXIII (February 1957), 260-63.
3. Bohnhorst, Ben A., and Sophia N. Sellars, "Individual Reading Instruction vs. Basal Textbook Instruction: Some Tentative Explorations," *Elementary English,* XXXVI (March 1959), 185-90.
4. Bond, Guy L., and Eva Bond Wagner, *Teaching the Child to Read* (4th ed.). New York: The Macmillan Company, 1966, Chapters 3, 5, and 6.

5. Bremmer, Neville, "First-Grade Achievement under Different Plans of Grouping," *Elementary English,* XXXV (May 1958), 324-26.

6. Bush, Clifford L., "Three Kinds of Grouping in the Same Classroom," *Improvement of Reading Through Classroom Practice.* International Reading Association Proceedings, 9, 1964, 50-51.

7. DeBoer, John J., and Martha Dallmann, *The Teaching of Reading* (rev. ed.). New York: Holt, Rinehart & Winston, Inc., 1965.

8. Denny, Terry, and Samuel Weintraub, "First-Graders' Responses to Three Questions about Reading," *Elementary School Journal,* 66 (May 1966), 441-49.

9. Frazier, Alexander, and Esther E. Schatz, "Teaching a Picture Book as Literature," *Elementary English,* XXXXIII (January 1966), 45-49.

10. Frymier, Jack R., "The Effect of Class Size Upon Reading Achievement in First Grade," *Reading Teacher,* 18 (November 1964), 90-3.

11. Gans, Roma, *Common Sense In Teaching Reading.* Indianapolis: The Bobbs-Merrill Company, Inc., 1963, Chapters 5, 6, and 7.

12. Goodlad, John I., "Ungrading the Elementary Grades," *NEA Journal,* XLIX (March 1955), 170-71.

13. ———, and Robert H. Anderson, *The Nongraded Elementary School.* New York: Harcourt, Brace & World, 1959.

14. Gray, William S., *On Their Own In Reading* (rev. ed.). Chicago: Scott, Foresman & Company, 1960.

15. Hanson, Irene W., "First Grade Children Work with Variant Word Endings," *Reading Teacher,* 19 (April 1966), 505-7.

16. McCullough, Constance M., "Groping or Grouping?" *Elementary English,* XXXI (1954), 136-38.

17. McKee, Paul, and William K. Durr, *Reading/a Program of Instruction for The Elementary School.* Boston: Houghton Mifflin Company, 1966, Chapters 1-5.

18. Mason, George E., "The Role of Phonics in the First Grade Program," *Challenge and Experiment In Reading.* International Reading Association Proceedings, 7, 1962, 27-9.

19. Murphy, Helen A., "A Balanced First Grade Reading Program," *Challenge and Experiment In Reading.* International Reading Association Proceedings, 7, 1962, 33-6.

20. Polkinghorne, Ada R., "Grouping Children in the Primary Grades," *Elementary School Journal,* L (May 1950), 502-8.

21. Robinson, H. Alan, "A Study of the Techniques of Word Identification," *Reading Teacher,* 16 (January 1963), 238-42.

22. Sister Marilyn, O.S.F., "Reading for Meaning," *Catholic School Journal,* 65 (September 1965), 56.

23. Sister Mary Alice, R.S.M., and Adma d'Heurle, "New Ventures In School Organization — The Ungraded School and Use of Teacher Aids," *Elementary School Journal,* LVII (February 1957), 268-71.

24. Sutton, Marjorie Hunt, "First Grade Children who Learned to Read in Kindergarten," *Reading Teacher,* 19 (December 1965), 192-96.

25. Tinker, Miles A., and Constance M. McCullough, *Teaching Elementary Reading.* New York: Appleton-Century-Crofts, 1962, Chapters 6 and 19.

26. Whipple, Gertrude, "Good Practices in Grouping," *Reading Teacher,* VII (1953), 69-73.

27. Worth, Walter H., and J. Harlan Shores, "Does Nonpromotion Improve Achievement in the Language Arts?" *Elementary English,* 37 (January 1960), 49-52.

bus driver

6 Teaching Reading in the Primary Grades

The term *primary reading* refers to the first three years of formal instruction. Having already discussed beginning reading, we are here concerned only with the later primary years. Primary reading is not to be thought of as a stage in the learning process which has fixed or rigid boundaries. It does not start with one particular aspect of the curriculum and end with another, but rather overlaps and blends with previous and later teachings. The teacher in the later primary grades will stress the same fundamental skills introduced in beginning reading instruction, but with the goal of expanding and broadening them. As pupils learn and master basic skills, new ones will be introduced.

A book on reading may be organized to discuss objectives, materials, and instruction grade by grade. This has value in that it gives a logical continuity to the steps of teaching reading in the order in which they are usually introduced. The disadvantage is that this method of organization reinforces the illusion that children in given grades have abilities which parallel the curricular materials designed for those particular grades. It is easy to accept the idea that the second-grade teacher teaches second graders and that third grades are populated by third graders. Experience in the classroom indicates that this idea is not very useful for instructional purposes since the classification of second or third grader does not define pupil achievement but merely identifies the room which certain pupils are currently occupying.

OBJECTIVES OF THIS PERIOD

The primary grades find the majority of pupils making rather rapid progress in reading. This period is often referred to as the period for gaining independence in reading. Significant changes which have an impact on reading are taking place among children. They develop abilities which are prerequisites for improving reading, and interests which enhance the value of reading ability. Pupils in the primary years acquire a large store of general information, a wider interest in events not directly involving their own lives, and an increasing ability to deal with the abstract. They are now mature enough to concentrate for relatively long periods, developing capabilities for both independent work and teamwork.

An almost unlimited number of objectives for primary reading instruction could be advanced. Many of those listed here cannot be thought of as belonging exclusively to the primary period. Some were important in beginning reading and others will continue to be important throughout the intermediate, junior high, and secondary school levels. These objectives are to help the child:

1. Develop a large sight vocabulary.
2. Expand his stock of concepts and word meanings.
3. Learn and apply phonic principles for sounding out unknown words.
4. Review and extend knowledge of language sounds associated with vowel and consonant combinations.
5. Use punctuation for smooth meaningful reading.
6. Develop the skill of reading several words together as thought units, either phrases or sentences.
7. Reduce the number of occurrences of reading errors such as hesitations, regression, repetition, substitutions, or omissions.
8. Develop the ability to recognize known root words in new word forms which include prefixes or inflectional endings.

9. Further develop the attitude that reading is always purposeful and that he must clarify his purpose in specific reading tasks.
10. Use the context as an aid in attacking unknown words.
11. Enjoy and appreciate the vicarious experiences which are open to him in reading.

THE INSTRUCTIONAL PROGRAM

Reading Growth is Developmental

The instructional program in grades two and three will continue to emphasize such skills as discrimination of initial consonant sounds and consonant blends, building sight vocabulary, profiting from pictures, and using context. Recognition of word endings *s, ed, ing,* taught in grade one, is followed by systematic instruction in extending this developmental task. In grade two, other suffixes will be dealt with including *er, y, est, ly, iest, less, ful;* later instruction will deal with *ment, tion, tive, sion,* and others.

Study in grade one of initial consonant blends, such as *cl, br, bl, scr, gr, str,* will be extended. Work on recognition of the contractions *aren't, I'll, won't, they're, can't, we'll, you'll,* etc., and of numerous compound words will receive attention.

In addition to a systematic effort to extend skills previously introduced, many new developmental tasks are undertaken. Particular emphasis is placed on phonic and structural analysis. A number of prefixes and suffixes are taught with an emphasis on both structural and meaning changes involved. Silent consonants (*k*nife, com*b*, i*s*land, li*gh*t) and other spelling irregularities will receive attention along with syllabication and simple alphabetizing.

Comprehension skills are developmental also and should be developed systematically in the primary grades. Context clues become more important as unknown sight words are met more frequently. It is essential to learn new connotations for many words, and literal meanings cannot be insisted on for figurative expressions. The reader must follow the sequence of ideas and see their relationship to each other. The ability to analyze the meaning of sentences must be extended to paragraphs and larger units so that the main ideas of these larger units of material can be grasped.

The pace at which reading skills are taught in the primary grades is increased and the progress expected of pupils in a given period of time, such as a semester or year, is practically doubled when compared with the goals of beginning reading. The program necessarily includes simultaneous emphasis on the development of the mechanics of reading and the development of those comprehension skills which make reading rewarding and satisfying. To attain the many objectives of the primary period, instruction must focus on four main activities:

1. Selection of materials and the teaching schedule.
2. Diagnosis of pupil achievement and instructional needs to serve as a basis for classroom organization and instructional emphasis.
3. The systematic expansion of skills in the mechanics of reading.
4. The development of comprehension skills and emphasis on recreational reading.

MATERIALS AND TEACHING SCHEDULE

Use of Basal Materials

The relation of basal reader series to the total reading program is much the same in grades two and three as in beginning reading. Growth in reading is developmental, and basal reader materials are designed with this fact in mind. Most facets of instruction are provided for in a logical sequence and each receives proper emphasis. The essence of primary-level instruction is continuity and a systematic building of skills. When a child's growth does not parallel the materials found at his grade level, it is the pupil's achievement and rate of growth, not the materials, that must determine the instructional program. The basal reader materials at this level not only stress the mechanical skills of reading but also emphasize comprehension, cultivating in the reader an attitude that demands comprehension from reading. While vocabulary is still controlled, the expansion of the reading vocabulary at this level permits practice in reading for information, organization of data, and interpretation and appreciation of literature. (3) These skills systematically taught in reading instruction should easily transfer to all reading situations involving subject area materials and textbooks. Instructional procedures for developing the mechanics of reading and comprehension skills are discussed later in this chapter.

Experience Charts and Other Supplementary Materials

While basal reader series can provide the foundation for systematic instruction at this level, these materials should not be thought of as *the* reading program. Certainly the continued use of experience charts is justifiable in grades two and three. Experience stories written by individual pupils, as well as charts produced by the class as a whole, can be used extensively at the primary level. Since the sight vocabulary of pupils has been enlarged, this particular problem in the use of experience charts is minimized in the upper primary grades.

Bulletin boards also have many potential uses since children can now engage in independent reading and find materials which bear on topics under discussion. Pictures and newspaper and magazine articles offer interesting sources of material. When children know that there is a certain space in the room reserved for the use of such materials, they are motivated to do outside reading to find appropriate display materials. The bulletin board can be particularly effective when the teacher is working with units. The unit approach may be used successfully at this level if enough supplementary reading material is available at the pupils' reading level. (For a discussion of the unit approach, see Chapter 10.) If such materials are not available in the various content areas, there is little reason why a wide array of materials cannot be provided for recreational reading.

Teaching Schedule

Teachers in the primary grades must have definite daily periods of time devoted exclusively to reading instruction. In addition to this regularly scheduled time, other periods may occasionally be used for reading instruction with particular groups. For instance, a number of poorer readers may be given extra practice in word-attack skills while those pupils fairly proficient in this skill read independently in a subject area text or for recreation. At other times the teacher may participate in the discussion of a story with a group of advanced readers while other pupils do seatwork on teacher-prepared lesson sheets.

There is no one specific amount of time per day which can be said to be ideal for systematic reading instruction. (4) Factors such as class size, pupils' achievement, the teacher's skill, and classroom organization would have to be considered in arriving at a schedule. In grade two, an hour each morning and possibly a slightly shorter period in the afternoon would certainly be considered a minimum amount of time for scheduled instruction. Other short periods throughout the week should be devoted to particular reading problems as they arise in other instructional activities. Problems in word meaning, word attack, punctuation, and exploration of concepts all involve reading instruction and should take place in any context whether the curricular task is in the area of arithmetic, health, or language arts.

RECREATIONAL READING

Reading for pleasure and satisfaction should be considered in any discussion of reading materials and schedules. By providing vicarious experiences that help them gain insight into their own problems, recreational reading is a means through which children can attain greater maturity.

Maturity, which is determined by the response that an individual makes in attempting to deal with his social and psychological needs, is never achieved once and for all. A child who is socially and emotionally mature at six may not be equally well-adjusted at age nine. Thus, recreational reading should be continually encouraged throughout the primary and intermediate grades. All the *potential* resources residing in reading will go unrealized unless the individual *reads*. Teachers must help children see reading as a resource for intellectual, social, and emotional growth.

There are many factors which influence the success of a recreational reading program. First, any child's participation in recreational reading will be determined by the degree to which he has mastered reading skills and habits. The child deficient in these skills is not likely to turn to reading, because reading will not be satisfying. Second, the variability in pupils' skills, needs, and interests makes the teacher's task difficult. She will have to be familiar with a great deal of reading material, and she will have to know something of the social and emotional environment of pupils if she is to have the right book at the right time for each pupil. At the very time the child is developing into an independent reader and might find great pleasure in reading, the school channels most reading experiences into textbooks and assigned reading in content areas. There is no doubt that in some instances the school's preoccupation with textbook subject matter may have a tendency to stifle outside reading for pleasure.

A third factor jeopardizing the success of recreational reading programs is the fact that many schools fail to provide supplementary reading materials at all reading levels. Today there are no areas of interest in which there is not a vast amount of reading materials. These materials parallel and supplement all subject matter found in the present-day curriculum. In science there are books devoted to subjects varying from rocks to rockets or snakes to satellites. There are biographies of men and women in such fields as medicine, exploration, invention, social work, politics, nursing, and sports. Well-written stories can be found that deal with other countries and other peoples. These must be made available to children in the schools.

Despite all of the values inherent in wide and wisely selected reading, recreational reading seems to be declining. This is certainly true among adults and appears to be a growing problem among adolescents. The school has the responsibility of guiding the growth of children and cannot possibly wait for a child's needs to drive him into recreational reading. Recreational reading is a special instructional problem because of the discrepancy between the tremendous potential residing in recreational reading and the actual values presently achieved in our schools.

MOTIVATING CHILDREN TO READ

There are many ways in which teachers can help children develop an interest in recreational reading.

1. One way to make reading attractive to children is to read to them. In many instances a teacher will want to read a book or story in its entirety. Sometimes she might read just enough to whet appetites, and children will want to read the book for themselves. When the teacher reads, she will have to be well-prepared. She must read with expression and feeling to provide a model interpretation.

2. Teachers must be prepared to guide children in selecting books which they are capable of reading and which they will enjoy. Nothing kills interest in reading so quickly as material for which one does not have an adequate background or in which one has no interest. Often the teacher can help supply these prerequisites. If the child is reading a biography, he should know something of the central character's background, accomplishments, and contribu-

tions. In dealing with fiction or historical works, he should be aware of events and conditions which would make the story more meaningful.

3. To guide the child toward wide reading is a worthy objective, but at the same time a balanced diet is not necessarily the first step. Children should be permitted to read what they enjoy. The teacher's preference does not always coincide with the child's interest. A child may not be ready for the classics or for great literature. If he reads extensively, he will soon become satiated with "series" books, mysteries, westerns, myths, or whatever he is currently engrossed in. Recreational reading is by definition an individual matter. There is little cause for fear that the avid reader will not gradually broaden his interests and taste. He should be guided in this direction but not pushed.

4. In some situations it may be necessary to use extrinsic motivations. Librarians and teachers have found that some children are favorably influenced by keeping a record of the books they read. Charts or graphs can be used to reflect the number of books or stories read. This extrinsic motivation is educationally justifiable, but teachers must remember its limitation. It can work for only a limited time. While it is being used and while it is serving as an ego satisfaction for the child, the real aim is to have the child develop a love for reading which in time becomes the reward itself. When this occurs, the child will no longer need the show of accomplishment in the form of a *record* of books read. Some children will need overt approval from the teacher as a reward for their effort in recreational or outside reading. These children should be permitted to tell the teacher or a group in the class about the story they have read. Acceptance and teacher approval then become associated with reading. If a child is adequately prepared, he may be permitted to read to a group during a free reading period or as part of a unit. This practice is certainly one of the chief uses of oral reading in the classroom.

ORAL READING

Instruction in oral reading must be considered in light of the purposes for which it is used, the materials used, and how it is incorporated into the total reading program.

Teachers of beginning reading will use oral reading for a number of purposes. Opinions as to the relative value of teaching oral reading have changed considerably during the present century. At one time oral reading was widely practiced without much attention to the justification of the classroom procedures that were followed. Oral reading was equated with the school's reading program. The term *oral reading* may call to mind children in a circle reading round robin from the same book with each child in the group reading silently along with, behind, or ahead of the child performing orally. The poorer reader took his turn along with the rest and sighed, mumbled, and coughed his embarrassed way through the allotted paragraph.

The evils that result from a particular educational practice may be remembered long after the practice has either been discontinued or substantially modified. In some cases oral reading was overemphasized and children spent most of their time reading aloud. As a result, they read slowly, putting all the emphasis on the mechanics of reading and little emphasis on meaning. Gray (9) tells of a boy reading a long passage orally. He read with expression and good interpretation. The teacher asked him a question about the content of what he had just read. His reply was that he could not answer because he "wasn't listening."

Another abuse was that oral reading was often advanced as an end in itself rather than a means to several desirable ends. Oral reading was practiced in artificial situations with little thought given to creating a true audience situation. As these abuses were pointed out in the literature on teaching reading, a reaction against oral reading took place. The disadvantages and potential weaknesses were stressed to the point where many teachers may possibly have thought that the issue was oral reading versus silent reading, rather than the *intelligent use* of oral reading. At the moment, the most popular position is the middle ground which embraces the position that a proper balance should be maintained between silent and oral reading. It is difficult to argue with the logic of this latter position; nevertheless, it is almost impossible to find what constitutes a proper balance. What is adequate and desirable for one teacher with a particular class may be an improper diet in another situation.

The values of oral reading can be found in many natural classroom situations. The most common situation is one in which a child reads aloud in order to convey information or pleasure to an audience of his classmates. Regardless of the situation, oral reading can be justified only when the purposes are logical, the goals educationally sound, and the preparation adequate to the occasion. There is much written in teacher's manuals about the preparation of students for reading tasks, but there are no reading tasks which make more justified demands for adequate preparation than does oral reading.

Reading in an audience situation can be an ego-building experience for the reader. Personal and social growth as well as self-confidence can be achieved. But the child must be able to read satisfactorily in order to elicit approval from others, and he should not be expected to read to a group unless adequately prepared. Furthermore, reading aloud from a book while children follow the same passage in their books minimizes the audience situation. Oral reading should, insofar as possible, make use of materials other than basal series used for instructional purposes with the class.

Oral reading can be an excellent means of teaching reading skills such as good phrasing, use of punctuation, reading with expression, and fluent reading without hesitations or repetitions. Oral reading is a logical extension of the language usage characteristic of children as they enter school. Practice in oral reading can help the child associate printed words with their speech equivalents.

It is often stated that oral reading provides an excellent opportunity for the diagnosis of reading skills and the discovery of pupils' reading weaknesses. This diagnostic function is a pupil-teacher situation centered around a teacher purpose and probably would not involve the child's reading to a group. It could be argued that this is not a true oral-reading situation since pupil purpose, informing an audience, is not paramount. However, reading to the teacher is a highly motivating audience situation for most children, providing the teacher is encouraging rather than critical.

It cannot be denied that oral reading provides many clues to the actual weakness in a child's reading. A child's response after reading silently may indicate that he is a poor reader, or that he is performing below a certain grade level. Such a diagnosis may not disclose *why* the child reads poorly. If the teacher can *hear* and *observe* the child's reading, she can discover important clues to his competence in sight vocabulary, attacking unknown words, use of context, use of punctuation, and whether he views reading as getting meaning. The teacher will not rely on only one sample of oral reading as an adequate diagnosis, but each instance of oral reading will be seen as a part of an ongoing diagnosis.

It is generally agreed that oral reading is a more difficult task than silent reading. Kovas (13) emphasizes this, pointing out that in oral reading the reader must know all the words and must get the author's point and mood so that he can convey it to the listeners. To do this he must use proper phrasing, paying heed to punctuation while at the same time reading loud enough to reach all his listeners. Children will inevitably face situations which call for reading aloud. Since almost all purposeful oral reading takes place in a social setting, these instances will be important to the reader, whose performance will place him in the position of being judged by others.

In summary, considerations which should be observed when using oral reading include:

1. The reader must have a purpose for the oral reading. He must have interesting data which he wishes to share with others.
2. The reader must be prepared. He must have mastered the mechanical skills required and have arrived at an acceptable interpretation of the author's intent.
3. Children are not always well-trained in our schools to *listen*. When children cannot listen critically, the primary justification for oral reading is missing.
4. Instruction during the actual oral reading situation will usually destroy the value of oral reading.
5. Too much oral reading can diminish its effectiveness. The stress should be on good oral reading not on an endurance contest for either readers or listeners.
6. Oral reading must not become so artificial or mechanical for the reader that he forgets that he is reading for meaning.
7. The teacher should be ready to provide a good model of oral reading when such a model is needed by the group or an individual child.
8. It should be remembered that the larger the group involved, the more the problems.
9. Oral reading may be a considerable threat to some pupils. These cases should be handled with sympathetic understanding.

DIAGNOSIS OF PUPILS' READING ABILITY

It has been pointed out that throughout the primary years ever-increasing differences are found among pupils in the same classroom. If some children in a second grade read at the primer or first-reader level, their teacher must function as a first-grade teacher. Some pupils in the same class will have mastered skills sufficient to read third grade materials. To teach these children where they are, the teacher, in effect, will be a third-grade teacher. Very few second-grade teachers enjoy the luxury of a group more homogeneous than depicted here. Third-grade teachers are confronted with even more heterogenous groups as far as reading ability is concerned. Figure 15 is a graphic representation of the overlap between grades and the range of reading abilities found in the primary grades.

FIGURE 15

GRAPHIC REPRESENTATION OF READING ABILITIES IN THE PRIMARY GRADES. (Note that the *Range* of abilities increases at each succeeding grade level.)

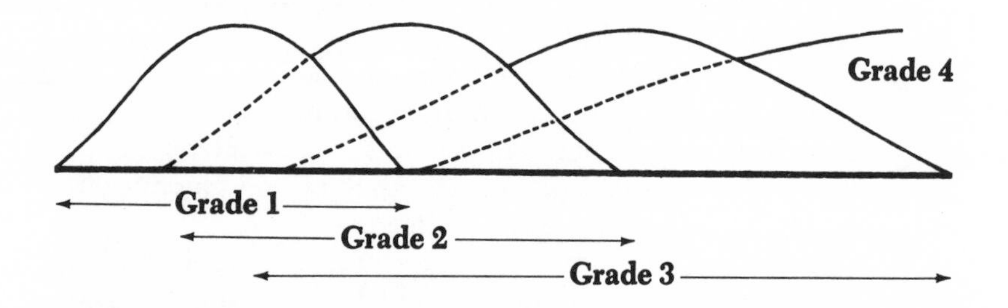

Teachers will have to be alert to differences among pupils in order to follow sound principles of teaching. Only through diagnosis will the teacher be able to assess needs and plan instruction for children whose needs vary considerably. Diagnosis should be thought of as continuous since children are changing rapidly. A diagnosis in September may be followed by a breakthrough on the part of the child in some vital skill or by a child's failure to master some new step in the reading process. In either case, the earlier diagnosis is obsolete.

Reading weaknesses and reading achievement can be assessed by either standardized or informal teacher-made tests. (18) Although tests are designed for use at every grade level, no purpose would be served in a reading textbook by a separate discussion of tests each time a different instructional level is under consideration. The following discussion of tests and testing applies to the various levels of the elementary school with the exception that reading readiness tests are dealt with in Chapter 2.

Standardized Tests

These are commercially printed tests which fall into two classes: those designed for group administration, and those designed to be administered individually. In both, credits are given for acceptable responses, and the child's score is determined by his correct responses, lack of errors, and rate of reading. Norms are usually provided, and any child's score can be translated into a grade-level equivalent. Usually sub-tests are scored separately, permitting the plotting of a profile which will indicate the areas of pupil strengths and weaknesses. Standardized tests are widely used in our schools, and a larger number of them are becoming available each year. Most of these have real merit, yet it is doubtful that reading instruction is improving as a direct result of these tests. This is paradoxical. If tests have real merit, how could their widespread use not result in appreciable improvement in reading instruction?

The answer to this question is to be found in the way the tests are used. (16) As pointed out in Chapter 1, the only justifiable purpose for the use of reading tests is to secure data about an individual's reading ability so that a reading program for the child can be built from the data secured. In actual practice some schools and some teachers gain comfort from the use of tests because they are convinced that testing programs per se have educational value. Testing becomes an end in itself rather than a basis for instruction. In some communities a metal filing cabinet "with a folder for each pupil" is interpreted as prima facie evidence of good teaching practices. This reaction suggests that the school has lost sight of the principle that diagnosis alone has no salutary effect on the pupil diagnosed.

Group Tests

Tests designed for groups have some very obvious weaknesses. A second-grade teacher testing a large number of children at one time cannot hope to find out much about any individual child's reading needs or weaknesses. Such a test will differentiate between poor and good readers, but using a formal testing situation may not be the most economical method of securing these data. A considerable amount of teacher time must be spent in learning the precise procedure for administering and scoring the test and in analyzing the results. The skilled teacher who uses equal time and effort in informal reading situations will certainly arrive at an equally reliable division of pupils. In addition, she will also have a better idea of what particular weaknesses certain children have developed. From the standpoint of instruction this is more important than simply knowing which children are impaired readers.

Another drawback to the use of group tests is that pupils' scores can be influenced by such factors as the misunderstanding of directions, guessing answers, and confusion in marking responses. If these go undetected in the group-administration process, the analysis of test scores will result in a distorted picture of the child's reading ability.

All achievement batteries designed to test pupils in the elementary school contain reading tests. Often these reading subtests are available in individual booklets which can be secured and administered independently of the rest of the battery. (The *California*, *SRA* and *Metropolitan* achievement batteries and the *Coordinated Scales of Attainment* are examples.) Since there are so many different reading tests, it is to be expected that many of them will measure virtually the same aspects of reading. Nevertheless, there are major differences among tests as to what they measure, the level of difficulty for which they are designed, the care which went into their construction, and the ease with which they are administered. Each of these factors affects two important attributes of reading tests—the consistency with which they measure reading skills, and the degree to which they actually measure the skills that they allegedly measure.

No full-time elementary teacher would have the time or the need to become thoroughly conversant with all standardized reading tests. However, it might be well to know where one can go for information about tests when that information is needed. Probably the most authoritative source for such information is *The Mental Measurements Yearbook*, edited by Buros.* Information regarding tests can also be secured from publishers of tests and sample sets of tests can be purchased. A number of publishers who issue descriptive test catalogues are cited at the end of this chapter. In addition, many universities and colleges maintain testing bureaus which are equipped to advise teachers and administrators concerning tests and testing programs.

---

*Oscar Krisen Buros, ed., *The Sixth Mental Measurements Yearbook* (Highland Park, N. J.: Gryphon Press, 1965).

Standardized Individual Tests

Individual tests can minimize some of the shortcomings attributed to group tests. Teachers can observe one child quite closely during the administration of the test. This permits much more precise knowledge of reading errors made and whether or not the child understands the test directions. Individual standardized tests range in content from a single paragraph of oral reading at each grade level to a number of subtests including silent reading, oral reading with comprehension questions, spelling, letter recognition, sounding of blends, word meanings, and rapid recognition of sight words in isolation. The most significant subtests are the oral reading passages at each grade level. These are usually relatively short reading passages upon which the grade norms are based and as a result tend to rate pupils higher than their actual reading level on sustained reading material. Table 2 presents data on the number of running words (total number of words in the reading passage at each grade level) found in several reading tests designed for use in the elementary grades.

TABLE 2

NUMBER OF RUNNING WORDS FOUND ON REPRESENTATIVE READING TESTS, GRADES 1-6

	Running Words Found on:		
Grade Level	*Durrell Analysis of Reading Difficulty**	*Gray Oral Reading Paragraphs Test†*	*Gilmore Oral Reading Tests**
1	21	49	26
2	51	49	50
3	55	49	51
4	72	62	67
5	78	62	107
6	97	62	107

*World Book Co., New York
†Public School Publishing Co., Bloomington, Indiana

Representative Tests

A brief description of a limited number of both group and individual tests follows. These tests are selected because they illustrate different types of reading tests and because, in most cases, they are recent publications or recent revisions.

Representative Group Tests.

1. *Gates-MacGinitie Reading Tests* (1965). *Publisher:* Teachers College Press, Columbia University, N. Y. Six separate tests are available for testing grades one through nine.

	Grade	*Subtests*	*Forms*
Primary A	1	Vocabulary, Comprehension	1-2
Primary B	2	Vocabulary, Comprehension	1-2
Primary C	3	Vocabulary, Comprehension	1-2
Primary CS	2.5-3	Speed, Accuracy	1-2-3
Survey D*	4-5-6	Speed, Vocabulary, Comprehension	1-2-3
Survey E*	7-8-9	Speed, Vocabulary, Comprehension	1-2-3

2. *Nelson-Lohmann Reading Test* (Grades 4-8). *Publisher:* Educational Test Bureau, Educational Publishers, Inc. This is a paragraph test using multiple-choice questions to measure the pupil's grasp of central ideas; word meanings derived from context, and details; and the pupil's ability to integrate ideas. There are separate tests for each grade level 4-8. Two comparable forms are available.

These tests are also part of the battery: *Coordinated Scales of Attainment.*

3. *S.R.A. Achievement Series* (1964). *Publisher:* Science Research Associates, Inc. These materials consist of three separate batteries for use at grade levels 1-2; 2-4; 4-9. There are subtests for each area of the curriculum. The following data refer only to the reading subtests.

Grades 1-2. The reading test contains 4 subtests: verbal-picture association, language perception, comprehension, and vocabulary. Forms C-D.

Grades 2-4. The reading test consists of two subtests: vocabulary and comprehension. Forms C-D.

Grades 4-9. Three separate batteries are published in a single booklet. Batteries are for grade levels as follows:

*Available in both hand-scored and machine-scored editions.

4.5 to 5.5
6.5 to 8.0
8 to 9

Subtests: Comprehension, Vocabulary. Forms C-D.

4. *California Achievement Test Batteries* (1957 edition with 1963 norms). *Publisher:* California Test Bureau.

A. Lower Primary, Grades 1-2
B. Upper Primary, Grades 3-4
C. Elementary, Grades 4-6
D. Junior High, Grades 7-9
E. Advanced, Grades 9-14

Reading skills measured: Reading vocabulary and reading comprehension are tested. Each is covered by several subtests which yield part scores. The reading tests, which are part of the achievement battery, are available as separate tests under the title *California Reading Test.*

Four forms: W, X, Y, Z

5. *Stanford Achievement Tests* (1964). *Publisher:* Harcourt, Brace & World, Inc. Five separate batteries cover grades 1-9. Each battery contains a number of subtests on reading.

Primary Battery I. Grades 1-2.5 (Word Reading, Paragraph Meaning, Vocabulary, Spelling, Word Study Skills).

Primary Battery II. Grades 2-3 (Word Meaning, Paragraph Meaning, Spelling, Word Study Skills, Language).

Intermediate Battery I. Grades 4-5 (Same subtests as above).

Intermediate Battery II. Grades 5-6 (Word Meaning, Paragraph Meaning, Spelling, Language).

Advanced Battery. Grades 7-9 (Paragraph Meaning, Spelling, Language).

Each of the above batteries is available in forms: W, X, Y, Z.

6. *Iowa Tests of Basic Skills* (Grades 3-9). *Publisher:* Houghton Mifflin Company (3 alternate forms). This achievement battery yields eleven separate scores in the following major areas: vocabulary, reading comprehension, language skills, work-study skills, and arithmetic skills.

All of the subtests for each grade, three through nine, are included in one spiral booklet of ninety-six pages. These booklets are reusable since responses are made on separate answer sheets.

The reading comprehension test requires approximately one hour for administration at *each* grade level. It consists of a number of stories of graduated length and difficulty. Comprehension is tested by means of multiple choice items, the reader selecting the one best answer from among the four available. As noted above, the reading comprehension test is available only as part of the entire Basic Skills Battery.

7. *American School Achievement Tests* (Part I, Test of Reading). *Publisher:* The Bobbs-Merrill Co., Inc.

A. Primary Battery, Grades 2-3
B. Intermediate Battery, Grades 4-6
C. Advanced Battery, Grades 7-9

Reading skills measured (all levels): Sentence and word meaning, paragraph meaning, and total reading score.

Four forms: D, E, F, G

Representative Individual Tests.

1. *Durrell Analysis of Reading Difficulty* (Grades 1-6). Major subtests include a separate series of paragraphs for oral reading and recall, silent reading and recall, and listening comprehension. Other subtests measure visual recognition of letters and words, ability to give sounds of letters and blends, and spelling. Each individual test folder contains an extensive checklist of potential reading difficulties. This test has several limitations: only one form is available; grade level norms are based on rate but not on comprehension; and comprehension questions rely heavily on recall of detail, thus slighting other facets of comprehension.

2. *Gates-McKillop Reading Diagnostic Tests.* (Grades 2-6, a 1962 Revision of the *Gates Reading Diagnostic Tests*). *Publisher:* Teachers Press, Teachers College, Columbia University. This test consists of subtests measuring oral reading, rapid recognition of whole words, untimed sight-word recognition, auditory blending, spelling, recognizing word parts and oral vocabulary (meaning). The total test yields 28 scores, is somewhat complicated to administer, and is time-consuming.

3. *Gilmore Oral Reading Test* (Grades 1-8). *Publisher:* World Book Company. This test consists of ten paragraphs, arranged in order of difficulty, which form a continuous story. Each paragraph, representing a grade level, is followed by five comprehension questions. There are two forms of the test, both of which are included in the same spiral-bound booklet. The test yields separate scores on rate of reading, comprehension, and accuracy (pronunciation of vocabulary). The individual record blank permits a detailed record of reading errors.

4. *Gray Oral Reading Test* (1963). *Publisher:* The Bobbs-Merrill Co., Inc. This test consists of a series of 13 paragraphs of increasing difficulty. As the subject reads orally, the examiner marks on an identical passage the errors noted such as mispronunciation, words not attempted, omission, substitution, repetitions, and the like. Comprehension of each paragraph is checked by a series of four questions. Each paragraph is timed. Scoring involves recording the number of errors, type of errors, time elapsed in reading each paragraph, and a comprehension score. Total score can be converted into a grade-equivalent score. There are four alternate forms of the test: A, B, C, D.

Informal Teacher-Made Tests

Teachers can devise informal tests for any classroom purpose. The simplest screening test might consist of having a child read a paragraph or two from a book to determine whether he can successfully read that particular book. (14) More thorough informal tests will yield important data about children's reading, and these tests have certain advantages for classroom use. First, they are simple to construct since the teacher has available graded reading materials from the pre-primer level through the upper grades. Second, the child can be tested over longer passages of sustained reading than are characteristically found on standardized tests. Third, the use of teacher-made tests avoids the formality of the usual test situation. Informal testing is not likely to arouse the pupil tensions which sometimes accompany testing and which occasionally influence pupil performance. In this respect, the informal test more closely parallels the actual reading situations which the child encounters in the classroom. (1) Finally, the teacher-made test is inexpensive and demands no more teacher time for administration and analysis than do other tests. At the same time it yields very specific data on each child's weaknesses and needs, as do the individual standardized tests. The following steps might serve as a guide in the construction of an informal test.

Step 1. Devise a checklist of reading behaviors. This is usually one page upon which the teacher can rapidly record reading errors and observations of related behavior. Figure 16 is an example which could be duplicated and filled out for each child in the class. The checklist can be used with any graded reading materials.

FIGURE 16

Reading Behavior Record

Name____________________ Age________ Grade________ Date________
School____________________ Teacher________________________
Examiner____________________

I. *Word Analysis*	Yes	No
A. Knows names of letters.		
B. Attacks initial sounds of words.		
C. Can substitute initial sound.		
D. Can work out initial blends.		
E. If root word is known, can get words formed by adding prefixes and suffixes.		

II. *Sight Words*	Yes	No
A. Knows words in context, but misses them in isolation.		
B. Knows a word one time, misses it later.		
C. Guesses at unknown words.		
D. Does not attempt unknown words.		
E. Frequently adds words.		
F. Omits words not known, reads on.		
G. Occasionally omits or skips words he knows.		

III. *General Reading Habits*

__________word by word __________does not utilize punctuation
__________poor phrasing __________points with finger
__________(other) __________(other)

IV. *Informal Reading Analysis:* Sustained Reading

	Book	*Grade Level*	*Approx. Number of Running Words*	*Number of Errors*
1.				
2.				

	Excellent	*Average*	*Below Average*
Attitude toward reading			
Self-confidence			
General background experience			
Language facility			
Recall or comprehension			

Step 2. Construct a simple test of sight words in isolation. The Dolch Basic Sight Word Test* could be used or a typed list of approximately one hundred words taken from pre-primers, primers, and first readers, omitting proper names. Almost any list made will contain words found on the Dolch list. Testing sight words in isolation will sometimes reveal that a child knows more words in actual reading than he does in the sight recognition of words in isolation. Often a child miscalls small words in sustained reading situations which he may be able to correct immediately. This indicates that he has not *mastered* these small "service words" as instant recognition sight vocabulary. The following 100 words are common to the pre-primers and primers of a number of widely used basal reader series. A child who has trouble with many of these words will find reading a frustrating task.

we	horse	they	boat
with	a	jump	to
yes	an	big	walk
stop	look	come	want
like	was	go	on
help	find	think	house
very	little	and	my
all	best	could	can
this	old	boy	talk
some	try	may	girl
the	see	again	said
ball	mother	pretty	will
friend	any	which	father
went	over	then	small
did	wagon	live	blue
good	not	run	had
in	play	arm	she
me	what	up	your
hat	do	each	after
man	ran	his	clean
that	new	got	many
saw	wish	red	most
you	dog	there	around
here	under	please	open
sure	ride	name	every

*Garrard Press, Champaign, Illinois.

Step 3. Secure materials for testing children on sustained reading. Short passages of 100 or more words from pre-primer through sixth-grade level can be used. Pages from books can be cut out and placed in order of difficulty in a teacher-made booklet, or the basal readers themselves can be used. Comprehension questions should be carefully developed for each passage. The child should not be permitted to read from a book which he is using in class or which he has used extensively in the recent past. Some teachers prefer to have typed copies of these passages so that they can mark the copies, showing each error and weakness observed while the child is reading. The checklist mentioned above is also used to its fullest advantage during this step of the informal analysis.

Judging the pupil's reading level for basal materials can be accomplished quite accurately by carefully noting his reading behavior on the sustained material test. Failure to pronounce as high as 7 or 8 different words per 100 running words at a given level would indicate this basal material is too difficult for independent reading. On the other hand, few reading errors on basal material at a given level does not assure that the reader will be successful in reading subject textbooks at this grade level. Textbooks in content areas are as a general rule more difficult than the basal-reader materials because in the former the vocabulary is not so rigidly controlled and more unknown concepts appear. A sustained reading test similar to that just described can be devised using representative passages from a geography or science text. Such a test should include carefully prepared comprehension and vocabulary questions.

Step 4. Include a subtest which deals extensively with word analysis skills. Attention has already been paid to these skills in the sight word test and the sustained reading, but further information will often be desired on a child's word-analysis skills. The sight word test included no inflectional endings but only common root words such as *look, run, walk, go, talk, come, like, want, see, play,* and *stop.* The child may now be tested with a series of cards containing these root words plus the common endings (Figure 17 A.). If the child reads at a level of difficulty above first grade, he can be tested with a number of derived forms, contractions, and compound words. (See Figure 17 B.) Performance on these tasks would determine whether the child should be tested on breaking words into syllables. Figure 17 C. uses words taken from spelling books at various grade levels. Separate duplicated work sheets can be made up for each grade level or one page might be developed which covers several grade levels. The child is asked to break the stimulus word found in Column A into syllables and write it in Column B.

FIGURE 17

Test of Word Analysis Skills

A. *Easy root words plus endings* s, ed, ing

running	seated	playing	comes	played
asks	talking	lived	wanted	going
looked	wants	jumps	talks	sees
helps	coming	lives	walking	helping
wanting	likes	pleased	talked	looks
sits	helped	finding	runs	sitting
living	stops	plays	seeing	jumped

B. *Contractions, compound words, and derived forms usually learned at second grade level*

happily	belong	I'll	slowly	behind	hadn't
bakery	didn't	friendly	report	surely	himself
princess	outside	loudest	I'd	everybody	believe
quickly	afternoon	return	herself	you'll	politely
I've	it's	really	suddenly	everyone	shouted
isn't	quickly	everything	doesn't	couldn't	yourself
beside	anything	can't	between	into	wasn't

Contractions, compound words, and derived forms usually learned at third grade level

expect	explain	disappear	comfortable	rapidly
afternoon	ourselves	happiness	halfway	sawmill
you've	discover	invite	safety	invisible
family	they'll	include	upward	Thanksgiving
enjoy	unless	gentleman	peaceful	eyebrow
funniest	experiment	foolish	enchanted	firecrackers
finally	we've	contentment	bathroom	telescope

C. *Words taken from spelling books at 3rd, 4th, and 5th grade level to test child's ability to break words into syllables. Pupil writes words in Column B. First word serves as sample.*

3rd Grade Level		4th Grade Level		5th Grade Level	
A	B	A	B	A	B
yesterday	yes ter day	grandfather	grand fa ther	citizen	cit i zen
money		beautiful		terrible	
birthday		lessons		interesting	
yellow		history		difference	
Easter		remember		medium	
stockings		arithmetic		average	
only		studying		frightened	
afternoon		geography		electric	

If the pupil's performance indicates a lack of ability in attacking words through phonic analysis, a most important step is to determine whether the child actually hears the different speech sounds in similar sounding words. Teachers can prepare auditory discrimination exercises consisting of three- or four-word series to check the pupil's ability to hear *initial sounds, initial blends, vowel sounds,* and *word endings.* The teacher pronounces each word in the series, and the child repeats the one word which does not belong or does not rhyme or begin with the same letter or letter blend. (See Figure 18.)

FIGURE 18

Test of Auditory Discrimination

(The teacher pronounces the four words in each series.)

A. Testing Ability to Hear Initial Consonants

Child repeats the one word that begins differently from the first word.

toy	pat	did	wind	dark	farm
tall	pet	kid	went	drink	warm
hall	cot	doll	bend	dash	find
tack	put	dull	well	bark	full
ball	hard	lack	kick	march	rode
pull	yard	lock	pick	much	load
back	hunt	lamp	kill	met	right
burn	hurt	damp	kind	net	race

B. Testing Ability to Hear Endings of Words

Child repeats the one word which does not rhyme.

pig	bake	ball	wet	bug	bag
dig	make	full	bet	hug	rug
big	bark	tall	pet	did	rag
bag	wake	wall	sat	mug	sag

pot	lick	leg	cut	fell	then
not	stuck	peg	hit	fill	hen
got	stick	lap	hut	sell	thin
God	kick	keg	but	bell	pen

C. Testing Ability to Hear Initial Blends

Child repeats the word which does not begin with the blend sound.

dress	sled	blue	step	tree	plan
drop	sack	blow	sack	truck	pain
draw	slip	bank	stop	train	place
down	slap	black	steep	turn	play

D. Testing Vowel Sounds

Child repeats word having short vowel sound.

mate	fan	fight	joke	cute	tell
mail	fame	mile	lock	dull	team
mad	table	fine	note	true	see
take	flame	skim	snow	tube	feed

USING TEST RESULTS FOR GROUPING AND INSTRUCTION

The results of diagnosis based on either standardized or informal tests can be used for various instructional purposes. The obvious uses are instruction based on pupil needs as disclosed by the diagnosis and grouping practices which might facilitate this instruction. (12) Pupils of widely varying achievement in a classroom will not profit equally from the same procedures applied to the group as a whole. Grouping, as stated previously, is a device which permits teachers to work with a smaller number of pupils who have similar instructional needs. Several factors which relate to grouping in the primary grades should be kept in mind. First, it is to be expected that some pupils will make substantial gains in reading during a period of weeks or months in the primary years. Therefore, neither reliance on a single initial diagnosis nor a rigid grouping arrangement would be desirable. Diagnosis must be ongoing and grouping practices flexible.

Second, the range of pupil abilities will inevitably place some children at the extremes of the achievement continuum outside of the conventional three-group or even a four-group structure. Fitting instruction to these extreme individual differences will call for a supply of materials at many difficulty levels and a variety of approaches to any given instructional objective. Third, since the total reading process is composed of a great number of related but specific skills, it is likely that some children will belong in one group when achievement in one skill is the criterion and in other groups for other instructional purposes. Few children, for example, will be equally deficient—or proficient—in phonic analysis, comprehension of what is read, and appreciation of literature.

The facets of primary reading dealt with in this chapter include the objectives of primary reading and its instructional program from the standpoint of materials, teaching schedule, recreational reading, oral reading, and formal and informal diagnosis. The two major tasks of dealing with the development of the mechanical skills of reading and the expansion of comprehension skills are discussed in the following chapter.

*A representative list of test publishers from whom descriptive catalogues or brochures may be obtained.**

Bureau of Educational Measurements, Kansas State Teachers College, Emporia, Kansas.

Bureau of Educational Research and Service, State University of Iowa, Iowa City, Iowa.

Bureau of Publications, Teachers College, Columbia University, New York, New York.

California Test Bureau, Monterey, California.

Consulting Psychologist Press, 577 College Avenue, Palo Alto, California.

Co-operative Test Division, Educational Testing Service, 20 Nassau Street, Princeton, New Jersey.

Educational Test Bureau, Educational Publishers, Inc., 720 Washington Avenue, S. E., Minneapolis, Minnesota.

Educational Testing Service, 20 Nassau Street, Princeton, New Jersey.

Harcourt, Brace and World, Inc., 757 Third Avenue, New York, New York.

Houghton Mifflin Co., 2 Park Street, Boston (2), Massachusetts.

---

*Source: Oscar Krisen Buros, ed., *The Sixth Mental Measurements Yearbook* (Highland Park, N.J.: Gryphon Press, 1965).

Ohio Scholarship Tests, Ohio State Department of Education, Columbus, Ohio.

Psychological Corporation, 304 East 45th Street, New York (17), New York.

Scholastic Testing Service, Inc., 3774 West Devon Avenue, Chicago (45), Illinois.

Science Research Associates, Inc., 259 East Erie Street, Chicago, Illinois.

Western Psychological Services, 10655 Santa Monica Boulevard, Los Angeles (25), California.

YOUR POINT OF VIEW?

Defend or attack the following statements.

1. Informal teacher-made tests can yield as much data about an individual child's reading as can standardized tests.
2. A careful study reveals that a certain per cent of third grade pupils do not see reading as a source of enjoyment. Complete the following statement so that it would apply to at least 90 per cent of these pupils:

   "These pupils ______________________________."
   (examples: "... are poor readers," "... do not read with expression," "... have experienced failure.")
3. In many schools the potential values which might be achieved from the use of standardized tests are lost because the school is more concerned with the ritual of administering tests than in "mining the test data."
4. Oral reading has little educational value in the primary grades.
5. One of the strengths of American schools is their success in arousing and maintaining pupil interest in recreational reading.
6. Using basal reader series as the basic instructional approach has less efficacy with accelerated readers than with those pupils who, on the basis of reading achievement, rank in the lower half of their grade.

BIBLIOGRAPHY

1. Austin, Mary C., and Mildred H. Huebner, "Evaluating Progress in Reading Through Informal Procedures," *Reading Teacher,* 15 (March 1962), 338-43.
2. Balow, Bruce, and James Curtin, "Ability Grouping of Bright Pupils," *Elementary School Journal,* 66 (March 1966), 321-27.
3. Bond, Guy L., and Eva Bond Wagner, *Teaching The Child to Read* (4th ed.). New York: The Macmillan Company, 1966, Chapter 6.
4. Brekke, Gerald W., "Actual and Recommended Allotments of Time for Reading," *Reading Teacher,* 16 (January 1963), 234-37.
5. Burnett, Richard W., "The Diagnostic Proficiency of Teachers of Reading," *Reading Teacher,* 16 (January 1963), 229-34.

6. Burns, Paul C., "Evaluation of Silent Reading," *Education,* 84 (March 1964), 411-14.
7. Cushenbery, Donald C., "Two Methods of Grouping for Reading Instruction," *Elementary School Journal,* 66 (February 1966), 267-72.
8. Della-Piana, Gabriel, "Analysis of Oral Reading Errors: Standardization, Norms and Validity," *Reading Teacher,* 15 (January 1962), 254-57.
9. Gray, Lillian, *Teaching Children To Read* (3rd ed.). New York: The Ronald Press, 1963, 276.
10. Johnson, Marjorie Seddon, "Reading Inventories for Classroom Use," *Reading Teacher,* 14 (September 1960), 9-13.
11. Karlin, Robert, and Hayden Jolly, "The Use of Alternate Forms of Standardized Reading Tests," *Reading Teacher,* 19 (December 1966), 187-91.
12. Kastner, Marie A., "Instructing and Motivating Pupils in the Light of Test Results," *Catholic Educational Review,* LVII (February 1959), 106-10.
13. Kovas, Helen, "The Place of Oral Reading," *Elementary English,* XXXIV (November 1957), 462-66.
14. McCracken, Robert A., "Using Reading As a Basis for Grouping," *Education,* 84 (February 1964), 357-59.
15. MacDonald, James B., and James D. Raths, "Should We Group by Creative Abilities?" *Elementary School Journal,* 65 (December 1964), 137-143.
16. Putt, Robert C., and Darrel D. Ray, "Putting Test Results to Work," *Elementary School Journal,* 65 (May 1965), 439-44.
17. Ruddell, Robert B., "Oral Language and the Development of Other Language Skills," *Elementary English,* XLIII (May 1966), 489-98.
18. Sheldon, William D., "Specific Principles Essential to Classroom Diagnosis," *Reading Teacher,* 14 (September 1960), 2-8.
19. Sipay, Edward R., "A Comparison of Standardized Reading Scores and Functional Reading Levels," *Reading Teacher,* 17 (January 1964), 265-72.
20. Trela, Thaddeus M., "What Do Diagnostic Reading Tests Diagnose?" *Elementary English,* XLIII (April 1966), 370-72.
21. Veatch, Jeannette, "The Materials and Diagnosis of Reading Problems," *Reading Teacher,* 14 (September 1960), 19-25.
22. Vite, Irene W., "Grouping Practices in Reading," *Elementary English,* XXXVIII (February 1961), 91-103.

Find the number
of syllables in each word.
granted coconuts Florida
1 2 3 4 1 2 3 4 1 2 3 4
native school television
1 2 3 4 1 2 3 4
plumber information climb
1 2 3 4 1 2 3 4 1 2 3 4

Teaching Reading in the Primary Grades (continued)

7

Following diagnosis, plans can be made for teaching each pupil the skills he needs. Since practically every skill is developmental, each must be extended at every level of instruction. For example, both instant recognition of words and phonic analysis are stressed in beginning reading, but the need for these skills becomes more acute in the primary and intermediate grades because new words are introduced with increased frequency at these levels.

In other contexts throughout this book, the point is stressed that all mechanical skills and reading habits are closely related to comprehension of printed material. This relationship is reaffirmed here because in the following materials particular skills are of necessity discussed separately. In the actual reading process, no skill is applied in isolation. One does not read simply to profit from punctuation, phrase material properly, or apply analysis skills.

DEVELOPING AND EXTENDING THE MECHANICAL SKILLS OF READING

The term *mechanics of reading* is used to refer to such skills as:

1. Extension of sight vocabulary
   a. Learning recognition of new words prior to silent reading
   b. Use of experience charts and pictures
   c. Picture-word cards
   d. Completing sentences by choosing proper word
   e. Rapid recognition of vowels in medial position
   f. Combining phrases into meaningful sentences
   g. Identifying root words and inflected forms
2. Word recognition skills
   a. Structural analysis
   b. Kinesthetic method
   c. Phonic analysis
3. Profiting from punctuation
4. Alphabetizing skills
5. Syllabication

Expanding Sight Word Vocabulary

Developing sight vocabulary is one of the most important goals in the primary reading program. The pupil who fails in this ability is in trouble as a reader. The child in the first grade will meet several hundred words on experience charts, on bulletin boards, and in basal readers. If he masters as sight words all the words he meets in the pre-primer, primer, and first reader of a given basal series, he will know between three and four hundred words, although this figure is too high to be used as an estimated average for all pupils beginning their second year of school. If at the end of the second grade, a child knew only the words met thus far in any one basal reader series, he would know between 800 and 1000 sight words. In the third year he would again double his stock of sight words. Throughout the primary period pupils read from a variety of sources, a practice which helps to expand sight vocabulary. (9)

A number of procedures and exercises for helping children extend sight vocabulary are found in basal reader workbooks. In many instances, teachers can devise additional seatwork lessons for pupils who need added experience. A few typical techniques follow:

1. Chalkboard work on new words which are introduced in the day's reading assignment. It is considered desirable to study these new words prior to having children read the story silently. The new words are pronounced as they are printed on the board *(stump, footprints, suddenly, ocean)*. Similarities to other words previously learned are pointed out, i.e., the *st* in *stump,* the word *foot* in the compound word *footprints,* the root word *sudden* in *suddenly.* Learning *ocean* as a sight word is stressed because of the difficulty of sounding it.

2. Using experience charts and personal experience records, labeling objects in the room, and matching captions with pictures. A series of pictures can be displayed and appropriate titles consisting of words, phrases, or sentences can be prepared on oak tag or cardboard. Children then match the proper written caption with each picture:

"The box is empty"	"A jet plane"
"Evergreens"	"Children in a school bus"
"A brown cow"	"Two boys"
"The tree has no leaves"	"A boy and a dog"

3. Using picture-word cards to teach "naming words." A picture of an object is pasted on one side of the card and the word for the picture printed on the other side:

house, car, tractor, bridge, shirt, television, giraffe, piano, dress, swing, policeman, cowboy, hammer, etc.

4. Introducing exercises which call for pupils to select the proper word to fill in a space left blank in a sentence. These exercises stress both meaning and differentiation between similar appearing words.

The kittens were asleep on the ________________.
stay, straw

The bird built its nest in the ________________.
tree, tray

They made a ________________ for the puppy.
bad, bed

Mr. Brown sells ________________ in his store.
hats, hates

A more difficult task is illustrated below where two similar appearing words are to be placed in two blanks in a sentence.

It was their ________ to go by ________. (plane - plan)
The ________ is about a ________ from here. (mile - mill)
The dog took the ________ to the ________. (bone - barn)
The train whistle went ________ ________. (toot-toot - two-too)
We must ________ to write on the ________. (line - learn)

5. Using word-drill periods and work sheets for seat work which stress seeing the difference between similar appearing words.

a. The easiest drill usually involves "family" words in which the initial letter or initial blend is the important visual cue:

*l*ake, *t*ake, *m*ake, *c*ake, *r*ake
*h*at, *c*at, *m*at, *f*at, *p*at, *r*at
*f*all, *c*all, *t*all, *b*all, *h*all, *w*all

b. A child is to supply a word containing the same ending as a pair of cue words.

make take
They used a boat to cross the l______.
told mold
The teacher showed them how to f______ the paper.

c. Practice may be provided in discriminating between common service words which have marked similarities.

their, there; where, when, which; stay, stop;
must, much; many, may; than, then, thin;
horse, house; every, very; think, thank.

d. Practice may be given in rapid recognition of vowels in medial position. (To be read orally):

pin, pen, pan, pun
men, tan, fun, fin, son
sack, sick, sock, suck
duck, kick, back, lock, neck
fell, fall, full, fill
bat, fit, hut, got, let

6. Combining phrases to form meaningful sentences. This exercise forces attention on both the configuration of words and their meanings. In a *finish the sentence* exercise, children draw a line from the phrase in Column A to the phrase in Column B which completes the meaning:

A	B
The car	is on his head.
Around the house	give us milk.
The horse	is a beautiful lawn.
A straw hat	moves down the road.
Cows	drink milk.
Cats	has a beautiful saddle.

7. Identifying root words in inflected forms. The child writes the root in the space provided.

taken	________	using	________
carried	________	goes	________
earlier	________	laziest	________
parties	________	angrily	________
reaching	________	wagged	________

Developing Word Recognition Skills

Word identification is one of the more important mechanical skills of reading. *Word analysis* includes all methods of arriving at the pronunciation of unknown words. Gaining independence in reading implies a mastery of those techniques which will permit a child to read a passage containing words which he does not recognize instantly as sight words. The reader in the primary grades will continue to use all methods of word analysis discussed in beginning reading, deducing words from pictures, context, and structural and phonic analysis. However, in the primary grades phonic and structural analysis become more important because of the reading tasks dealt with.

As taught in the primary grades, *structural analysis* involves a review and extension of the child's experience with:

common word endings
compound words
doubling consonants before adding endings beginning with a vowel
adding *es* to form some plurals
forming plurals of words ending with *y*
contractions
recognizing prefixes and suffixes added to root words
syllabication

Compound words will not be difficult for the child who forms the habit of examining unknown words. The compound words he meets will be composed of shorter words that he has already learned. Basal reader series introduce a few compound words at first-grade level and provide drill on recognition and analysis at each succeeding grade level. Plurals formed by *s*, *es*, and *ies* are usually not introduced until after the child has learned the root words.

There are a number of rules which apply to inflectional endings: an apostrophe followed by an *s* is used to form possessives; when root words end in *y*, the *y* becomes *i* in forming plurals; *e* is dropped before adding a suffix beginning with a vowel; some single consonants preceded by a single vowel are doubled at the end of root words before adding suffixes beginning with a vowel. Many words and inflected forms are learned as sight words before any of these rules are taught. After the child has had a number of experiences with each of the procedures described above, the rules or generalizations are taught. Exercises dealing with some of these changes which take place in words are illustrated in examples 1 through 5 below.

1. Noticing the structure of compound words.

   a. The two words in columns 1 and 2 can be placed together to form one word. Write the two words together under 3 and say the compound that is formed.

1	2	3
after	noon	afternoon
with	out	______
every	one	______
club	house	______
air	plane	______
door	way	______
some	time	______

   b. Each word under 1 can be placed with a word under 2 to make a compound word. The first one is done for you.

1	2	3
*after	way	afternoon
with	time	______
every	plane	______
club	one	______
air	*noon	______
door	out	______
	house	______

2. Doubling the final consonant.

   A number of one-syllable words ending with a consonant are given below. Double that consonant before adding the endings which begin with a vowel.

can	canned	canning
plan	______	______
skip	______	______

pop	______	______
drag	______	______
stop	______	______
slam	______	______
chop	______	______

3. Forming plurals by adding *es*.
Many plurals are formed by simply adding s, *as in* boys, girls, trees, farms, cats. *In many words* es *is added to form plurals.*

fox	foxes	inch	inches
box	______	dress	______
dish	______	lunch	______
brush	______	mix	______
potato	______	match	______
class	______	fish	______

4. Forming the plural of words ending in *y*.
Change the y to i, *then add* es.

funny	funnies	body	bodies
fly	______	army	______
baby	______	party	______
puppy	______	cherry	______
lady	______	family	______

5. Recognizing contractions.
The two words in column A are often combined to form a different word found in column B. The apostrophe (') *in these words indicates that a letter or letters have been omitted in forming the new word.*

A		B
I am	=	I'm
I will	=	I'll
he will	=	he'll
he is	=	he's
has not	=	hasn't
I have	=	I've
have not	=	haven't

(In follow-up work sheets only column A is presented and the child writes the contraction.)

do not	______
was not	______
they have	______
you will	______
it is	______
does not	______

The structure or visual stimulus pattern of words is changed by a syllable added either at the beginning or at the end of that word. A child may know the symbol *load* as a sight word, but the first few times he sees *unload, reload,* or *unloading,* he may not see what is familiar. Instead, he may see the whole new configuration as unfamiliar. Thus, recognizing common prefixes will be an aid in learning new words where the root word is known. (17) Children use words which contain prefixes and suffixes in spoken language long before coming to school. These words are often learned as sight words before formal instruction deals with the meanings of these suffixes.

Instruction cannot deal exclusively with the structural changes resulting from the addition of prefixes or suffixes. Exercises should force attention both to the structural change and the modification of meaning. Workbooks of all basal series have lessons devoted to the study of prefixes, but the teacher does not have to wait for a particular time or page in a workbook. The curriculum of the modern school does not impose such rigidity. It is just as appropriate to show pupils that prefixes change the meanings of words in a science, arithmetic, hygiene, or geography class as it is to discuss this point during the period devoted to reading instruction.

Figure 19 illustrates exercises which teachers can develop and duplicate. Introductory exercises can deal with one prefix. These can be followed by exercises using all of the prefixes taught thus far. Having the pupil make a sentence using the base word, then a sentence with the same word plus the prefix, emphasizes the meaning of the prefix.

FIGURE 19

1. *Make a sentence with each of the following words. What happens to the meaning of each word lettered* b? *What can you say about the prefix* un?

   a. clean
   b. *un*clean
   a. fair
   b. *un*fair
   a. load
   b. *un*load
   a. kind
   b. *un*kind

2. *Make a sentence with each of the following words. What happens to the meaning of each word lettered* b*? What can you say about the prefix* re*?*
   a. fill
   b. *re*fill
   a. read
   b. *re*read
   a. visit
   b. *re*visit

3. *Make a sentence with the following words. Each word lettered* b *has a prefix. Explain what each prefix does to the word meaning.*
   a. view
   b. *pre*view
   a. ability
   b. *in*ability
   a. agree
   b. *dis*agree

Suffixes are word endings which give root words different shades of meaning (*er, or, ist, an, al, ure, ty, ment, ism, age, is, en, el, ive, ish, ant, ful, ly, less,* etc.). Since there are a great number of suffixes and very few have an absolutely fixed meaning, an attempt to teach concrete meanings for the majority would probably produce more confusion than learning. If a child develops the habit of *seeing* the more common endings so that he is not prevented from recognizing known root words, the new word is not likely to cause trouble. Composing sentences using the different forms of a word is a better method of teaching than having the child attempt to tell the precise difference between words like joy*ful*, joy*fully*, joy*ous;* depend*ent*, depend*able*, depend*ency*.

The English language is rich in the number of prefabricated units that can be attached to any number of root words to form new words:

heat: heated, preheated, reheat, preheating, heatedly
war: postwar, warlike, warring, prewar, wartime
luck: lucky, unluckiest, luckily, unlucky
place: placing, displace, replaced, replacable

Assume that the word *happy* is a known sight word. Identifying the word *unhappily* theoretically calls for these skills: recognizing the prefix *un* and the suffix *ly* as units, perceiving the root word *happy*, applying the rule that words ending in *y* change *y* to *i* before adding an ending, and understanding syllabication — i.e., prefixes and suffixes usually stand as syllables and two like consonants usually divide, thus giving the pronunciation *un hap pi ly*. It is doubtful, however, that any reader goes through all of these mental steps since the process would be most uneconomical. The reader also has the context to suggest the word, and after he has met a word on several occasions, he will probably have mastered it as a sight word and will not have to resort to analysis.

The Kinesthetic Method. The kinesthetic method is sometimes used to help children recognize words. This approach is also referred to as the *tracing method* or a *visual-motor method*. (6) In this approach the sense of touch is added to sight and hearing in an effort to help the child who has extreme difficulty in learning to recognize words. The method usually employs the following steps but could be varied with individual children.

a. A word is written or printed on a card.
b. The teacher says "This is the word *farm* — say it with me."
c. The child traces his finger over the word one or two times saying, "the letters *f-a-r-m* is *farm*."
d. With the stimulus card out of sight, the child attempts to write the word from memory.
e. The child compares his efforts with the original and repeats the tracing and sounding until the word is mastered.

In addition to use with severely impaired readers, the kinesthetic method could be used with any child who consistently confuses certain words (*these, those; were, where*) or who reverses words (*was, saw; no, on*). It can also be used in learning difficult spellings. As a method of teaching reading this approach would probably not be used except in extreme remedial cases. Since it is very time-consuming, it would be uneconomical to use the method with children who could learn by faster methods. The kinesthetic approach as a remedial technique is discussed at length by Fernald. (7)

Phonic Analysis. Phonics instruction may be the most important of the mechanical skills taught in the primary grades for helping the child expand his sight vocabulary and become an independent reader. All steps taught at any given grade level must be reviewed and retaught in the following grades if there are pupils who need this instruction. It is important that teachers do not associate particular phonics instruction too closely with a particular grade level. In order to present an over-all view of the phonics program in the primary grades, Chapter 9 is devoted to this topic.

It should be emphasized that phonics is only one of many skills needed for facile reading. For instance, when a child does not know the meaning of a word, arriving at its *exact* pronunciation through phonic analysis will not help him. In the following sentence there is an unknown symbol:

The man was attacked by a marbohem.

Everyone reading this page can sound out *mar-bo-hem,* but no one knows what attacked the man since saying *mar-bo-hem* does not convey meaning to the reader. Words can be substituted for *marbohem,* and some readers would still have trouble with the meaning even though they successfully analyze the speech sounds in the words. For example:

1. The man was attacked by a peccarry.
2. " " " " " " freebooter.
3. " " " " " " iconoclast.
4. " " " " " " fusilier.
5. " " " " " " hypochondriac.

Analysis is only a tool for use in the reading process and should not be confused with the process. It is a valuable technique in reading, but is not in itself a method of teaching reading.

Context and Methods in Combination

At practically all points on the reading continuum, the one ability that sets the good readers apart from poorer readers is the degree to which the context helps the reader get unknown words. When children do not profit from context clues, this weakness is easy to detect by observing their reading behavior — either they do not "try" words or they insert words which do not belong. On the other hand, when a passage is read correctly, it is difficult for an observer to determine to what degree dependence on context clues contributed to the successful reading.

The good reader keeps in mind what has been read and how the sentence he is reading builds on this meaning. If context is not enough, he glances through the word to detect a prefix, the root word, or an inflectional ending. When no prefix is found, the first syllable is isolated. This may unlock the word. If not, he will work further through the word. These operations are performed so rapidly by a good reader that there may be no perceptible pause between the different modes of attack. If the word is not solved by this attack, the reader may go on past the word for additional context clues. This step may call for rereading the sentence, but if it is successful, meaning will have been reached.

When each method of attacking unknown words is discussed and examined separately, one might conclude that in a given situation a reader uses only one method. The exclusive use of one method in this way makes for slow and inefficient reading, although some children approach reading in this manner. The more ability a reader has in profiting from structural, phonic, and context clues, the less likely it is that he can tell which one was the key in helping him solve a particular word. The smooth, facile reader is one who attacks an unknown word simultaneously on every front on which it is vulnerable to analysis. Early in the first grade the child learns to sound the initial letters of words. This skill, plus pictures and context clues, makes it possible to eliminate many of the words that might otherwise have been plausible choices.

The more difficult the level of the material, the less likely it is that the immediate context alone will be an adequate tool for getting unknown words, but often with the smallest additional clue the word is easily solved. Assume that the pupil meets a sentence containing an unknown word: "Jack was sure his ______ would let him go." This is the opening line of a story and the author has yet to unfold the plot or background. There are many words which might complete an idea when this is all we know. Is Jack being held a prisoner? The word could be *captors*. Is he thinking of "getting permission?" The word might be *mother, father, friends, teacher*. If the reader notes something about the unknown word, he may get a valuable clue. For instance, "Jack was sure his p______ would let him go." *Mother, father, teacher, friends* are eliminated if the reader can use initial sounds. Several possibilities remain, such as *pal, playmates, principal, parents*. The word *play* is known as a sight word. It is not found in this unknown word, so playmates is not suggested. It is possible that word configuration (length of word) might help the reader decide between *pal* or *parents*. With enough skill at phonic analysis to work his way through the first syllable, the reader is almost assured of arriving at the correct response. If he should try PA rents or PAR ents, either pronunciation will be close enough to suggest the correct word.

" It's my ______," said Jimmy. Here a number of possibilities occur to the reader: my *idea, turn, guess, opinion* or any number of possessions. This sentence alone does not provide enough context, but rarely does such a sentence stand alone. As we take into consideration the context supplied by several previous sentences, the unknown word falls into place.

> The boys searched everywhere but they did not find the little lost puppy. "I hope Blackie doesn't get hit by a car," said Billy. Jimmy was very sad. He had been thinking all afternoon about not closing the gate when he had gone to mail the letter. The puppy must have gotten out when he left the gate open. "It's my ________," said Jimmy. Then he told about the gate.

Punctuation

Learning to profit from punctuation in reading is a skill which greatly influences comprehension. The lack of ability to use punctuation in making reading a smooth and meaningful process appears with surprising frequency among impaired readers. Experience in working with poor readers indicates that this habit is not exceptionally difficult to eradicate. Ignoring punctuation is one of the easiest defects to detect on any reading analysis, a fact which suggests that the importance of learning to use punctuation is underrated in reading instruction.

One of the most effective methods of dramatizing the utility of punctuation is through the use of a tape recorder. On the playback the reader follows the reading passage as he listens to his recorded version. Errors are easily detected and insight comes a little easier when the child acts as his own critic.

Another procedure is to deliberately displace punctuation in a passage and thus illustrate how the meaning becomes lost. The same passage can be reproduced several times with varying degrees of distortion. The pupil sees how difficult it is to get meaning from a passage so treated. In Figure 20 the first copy completely obscures the meaning, the second copy is frustrating but not impossible, and the third is reproduced correctly.

FIGURE 20

How Punctuation Helps the Reader

> Billy listened, carefully as the teacher. Explained how punctuation helps. The reader commas periods exclamation marks and question marks? All help a reader get meaning. From the printed page. Billy wondered what would happen. If the printer

got the punctuation marks mixed. Up it was hard for him to imagine. What this would do to a story.

Billy listened carefully as the teacher explained. How punctuation helps the reader. Commas periods, exclamation marks and question marks all help. A reader get meaning from the printed page. Billy wondered. What would happen if the printer got the punctuation marks mixed up. It was hard for him to imagine what this would do. To a story.

Billy listened carefully as the teacher explained how punctuation helps the reader. Commas, periods, exclamation marks, and question marks all help a reader get meaning from the printed page. Billy wondered what would happen if the printer got the punctuation marks mixed up. It was hard for him to imagine what this would do to a story.

Simple Alphabetizing

In the primary grades the initial steps in developing this mechanical skill are dealt with. Only the basic alphabetizing skills needed in using the dictionary are taught.

These include:

1. Teaching the alphabet in order

   Exercises might include having the child:

   a. write the alphabet in sequence.

   b. fill in the letters which are missing:

   AB__DEF__IJK__NO__QR__UV__X__Z.

   c. write the letters which come before:

   __D; ____K; ____N; ____T; ____W.

2. Arranging a series of words in alphabetical order using the initial letter only

   In column B write in alphabetical order the words found in column A.

A	B
almost	______
earth	______
puppy	______
rain	______
milk	______
drive	______
change	______
geese	______
few	______

Later instruction will deal with alphabetizing by the first two letters, three letters, and through the entire word.

Syllabication

The ability to break words into the syllabic components is one of the mechanical skills which receives attention at various levels of instruction. A limited number of rules of syllabication are introduced at the primary level. The major emphasis on syllabication is found in the intermediate grades where dictionary skills are stressed. Pupils have a number of experiences with words from which they might generalize a number of rules. Whether or not these rules are memorized, most children will learn more effectively if the rules are presented verbally. How well a child masters the basic pattern of syllabication will influence his progress in independent reading. The first step in the process is the ability to hear the number of distinct sounds in a word, or the number of syllables it contains. A few rules and illustrations follow.

1. Every syllable contains a sounded vowel. (Exceptions are the syllables *dle, ble, zle, tle, cle,* etc., at the end of words. These particular endings are syllables but do not contain one of the conventional vowel sounds.)
2. The number of vowel sounds in a word determines the number of syllables in the word.
3. A syllable may be a single vowel such as *a*-ble, *o*-boe, vi-*o*-let, ed-*u*-ca-tion; or a syllable may contain a vowel digraph plus one or more consonants — *rain, meet, see.*
4. In general, when two consonants fall between the two vowels, the division of syllables is between the two consonants: *af-ter, sis-ter, win-dow, gar-den, pen-cil.*
5. Double consonants are usually separated: *lit-tle, val-ley, let-ter, sum-mer, cot-ton, din-ner.*
6. Prefixes and suffixes which are syllables should be learned and recognized as units — *un, ex, pre, ment, tion, tive, ly.*
7. Consonant blends are usually not divided when breaking words into syllables: tea-*cher,* ta-*ble,* wea-*ther,* re-*ply.*

COMPREHENSION SKILLS

The mechanics of reading are of necessity closely related to the comprehension of material read. Learning to use punctuation might appear to be totally within the framework of mechanics, yet nothing can more quickly distort meaning than the inability to profit from the clues that punctuation provides. Word-by-word reading has implications other than just in the skills area. In addition to slowing the reading rate, this habit tends to force attention on words rather than larger units. It is the sentence which carries meaning, and when a child spends too much time on word units, he may easily lose the thought of the sentence unit.

All mechanical skills and reading habits are related to comprehension of printed material. Here visual aids encourage enthusiastic participation in a reading group. (Courtesy of San Diego City Schools.)

In the transition from beginning reading to independent reading, quite noticeable changes take place in the materials which children read. Pictures will still be found in basal readers, but there will be fewer of them, and the decline of the importance of pictures in providing context clues will be quite obvious. Stories will be much longer, will be more interesting, and will include more concepts. These will not be built around the "one family" theme. There will be fairy tales and tales of animals who think and talk and have feelings. There will be stories of children who live in different lands and do unusual things. The lives and contributions of great men and women will be studied. Materials at this level call for the reader to make interpretations. He must detect clues to the mood of characters, see the relationship between events, and grasp the intended meaning of figurative or idiomatic expressions. (18) Humor may not always be overt, and inferences may have to be drawn in the absence of absolute statements. The ability to read each word in a passage is not the only criterion of reading. The child must also be able to tell "if grandfather was serious or just playing a joke on the boys" or "if Jerry was frightened by what he overheard" or "how the storm affected the plans for a vacation."

MISCONCEPTIONS

During the latter stages of the primary years, many children will encounter a number of words and concepts which will puzzle them. Many such instances will occur in subject-matter texts as well as in basal readers. Whereas the child comes to school with the "meanings" which are adequate for dealing with beginning reading, he is by no means familiar with the various connotations of the words with which he must cope in the primary and intermediate grades. A lack of concepts and insufficient knowledge of various connotations of words is not the only problem with which the teacher must deal in expanding meaning. A related problem is that of misconceptions harbored by pupils. The school cannot be held responsible for misconceptions which children have picked up elsewhere. It may be impossible in overcrowded classrooms to prevent misconceptions from arising or going undetected. Nevertheless, the extent to which this problem exists should motivate teachers to seek ways of modifying instructional techniques, for the confusion of meanings is a barrier to reading and learning.

One of the axioms of teaching reading is that "new" words in a lesson should be mastered both as sight words and as meaning-bearing units before the child is expected to read that lesson. Often little attention is given to mastering shades of meaning, and too much is taken for granted when the child is able to "call the word." As a result, many teachers would be shocked at the misconceptions still harbored by some children in their classes. The following responses on vocabulary tests illustrate some rather striking misconceptions, even though it is not difficult to imagine how some of these arose. The responses are given verbatim.

regard-	*a.* like you were guarding something
	b. to think of someone as a cousin
	c. to re-do your work
priceless-	*a.* something that doesn't cost anything
	b. you want to buy something and you think it's not worth it
brunette-	*a.* a kind of permanent
	b. a girl that dances
	c. a prune
shrewd-	*a.* when you're not polite
	b. being kind of cruel
	c. guess it means rude
lecture-	*a.* 'lected for president

When asked to give the meaning of "conquer," one boy volunteered, "It means like to *konk her* on the head." Another, when meeting the written word *mosquitoes* for the first time, concluded it was the name of a fairy — "most quiet toes." A pre-school child hearing an older sibling make a reference to a dinosaur immediately responded, "I like to go to the *dime store.*" An eight-year-old listening around Christmas time to a choir on television asked, "What does the *si door im* mean?" His parents were at a loss until he repeated the line, "Oh come let us si door im."

Some of these examples illustrate what takes place when a child is confronted with concepts beyond his present grasp. He usually changes them to a more concrete meaning which is known to him. Although illustrating how the child deals with unknown words which he *hears,* these examples can also provide us with insight into what happens when a child *reads* unknown words.

EXPANSION OF MEANINGS

Children's development of concepts cannot be left to chance. The school deliberately seeks to provide an environment which will lead to the development and expansion of concepts in every area of the curriculum. The following procedures can be used in helping children develop meanings. They are not limited to a particular grade level. While many of these techniques are used in the formal reading program, they are appropriate for teaching terms and concepts in all subject areas.

Using Pictures

The use of pictures is an excellent method of expanding concepts and clearing up misconceptions. The role of pictures in beginning reading has been discussed previously in relation to helping pupils master sight words by suggesting context. Here we deal with the utility of pictures in developing and expanding concepts. A picture of an eroded hillside is much more effective in fixing the concept of *erosion* than is a word definition of the term. Early basal readers rely heavily on pictures, but it is actually in the content areas that pictures have greatest value. Pictures are more likely to fix accurate concepts of *colonial architecture*, the *iron-plated Monitor*, an *ant-eater*, a *Chinese junk*, *terrace farming* or the *human circulatory system* than is language alone.

The same picture can be used at different levels for teaching words and meanings. For example, let us imagine a picture which would be available to almost any teacher. The picture is a down-town scene in a small city. We see a bus, a boy on a bicycle, various store fronts and offices, a policeman directing traffic, a fire hydrant, the city hall across from a parking lot.* Without going into more detail, we might build a hierarchy of concepts.

> *"Where is the policeman?"*
> "In the *street*."
> "Yes, he is really standing in the middle of where two streets cross — what is that called?"
> "That's an *intersection*."
> (The class level will determine whether the teacher should explain the term intersection.)
> *"How many kinds of travel or transportation do we see?"*
> "Some people are *walking*."
> "A boy on a *bicycle*."
> "There's a *bus*. It's a city bus."
> "There are lots of *cars*."
> "I see an *airplane* above the city."
> *"What kinds of transportation are not seen in the picture?"*
> *"Trains."*

---

*This is a description of the poster picture "The City" found in *Readiness Pictures* (New York: The Macmillan Company).

"Don't see any *boats.*"

"There are no big *trucks* — big trailers."

(Teacher points to the symbol which identifies the telephone company office.)

"What is in this building?"

"That must be the telephone office."

"What's this sign across the street?"

"City Water Company, it says."

"What do we call these types of businesses?"

(no response)

"Did you ever hear the term *utilities* or *public utilities?"*

(The teacher prints the word on the board.)

"What other *utilities* do you think this city has — what others besides telephone company and water company?"

"Electricity."

"That's right — what other name might it have?"

"Light Company"

"Power Company"

"Do you think of any other *utility* companies? Would there be a gas company?"

Other meanings the teacher can lead into are:

"Four stories high"

"This canvas over the sidewalk is an *awning* or a *canopy.*"

"This is a parcel post truck. Its purpose is to serve the people. How is it like the power company? How is it different?"

The picture we have attempted to visualize is a simple one which could be used at various grade levels. Through its use the teacher can stress:

1. Noticing details
2. Symbols standing for things (the telephone symbol on a window)
3. Many different *names* standing for the same things
    a. Power company, public service company, utility company, etc.
    b. Canopy, awning
4. The same word having different meanings according to usage (i.e., *meter:* parking meter, gas meter, electric meter; meters in cars: speedometers, gas meter, and mileage meter)

The value of pictures lies in their wealth of detail and the fact that they stay in focus or can be referred back to after a discussion has led away to other things.

DEVELOPING DIFFERENT MEANINGS FOR THE SAME WORD

The child's early language development is characterized by mastery of the concrete first and then a gradual moving up the ladder of abstraction. He may know such words as *air, blue, mine, broadcast, fence,* and he may know several meanings for each word; yet he will not be familiar with all the meanings of these words. The child will probably have mastered a number of meanings for the word *air.*

1. My daddy put *air* in the tires.
2. We hang clothes outside to *air* them.
3. We breathe *air.*

The same child may be confused by the following:

1. If asked to "*air* his views."
2. To hear that "his older brother gave his girlfriend the *air.*"
3. That Mrs. Jones is disliked in the neighborhood because "she puts on *airs.*"

The child may understand what is meant by *blue* in the sentence, "The boy had a *blue* boat." He may not be familiar with "The boy felt *blue* when his aunt left." He may understand "Grandfather rode the *horse,*" but not have a concept of "The coach warned the boys not to *horse* around" or the expression "That's a *horse* of a different color" or "The mayor accused the council of beating a dead *horse.*"

He may know one or two meanings of *mine* but some of the usages or concepts involving the word *mine* will undoubtedly be beyond him.

a. "The book is *mine.*"
b. "Joe's father worked in the coal *mine.*"
c. "That corner store is a gold *mine.*"
d. "The tank was damaged by a land *mine.*"
e. "Don't under*mine* the confidence of the people."
f. "Our break is over, let's get back to the salt *mine.*"
g. "He was stationed aboard a *mine* sweeper."

The above examples point up how difficult it is to measure "size of vocabulary," for each child has several different kinds of vocabularies. The word *mine* would be in a child's meaning, speaking, and reading vocabularies if he could read sentence (a) above, even though that was the only usage which was familiar to him. And in some instances, if the child could "read" — that is, correctly say all the words in the sentence (d) — it would be concluded that *mine* was in his *reading vocabulary* whether or not he could explain the sentence. Inability to explain the usage would indicate only that the child did not understand this particular concept.

Adults' meaning vocabularies are larger than their speaking, writing, or reading vocabularies. The sounds "klee-shay" may conjure up meaning for an individual when he hears the word used in context, yet the written symbol cliché may be meaningless if he sounds "clish." The word *cache* may be mispronounced in reading but still produce meaning in the sentence "The bandits, under cover of darkness, returned to the mountain cache for their stolen loot." Meaning may escape the individual when the T. V. badman says, "Let's go, boys, we have to beat the posse to the *kash*."

Learning meanings is a fascinating and highly motivating experience for children. The teacher can point out that most words carry several different meanings according to how they are used. She might illustrate with simple words like *can, stick, run,* or *set.* As the teacher asks for different usages, she will write the children's responses on the board, at the same time attempting to fix the various meanings by using other known words.

"I *can* spell my name." — *can* means *able*

"I bought a *can* of beans." — *can* means a *container*

"Put the garbage in the *garbage can.*" — another type of *container*

"My mother said, 'Tomorrow I will *can* the peaches.' " — *can* means to *preserve food.*

The last example may not be given by any child in an early elementary grade in an urban locality, but this usage may be known to almost every child in the same grade in another locality. Some other usages of the word *can* may not be appropriate for an early grade level, but would be at a higher grade level.

"Can it, Mack." — an order to stop talking

"If you leave now, the boss will can you." — dismiss from job

"Why don't you trade in that old tin can and get an automobile?" — a battered old car

After several group exercises which stress that the objective is to supply different meanings of a word, not simply different sentences, the teacher can suggest a written game. Each child works independently, selecting his own words for illustrating different usages. In order not to handicap the poorer spellers, the teacher may offer to spell any words the children want to use in their sentences. "Just hold up your hand and I'll come to your desk and write out the word you want to use." This exercise has considerable diagnostic value in that it yields data on spelling ability, language facility, legibility of handwriting, ability to follow directions, and ability to work independently.

Some specific findings reported by one teacher include:

1. Despite what appeared to be a thorough explanation of the objective, a number of pupils missed the point of the exercise and wrote different sentences using the same meaning of the word selected.
2. Several pupils misspelled words which they could spell correctly when the teacher pronounced or dictated these words. (The pupils slurred or omitted syllables when they said these words silently.)
3. The papers revealed many words misspelled *which the pupils thought they spelled correctly*. This data served as a basis for spelling review.
4. The handwriting was inferior to that which the child would do on a writing test.
5. This exercise disclosed great differences among pupils in their ability to use expressive language as well as exposing paucity of concepts among some pupils.
6. Misconceptions were found on many pages. These could be corrected individually with the pupil.

SYNONYMS

The pupils are reminded that words which have the same meaning are called *synonyms*. "Give me another word that means the same as *big, work, fast*" will as a rule elicit responses from everyone in the group. Exercises that permit group participation can be followed by individual work involving a series of three-by-five cards each containing the directions "Go to the board and write the word ______. Under it write as many synonyms as you can." Another series of cards may include a number of words some of which are synonyms for the stimulus word. The pupil selects the synonyms and writes them under the stimulus word. This latter task is the easier of the two and permits pupils of differing ability to participate. (See Figure 21.)

FIGURE 21

Expanding Meanings through Practice with Synonyms and Antonyms

Write the word *timid* on the board. Under it write as many synonyms as you can think of.

Write the word *rapid* on the board. Under it write any word from the following group which is similar in meaning:

quick	speedy
shave	light
fast	fleet
grasp	throw
inquire	reduce
hastily	swift

On the board write the word *release* and under it write any word in the following group which is nearly the *opposite* in meaning:

grasp	trap
relief	free
hold	captive
clutch	repeat
dismiss	catch
receive	keep
mistake	

Another exercise might call for the child to underline two words in a series which are similar in meaning:

almost	together	certainly	*nearly*
thrilling	spinning	exciting	frightening
nonsense	terrible	scolding	awful
matches	money	penny	postcard

Work sheets of varying difficulty can be used with pupils of different ability levels in a class. Similar exercises are applicable to expanding word meanings by teaching words of *opposite meanings.* The objective should always be to work out lesson plans that will assure that the pupils:

See the words
Hear them pronounced
Experience their use in sentences

Sentence comprehension exercises can be used in which the child reads to determine whether two sentences carry the same meaning:

> Read the two sentences below marked A. Do they have the same meaning? If so, write *S* in the box to indicate they have the *S*ame meaning. Write *D* if the sentences have a *D*ifferent meaning. Do the same for sentences B, C, D, etc.

A Bill took his dog for a ride. ☐
A Bill took his dog in the house.
B The park is not far from where Mary lives. ☐
B Mary's house is near the park.
C Tom has a cat and a pony at the farm. ☐
C Tom has a pet goat at the farm.

HOMONYMS

Homonyms are words which sound exactly alike and are spelled differently. They are potential sources of trouble to young readers since both sight recognition and meanings may be confusing. Many common homonyms look very much alike (*their, there; see, sea; hear, here; beat, beet; dear, deer; course, coarse*). The reader in the primary grades gets meaning from hearing the following sounds in these combinations, but he may not recognize all of the written symbols.

1. *Their* coats are over *there.*
2. The *plane* landed safely on the *plain.*
3. *Would* you please carry in some *wood?*
4. He felt *weak* for a *week* after he was sick.
5. "*Oh,*" he said, "how much do I *owe* you?"
6. The boy *ate eight* pieces of candy.
7. *See* the ship on the *sea.*
8. *No,* I do not *know* where it is.

One method of expanding both sight and usage vocabularies is to list homonyms in columns with the word the child is most likely to be familiar with on the left. An exercise calling for the use of each word in a sentence will provide a check on the mastery of meanings.

The words in columns A and B are pronounced the same.

A	B	A	B
do	dew	sail	sale
dear	deer	hair	hare
way	weigh	made	maid
hall	haul	one	won
pair	pare	poor	pour

For children who have trouble with these words, simple card games can be devised for two or more players in which one word of each pair is included in a draw pile and the other words shuffled and dealt to the players. When a card in the draw pile is turned up, whoever has the homonym for it in his hand pronounces the word on the stack and gives its meaning, then gives the meaning for the word in his hand. If he does each without help, he "takes" both cards. There are many variations which can be used with such cards.

Following is a list of easier homonyms which the child usually meets in the primary grades.

beat	beet	red	read
know	no	ring	wring
do	dew	would	wood
dear	deer	whole	hole
to two	too	sail	sale
knew	new	hall	haul
mail	male	pair	pare
road	rode	tail	tale
wait	weight	steal	steel
there	their	birth	berth
sun	son	ate	eight
oh	owe	some	sum
waist	waste	pain	pane
rap	wrap	so	sew
bee	be	by	buy
one	won	not	knot
see	sea	hear	here
hair	hare	our	hour
week	weak	maid	made
fair	fare	piece	peace

FIGURATIVE LANGUAGE AND IDIOMATIC EXPRESSIONS

Figurative language and idomatic expressions are quite widely used both in basal readers and in subject texts. (11) These expressions pose virtually no problem for some readers, but can be stumbling blocks for other children in getting the meaning. This occurs because some readers have developed the habit of expecting the words they read to have literal meanings. It has also been noted that some children can both use and understand such expressions in oral communication but are still confused or misled when they attempt to read them. (12)

Some examples of expressions that will be met in the primary or elementary grades follow. The mere fact that a child can read these correctly is not assurance that he interprets them correctly.

The old sailor *spun a yarn* for the boys.
Soon *night fell.*
Don't *throw your money away* at the circus.
Before long they were driving through *rolling hills.*
The *rich earth* spread for miles along the river.
He returned *heavy-hearted.*
The waves *pitched the boat* up and down.
Give me a *lift.*
They *picked themselves up.*
He *made his mark* as a successful coach early in his career.
The captain *barked* his orders.
A *finger* of light moved around the airport.

Workbooks have a limited number of exercises which attempt to give practice in interpretation of figurative language. The teacher must be alert when these exercises are used, however, for a pupil may check the correct response without clearly understanding the intended meaning. When a child makes an error in interpretation and his response is marked wrong by the teacher, all he has to do is erase his X and place it in the remaining choice, thus "correcting his error." Learning may not have taken place even though the exercise is corrected.

Although teachers understand that some pupils will need extra practice in developing skills, they often do not find the time to construct teacher-made work sheets. If exercises are duplicated, one preparation can be used with successive classes, and if several teachers at various grade levels co-operate, they will find work sheets designed for use at one grade level are appropriate for particular children in other grades. Pooling their effort will save time, add variety, and enhance the teaching in that school. Figure 22 contains examples of exercises designed by teachers in grades three through five in one elementary school. These were then made available to all teachers.

FIGURE 22

Working with Expressions

What is the meaning of the words that are underlined? Write "same" before the sentence which explains the underlined words.

1. Father said: "I was walking through the park and Mr. Brown gave me a lift."

   ________ picked father up in his arms.
   ________ lifted father off the ground.
   ________ gave father a ride home.

Finish the sentence with the one group of words (phrases) that makes the best meaning.

1. The stones in the show case were ________.

   as big as watermelons.
   as high as a mountain.
   as shiny as diamonds.

Can you tell in your own words what each of the following expressions means? If any puzzle you, ask the teacher for help.

1. A wolf in sheep's clothing.
2. Keep the wolf from the door.
3. Flew into a rage.
4. The ship was water-tight.

Analyzing Stories

Some stories need to be analyzed and discussed. The discussion should not be conducted from the standpoint of "who remembers something from the story" but by skillfully leading the children to see how the author is able to picture each character and show the type of person he is, how he conveys the characters' attitudes toward each other and toward themselves, how the reader is led to see the difference between unkindness and thoughtlessness, to see how people feel after making mistakes, what they do about them, and why it is not always possible to do exactly what one wants. Analysis of stories is not a testing period or a time for the recitation of facts. Analysis should lay the foundation for the type of insight Emily Dickinson developed before she could write, "There is no frigate like a book to bear us lands away."

Dramatizing Stories

Dramatizing stories or incidents from stories helps children develop understanding, imagination, and appreciation. To dramatize a story or scene, children must read the material critically and understand the author's purpose and the feelings he wishes to convey. In the dramatization these would find expression through tone of voice, emphasis, gesture, facial expression, and the like. In selecting material to be acted out, children will have to make correct judgments on the dramatic potential of various stories or situations. A story about a man lost on a mountain might be extremely interesting reading, but it is not well-suited to a third-grade dramatic production. One drawback is that only one character is involved.

Choral Reading

Choral reading is sometimes thought of as an activity reserved for expert readers. Actually, choral reading can be used at a number of instructional levels. The reading ability of the participants simply determines the materials which might be used successfully. For example, a teacher discovered quite by accident that choral reading had extremely high motivational value for her third-grade class. She was showing a text-film of a story that the class had not read before. Each frame consisted of an attractive picture in color and two or three lines of text. She would call on individual children to read this material but would occasionally say, "Let's all read." The response was so enthusiastic that she printed on chart paper poems such as "The Wind," "Watching Clouds," "Railroad Reverie," "The Owl and the Pussy Cat," "Hold Hands," or any number of limericks. Later she prepared duplicated sheets which contained several pieces of material appropriate for choral reading.

She observed that choral reading was always the motivational peak of the day's activity.

Choral reading has many justifications — possibly the chief one being that it is enjoyable. Other values often cited are that choral reading:

1. Is a good technique for getting all children to participate.
2. Can be a means of motivating children to want to read. The shy child or the poor reader is not likely to experience failure or frustration in this type of group reading experience.
3. Provides an opportunity to teach good pronunciation and reading with expression.
4. Permits the use of different materials for emphasizing different objectives such as phonic analysis, profiting from punctuation, and proper phrasing.
5. Can be a creative experience since children can suggest different ways a poem or passage can be interpreted.
6. Helps develop an appreciation for fine literature or poetry.

CONCLUSION

Reading instruction in the primary grades is extremely important because of the nature of the learning tasks found there and because of the variety of growth patterns characteristically found among children during this stage of their development. In order to provide pupils with the instruction they need, it is necessary to reach a thorough individual diagnosis of reading achievement based on either standardized or informal tests or both. Diagnosis as the basis for a program is quite essential at this instructional level because children are going through a stage of rapid development and are entering into independent reading. Furthermore, the curricular materials are used and designed with the assumption in mind that pupils have achieved a certain level of competence in reading.

In the primary grades children meet a number of concepts in their reading which are strange or unknown. They encounter an increasing number of words not in their sight vocabulary, a fact which calls for a higher level of word recognition skill. The accelerated pace at which new tasks are introduced makes it essential that sound principles of teaching reading be followed. Growth in reading must be treated as developmental. Practically all skills previously taught must now be reinforced and extended. Mechanical and comprehension skills must be developed simultaneously and at a rate of growth which is considerably beyond that found in beginning reading. To prevent both gaps in learning and overemphasis of particular skills, instruction must be systematic and planned.

The primary grades are a period in which children's experience with reading will mold their later attitudes and reading habits. Great damage can be done to some children by expecting them to read materials which at the moment they are incapable of handling. Other children may form mal-attitudes if they are forced to perform mechanical activities when they are capable of wide and extensive reading for pleasure and profit. Thus, a successful program in the primary grades, probably as much as at any instructional level, depends on the right combination of instruction in all facets of reading.

YOUR POINT OF VIEW?

Would you prefer to defend or attack the following premises? Why?

1. What would you have to add to the following statement to make it consistent with your present beliefs:

   The purpose and function of formal education is to help the child develop and expand concepts along with the language tools necessary for this activity.

2. At each successive grade level, a smaller percentage of children are avid readers, i.e., fewer children love to read as a free-choice activity.

3. Misconceptions are more likely to arise in the content areas than in the materials used for reading instruction.

4. *Data:* A child made normal progress in beginning reading, but is now experiencing considerable difficulty in reading in grade two. The most tenable hypothesis as to his problem is that he has failed to master letter-sound relationships.

BIBLIOGRAPHY

1. Amster, Harriett, "Concept Formation in Children," *Elementary English,* XXXXII (May 1965), 543-52.
2. Bond, Guy L., and Eva Bond Wagner, *Teaching the Child to Read* (4th ed.). New York: The Macmillan Company, 1966, Chapters 8, 9, and 12.
3. Buelke, Eleanor, "The Drama of Teaching Reading Through Creative Writing," *Reading Teacher,* 19 (January 1966), 267-72.
4. Byers, Loretta, "Pupils' Interests and the Content of Primary Reading Texts," *Reading Teacher,* 17 (January 1964), 227-33.
5. Dechant, Emerald V., *Improving The Teaching of Reading.* Englewood Cliffs, N. J.: Prentice-Hall, Inc. 1964, Chapter 9.
6. Durrell, Donald D., *Improving Reading Instruction.* New York: World Book Company, 1956, pp. 202-204.
7. Fernald, Grace M., *Remedial Techniques In Basic School Subjects.* New York: McGraw-Hill Book Co., Inc., 1943.

8. Frame, Norman, "The Availability of Reading Materials for Teachers and Pupils at the Primary Level," *Elementary English,* XXXXI (March 1964), 224-30.

9. Gates, Arthur I., "The Word Recognition Ability and the Reading Vocabulary of Second- and Third-Grade Children," *Reading Teacher,* 15 (May 1962), 443-48.

10. Gray, William S., *On Their Own in Reading* (rev. ed.). Chicago: Scott, Foresman & Company, 1960.

11. Grosbeck, Hulda, *The Comprehension of Figurative Language by Elementary Pupils: A Study of Transfer.* Unpublished Doctoral Thesis, Oklahoma University, 1961.

12. Holmes, Elizabeth Ann, *Children's Knowledge of Figurative Language.* Unpublished Masters Thesis, Oklahoma University, 1959.

13. Kerfoot, James F., "The Vocabulary in Primary Arithmetic Texts," *Reading Teacher,* 14 (January 1961), 177-80.

14. Monroe, Marion, "The Use of Picture Dictionaries in the Primary Grades," *Elementary English,* XXXXI (April 1964), 340-45.

15. Olson, Arthur V., "An Analysis of the Vocabulary of Seven Primary Reading Series," *Elementary English,* XXXXII (March 1965), 261-64.

16. ———, "School Achievement, Reading Ability, and Specific Visual Perception Skills in the Third Grade," *Reading Teacher,* 19 (April 1966), 490-92.

17. Otterman, Lois M., "The Value of Teaching Prefixes and Word Roots," *Journal of Educational Research,* XLVIII (April 1955), 611-16.

18. Painter, Helen W., "Critical Reading In The Primary Grades," *Reading Teacher,* 19 (October 1965), 35-9.

19. Parke, Margaret B., "Picture Dictionaries — Tools for Primary Grades," *Education,* 84 (September 1963), 23-9.

20. Piekarz, Josephine A., "Getting Meaning from Reading," *Elementary School Journal,* LVI (March 1956), 303-9.

21. *Reading in the Elementary School,* Forty-eighth Yearbook, Part II, National Society for the Study of Education. Chicago: University of Chicago Press, 1949.

22. Russell, David H., *Children Learn to Read* (2nd ed.). Boston: Ginn and Company, 1961, Chapter 7.

23. Schonell, Fred J., *The Psychology and Teaching of Reading* (4th ed.). New York: Philosophical Library, 1961.

24. Sister Josephina C.S.J., "Reading Accomplishment of Gifted and Average Pupils," *Educational and Psychological Measurement,* XVIII (1958), 867-71.

25. Spache, George D., *Reading In The Elementary School.* Boston: Allyn and Bacon, Inc., 1964. Chapter 8.

26. Smith, Henry P., and Emerald V. Dechant, *Psychology In Teaching Reading.* Englewood Cliffs, N. J.: Prentice-Hall, Inc., 1961.

27. Wilson, Louis Ada, "Children's Realistic Vocabulary," *Elementary English,* XXXX (January 1963), 37-42.

SURVEY QUESTION
Row 1
Row 1
A HERO OF THE AIR

Linguistics and Reading

8

Linguists are justifiably sensitive about non-linguists attempting to summarize or popularize linguistic discoveries. The purpose here is not to interpret the technical findings of this discipline but rather to examine the suggestions made by certain linguists relative to reading instruction. In order to understand what linguists have proposed, why they disagree about reading instruction and why linguists as a group will never develop *The* Linguistic Method of Teaching Reading, we must have some understanding of the terms linguist and linguistics.

In attempting definitions of these terms one might keep in mind a linguist's advice, "We must define a linguist rather strictly because the term has become dangerously popular, emulating the more extensive term scientist."*

Linguists are trained individuals who make a scientific study of human language. Such study implies accurate observation and recording of data.

---

*Raven I. McDavid, Jr., "The Role of the Linguist in the Teaching of Reading," *Changing Concepts of Reading Instruction*. International Reading Association Proceedings, 6 (1961), 253-56.

The linguist studies and identifies the building blocks of language called speech sounds or phonemes. He discerns how these are combined into words and word parts which have assigned meanings (morphemes). This is the groundwork for further study of language, namely the *patterns* in which words may occur and those which cannot occur in a particular language. When these discoveries are made, one has the key to the structure or the grammar of a language.

The linguist discovers facts which are unique to each language and others that are common to various languages. The layman can verbalize some of these findings without grasping their full significance. For instance, the linguist states, *language is arbitrary*. This applies to all facets of language. The normal child growing up in an English-speaking environment learns to make many speech sounds which he will have to discard if he restricts his language usage to English. The sounds he will use is not a matter of individual choice. This matter has been arbitrarily established, along with the patterns or sequence in which sounds may be combined.

The order in which words may be combined into utterances has also been established. Language has a definite structure. The linguist notes that this structure permits a sentence like, "I runned all the way home," but that common usage dictates, "I ran all the way home," and English structure cannot accommodate, "I all the ran home way." While six year old children have mastered a tremendously large portion of English grammar, they project certain characteristics into word meanings which do not exist. When asked Piagets' question "Can the sun be called the moon?" they answer: "No, because the moon comes up at night," or "No, because the sun is brighter." This reaction that the meaning resides in the word is not confined to children.

Adults can also have hazy concepts about language. An example is the manner in which adults think the grammar of a language might best be taught to students who have already mastered it in practice. Fries (15) states that traditional grammar starts with the assigning of meaning to any given sentence and then moves to the labeling of words or groups of words and whole utterances. Thus, sentences become *declarative*, *interrogative*, or *imperative*. Within each sentence there is a subject and verb; to this may be added a direct object and an array of modifiers attached to each of those parts.

This approach, according to Fries, starts with an assumption that *grammatical meanings* are intuitive. A number of structural linguists reject this assumption. They posit that "grammatical meanings" are of considerable importance and that meanings are conveyed by signal or structure words which permit certain meanings and exclude others. A few examples of these structure words are *a* man, *the* man, *these* men, *that* man, *this* man, *some* men, *no* man. A further discussion of structure words will be found later in this chapter.

Linguistics is a broad term which can cover many orientations to language study. One linguist may be primarily interested in comparing different languages, another with the sound patterns of a language, another with the structural (grammatical word order) features of one or more languages, and another in the changes (phonological and structural) which occur in any living language. While linguists rarely deal with only one isolated facet of language, they do tend to become somewhat specialized.

THE APPLICATION OF LINGUISTIC FINDINGS TO READING INSTRUCTION

Linguists as scientists are in no way responsible for finding applications for their discoveries. Few have actively engaged in relating their discoveries to the school curriculum. As a result, linguistics has had little impact on the content of the curriculum, particularly at the elementary level. University faculties have devised courses of study for students whose educational goal is to become linguists or specialists in a particular language. Certain related fields, such as speech therapy, draw heavily on linguistics since therapists must distinguish speech sounds and understand the anatomical involvement in their production.

How children learn to read and how the reading process should be taught is not a part of linguistic science. However, there is little doubt that certain linguistic insights can be analyzed in such a way as to be extremely useful in reading instruction. Recently some linguists have turned their attention to the reading process, and there were high hopes that a significant instructional breakthrough would be achieved fairly rapidly. This optimism was soon tempered by reality when it was discovered that a real communication barrier separated linguists and reading teachers.

Linguistic science has moved rapidly in the past fifty years because linguists were able to agree on the precise meaning of many crucial terms. Linguists were the first, and possibly the only, group who thus far agreed on the definition of language. Their definition is that "language is oral." To reading specialists, psychologists, and general semanticists, this definition may seem to be somewhat narrow, but the mark of a science is that its basic terms are unequivocal.

On the other hand, the field of reading provides many examples of terms which are used frequently but for which there is no universal agreement as to meaning. Examples include *reading, phonics method, individualized reading, critical reading, sightword method, reading disability, traditional method, remedial reading* and *phonics instruction.* All of these represent concepts, but none have a fixed meaning for all of the people who use them. Obviously, confusion results. The problem is accentuated when persons in different disciplines attempt to co-operate in the absence of an agreement on the meaning of the terms which both groups use. An illustration is provided in the use of the term *language* at a recent national reading conference.

A linguist, speaking to teachers of reading, remarked that he had little patience for the educators who made such absurd statements as, "English is not a phonetic language," or "English is not phonetically lawful." He stated that "English is perfectly phonetic — 100 per cent phonetic." He was followed on the same platform by a teacher of reading who, probably not having heard his predecessor, stated: "One of the major problems of teaching children to read is the fact that English is not phonetic. The language contains a large number of phonetically irregular words."

Each of the speakers started from different premises based on different connotations for the words he used. Each was correct if one granted his original premise. The linguist worked from the linguistic definition of language that "language is oral — language is speech." Thus, all English language (speech) is 100 per cent phonetically regular. Such words as *freight, light, come,* and all other words can be transcribed within the framework of English phonemes.

The teacher of reading used language to mean written English. The linguist, of course, would refer to this as "a graphic representation of language." The teacher of reading meant that many English spellings were irregular; that there was not a one-to-one relationship between printed letters seen and speech sounds heard when one is reading English. With this the linguist would agree, but he would convey this information by using the terms *phoneme-grapheme relationship.*

Communication between reading teachers and linguists depends on each making an effort to understand the other. In recent years terminology from the science of linguistics have been used frequently in material addressed to the reading teacher. These terms have fixed meanings, and there is little point in not adopting them for use in discussion of reading instruction.

Phoneme: The smallest unit of sound within a language. When the word *man* is pronounced, three phonemes are utilized: /m/ /ae/ /n/. The basic consonant and vowel sound are called *segmental phonemes*. In addition to these 31 to 33 basic sounds, the English language utilizes twelve intonational phonemes.

Intonation: In addition to the consonant and vowel phonemes just mentioned, English utilizes a number of intonational phonemes. Speech consists of a flow of words arranged in particular patterns which result in distinctive rhythms or melodies which are unique to English. The melody is created in part by several levels of pitch, several degrees of stress or emphasis on word components, and by pauses or stops in the flow of speech.

Individuals learn the intonation patterns of their native tongue without being aware of the significance of these signals; and certainly without any conscious labeling of the variations in pitch, stress, and pace. The pre-school child with normal hearing inevitably "picks up" the intonation patterns of English or the particular dialect he hears around him. Later, as an adult he may experience considerable difficulty in mastering the intonation patterns of a foreign language. He may have little difficulty in learning the pronunciation and meaning of *words* (vocabulary). The problem lies in stringing the words together, in acquiring the flow or the melody of the new language.

English writing, and the act of reading this writing, poses a somewhat similar problem. First, writing is an imperfect representation of speech. One cannot accurately depict intonation or melody of speech. Many nuances are lost in setting down the graphic representation of speech. The reader's task now becomes that of putting the intonation back into the graphic signs. He has some very useful hints in the form of punctuation which suggests some pauses and stops. He is aided by other orthographic devices such as underlined or italicized words. But in the final analysis the reader is left to project or "think in" much of the meaning-making melody which is not depicted in print. The following discussion provides brief illustrations of the three major intonational components: juncture, stress and pitch.

Junctures and terminals: Speech includes a number of pauses which serve as signals to the listener. In general four classes of junctures and terminals are identified in English speech, these are:

Open Juncture / + / which represents the most minute interruptions which occur between some syllables within words and between words. These breaks in speech enable one to follow such patterns as:

> "I *am a Tory* but not an *amatory* Tory."
> "He used a jar to keep the door ajar."
> *(amiss - a miss; a bet - abet; add dresses - addresses).*

Level juncture is a pause between parts of a total utterance, in which the pause does not demand a rise or falling off of pitch. In the following illustrative sentence, examples A and B represent level terminal where everything preceding the phrase *was blind* is spoken without noticeable variation in pitch. Example C indicates a different reading.

A. The man → speaking to me → was blind.↘
B. The man speaking to me → was blind.↘
C. The man speaking to me ↘ was blind.↘

Rise and fall terminals are examples of speech signals which terminate all sentences, and which are frequently found separating major groupings of words within sentences. (Sentence C above.) The symbol / ↘ / represents a falling off or fading pitch accompanied by a pause which characteristically terminates declarative sentences. Many interrogative sentences end with a fading, higher pitch, indicated by the symbol / ↗ /. Both of these terminals contain a signal which goes beyond the mere pause in the flow of words.

> "The train arrives at six o'clock."↘
> "What time does the train leave?"↗

Pitch, as this term is used in describing a particular characteristic of human speech, should be thought of as a continuum. However, this continuum does not consist of innumerable points, but rather a discrete number of segments or ranges. These ranges have been labeled low, normal, high, and extra high, and are frequently designated by the numbers 1 - 2 - 3 - 4. The absence of pitch variations in speech is called monotone, or in essence, one-level-pitch.

Pitch interacts with stress and juncture and every statement in English has a "pitch contour" which can be plotted using one or another marking system such as /1-234/;/low normal high etc/.

Stress indicates the degree of emphasis placed on syllables or words in utterances. As in the case of pitch there are four levels or degrees of stress: heavy, medium, light, weak.* As noted earlier, the graphic representation of speech provides a rather incomplete record of intonation. Stress, pitch, and juncture are represented only partially by means of punctuation marks such as beginning a sentence with a capital letter and the use of the comma, semi-colon, period, exclamation mark, and question mark. In addition, one may indicate emphasis through underlining or italicizing a particular word.

> *He* was really a tall man.
> He was *really* a tall man.
> He was really a *tall* man.

Morpheme: The smallest meaningful units of language. Thus, *son* is a morpheme composed of three phonemes. If one adds an *s* to form a plural, *sons*, the final *s* in this situation is a morpheme. Here, the same grapheme (s) functions in the initial part of the word as a phoneme, and when it is used at the end of the word to change the meaning to "more than one son," it functions as a morpheme. When used to show possession, *his son's house*, it illustrates another morpheme.

There are two classes of morphemes determined by function. A *free morpheme* is one that functions independently in larger language units (cat, man, son). *Bound morphemes* must combine with another morpheme. This class includes affixes and inflectional endings. The prefix *un* in *un*lock is a bound morpheme while the same graphemes in *union* stand for two phonemes.

Alphabetic Principle: English is one of the many languages for which an alphabet has been devised for writing. We use 26 letters to graphically represent the sounds of English. Thus, English is an alphabetic language. English writing follows an alphabetical principle, i.e., certain graphic signs represent speech sounds. However, English spellings used in writing of words do not follow a one-to-one relationship of grapheme seen, phoneme heard. Exceptions are discussed in relation to phonics instruction (Chapter 9).

---

*Levels of stress are also designated as primary (/), secondary (∧), tertiary (\) and weak (∪). See Henry Lee Smith, Jr., "The Teacher and The World of Language," College English, 20, (January, 1959), 172-78.

The irregular spellings of English words creates a problem for the person attempting to learn to write or read English. The fact that a large majority of English words follow regular grapheme-phoneme patterns leads some individuals to minimize the effect of irregular spellings on learning these two derived language processes. Establishing what per cent of the 10,000 most frequently used words happen to be regular in grapheme-phoneme relationships and then generalizing from this data to the reading process ignores the *frequency of the use* of irregularly spelled words. This point becomes clearer as we examine structure words.

Structure words is a term used to cover some three-hundred or more frequently used words which have no concrete referent. Various other descriptive terms have been used to describe these words. These include "signal words," "glue words," "service words," and for reasons discussed below, they have also been referred to as "basic sight words." Each of the above have some validity. Structure words do signal the listener, or more important, the reader, that a particular syntactical pattern is coming.

LeFevre (29) refers to structure words as "empty" words used primarily to signal the coming use of noun or verb phrases, dependent clauses and questions. In one analysis he indicates that approximately half of the words on the Dolch Basic Sight Word Test* are structure or "empty" words. A few examples of markers are:

Noun markers: *my* house, *any* house, *this* house, *a* house, *some* houses, *the* house

Verb markers: *am* coming, *are* coming, *is* coming, *was* coming

Clause markers: *now, like, until, if, although, since, before, however*

Question indicators: *when, where, who, which, why*

It is easy to see why structure words have been called "the glue words of the English language," or "service words." Both of these concepts are consistent with the way these words function in sentences. They both introduce and bind together utterances while not conveying meaning in and of themselves. Many structure words have irregular spellings which accounts for their being designated "sight words." Both their irregular spellings and their high frequency of usage make it mandatory that they be instantly recognized in print.

---

*The Dolch Basic Sight Word Test consists of 220 words and is available from Garrard Press, Champaign, Illinois.

The frequency with which particular words are used will of course vary with the material under consideration. The previous sentence uses eight different structure words for a total of eleven running words (the, with, which, and, used, will, of, course, with, the, under). Whether one is talking about reading material specifically designed for the primary grades, or the professional writing of historians and linguists, these words will comprise from 25 to 50 per cent of all running words, regardless of how many different words are encountered.

Structure words pose no problem for facile readers. But with seriously impaired readers, these are the words they have been unable to learn or recognize even after hundreds of experiences of seeing them in print and various types of drills designed to facilitate their becoming "sight words."

Syntax is a term used to describe the meaning patterns found within any language, in essence, the *grammar* of that language. Syntax includes the various word order patterns in which words can be strung together. The following word orders represent a correct sentence in English, an extreme regional expression and a non-English pattern. "I go up the steps"; "I go the steps up"; "Up the go I steps."

Syntax includes the ways in which words may function in different patterns. The same word may function as a verb, noun, or adverb. *Light* the fire. She saw the *light*. He danced *lightly* across the ring and threw a *lightening* punch. English syntax rules out "He danced *lightening* across the ring and thrown a *lighted* punch." A careful study of the syntax of a language will permit one to describe the basic sentence patterns which occur in that language, as well as the ways in which these patterns may be varied by means of expansion, substitution, and inversion.

Linguists have made a thorough and scientific analysis of the English language, and their writings should be consulted by individuals interested in linguistic findings. The purpose of the preceding discussion was to provide a few definitions which might be useful to non-linguists.

PHONOLOGY AND READING

The noted linguist Leonard Bloomfield was probably the first linguist to concern himself with the application of linguistic findings to the teaching of reading. In 1942 he outlined in the April and May issues of *The Elementary English Review* what in essence was later expanded and published in 1961 under the title *Let's Read—A Linguistic Approach.** This approach involves the teaching of beginning reading through the process of teaching only those words which follow "regular spellings" in English.

Regular spellings are words in which each grapheme (written letter) represents only one phoneme (sound), and the sound is the one most frequently associated with a given grapheme. The rationale of the Bloomfield approach is that beginning reading instruction should focus entirely on associating and producing the regular sound each time the reader sees a given grapheme or printed letter. A "lesson" consists of a series of words and nonsense syllables, each of which contains a given vowel sound plus any combination of regular consonant phonemes before and after the vowel. Subsequent lessons introduce only one new pattern but may review patterns previously introduced.

For example, lesson one deals primarily with three letter words all of which contain the short *a* sound and end with *n* (*can, fan, man, pan, ran, tan, Nan, Dan, van*). The second lesson introduces words ending with the *at* phonogram. With the exception of *a an at* all words follow the consonant-vowel-consonant (CVC) pattern.

The separate words differ only in the initial grapheme-phoneme. The child is to see and hear these "minimal contrasts" in words. When all the words in lesson one are mastered, the child meets sentences such as:

Dan ran. Nan ran. Nan can fan Dan. Can Dan fan Nan?

Lesson two includes sentences such as:

A fat cat ran. A fat man ran. Can a fat man pat a cat?

Pre-Reading

Prior to working with words, the child is to learn the following:

1. He should learn to identify (name) the letters of the English alphabet.
   A. Capital letters are learned first.
   B. Small or lower case letters follow.
   C. Letters are taught in alphabetical order stressing reading from left to right.

---

*Leonard Bloomfield and Clarence L. Barnhart, *Let's Read—A Linguistic Approach* (Detroit: Wayne State University Press, 1961).

2. Next the child is to learn to pronounce "combinations of letters" including words, but the child need not be told that these combinations represent words.
3. Lesson one consists of the words *can, Dan, fan, man, an, pan, ran, tan, Nan, van.*
4. The word *can* is printed on the chalkboard.
   A. The child is asked to "read the letter names in the order of their appearance—See-aye-en.*
   B. The teacher says "We have spelled the word. Now we are going to read it. This word is *can.* Read it—*can.*"
5. Each new word in the lesson will be presented in the above manner.
6. Bloomfield cautions: "The early reading lessons should not be very long, for they demand a severe intellectual effort. It may be well to take up only two words in the first lesson." It is not implied that this is an overstatement. The difficulty of this task stems from the fact that children have had no previous language experience which relates to it. In mastering much of the complicated structure of their native tongue they have met no patterns such as "see-aye-en-spells can, read it—*can.*"

The preceding discussion has, without dealing extensively with lesson material, briefly outlined the Bloomfield-Barnhart approach. Further questions which should be dealt with include: What does this system attempt to accomplish? What questionable methodological weaknesses are tolerated in order not to dilute its alleged strength?

Bloomfield's approach aims at protecting the child from the irrational spelling patterns which have been allowed to occur and to continue in English writing. Of course the child cannot be protected long. The shock of reality can only be postponed. Bloomfield states, "learning to read consists of learning the very abstract equation printed letter-speech sound to be spoken."** This equation fits the words taught initially but does not hold for the irregular words which soon are to come.

Interestingly enough, there is no Bloomfield Methodology for reading instruction once these regular patterns are exhausted. In the introduction to Part IV, *The Commonest Irregular Words,* one finds, "when it comes to teaching irregular and special words,

---

*Ibid, p. 41.
**Ibid, p. 36.

each word will demand a separate effort and separate practice"* (emphasis added). It is difficult to see how this differs from the "word method" which Bloomfield misconstrues but abhors.**

Another issue of considerable importance is the number of words which have regular spellings as compared with those which have irregular spellings. Of the 5,000 English words introduced in the reading program outlined in *Let's Read,* only 37 per cent were words which met the author's criteria for regular spellings. However, it should be pointed out that Bloomfield's criteria were much more stringent than the average reading teacher would apply.

REGULAR SPELLING VS. PHONICS

Bloomfield's opposition to phonics instruction rests on several premises about phonics instruction which have little relevance to current instructional practice. The first of these is that phonics aims to teach the child *how* to pronounce words by teaching him how to make speech sounds. "If a child has not learned to utter the speech sounds of our language, the only sensible course is to postpone reading until he has learned to speak."*** The fact is that phonics instruction aims at having the child associate speech sounds with their graphic representations so that he will pronounce written English patterns he already knows as speech patterns. Present day phonics instruction rests solidly on Bloomfield's equation: printed letter-speech sound to be spoken.

The second misconception is that phonics instruction in the schools teaches that letter sounds be pronounced in isolation. This malpractice was one of the chief reasons for the "revolt against phonics" which occurred before the publication of Bloomfield's article in 1942. Assuming there existed some justification for his error at that time, there was none for letting this specious argument appear in the 1961 printing of *Let's Read* (p. 28). Even at its worst (which was very bad) phonics instruction avoided the ritual "see-aye-en-read it *can*." Bad phonics instruction would have had it: "Kuh-ah-en makes can."

STRUCTURAL LINGUISTICS AND THE READING PROCESS

A language has a total structure within which will be found a number of sub-structures. The phonemic sub-structure determines

*Bloomfield and Barnhart, *Let's Read.* p. 206.
**Ibid, pp. 28-30.
***Ibid, p. 27.

which speech sounds are found in the language and the patterns in which these may be combined in words. However, the total structure cannot be grasped by focusing on the identifiable sounds in words or even by studying words as units. The larger or controlling structure is that which governs the possible word combinations found in utterances—the variations in which words may be strung together.

Structural linguistics is one of the broad fields of language research. It is an integral part of linguistic science which deals with how a given language actually functions when used by persons who learned it as their native tongue. Structural linguistics is often equated with the grammar of a language. This is not to be confused with a course of study usually found in English courses which has come to be labeled "traditional grammar." The structural linguist is concerned with *how* language is used, not with formulating theories as to how it *should* be used.

Individuals who would apply structural linguistics to reading instruction suggest that emphasis be placed on having the learner see the relationship between his use of spoken English and the decoding of written English. A statement frequently met is that "speech is primary and reading is secondary—or a derived process." This statement means more than that speech is learned before one learns how to read. In so far as structural linguistics relates to reading instruction, this concept implies that speech is involved in the reading process. If the child does not grasp that in his reading he must reproduce the intonation patterns of English speech, he will not arrive at the meanings which are graphically represented.

LeFevre, (29) in *Linguistics and the Teaching of Reading*, has attempted to build a communicative bridge between the structural linguist and the reading teacher. While stating his awareness of the complex nature of reading problems and the possibility of a number of casual factors, he states that, "The basic fault in poor reading (viewed as a crippled language process) is poor sentence sense, demonstrated orally in word-calling, or in reading various nonstructural fragments of language patterns as units." If a child reads word by word, he treats each separate word as an utterance and will utilize a fade-fall terminal /↘/ after each word.

The/↘boy/↘went/↘to/↘the/↘store/↘.

This habit will inevitably destroy the melody of spoken English and thus preclude reading for meaning.

Structuralists point out that single words are rarely meaning-bearing units. Words work together in larger wholes. It is with larger language patterns that the structural linguist wishes to begin reading instruction. Not words-to-phrases-to-sentences, but rather he wishes to begin with the sentence as the *basic* meaning-bearing pattern. The structuralists feel that the child must start with oral reading of sentences with instructional emphasis on his noting and practicing intonation patterns he already recognizes and uses in his speech.

The reading teacher, not aware of the vast body of knowledge encompassed by the linguists in the use of the term "intonation pattern," may feel that structural linguistics has staked out a rather narrow foundation for reading instruction. But intonation—which consists of pitch, stress and juncture — accounts for the rhythm and melody of American English. The term "melodies of speech" has a special connotation for the linguist.

Tyler (41) makes a number of references to the melody one must seek out when reading. "A writer wants his reader to hear the unspoken melody of his words"; primary-grade pupils have "an extensive lexicon of sentence melodies." Stress patterns are referred to as an "upward-downward melody." Lloyd (31) states, "*The ability to relate the melody of speech to the written page is the key to good reading*. Good readers do it; poor readers don't do it." Stevens (39) suggests that once pupils are able to recognize word in print, "they must be taught to see the sentence that they already hear. Only with help in perceiving this melody in its varied patterns will they ultimately become literate."

This concept of melody of language does not concern itself with the selection of words but rather with the structural arrangements found in English. The child comes to school with an ear for this melody already developed. His use of oral language fits the pattern, and his understanding of oral English rests on this tremendous accomplishment. The seven-year-old speaks a melodic English comparable to his teacher. Both have learned the same structure.

In another sense the child has much to learn from his teachers and from experience which will enhance his use and understanding of the melody of language; this is in the choice of words which he can fit into the sentence structures permitted in the English language. This is illustrated by the title of a book of poems by Emily Dickinson, *Bolts of Melody*.* This is a most apt choice of words to describe the poet's art; the manipulation of language.

**Bolts of Melody — New Poems of Emily Dickinson,* Mabel Loomis Todd and Millicent Todd Bingham, eds., (New York: Harper & Row, Publishers, 1945).

EVALUATION OF LINGUISTIC PROPOSALS

It would be difficult to find two more diametrically opposed approaches to beginning reading instruction than the "regular spellings" and the structural "melody of language" schools discussed above. Barnhart's statement that "a linguistic system separates the study of word form from word meaning" seems to imply that *all* linguistic approaches would of necessity start with materials in which the vocabulary consisted of regularly spelled words. Many linguists reject this thesis.

There can be no official linguistic approach to reading instruction because the science of linguistics is not concerned with teaching children to read. However, any linguist is free to theorize and experiment in the area of reading instruction. Such experiences on the part of linguists may result in insights which eventually lead to significant changes in reading instruction.

The science of linguistics has not established that beginning reading instructional materials should deal only with regular spellings, or that pictures should be omitted from children's books. These are pedagogical decisions unrelated to linguistic science. These and other suggestions may prove to have merit, but their validity must be tested in the classroom like any other proposals. Their efficacy is not established a priori because they are labeled "linguistic approach." Raven McDavid (33) makes this point most succinctly by suggesting that the layman may have difficulty in distinguishing between when the linguist is speaking from his professional competence and when he is speaking as any other citizen. "When the linguist attempts to produce (basal) readers, he can expect them to be criticized on both linguistic and other grounds."

In discussing Bloomfield's and Fries' phonological approach to reading instruction, it might be pointed out that their linguistic scholarship was immensely broad; but the segment of linguistic knowledge they choose to utilize in their approach to reading instruction is extremely narrow. Bloomfield's ignoring of much of his own significant research (inflection patterns, signaling devices, sentence type, and word order), in the words of Lefevre (27) constitutes "an unsolved mystery of twentieth century linguistic scholarship."

It would appear that based on training and experience, any linguist might evolve any one of a number of approaches to reading instruction. This would indicate that suggestions about how reading should be taught are less influenced by linguistic training than by one's own concept of "what is reading." This leads to an important educational issue posed by certain newer materials. Should the materials and methodology used in beginning reading be evaluated from the standpoint of the concept of reading which they inculcate in beginning readers?

THE READERS "SET" IN BEGINNING READING

The proponents of the phonological approach to beginning reading instruction are unequivocal in their rejection of the thesis that "beginning reading instruction should be a meaning-making process." In the words of Clarence Barnhart, co-author of *Let's Read*, "We find Bloomfield's system of teaching reading is a linguistic system. Essentially a linguistic system of teaching reading separates the problem of the study of word form from the study of word meaning." (p. 9) Bloomfield concurs; "Aside from their silliness, the stories in a child's first reader are of little use because the child is too busy with the mechanics of reading to get anything of the content . . . . This does not mean that we must forego the use of sentences and connected stories, but it does mean that these are not essential to the first steps. We need not fear to use disconnected words and even senseless syllables; and above all we must not, for the sake of a story, upset the child's scarcely formed habits by presenting him with irregularities of spelling for which he is not prepared." (p. 34)

Fries, (15) in *Linguistics and Reading*, states: "Seeking an extraneous interest in a story as a story during the earliest steps of reading is more likely to hinder than to help the efforts put forth by the pupil himself." (p. 199) A non-linguist who supports the methodology under discussion writes, "Reading, thus, is the act of producing correct sounds from symbols. If the reader does not know the meaning of a word he can still 'read' it if he knows the alphabetical system. The reader of English can read 'gan' and 'foggle' and many other nonsense and real words because he knows the alphabetical system." (11)

That Fries (16) is bothered by the issue of meaning is evidenced in a later writing where he states: "As a matter of fact the primary *objective* of our materials built upon linguistic understanding *is the ability to read for meanings*." The better part of a page is devoted to an explanation of the cumulative meanings the child must grasp in reading the material:

Nat is a cat.
Nat is fat.
Nat is a fat cat.

Recently there has been considerable emphasis on research related to beginning reading. The chief goal of much of this research has centered on identifying those materials and methodology whose use would result in higher achievement test scores at the end of grade one. In addition to their impact on initial achievement, materials and methodology will also influence pupils' perception of reading.

Concomitant with the interest in beginning reading, there has been a tendency to lose sight of the fact that learning to read is a long-term developmental process. The habits, attitudes (and "set" as to what is involved in reading), which a child acquires during this period can have a significant impact on all future reading behavior. If educators become overly concerned with pupils achieving a fast start in reading, it is possible that they might fail to note that achieving this initial rapid growth under certain methodological conditions might also produce side effects which lead to later problems for the reader.

It is not suggested here that lesser achievement in grade one is a virtue, but rather that it is possible to achieve an initial spurt at the expense of the long-term goal of producing facile, critical readers. There is no suggestion that "cracking-the-code" is not an essential part of the beginning reading process; but the issue centers on whether certain methodology and materials maintain a proper balance between this facet of instruction and teaching reading as a meaning-making process.

CONCLUSION:

Linguistics is the scientific study of language. Without doubt, reading instruction can be strengthened as teachers acquire some of the important insights which linguists have discovered. On the other hand, linguists as scientists are in no way responsible for finding applications for their discoveries. Few have actively engaged in relating their discoveries to the school curriculum. As a result, linguistics has had little impact on the content of the curriculum particularly at the elementary level.

Recently there has been an awakening of interest in the question of how linguistic findings might aid the school in developing more meaningful educational experiences. Some linguists have turned their attention to the teaching of the reading process. It has been difficult for these linguists to apply the same scientific rigor to reading instruction that they applied to the study of language.

Linguists have evolved theories relative to instructional materials and methodology, but these have not been tested longitudinally in the classroom. There is little research data upon which to base conclusions. Linguistic science has not been concerned with the issue of *how children learn to read,* and some linguists have started with an assumption of how they *should* learn this process. This factor, ignoring the learner, may inhibit the efficacy of some suggestions advanced by linguists.

There are certain important concepts which do relate to reading which may have been slighted in past and current methodology. The following are illustrative:

1. Despite irregularities in English spelling, important phonemegrapheme *patterns* do exist, and possibly these should be exploited to a larger degree in reading instruction.
2. Reading instruction can overemphasize dealing with words as units. Graphic symbols must be read to parallel normal sentence tunes. The reader must "put together meaning bearing patterns."
3. The printed page represents language which is oral. The child beginning to read knows the melody (i.e., grammar or syntax) of oral language. However, the printed pages do not contain all the language clues found in speech. The "graphic representation" of language does not indicate various levels of pitch and stress. Punctuation (which indicates junctures) is the only graphic intonational help that is provided; and it too is somewhat imperfect. Intonation-juncture, stress and pitch are part of the language, not optional additives.
4. The purpose and function of structure words need to be better understood for the mastery of the reading process. These approximately 300 words, sometimes referred to as "glue words" or "service words," have little or no meaning in and of themselves; but they provide significant clues as to the type of patterns they introduce (questions, noun markers, verb markers, parallel constructions).

YOUR POINT OF VIEW?

Defend or attack the following statements.

1. Evidence is lacking that if children learn to read using materials which present only "regular spellings," that they will master the recognition of irregularly spelled words faster because of this initial experience.
2. No branch of linguistics deals with the phenomenon of how children learn to read.
3. The study of *language* is unquestionably neglected in our schools.
4. Based on training, psychologists, linguists, sociologists, and novelists should be approximately equally adept at preparing reading materials for six-year-olds.
5. All reading-instruction materials which follow the structure and patterns of English usage can be said to be "linguistically sound" or "linguistic methods."
6. Approximately the same percentage of sixth graders have mastered the "melody of language" in their reading as have first graders in their oral language usage.

BIBLIOGRAPHY

1. Allen, Robert, "An Approach to Better Reading Through Recognition of Grammatical Relationships," *Improvement of Reading through Classroom Practice*. International Reading Association Conference Proceedings, 9, 1964, 224-25.
2. ———, "Better Reading Through the Recognition of Grammatical Relationships," *Reading Teacher,* 18 (December 1964), 194-98.
3. Bateman, Barbara, and Janis Wetherell, "A Critique of Bloomfield's Linguistic Approach to the Teaching of Reading," *Reading Teacher,* 18 (November 1964), 98-104.
4. Betts, Emmett A., "Structure in the Reading Program," *Elementary English,* XXXXII (March 1965), 238-42.
5. Bloomfield, Leonard, *Language*. New York: Holt, Rinehart & Winston, Inc., 1933.

6. ———, and Clarence L. Barnhart, *Let's Read — a Linguistic Approach*. Detroit: Wayne State University Press, 1961.

7. Botel, Morton, "What Linguistics Says to This Teacher of Reading and Spelling," *Reading Teacher*, 18 (December 1964), 188-93.

8. Cameron, Jack R., "Traditionalists, Textbooks, and Non-English Grammar," *Elementary English*, XXXXI (February 1964), 145-48.

9. Carroll, John B., *Language and Thought*. Englewood Cliffs, N. J.: Prentice-Hall, Inc., 1964.

10. Creswell, Thomas J., and Virginia McDavid, "Linguistics and the Teaching of Reading," *Elementary English*, XXXX (January 1963), 93-6.

11. Dawkins, John, "Reading Theory — An Important Distinction," *Elementary English*, XXXVIII (October 1961), 389-92.

12. ———, "Linguistics in the Elementary Grades," *Elementary English*, XXXXII (November 1965), 762-68.

13. Durkin, Dolores, "Linguistics and the Teaching of Reading," *Reading Teacher*, 16 (March 1963), 341-46.

14. Edward, Sister Mary, P.B.V.M., "A Modified Linguistic Versus a Composite Basal Reading Program," *Reading Teacher*, 17 (April 1964), 511-15.

15. Fries, Charles C., *Linguistics and Reading*. New York: Holt, Rinehart & Winston, Inc., 1963.

16. ———, "Linguistics and Reading Problems at the Junior High School Level," *Reading and Inquiry*. International Reading Association Proceedings, 10, 1965, 244-47.

17. Goodman, Kenneth S., "Dialect Barriers to Reading Comprehension," *Reading and Inquiry*. International Reading Association Proceedings, 10, 1965, 240-42.

18. ———, "The Linguistics of Reading," *Elementary School Journal*, 64 (April 1964), 355-61.

19. Hall, Robert A., Jr., *Linguistics and Your Language*. Garden City, N. Y.: Anchor Books, Doubleday & Company, Inc., 1960.

20. Hanna, Paul R., and Jean S. Hanna, "Applications of Linguistics and Psychological Cues to the Spelling Course of Study," *Elementary English*, XXXXII (November 1965), 753-59.

21. Hildreth, Gertrude, "Linguistic Factors in Early Reading Instruction," *Reading Teacher,* 18 (December 1964), 172-78.

22. Hodges, Richard E., "Linguistics, Psychology, and the Teaching of English," *Elementary School Journal,* 66 (January 1966), 208-13.

23. Hunt, Kellogg W., "Recent Measures In Syntactic Development," *Elementary English,* XLIII, (November 1966), 732-39.

24. Keislar, Evan, "Conference on Perceptual and Linguistic Aspects of Reading," *Reading Teacher,* 18 (October 1964), 43-52.

25. Lefcourt, Ann, "Linguistics and Elementary School Textbooks," *Elementary English,* XXXX (October 1963), 598-601.

26. Lefevre, Carl A., "The Sounds and Tunes We Read By," *New Dimensions in Reading.* University of Pittsburgh Conference Proceedings, 19, 1963, 61-68.

27. ———, "A Longer Look at Let's Read," *Elementary English,* XXXI (March 1964), 199-206.

28. ———, "A Comprehensive Linguistic Approach to Reading," *Elementary English,* XXXXII (October 1965), 651-60.

29. ———, *Linguistics and The Teaching of Reading.* New York: McGraw-Hill Book Company, 1964.

30. Lester, Mark, Graphemic-Phonemic Correspondences as the Basis for Teaching Spelling," *Elementary English,* XXXXI (November 1964), 748-52.

31. Lloyd, Donald J., "Reading American English Sound Patterns." New York: Harper & Row, Publishers, 1962, Monograph No. 104.

32. McDavid, Raven J., Jr., "The Role of the Linguist In The Teaching of Reading," *Changing Concepts of Reading Instruction.* International Reading Association Proceedings, 6, 1961, 253-56.

33. ———, "Remarks on B. Robert Tabachnick's Paper," *Reading and the Language Arts,* H. Alan Robinson (ed.), Supplementary Educational Monographs No. 93. Chicago: University of Chicago Press, 1963, 112.

34. Owen, George H., "Linguistics: An Overview," *Elementary English,* XXXIX (May 1962), 421-25.

35. Reed, David W., "A Theory of Language, Speech and Writing," *Elementary English,* (December 1965), 845-51.

36. Rystrom, Richard, "Whole-Word and Phonics Methods and Current Linguistic Findings," *Elementary English,* XXXXII (March 1965), 265-68.

37. Soffietti, James P., "Why Children Fail To Read: A Linguistic Analysis," *Harvard Educational Review,* 25 (Spring 1955), 63-84.

38. Stegall, Carrie, "Linguistics and I," *Elementary English* (April 1961), 229-31.

39. Stevens, Martin, "Intonation in the Teachings of Reading," *Elementary English,* XXXXII (March 1965), 231-37.

40. Strickland, Ruth G., "Implication of Research in Linguistics for Elementary Teaching," *Elementary English,* XXXX (February 1963), 168-71.

41. Tyler, Priscilla, "Sound, Pattern and Sense," *Changing Concepts of Reading Instruction.* International Reading Association Proceedings, 6, 1961, 249-53.

42. Wilson, Rosemary Green, "A Linguistic Approach to Beginning Reading Based on Fries' Principles," *Improvement of Reading Through Classroom Practice.* International Reading Association Proceedings, 9, 1964, 225-27.

prefix
word
away
SIGNS
OF

Phonics Instruction

9

The child's ability to associate letters with sounds is second in importance to no other skill in helping him become an independent reader. Starting from this premise, one might still have reservations to some of the phonics instructional materials presently available and to certain practices they advocate.

The problem of determining what is the proper role of phonics in reading instruction is not new. Undoubtedly the pressures on schools and teachers today which are tracable to this issue are unprecedented. During the past decade the most vociferous critics of present-day reading instruction started from a number of erroneous premises, chief among these were:

1. There is a sight word method of teaching reading which makes little or no provision for teaching phonic analysis skills.
2. All words met at various instructional levels are taught exclusively as "sight words."

3. Phonics instruction is "good" and children cannot get too much of a good thing.
4. If we were to go back to the phonics emphasis of the 1890's, reading problems in our schools would disappear.

For illustrative purposes one might cite the views of the *Council on Basic Education*, a non-profit organization dedicated to the improvement of American education. In their concern with reading instruction, the Council has focused entirely on the issue of phonics. In the January, 1964, *Bulletin* of the Council we read, "Perhaps the most encouraging development of the year (1963), was the increasing understanding on the part of the public of what the phonics versus sight reading controversy is all about. The issue has often been confused in the public mind, especially when the advocates of the sight, or look-and-say method, insist that they also are believers in phonics instruction."

In the C.B.E. *Bulletin*, February, 1962, one finds, "From our observation of good teachers in the fields of reading and language, we discern a few guiding principles and methods of operations. The good teacher of beginning reading, where she is not bound by an imposed methodology, operates on the theory that *beginning* reading is not a 'thought getting' process but is based on translating letters into sounds." No evidence was cited as to the source of this data.

HOW EFFECTIVELY ARE PHONICS SKILLS TAUGHT?

While certain critics have erred in stating that phonic analysis is ignored in both instructional materials and practices; they would undoubtedly have been justified in raising questions as to how well these skills are taught. There has been, and still is, considerable confusion and insecurity among a number of elementary teachers about teaching phonics. This is reflected in the titles of numerous journal articles such as: "Am I Teaching Phonics Right?" "Some Misconceptions Concerning Phonics," and "Is English a Phonetic Language?"

A number of recent studies suggest that teachers' limited knowledge of phonic principles, as these relate to letter sounds, might be a factor in the uneasiness about teaching phonics. A study by Aaron (1) reports that a group of prospective and experienced teachers were able to correctly answer approximately 60 per cent of the items on a phonics test. This study was replicated by Spache and Baggett (37) who, although reporting somewhat higher means for teachers, state that their data confirmed the need for more intensive instruction in phonics.

Other investigations did not employ actual testing of teachers' knowledge, but invited teachers to identify their needs for further learning about any specific aspects of reading instruction. Reporting data from such studies, Haggard (18) and Adams (2) indicate that teachers consistently state that one of their greatest needs is an understanding of phonics.

This data suggests that there is some justification for a chapter devoted exclusively to the elementary phonics program. This permits the teacher to have an overview of the total program without weakening the premise that the actual teaching of phonics should be integrated with all other techniques for solving unknown words. The remainder of this chapter is concerned with teaching the major phonic analysis skills.

BRIEF REVIEW OF PAST PRACTICES

Some knowledge of the history of phonics teaching in American education is undoubtedly helpful in understanding some of the problems, attitudes, and misunderstandings observable in education today. The following discussion is a very brief summary of phonic practices advocated in the past.*

Beginning around 1890 and continuing for a period of thirty or forty years, the cornerstone of reading instruction in American schools was a synthetic phonics method. Previous to this era much time was spent on the rote learning of the ABC's. Emphasis now shifted from drill on "letter names" to drill on the "sounds of the various letters." Here we have a form of phonics drill unrelated to meaning and in some instances unrelated to words in English. Children drilled on isolated sounds as illustrated below:

da ha la ma pa ra
be se te ne le re
pi mi ti si li ri

*The reader who wishes a more detailed account of past practices will find the following sources helpful:

Nile B. Smith, "Phonics Then and Now," *Education* LXXV (1955), 560-65.

W. S. Gray, *On Their Own in Reading,* (Chicago: Scott, Foresman & Co., 1948), Chap. 1.

E. A. Betts, "Phonics: Practical Consideration Based on Research," *Elementary English,* XXXIII (1956), 357-71.

This drill was not in context with reading, since the drills preceded the child's learning of words. It is easy to see that this type of introduction placed little, if any, emphasis on reading as a process of discovering meaning.

Rebecca Pollard's synthetic method, introduced about 1890,* advocated reducing reading to a number of mechanical procedures, each of which focused on a unit smaller than a word. Reading became very mechanistic and, when mastered, often produced individuals who were adept at working their way through a given word. The result among both teachers and pupils was that facile reading became equated with "facility in calling words." A few of the recommended procedures of this method were:

1. Drills in articulation were to precede any attempt at reading. The child was to drill on the "sounds of letters." Then he would be able, it was reasoned, to attack whole words.
2. Single consonants were "sounded." Each consonant was given a sound equivalent to a syllable. Thus *b, c, d, p, h,* and *t* were sounded *buh, cuh, duh, puh, huh,* and *tuh.*
3. Drill on word families was stressed. This was unrelated to meaning. Sometimes children memorized lists of words ending in such common family phonograms as *ill, am, ick, ate, old, ack.*
4. Diacritical markings were introduced in first grade, and children drilled on "marking sentences." For example:

> The ghŏst wăs ā cŏmmŏn sīght near the wrĕck. He knew the īslănd was ĕmpty.

A number of widely used reading texts adopted the suggestions of Pollard and, in many cases, extended them. For instance, if the objective of a unit were to teach the phonogram or "family" *ick,* a story might be built primarily from words in that family, regardless of meaning or lack of it in the passage. The following example is illustrative and, it is hoped, exaggerated.

> Nick, flick the tick from the chick with a stick. Prick the tick from the chick with a thick stick. Nick, do not kick the brick, kick the stick.

The discerning reader will see the close relationship between this practice and one of the linguistic approaches to beginning reading which has recently enjoyed widespread publicity (see Chapter 8).

*Rebecca S. Pollard, *Pollard's Synthetic Method* (Chicago: Western Publishing House, 1889).

It is not implied that teaching word families is an indefensible practice but rather that some practices seem to have more merit than others. Drill on a column of words entirely unrelated to meaningful reading might be a poor learning technique. On the other hand, when children have learned the words *make* and *take* as sight words, and they meet the new word *lake* in a reading exercise, it would not be poor instruction to point out that this word, and certain others whose meanings are known, contain the common letters *ake* which in every case represent the same speech sound (*cake, bake, wake, snake, rake, shake*).

There is little point in opposing the teaching of "family groups" on the basis that a relatively small number of English words contain these families. This is not a sound argument because so many small, often used words *are* formed from some thirty such families, and these words are among those most frequently occurring in beginning reading materials (specifically such families as *an, at, it, am, in, as, ate, ake, et, ick, eat, arm, en, ing, ot, est, un, all, ell, and ame*). There are enough common or service words which are *not* phonetic to be learned as sight words that any clue, such as word families, that a child can pick up early in learning to read can be useful.

LITTLE WORDS IN BIG WORDS

Since some of the regular spelling families are also words (*am, is, and, ate, an, all, old, it, at, eat*), the practice of "looking for small words in large words" was advocated. The justification for this practice was that the little words were familiar to the child, and he could pronounce them. If he found little words he knew in larger unknown words, he had a start toward mastering the unknown larger word.

The procedure of looking for small words in larger words fails for two reasons. First, there is little logic in having the child see the word *ill* in the monosyllabic words *will, Bill, fill, mill, kill,* and *pill,* unless it is the association of *ill* with *pill,* which leaves much to be desired. In teaching reading today, the clue will not be the word *ill* but the sound of *ill* in conjunction with the sounds of various initial letters: *w, b, f, m, g, k, p,* and *h.*

The second charge against "finding little words" appears to be so serious as to remove the practice from the list of justifiable procedures. Many of the little words which retain some degree of pronounceable autonomy in single-syllable words lose this characteristic in words of more than one syllable. In *pan, can, man, fan, tan, ran* or in *ham, jam, Sam,* noting the little words *an* and *am* would not destroy the pronunciation of the words. However, seeing or pronouncing the *am* in *am*ong, *am*end, *am*en, *am*use, *am*ass would prevent a correct phonic analysis. Likewise, seeing or saying the word *as* in *as*hore, *As*ia, *as*ide, *as*leep; *it* in *it*em; *at* in *at*omic and *at*hlete; or *all* in *allow* or *allege* would hinder attempts at word analysis.

The "total emphasis" on phonics brought the method into disrepute during the 1920's. Reform was not advocated, but rather discarding the teaching of phonics. It was commonly alleged that the abuses of phonics teaching were responsible for the reading problems found at that time. Thus, what was *pre*scribed at one moment was *pro*scribed the next. There was much confusion among teachers, and this confusion seems not to have abated perceptibly today.

Association of letters with sounds is of primary importance to independent reading. Here children use phonic clues as a means of arriving at the pronunciation of words. Each child works with materials which are selected for his individual needs. (Courtesy of Bexley Schools, Bexley, Ohio; photographer: Arthur Burt, Inc.)

TASKS INVOLVED IN PHONICS INSTRUCTION

There are a series of instructional tasks which taken together constitute the phonics program. Different phonic teaching materials will include a number of techniques which are common to all approaches. They may differ as to the sequence in which skills are introduced, the emphasis on children learning rules, the number of different steps taught and how much phonics instruction is included in beginning reading. An outline of the major phonics tasks which must be taught would include:

1. Auditory discrimination of speech sounds in words.
2. Written letters are used to represent these speech sounds.
3. The sound represented by a letter or letters in a known word can be used to unlock the pronunciation of unknown words in which these particular letters occur.
4. Sounds of consonants.
    a. Initial position in words
    b. Final position in words
5. Consonants which are blended.
6. Special consonant digraphs (*th*, *ch*, *sh*, *wh*).
7. Vowel sounds.
    a. Short vowel sounds
    b. Long vowel sounds
    c. Double vowels
        (1) Digraphs
        (2) Diphthongs
    d. Vowels followed by *r*
    e. Effect of final *e*
    f. Final *y* sounded as long *i*
8. Silent consonants.
9. Syllabication.
10. Accent.

It should not be inferred that each of the above steps is of equal importance in learning to read, or that each should receive the same amount of instructional time. The steps listed are simply the framework, since some steps include many specific tasks. For instance, under syllabication one would deal with such teachings as "prefixes and suffixes are usually syllables; there are as many syllables as sounded vowels; two consonants coming between vowels usually divide (*gar•den*); double consonants usually divide (*let•ter,sum•*

mer); the letter combinations *cle, ble, gle, dle, kle,* and *tle* at the ends of words are single syllables." There is no agreement as to the number of such rules or principles that should be taught in the reading process. Even a summary of all the suggestions found in the literature of teaching reading would be beyond the scope of this book.

The actual learning of phonics as it relates to reading usually begins quite early in the pre-school years. The child learns a sound like *mommy,* and can easily differentiate it from similar sounds. He may have a pet *kitty* and a playmate *Kathy* and will differentiate if asked "where is *Kathy?*" even though the kitty is also present. Phonics instruction begins when an adult talks with an infant, thus providing the child a model.

When a child associates sounds with objects and does not confuse sounds that are very similar such as *mommy, money, monkey,* and *maybe,* he is mastering auditory discrimination, which is a prerequisite for phonic analysis in the reading process. None of the later "steps" in learning phonics can take place in the absence of mastery of this basic language function. Beginning reading instruction in the school builds on the child's previous language experiences. In reading, the child will have to make visual discriminations between written word symbols and learn that the written symbols represent the speech sounds of words he speaks and understands.

Teaching Consonant Sounds

Why Begin with Consonant Sounds? A large majority of instructional materials used in beginning reading advocate that the teaching of letter sounds begin with consonants. This position is supported by the following factors:

1. A number of consonants (*b, f, d, h, j, k, p, m, l, r, t,* etc.) have only one sound. Once the child masters these letter-sound associations, this skill can be transferred in attacking other words in which these letters occur. On the other hand, vowels in written words are notoriously inconsistent as to the sound they represent.
2. Children must learn to read from left-to-right. Since most English words begin with consonants, the first letter or letters a child must sound out in an unknown word will be consonants.

3. If a reader uses context along with sounding, the initial sound in the word helps eliminate most alternative possibilities. To illustrate, each of the following blank lines represents an unknown word.

   A. ____________

   B. n____________

   The blank space in (A) can represent any word in English, while in (B) *all* words which do not begin with the /n/ sound are eliminated. Below, each sentence contains a different unknown word. It is likely that the one-sentence context and the initial consonant will permit you to solve the unknown word. Larger contexts would make the task easier.

   C. "Pull that n______ out of the board," said Grandfather.

   D. "What's the n______ of that song?" asked Mary. "It's on the n______ record I bought yesterday."

   E. "The big right hander struck out in the last of the n______."

The rationale for introducing vowel sounds first rests on the following assumptions. These have been gleaned from writings favorable to this practice and represent all of the justification this writer has found to date.

1. All words contain one or more vowels.
2. Vowels provide more important clues to pronunciation of words.
3. Consonants are blended with vowels and thus should not be sounded in isolation.

At first glance the above statements appear to have validity, but upon analysis they are seen to be relatively weak arguments. One might reverse the first statement and say, "all words contain consonants," but this is not a reason for teaching either consonants or vowels first. In the following sentence all consonant clues are removed. _e_ _ _ _y _o _ou_ _ _ _e_e _o_ _ _. It would be a most difficult task to decipher the preceding sentence. The following sentence shows consonants and omits vowels. L_ts tr_ t_ s_ _nd th_s_ w_rds. Reading this sentence is a much simpler task. Many other samples could be cited and the result would be to cast doubt on the premise that vowels provide the most important clues to pronunciation.

In regard to the third point above, *neither* consonants nor vowels should be sounded in isolation (*cat* = kah-ah-tuh). Since no instructional materials, with the exception of the Carden Method,* advocate sounding letters in isolation, the statement has little relevancy as an argument for teaching vowels first. It should be kept in mind that one of the most important clues to the sounds of vowels is provided by consonants which follow vowels. A consonant-vowel-consonant pattern usually results in a short vowel sound — *cat, den, can.* The same is true if the vowel is followed by two consonants (*cattle, dentist, canvas*).

Simultaneous Learning of Sight Words and Analysis

Teaching a limited number of sight words in beginning reading has been justified on the basis of the following rationale. First, the child has already mastered oral language in which he utilizes global word sounds rather than letter sounds. He has learned language as a meaningful process. Recognizing whole words builds on the child's previous language experience. That is, the child is taught the sight symbol *man* before he is taught the sounds of symbols *m, a,* and *n.* The word *man* is much more meaningful than the three symbols of which it is formed because the child:

1. Understands the meaning of the sound *man* in many contexts.
2. Can make this sound himself and associates it with its referent.
3. Can recognize a picture (sight symbol or representation) of a *man.*

Thus, it easy to move from what is known to the new and unknown — the printed word *man* used in any context familiar to the child.

Second, any word instantly recognized will serve as a phonic model for analyzing identical letter-sound combinations found in other words. This is predicated on the child's ability to recognize printed letters and associate a particular sound with that letter.

This discussion is not intended to suggest that teaching sight words without recourse to sounding letters goes on for any lengthy, fixed period of time. Building a sight vocabulary and utilizing sounding techniques (which should lead to further expansion of

---

*Mae Carden, *The Carden Method,* Glen Rock, New Jersey.

one's sight vocabulary) are parts of the same process. The most difficult task in beginning reading instruction is to arrive at the proper emphasis of both skills.

Teaching Initial Consonant Sounds. Starting from the premise that the child has learned to recognize a few words, which for illustrative purposes we will assume includes any of the words *be, back,* or *ball,* he is now ready to associate the sound of *b* in these words with the written symbol *b.*

> The teacher prints a capital *B* on the chalkboard and says, "Today we will learn all about the letter *B.* Next to the big *B* I will print a little *b.* This big *B* is called a capital *B.* Now I am going to write some words which begin with *b.*" (She writes *be, back,* and *ball.)* "Who can give us another word that begins with the *b* sound? Yes, *bear, boat, big* — *Bobby* we write with a large (or capital) *B* because it is somebody's name."

B	b
	be
	back
	ball
	boat
	Bobby

When a number of examples have been given, the teacher asks, "What do we notice about the sound of each of these words?" "That's right, they all begin with the sound of *b* — *bear, ball, boat, bat, big, bomb.*" As the words are called out by the children, they are added to the list on the board and the teacher asks, "What do we *see* that is the same in all of these words? That's right, they all begin with *b.*" It should be noted that in no instance were the children asked to sound the letter *b* in isolation, although it may have been emphasized without distortion.

In addition to the group work just described, there will be workbook exercises giving each child an opportunity to do seat work which parallels the concept taught. These exercises use both visual stimuli and sounds associated with pictures, letters, and words. A few typical examples are:

1. In the row of pictures, the child is to mark pictures of objects whose names begin with the same sound as the name of the object in the picture on the extreme left. (See Figure 23.)

FIGURE 23

2. A picture of a familiar object is shown along with the word represented by the object in the picture. The example is a bell (Figure 24). Here the child can see and hear the *b* sound. He is then to mark all the other words in a supplied list which begin with the same sound.

FIGURE 24

3. Figure 25 shows a series of words in columns, some of which begin with the same sound and the same letter. The child is to draw a line from the word in column *A* to the word in column *B* which begins with the same sound.

FIGURE 25

A word of caution should be injected here to point out that many exercises found in workbooks which aim to provide auditory practice can result in nothing but visual discrimination exercises, unless the teacher is careful to see that each child actually *sounds* the word symbols which are given as stimuli. To illustrate, the following exercise is patterned after Figure 25 and can be correctly marked using only visual clues. Incorporating auditory practice would require associating sounds with each initial symbol.

FIGURE 26

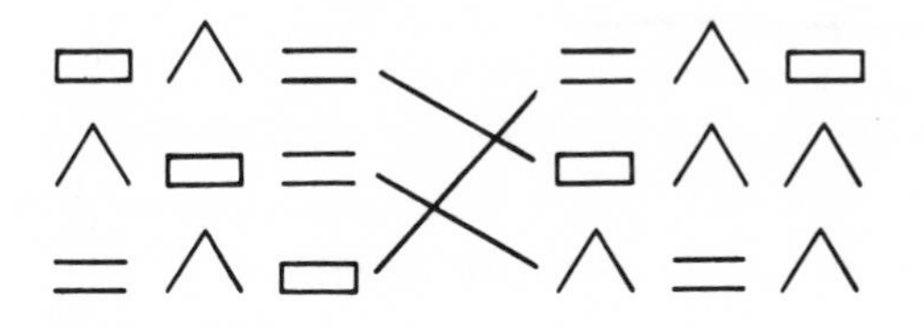

4. A pictured object is shown, followed by four words, none of which stand for the picture, but one or more of which begin with the same sound as the name of the pictured object.

FIGURE 27

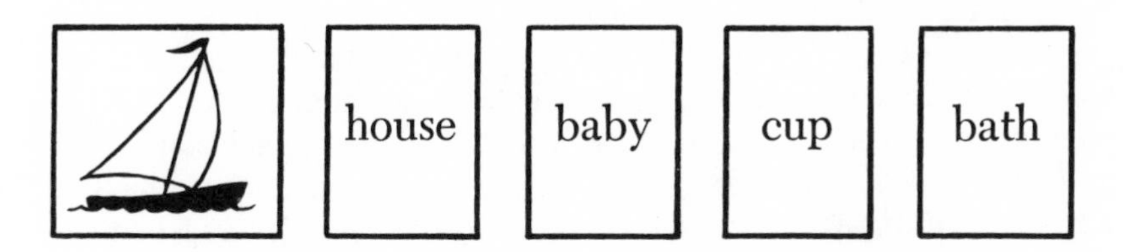

5. A series of boxes is shown, each containing three words. The teacher pronounces one of the words and the pupil underlines the word pronounced. (See Figure 28.) He need not know all of the words as sight words, provided he is familiar with the initial sound of each. In the following example, the teacher could pronounce *bank, tell, bill, may,*

bat. There are many other types of exercises and many variations of those illustrated.

FIGURE 28

1	2	3	4	5
call	*tell*	hill	*may*	hat
bank	sell	fill	pay	show
play	fell	*bill*	say	*bat*

Substitution of Initial Sounds

The next important skill to be learned is to substitute known letter sounds in attacking unknown words. Assume the child knows the words *take* and *make* and meets the unknown word *rake*. He should be able to combine the *r* sound (which he knows in words like *run, rain* or *ride*), with the sound of *ake* in *take*. By this process of "thinking the sounds," he should unlock the new word. (16) If the reader has mastered the steps in phonics previously introduced, this step also starts from that which is known, i.e., sight words and the sounds initial consonants contribute to words.

In beginning reading it is a common practice to teach a number of monosyllabic words which contain frequently used phonograms. Practically all workbooks use these "word families" as a means of teaching new words. Work on the substitution of initial consonants parallels the primers and first readers. Moving through the primer, the child meets such words as *back, came, day, fun, gate, hand, just, king, lake, met, not, pin, rest, sun, tall,* and *wet*. Each of these words contains a familiar and often occurring phonogram. Children should not receive drill on these word endings in isolation (*ack, ame, ay, ate, est, ust, ing, ake, ot, in, un, all, et*). Nevertheless, a number of important words can be solved independently when the child knows some sight words containing often used letter combinations and can substitute initial letter sounds.

Substitution of Single Consonant Sounds at the Ends of Words

Some teachers prefer to teach consonant sounds at the ends of words at the same time that they deal with a particular initial consonant sound. Other teachers work through the initial sounds and then work on single consonant sounds at the ends of words. Regardless of which procedure is followed, the child is taught to notice visually and auditorily the final consonants in short words. He knows words such as *men, log, pen, bold, leg* and the sounds of letters, including *t*. He is now asked to substitute the *t* sound at the end of the words to get *met, lot, pet, bolt,* and *let.*

Initial Blends

In dealing with many words that the child will meet early in the process of learning to read, sounding only the initial consonant will result in confusion. These words fall into two classes: simple consonant blends, and a smaller group of two-consonant combinations representing special speech sounds in English (*th, sh, ch, wh*).

The twenty-five two- and three-letter blends may be divided into three major groups on the basis of a common letter:

1. Those which begin with *s: sc, sk, sm, sn, sp, st, sw, str*
2. Those which conclude with *l: bl, cl, fl, gl, pl, sl, spl*
3. Those which conclude with *r: br, cr, dr, fr, gr, pr, tr, scr, spr, str*

The above arrangement is not intended to suggest a particular order in which blends should be taught. A logical sequence would probably be determined by the vocabulary found in the instructional materials actually used in beginning reading.

There is a great deal of variance among teachers as well as among basal readers as to (a) when blends are dealt with, (b) which are taught first, and (c) how rapidly the blends are covered. Most materials suggest teaching initial blends first and later stressing blends and special consonant sounds at the ends of words (chur*ch*, tra*sh*, che*st*, che*ck*, fla*sh*, fre*sh*, fro*st*, smoo*th*, whi*ch*, thi*ck*). While there are numerous approaches for teaching consonant blends, the objectives of all methods are to lead the child:

1. To see the printed letters involved.
2. To understand that in every instance the letter sounds combine into a blended sound.
3. To auditorily discriminate between the sound of individual letters and blends — *d*ug, *r*ug, *dr*ug; *s*old, *c*old, *sc*old.

Any procedure for teaching initial consonant sounds can be utilized for teaching each of the different consonant blends. A few techniques are illustrated below.

1. Secure a number of pictures of concrete objects whose names begin with a blend. Show the pictures one at a time and have the children write, or say orally, the blended letters. (They are not to simply name the picture.) Examples: *sk*ate, *tr*ain, *br*idge, *pl*ate, *gr*apes, *sl*ed, *fr*og, *cl*ock, *st*ar, *bl*anket, *sn*ake, *st*ore, *pl*ow, *cl*own, *sw*ing, *sc*hool.
2. Prepare and duplicate a series of sentences which contain a number of blends. Have pupils underline each blend.
   A. The *bl*ack *cr*ow *fl*ew away *fr*om the *tr*ee.
   B. *Pr*etty *br*ight *fl*owers *gr*ew near the *br*idge.
   C. What is the *pr*ice of the *gr*een *dr*ess in the *st*ore window?
   D. We will re*st* when we rea*ch* the coa*st* about du*sk*.
3. Add one of the letters *c, g, p, t* in front of each word to produce a consonant blend. Underline the letters which blend.

__reat	__roud	__rain	__rop
__reek	__rail	__rice	__ruly
__rint	__reen	__row	__rize
__rip	__rack	__ree	__rand

Teaching Consonant Digraphs

A digraph is a combination of two letters which when pronounced results in one speech sound. This sound is neither a blend of the two letters nor the characteristic sound of either. Some digraphs have more than one sound (*ch* = *k* in character; *sh* in chiffon; *ch* in church). Techniques used in teaching consonants and blends and the illustration of teaching *ch* which follows will apply to teaching other digraphs.

Teaching the Sound of ch

1. Place words beginning with *ch* on the board.
2. Direct children's attention to these initial letters.
3. Pronounce each word, inviting pupils to *listen* to the sound of *ch* in each word.

Ch
chair
child
chance

4. In pronouncing, emphasize but do not distort the *ch* sound.
5. Have pupils pronounce words.
6. Ask class to provide other words which begin with the *ch* sound heard in *chair, child,* etc.

At a later time children will be taught that:

ch = k: *ch*orus, *ch*emistry, *ch*rome, *ch*aracter.
ch = *sh: ch*auffeur, *ch*amois, *ch*ef, *Ch*icago.
Other frequently met digraphs include *sh, wh, th, gh, ng, ph.* The sounds of these letter combinations are:
sh = Sound heard in *sh*oe, *sh*op, *sh*ell, *sh*ort, wi*sh,* fi*sh.*
wh = hw: when — hwen; wheel — hweel; which — hwich.
wh followed by *o,* the *w* is silent: whole — hole; whose — hooz; whom — hoom.
th = two sounds, voiced: them, there, they, with.
voiceless: thin, three, throw, cloth.
gh = sound of *f* in: laugh, tough, cough, etc.
silent in: night, bough, eight, thought, etc.
ng = sounded as in: sang, wing, song, rung.
ph = usually sounded as *f: ph*one, ne*ph*ew, gra*ph.*

TEACHING VOWEL SOUNDS

Phonic "Rules" Which Govern Vowel Sounds

Teaching vowel sounds is a challenge because vowel sounds in English spellings are represented by a most irrational conglomeration of letters. When an attempt is made to advance rules which cover all vowel situations, the resultant list is lengthy and contains numerous exceptions to the rules. Oaks (29) has analyzed the vowel situations occurring in the primer-through-third-grade materials in fourteen basal reader series. She presents eight principles that apply often enough in vowel situations to merit their being taught. In her study, the eight rules were applicable in only about 50 per cent of the total vowel situations.

A recent study by Clymer (11) tested the per cent of cases in which various rules or phonic generalizations actually applied in words met in four basal series (grades 1-3), plus the words on the Gates Primary Reading Vocabulary (not found in the basals). Some twenty-six hundred words constituted the sample. Forty-five phonic generalizations were applied to these words to determine what per cent of the words followed the rule and what per cent were exceptions.

Clymer suggested that two criteria be met in order for a rule to be classified as useful. First, the situation covered by a rule must occur in a minimum of 20 words found in the twenty-six-hundred-word sample; second, the rule should apply in at least 75 per cent of the cases it was designed to cover. Of the forty-five phonic generalizations studied in the study, twenty-three covered vowel situations. Only five of this number met the criteria stated above. Ten vowel rules applied in less than 50 per cent of the cases; seven rules applied more than 50 per cent (but in fewer than 3 out of 4 instances); and one rule-situation occurred in only ten words in the entire sample.

Burrows and Lourie (9) report an intensive study of the frequency with which one widely taught vowel rule applied to the five thousand highest frequency words on the Rinsland List. The rule under discussion states, "when there are two adjacent vowels in a word, the first usually has its long sound and the second is silent." Children are often taught this rule as, "when two vowels go walking, the first does the talking." In the five-thousand-word sample a total of 1,728 words met the two-vowel criterion. However, only 628 (approximately 40 per cent) followed the rule.

Data from these and other studies, regardless of word samples or the precise criteria used for arriving at the utility of phonic rules, show a marked agreement that vowel rules have limited efficacy for sounding out English words. It is not suggested here that no rules be taught but rather that one keep in mind the limitations of vowel rules. The implication is strong that children should not be taught to *overrely* on rules; and that many rules which have very limited application need not be taught.

Leading the child to see relationships between letters-and-sounds is an absolute essential. The purpose and function of the teacher and school are to provide guidance, and most children gain proficiency in phonic analysis more quickly and more surely with guidance that leads to insights. To require rote memorization of a great number of rules will hinder some children in understanding the relationship between the rule and their reading. They may become so involved with learning the rules that they miss the application. On the other hand, having a generalization verbalized is often a big help to learning.

Sequence of Teaching Vowel Sounds

Some authorities suggest that the long sounds of vowels be taught first, since the long sound is the name of the vowel. Others suggest that beginning with the short sound is the most logical, since the majority of words learned thus far have the short sound, particularly the smaller, one-vowel words. Another suggestion is to teach both the long and short sound of a vowel together, since the child can compare and contrast these sounds in words he has already learned. Suggestions vary as to the order in which the vowel sounds are to be introduced. When teachers have a clear concept of the aims of phonic instruction, it is doubtful that practices involving the variables just mentioned would of themselves materially influence reading achievement as it is measured at the end of the third or fourth grade.

When teaching vowel sounds, a teacher should follow the same pattern as in each preceding step in phonic analysis — moving one short step from what is already known to what is unknown. The child knows a number of words having the short sounds of vowels, and some having the long sounds. At this point the objective is to focus on these sounds, causing the child to notice the vowel symbol and hear its various sounds. Using the vowel *a*, illustrations of teaching the long sound of vowels, short sound of vowels, and vowels followed by *r* and *l* are given here.

First, attention is directed to the vowel *a* in words which the children know as sight words. A column of words containing the long sound of *a* as the initial letter is placed on the chalkboard (Figure 29, column A). Children are asked to say each word and listen to the sound of the *a* in these words. The teacher explains that the vowel "saying its name" is called the long sound, and long vowels are marked *ā*. The class is now asked to supply other words which begin with the long sound of *a* as heard in *age*, *able*, and *ape*. Probably not many words of this kind will be suggested. The teacher can then emphasize that most words learned so far have the short sound.

Another column of words beginning with the short sound of *a* can be placed on the board (Figure 29, column B). As the words are pronounced, the children listen in order to distinguish between the short and long sounds. Next, known sight words containing the vowel in medial position are put on the board and children are asked to tell which sound of *a* they hear (Figure 29, column C).

FIGURE 29

Teaching long and short initial vowels; short vowels in medial position.

A	B	C
āble	ăndd	hăd
āge	ăct	căn
āid	ăpple	flăg
āgent	ăsk	băck
āpe	ăt	lămp
ācorn	ădd	măn
ā	ăny	măd
āte	ăbsent	cămp
Āpril	ăm	căp
āim	ăbout	hăt

Pupils are now invited to give other words which contain only the single vowel *a* in the middle of the word. Many such words can be suggested (*had, cap, bag, sand, pack, rat, plan, dad, flag, has, bad, cat, fast, hand, sack, mad, fat, than, sad, band,* etc.). At this point a rule can be stressed:

"One vowel in the middle of a word (or syllable) *usually* has its short sound."

The Effect of the Final e

To teach the effect of the final *e* on vowel sounds, the words *name, came, take, made, grade, place, gave, make, game, hate,* and *cane* may be placed on the board. All of them contain the vowel *a* in medial position, have a final *e,* and should have been learned previously as sight words. Children say the words and listen to the sound of *a* in each word. The fact is stressed that in each word the long sound of *a* is heard. Pupils are then led to observe that each word ends with the vowel *e,* but that the final *e* is not sounded when the word is pronounced. The rule is then stated: "In short words containing final *e,* the *e* is silent, and the previous vowel usually has its long sound."

A concrete method of illustrating the role of the final *e* is to use words having the short vowel sound and which (upon addition of final *e*) become different words now having the long vowel sound.

hat	*hate*	*hop*	*hope*
mad	*made*	*not*	*note*
can	*cane*	*rob*	*robe*
rid	*ride*	*cut*	*cute*
fin	*fine*	*hug*	*huge*
hid	*hide*	*tub*	*tube*

Some words will be suggested by the children that do not follow the rule (*love, come, give, some*). These words can be used as a means of pointing out that there are some words that are exceptions.

Long Vowel Sounds at the Ends of Words

Children will have learned a number of sight words containing a single vowel at the end of the word. In such cases the vowel sound is usually long (*go, me, my, so, no*). Vowels which end syllables are usually sounded long (*ti* ger, *mo* tel, *fa* tal, *to* tal); the generalization to be taught is, "A vowel at the end of a one-vowel word or syllable usually has the long sound." Final *y* at the end of a word containing no other vowel has the long sound of *i* (*my, dry, cry, try, why, by, fly*). This principle can be taught either in conjunction with long vowel sounds at the ends of words, or when dealing with the long and short sounds of the vowel *i*.

Adjacent Vowels

When two vowels come together and stand for a single sound, they are referred to as vowel digraphs. When two adjacent vowels are both sounded in the same syllable, they are called diphthongs. The most widely advocated generalization to cover vowel digraphs is: When two vowels come together the first is usually long and the second is silent. When this rule is applied to all two-vowel situations, there are about as many exceptions as instances when it applies. Clymer (11) found this rule as stated above to apply in 45 per cent of his word sample but for specific vowel situations it will hold more frequently, for instance, *ee* (87 words) 98 per cent; *oa* (35 words) 97 per cent; *ea* (152 words) 66 per cent; *ai* (67 words) 64 per cent.

Contrasting Single-Double Vowel Situations

Pupils can be reminded that the vowel sound is usually short in one-vowel words where the vowel does not end the word. Figure 30 shows a column of familiar sight words which follow this rule.

FIGURE 30

A single vowel with a short sound.	Two vowels together. First is sounded long; second is silent.
cot	coat
mad	maid
lid	lied
men	mean
fed	feed
set	seat
got	goat
met	meet
did	died
pan	pain

In the second column a vowel is inserted in each word, making a new word containing two adjacent vowels. The first vowel has the long sound and the second is silent. Lest the child over-generalize from this rule, the instances where it does not apply should be reviewed. This would include the vowel digraphs *au, eu, aw, ew, oo,* where two vowels result in a single sound but not the long sound of the first vowel. For example:

au: haul, cause, haunt, caught
eu: feud, neutral, deuce, neutron
aw: lawn, hawk, draw, trawler
o͞o: goose, tooth, spoon, broom
o͝o: good, took, look, wood

Diphthongs are two adjacent vowels, each of which is sounded, as the *ou* in *house, oi* in *oil, oy* in *boy, ow* in *how* (but not the *ow* in *blow, grow, throw,* or *sow,* where the sound is long *o*). It is doubtful that teaching diphthongs is of major importance in the total phonics program. These sounds are met in a number of words that are learned as sight words, and certain of these words can serve as key words to help the pupil hear the sound (h*ou*se, *oi*l, b*oy*, h*ow*).

Vowels Affected by Particular Consonants

The long and short vowel sounds are by far the most important vowel clues in helping children unlock the pronunciation of words.

In addition, there are other vowel situations which should be explained, even though they may be of lesser importance in phonic analysis. When a vowel is followed by *r*, the sound of that vowel is affected by the *r*. Usually a blend results, which is neither the long nor the short sound of the vowel (*car, curl, fir, for, park*). When the vowel *a* is followed by *l* or *w*, the resultant sound is a blend (*awl, tall, awful, talcum, awning, ball*). These particular instances of vowel controllers are of minor importance.

SUMMARY OF RULES RELATED TO VOWEL SOUNDS

1. Long vowel sounds are usually identified as the names of the vowel letters *a, e, i, o, u.*
2. A single vowel followed by a consonant in a word or syllable usually has the short sound: *can* in *cancel.*
3. A single vowel which concludes a word or syllable usually has the long sound (*me, ti ger, lo co mo tive*).
4. In the vowel digraphs *oa, ea, ee, ai, ay,* the first vowel is usually long and the second is silent (*coat, reap, lead, wait, play*). The digraphs *oo, au,* and *ew* form a single sound which is not the long sound of the first vowel (*food, good, haul, few*).
5. In words containing two vowels, one of which is final *e*, the final *e* is usually silent and the preceding vowel is long.
6. Single vowels followed by *r* usually result in a blend sound (*fir, car, burn, fur*). The vowel *a* followed by *l* or *w* usually results in a blend sound (*awl, tall, claw, awful*).
7. The letter *y* at the end of words containing no other vowel has the long sound of *i* (*my, try, sky, shy*).
8. Diphthongs are two-vowel combinations in which both vowels contribute to the speech sound (h*ou*se, b*oy*, c*ow*).

SYLLABICATION

A syllable is a vowel, or group of letters containing a vowel, which is pronounced as a unit. A child must be able to break unknown polysyllabic words into syllables if he is to approximate the pronunciation of these words. This ability grows out of knowing both the structural and the phonetic features of words.

Structural analysis involves a deliberate attempt to see and recognize familiar units or parts of a word such as prefixes, endings, and root words: *re* read *ing*, *pre* heat *ed*, *bi* week *ly*, *un* wholesome *ness*, *dis* appear *ance*. Children should learn to recognize those word beginnings and endings, which are usually pronounced as units: *bi, re, dis, pre, in; ly, ness, ing, tion, ment, ful, tive, less* and others.

A knowledge of vowel behavior within words is the second major aid in breaking words into syllables. The sounds of vowels and letter combinations are not as consistent as prefixes and suffixes. Nevertheless, many phonetic generalizations are useful. Although the following examples are not words, the letter combinations can be broken into syllables: *comration, ragmotex, obsebong, fasnotel.* The likely syllabication is: *com•ra•tion, rag•mo•tex, ob•se•bong, fas•no•tel.* Most facile readers would pronounce these nonsense words in substantially the same way. These readers probably would not recite rules to themselves before attempting to pronounce the above words, but they would probably be subconsciously influenced by rules they had learned.

When generalizations applicable to syllabication are taught, children should be provided with a number of examples and then led to see for themselves what happens. Out of this experience rules can develop. Starting with the question, "What usually happens when two consonants come between vowels?" the teacher can place on the board a number of words such as:

af ter	win dow	rab bit	let ter
gar den	can dy	din ner	sum mer
fas ter	pen cil	lit tle	cot ton

The generalization will then emerge that "when two consonants come between vowels the syllable division comes between the consonants" or "one consonant goes with each vowel." It should be pointed out that this rule will not always hold, but that it is the best guess to make when trying to pronounce an unknown word. In the case of double consonants (le*tt*er, su*mm*er), there are few exceptions to the rule.

To teach what happens when one consonant comes between two vowels, a list of known sight words may be placed on the board:

be gin	fe ver	to tal	de cide
o ver	di rect	ti ger	me ter
fa tal	mo ment	pu pil	ho tel

From these examples children will both see and hear that "the single consonant goes with the following syllable." They will also note that when "the syllable is a vowel or ends with a vowel, it usually has the long sound." These two generalizations should be taught together because they work together. In cases where the first of two vowels separated by a single consonant has its short sound, the single intervening consonant closes the first syllable (*cam el, mag a zine*).

A few generalizations about common word endings as they relate to syllabication might be taught. Children have had experience with prefixes and suffixes and may follow these rules even though they are not able to verbalize them.

1. Common endings which begin with a vowel such as *ing*, *est*, or *er* are usually sounded as syllables (look *ing*, long *er*, long *est*). This is not true of *ed* except when preceded by *t* or *d* (wanted, needed).
2. Most one-syllable words remain intact as syllables when endings are added. In many instances this violates the "divide between consonants" rule stated earlier. This is not a problem to children if they have learned to see prefixes and suffixes as units. Examples might include spell *ing*, want *ed*, tell *ing* (not spel *ling*, wan *ted*, tel *ling*).
3. Certain letter combinations, when found at the ends of words, are rarely divided and thus stand as the final syllable.

un *cle*	fa *ble*	bu *gle*	sad *dle*	an *kle*
cir *cle*	tum *ble*	sin *gle*	can *dle*	spar *kle*
bicy *cle*	mar *ble*	ea *gle*	nee *dle*	wrin *kle*
mus *cle*	dou *ble*	strug *gle*	bun *dle*	twin *kle*

sam *ple*	gen *tle*	puz *zle*
tem *ple*	rat *tle*	daz *zle*
sim *ple*	whis *tle*	muz *zle*
pur *ple*	ti *tle*	

The generalizations are:

1. The letter combinations *cle, ble, gle, dle, zle, kle, ple, tle* at the end of words usually stand as the final syllable.
2. The final *e* is silent, and the sound contains the *l* blended.
3. This final syllable is not accented.

ACCENT

Certain words in sentences receive more stress than others, and this is also true of syllables in polysyllabic words. The child as he learns his native language masters the stress and intonation patterns of sentences and longer words. To say that a child knows the pronunciation of a word implies that he knows its pattern of stress in normal speech. However, when one is attempting to sound out a word not known as a sight word, determining the syllables stress is important.

Teaching accent is usually one of the later steps in phonic analysis primarily because the learner must be at a stage of development where he can use a dictionary and note primary and secondary accent marks. Memorization of a set of rules to apply in determining accent is probably not desirable since there are numerous exceptions to most of such rules. However, structuring learning situations in which the child is invited to make observations and note certain "pronunciation clues" is undoubtedly defensible. To facilitate such learnings, one might provide brief lists of words and have the child or class mark the accent and then state an observation which applies to the group of words. Several illustrations follow.

1. *Two-syllable words*

dentist	den′ tist	anvil	an′ vil
barley	bar′ ley	wisdom	wis′ dom
wizard	wiz′ ard	column	col′ umn
journal	jour′ nal	local	lo′ cal
symbol	sym′ bol	tailor	tai′ lor

Observation: In two-syllable words the first syllable is usually accented. Present following new data:

appoint	ap point′	parade	pa rade′
subdue	sub due′	complain	com plain′
receive	re ceive′	reveal	re veal′
proceed	pro ceed′	astound	a stound′

Modify observation: In two-syllable words the first syllable is usually accented *unless* the second syllable contains two vowels, in which case it is usually accented.

2. *Compound words*

evergreen (ever′ green)	underdog (un′ der dog)
newscast (news′ cast)	makeshift (make′ shift)
shoehorn (shoe′ horn)	passport (pass′ port)
censorship (cen′ sor ship)	drawbridge (draw′ bridge)
waterfall (wa′ ter fall)	

Observation: Three-syllable words are usually accented on the or within the first word.

3. *Three syllable words*

an′ ces tor	sta′ di um	syl′ la ble
cap′ i tal	fan tas′ tik	ho ri′ zon
sat′ el lite	pa′ tri ot	in′ ci dent
in dig′ nant	col′ o ny	chem′ is try
fi na′ le	bat tal′ ion	al′ ma nac

Observation: Three-syllable words are usually accented on the first or second syllable.

4. *Words containing primary and secondary accent*

con′ den sa′ tion	su′ per sti′ tions
op′ po si′ tion	ad′ van ta′ geous
sep′ a ra′ tion	in′ ter mis′ sion
sen′ ti men′ tal	mi cro scop′ ic

Observations: (a) Words of four or more syllables have a primary and secondary accent.
(b) The primary accent usually falls on the syllable preceding suffixes such as *tion, ous, al, ic, sion.*

5. *Shift in accent*

sep′ a rate ⟶ sep a ra′ tion
re spon′ si ble ⟶ re spon si bil′ i ty
sen′ ti ment ⟶ sen ti men′ tal ⟶ sen ti men tal′ i ty

Observation: Primary accent often shifts in derived forms of root words (adding suffixes).

CONCLUSION AND YOUR POINT OF VIEW?

Space limitations prohibit a thorough discussion of all of the educational issues involved in phonics instruction. Therefore, as a conclusion to this chapter a number of questions will be posed, followed by brief answers which do not cite research findings. In some instances these questions and answers may serve as a stimulus for further discussion and library research.

1. In learning to read, how important are phonic (letter-sound analyses) skills? The child learning to read English writing *must* learn to associate printed letters with speech sounds. One cannot become an independent reader without this skill. It follows that if a cluster of skills are this important, they should be well taught.

2. What is the purpose of phonics instruction as it relates to learning to read? Applying phonic skills permits the reader to "work out" the pronunciation or the approximate pronunciation of printed words NOT known as sight words. The child is not learning "how to pronounce" the word in question, he is learning that a particular series of letters represents a particular word which is part of his speaking vocabulary.

3. Should children be taught to learn words-as-wholes (sight words)? All facile readers at *every* grade level recognize words as wholes and their stock of sight words is constantly enlarged month by month and year by year.

4. Is it possible to teach children to overrely on phonic analysis? It is possible to teach children to overrely on any word recognition technique (sight words, context, letter analysis). Learning to read involves the *simultaneous* application of all of these approaches; each is part of a unitary process called *reading*. When children overrely on phonics analysis, they have a "set" to sound out each word (a habit which precludes getting meaning from larger language units). They sound out the same words many times, continuing to do so long after they should have learned the word as a unit. The child who sounds out every word in a story *is a seriously impaired reader.*

5. Does every child need the same amount of phonics instruction? Since the answer here is obviously no, the question is posed mainly to focus on phonic instructional materials which tend to ignore this issue. These types of materials suggest that lengthy periods of time

be devoted to phonics each day. All children perform the same tasks and in so doing many are subjected to much more than the optimum amount of such instruction.

6. What is the optimum amount of phonics instruction? The optimum is the minimum amount of phonics which permits the child to become an independent reader. On-going diagnosis provides the teacher with information as to what skills are needed.

7. What is the relationship between memorizing "phonic rules" and applying them in reading situations? It is likely that some children profit from familiarity with certain phonic generalizations. On the other hand, it is known that some children can memorize "rules" and yet be unable to apply them in reading situations. It is debatable whether children should be asked to memorize rules which have very limited application to words they will meet in reading.

Two For You!

1. Is the sequence in which phonic skills are taught of any significance?
2. Should beginning reading instruction stress that reading involves meaning? (see Chapter 8, "Linguistics and Reading.")

BIBLIOGRAPHY

1. Aaron, Ira E., "What Teachers and Prospective Teachers Know About Phonic Generalizations," *Journal of Educational Research,* 53 (May 1960), 323-30.

2. Adams, Mary Lourita, "Teachers Instructional Needs in Teaching Reading," *Reading Teacher,* 17 (January 1964), 260-64.

3. Agnew, Donald C., *Effect of Varied Amounts of Phonic Training on Primary Reading.* Durham, N. C.: Duke University Press, 1939.

4. Bear, David E., "Two Methods of Teaching Phonics: A Longitudinal Study," *Elementary School Journal,* 64 (February 1964), 273-79.

5. Bliesmer, Emery P., and Betty H. Yarborough, "A Comparison of Ten Different Beginning Reading Programs In First Grade," *Phi Delta Kappan,* (June 1965), 500-504.

6. Bloomer, Richard H., "An Investigation of an Experimental First Grade Phonics Program," *Journal of Educational Research,* LIII (January 1960), 188-93.

7. Bond, Guy L., and Eva Bond Wagner, *Teaching the Child to Read* (2nd ed.). New York: The Macmillan Company, 1966, Chapter 8.

8. Brzeinski, Joseph E., "When Should Phonics Instruction Begin?" *Reading as an Intellectual Activity.* International Reading Association Proceedings 8, 1963, 228-32.

9. Burrows, Alvina Trent, and Zyra Lourie, "Two Vowels Go Walking," *Reading Teacher,* 17 (November 1963), 79-82.

10. Chall, Jeanne, Florence G. Roswell, and Susan Halm Blumenthall, "Auditory Blending Ability: A Factor in Success in Beginning Reading," *Reading Teacher,* 17 (November 1963), 113-18.

11. Clymer, Theodore, "The Utility of Phonic Generalizations in the Primary Grades," *Reading Teacher,* 16 (January 1963), 252-58.

12. Cordts, Anna D., "When Phonics is Functional," *Elementary English,* XXXX (November 1963), 748-50.

13. ———, *Phonics for the Reading Teacher.* New York: Holt, Rinehart & Winston, Inc., 1965.

14. Fry, Edward, "A Frequency Approach to Phonics," *Elementary English,* XXXXI (November 1964), 759-65.

15. Goodman, Kenneth S., "A Linguistic Study of Cues and Miscues in Reading," *Elementary English,* XXXXII (October 1965), 639-43.

16. Gray, William, *On Their Own in Reading* (rev. ed.). Chicago: Scott, Foresman & Company, 1960.

17. Gurren, Louise, and Ann Hughes, "Intensive Phonics vs. Gradual Phonics in Beginning Reading: A Review," *Journal of Educational Research,* 58 (April 1965), 339-46.

18. Haggard, J. Kendall, "Phonics in Directed Reading Activities," *Reading Teacher,* IX (December 1955), 90.

19. Hanson, Irene W., "First Grade Children Work with Variant Word Endings," *Reading Teacher,* 19 (April 1966), 505-7.

20. Heilman, Arthur W., *Phonics In Proper Perspective.* Columbus, Ohio: Charles E. Merrill Publishing Company, 1964.

21. Hildreth, Gertrude, "Reading Methods for the English Language," *Reading Teacher,* 15 (November 1961), 75-80.

22. Hunt, Lyman, "The Right Questions About Phonics," *Education,* 82 (May 1962), 540-44.

23. King, Ethel M., and Siegmar Muehl, "Different Sensory Cues as Aids in Beginning Reading," *Reading Teacher,* 19 (December 1965), 163-68.

24. Levin, Harry, "Reading Research: What, Why and For Whom?" *Elementary English,* XXXXIII (February 1966), 138-47.

25. Lineham, E. B., "Early Instruction in Letter Names and Sounds as Related to Success in Beginning Reading," *Journal of Education,* CXL (February 1958), 44-48.

26. Marchbanks, Gabrielle, and Harry Levin, "Cues by Which Children Recognize Words," *Journal of Educational Psychology,* 56 (April 1965), 57-61.

27. Mason, George E., "The Role of Phonics in the First Grade Program," *Challenge and Experiment In Reading.* International Reading Association Proceedings 7, 1962, 27-29.

28. McCollum, John A., "An Evaluation of the Carden Reading Program," *Elementary English,* XXXXI (October 1964), 600-12.

29. Oaks, Ruth E., "A Study of the Vowel Situations in a Primary Vocabulary," *Education,* LXXII (May 1952), 604-17.

30. Piekarz, Josephine A., "Common Sense About Phonics," *Reading Teacher,* 18 (November 1964), 114-17.

31. Ramsey, Z. Wallace, "Will Tomorrow's Teachers Know and Teach Phonics?" *Reading Teacher,* 15 (January 1962), 241-45.

32. Robinson, H. Alan, "A Study of the Techniques of Word Identification," *Reading Teacher,* 16 (January 1963), 238-42.

33. Rystrom, Richard, "Whole-word and Phonics Methods and Current Linguistic Findings," *Elementary English,* XXXXII (March 1965), 265-68.

34. Sabaroff, Rose, "Breaking The Code: What Method? Introducing an Integrated Linguistic Approach to Beginning Reading," *Elementary School Journal,* 67 (November 1966), 95-103.

35. Scott, Louise Binder, and J. J. Thompson, *Phonics.* Manchester, Mo.: Webster Publishing, 1962.

36. Smith, Carl Bernard, "The Double Vowel and Linguistic Research," *Reading Teacher,* 19 (April 1966), 512-14.

37. Spache, George D., and Mary E. Baggett, "What Do Teachers Know About Phonics and Syllabication?" *Reading Teacher,* 19 (November 1965), 96-99.

38. Staiger, Ralph C., "Agreements About Phonics," *Elementary English,* XXXXI (March 1964), 204-6.

39. Stone, Clarence R., "Questionable Trends in Beginning Reading," *Elementary School Journal,* 66 (January 1966), 214-22.

40. Stone, David R., "A Sound-Symbol Frequency Count," *Reading Teacher,* 19 (April 1966), 498-504.

41. Wardhaugh, Ronald, "Syl-lab-i-ca-tion," *Elementary English,* XLIII (November 1966), 785-88.

42. Weintraub, Samuel, "A Critique of a Review of Phonics Studies," *Elementary School Journal,* 67 (October 1966), 34-41.

Linda
Luke
Lois
pretend
jail
victim
arrest
lawyer
curtain
principle
dispute
midnight
burglar
scale
ladder
ridge
GEORGE CARVER
BOY SCIENTIST
by AUGUSTA STEVENSON
DRAWINGS by CLOTILDE EMBREE FUNK
DAVY CROCKETT
Rifleman
Boy Minstrel

The Intermediate Grades

10

The intermediate grades constitute one of the crucial instructional periods in the child's education. The curriculum for this period has developed out of a series of adult concepts and theories as to what children *should* be learning. Theory, however, often does not take into account all aspects of the learning situation. As a result some goals and classroom practices of the school fit children as we wish them to be, rather than as they actually are.

Instruction is sometimes characterized by confusion. This becomes apparent as we examine the relationship of reading instruction to the total school curriculum — practically all of which is based on reading ability. An illustration of this confusion is the frequently met concept that the intermediate grades represent the point in the educational continuum where stress on the development of reading skills should ease off with students spending more of their time in an activity labeled "functional reading," that is, the "mining" of the various content areas such as health, arithmetic, science and geography. Unfortunately, this philosophy is put into practice in many schools. Whatever effort is focused on improving reading ability is done in classes devoted to "the reading of reading materials." When a bell rings, pupils move into other activities such as the *study* of science or geography. Prior to the bell they were "learning to read" — post-bell and for the rest of the day, they are "reading to learn." Philosophically, most teachers reject this dichotomy, but few schools could deny that existing classroom practices actually support it. Root (35), in discussing the teaching of skills *vs.* teaching literature, states, "Such a program is schizophrenic in nearly all of its dimensions."

LEARNING TO READ IS A LONG-TERM DEVELOPMENTAL PROCESS

The structure of American education is embedded in, and influenced by, the grade level system. The development of curricular materials for use in all grades is to some extent patterned on growth gradients in all subject areas. An underlying premise of the graded system is that students finishing a given grade have mastered the language skills and concepts that will prepare them for the developmental tasks of the next grade.

The theory is sound, but in actual practice the theory of the grade level structure is not adhered to. A large number of students in the intermediate grades have not mastered reading skills *commensurate with the tasks they will be asked to perform in these grades.* Another group of students may be fairly close to the expected growth level, but as months and years go by, they fail to *advance* in reading ability at a pace equal to the reading demands placed upon them.

The recognition of a problem is the first step in arriving at a solution. Unfortunately, the problem under consideration is so large and so complex that little progress has been made in alleviating it. Since there are no easy solutions, educators at various levels (elementary, junior high, secondary, and teacher training institutions) all live in the hope that some other group than themselves will tackle the problem and evolve a solution.

The statement of *how* we might solve the reading problem in our schools deceivingly makes the task seem simple: The solution would be: "we must systematically teach reading more effectively and more extensively than is our present practice." Achieving this goal, up to the present at least, has escaped fulfillment. No teacher or educational administrator at any educational level argues against the importance of reading ability; however, many have not as yet become personally involved in helping to devise programs and guidance in the development of reading skills in all areas of the curriculum.

Undoubtedly, one of the causes of the reading problem is the failure of the teacher to understand the nature of the reading process. The purpose here is to discuss the developmental nature of reading. In recent years the statement, "Reading is a developmental process," has been repeated so often that it now runs the risk of becoming a cliché. This concept deserves more respect and attention than it has received. "Reading ability is a developmental process" means that the very complicated process of learning to read is not mastered at any particular time such as age ten or twelve. Nor can it be assumed that one's ultimate ability to read critically is achieved at any particular point on the educational continuum such as grade six, eight, or ten.

Thus, an adequate reader at grade three may be considerably less efficient at grade four and be in serious trouble by grade six. The statement implies recognition that the nature of human learning and the nature of the reading task precludes the possibility of mastering the reading process by a given chronological age or a designated number of years of formal schooling. The developmental aspect of various reading skills is discussed in the following section.

ILLUSTRATIONS OF GROWTH GRADIENTS IN READING

Any of the dozens of reading skills and habits could serve as examples of how growth must take place at higher levels of efficiency.* Reading is an integrated total response which is made up of a very large number of separate skills, abilities, memory patterns, and the like. Without attempting to determine how many separate skills go into reading, we can isolate a few and illustrate how each is developmental in nature.

---

*There are a few skills which might be considered exceptions. That is, once learned they need not be extended — learning to read from left to right; learning the function of punctuation and the like. However, it will be noted that these are few in number and relate purely to mechanical factors.

Acquisition of Sight Vocabulary

The development of a sight-word vocabulary is probably one of the more obvious examples of what is implied by the term "developmental process." Instant recognition of words is a basic skill which is a prerequisite for reading at any level. Although it is true that mere recognition of words is not reading, it must be remembered that the absence of this ability precludes reading. For example, the individual who has no sight-recognition vocabulary is not a reader. One who fails to recognize as few as 5 per cent of the words in a passage is handicapped; one who is stopped on 10 per cent is a seriously impaired reader. For these people, frustration is inevitable.

For practical purposes, the continuum representing the learning of sight words extends from the first word learned to infinity. Actually there is a limit of English words (about 600,000 words), but no reader has ever achieved the ultimate of instant recognition of all of these words. Wide or extensive reading in a variety of subject areas such as history, biology, sociology, chemistry, and literature will usually result in an expansion of both sight and meaning vocabularies.

Some indication of the growth gradient for developing sight vocabulary might be gained by a look at the sentences below. These examples were taken from a basal reader series, grades one through six. This material does not reflect the introduction of specialized vocabulary in the various content areas such as health, science, mathematics, geography, and the like.

Grade 1 "I will run and bring some water."

Grade 2 "I know where the field mouse lives down by the brook."

Grade 3 "The next night, when his father got home, Bob said, "I read that book about the other Bob."

Grade 4 "Sir," said the duck, who was trying to recover his dignity while hopping around on one foot—not an easy thing to do, "Sir, I am minding my own business and I suggest that you do the same."

Grade 5 The missile range was known as Station One, and when the men talked over the radio from there they would say, "This is Station One," or just, "This is One."

Grade 6 "We can be sure that the Trojans, on hearing this, will not risk bringing her wrath down upon themselves by destroying our offering."*

Word Analysis Skills

The beginning reader will probably learn some whole words such as *man, like,* or *hand* before he begins analyzing letter sounds. With these words serving as models, he will learn the sounds that the various letters contribute to the pronunciation of words: *M* in *m*an, *L* in *l*ike, *H* in *h*and. Later he will learn the sounds of vowels and vowel digraphs, and in the process certain generalizations which relate to vowel sounds will be learned:

> One vowel in medial position usually has its short sound (man, ship, drum, chop). The final e in two-vowel words is usually silent and the previous vowel has its long sound (*līke̸, lāke̸, cūte̸*).
> Two adjacent vowels (ee, oa, ea, ai) usually has the first sounded long and the second silent (kēe̸p, lōa̸d, drēa̸m, chāi̸n).
> When the only vowel in a word comes at the end of the word, it usually has its long sound (*gō, shē, crȳ*).

Soon the reader deals with inflectional endings (*s, ed, ing*) and a number of prefabricated language units called prefixes and suffixes. These latter are usually pronounceable units added to words which permit the formation of thousands of new or different words:

> like: *un* like, like *ly, dis* like, *un* like *ly hood.*
> heat: *pre* heat, *re* heat, heat *edly*, *re* heat *able.*

From first grade through high school, the reader will continue to meet root words which are combined to form compound words. From simple beginnings such as *anyone, upon, sailboat, flagpole, notebook,* the learner moves to new and more difficult terms such as *praiseworthy, homespun, foreshadow, headlong, flashback, floodgate, masterpiece.* The ability to break words into syllables and to arrive at the proper accent on syllables in polysyllabic words rounds out the developmental series of word-attack skills.

---

*David H. Russell et al., *The Ginn Readers* (Boston: Ginn and Company, 1961).

Expansion of Word Meanings and Concepts

Although language is a system of agreements as to what words mean, language is not static. Within limits, the meanings of words have been established by previous generations over a period of many centuries. Nevertheless, each individual who uses language, whether receptively or as a form of expression, participates in a potentially creative act. This is analogous to the 20th century artist using a chisel upon a block of marble. He did not invent the chisel, the hammer, or the art form of sculpture; yet what he does can be creative because the media is open-ended.

Language is both the raw material and the working capital of the learning process. Practically all of the subject matter taught in the school is presented to the potential learner by means of language. The learner in turn must "break the code" of written language and assimilate word meanings and concepts. In essence, the educational process consists of transmitting meaning from the knower (author, teacher, etc.) to the learner.

When children enter school, they are able to understand and use several thousand words in their speech. From the standpoint of intellectual growth, the single most important educational achievement from kindergarten through college post-graduate work is the progressive mastery of word meanings and the acquisition of concepts which are fixed by words. The acquisition of concepts is based primarily upon experiences with language. The process of mastering language is much the same for individuals within a given language or culture; yet the rate of acquisition and extent of mastery vary tremendously.

As stated above, word mastery depends heavily upon experience which, in turn, provides background knowledge for understanding abstract words and concepts. Within limits, "word meanings" can be arranged in order of ascending difficulty. When one attempts to make such an arrangement of words, he will note the developmental nature of "learning meaning vocabulary." The following lists of terms serve as examples of growth gradients for concepts in mathematics, social studies, and health:

Mathematics	*Geography*	*Health*
number	trees	germ
addition	forest	vaccination
plus	timberland	microbe
circle	lumbering	antiseptic

plane	pulpwood	fumigate
circumference	hardwoods	infection
angle	coast redwoods	disinfectant
perimeter	giant sequoias	microorganism
formula	timberline	immune
theorem	resources	inoculate

The fact that many words have a large number of connotations adds to the problem of developing a precise order of difficulty of words, or the order in which words should be introduced and taught. Thus, the word *rhinoceros*, while very concrete in meaning, might be considered more difficult than the word *heavy*—but only if one is discussing a particular and limited connotation for *heavy*.

A child may acquire *a* meaning for *heavy* (opposed to light in weight) before he acquires a concept for, or the ability to, pronounce the term *rhinoceros*. But once he has had the experience of seeing a rhinoceros, or even a picture of one, he will have established a workable concept. Nevertheless, he can learn many more details about this animal such as its average weight, height, habitat, feeding habits, agressiveness, and economic value.

The word *heavy* has dozens of connotations which range from fairly concrete to highly abstract.

They had a *heavy* load on the wagon.
The voters registered a *heavy* vote.
The guide led them through a *heavy* fog.
Meet the new light *heavy* weight champion.
Time hung *heavy* on his hands.
Their eyes became *heavy* with sleep.
He carried a *heavy* load through life.
The sad news made him *heavy*-hearted.
The actor complained, "I am always cast as the *heavy*."

Figurative Language. Some of the above usages are figurative expressions, a type of word usage that is a specific example of vocabulary, the mastery of which is developmental in nature. Children are exposed to figures of speech long before they begin their formal schooling. Seldom do they have trouble learning the meanings of often repeated phrases such as, *lost his temper, flew down the stairs, fast as lightning, grouchy as a bear,* and *heavy-hearted.*

Eventually the student will be exposed to, and may learn the definitions of, less familiar words such as hyperbole, simile, metaphor, and euphemism. As he moves upwards through the grades and reads widely, he will meet hundreds of figurative expressions whose meaning must be grasped in order to follow the author's thought.

Study Skills

The term study skills is applied to a wide array of reading abilities which students must continue to master on progressively higher levels.*
The first teaching of many of these skills is found in the primary grades. At this level the depth and degree to which they are taught are limited by the curricular materials the student uses.

The reading-study skills are usually classified under broad headings such as:

1. Location of Information
2. Interpretation and Evaluation of Material
3. Organization and Summarization
4. Retention of Pertinent Data
5. Flexibility and Rate of Reading

The four examples cited above (sight vocabulary, word analysis, word meanings, and study skills) represent rather broad classifications. Each could be broken down into a number of specific developmental skills such as syllabification, accent, diacritical marks, pronunciation keys, guide words, card catalogue, *Readers Guide*, and the like. The point is, a given reading skill is not taught once and for all or learned upon first presentation. The entire instructional program of the school is posited on pupils' growth in, and extension of, all skills. When systematic instruction is not provided, the inevitable result is that for some students a serious gap develops between reading ability and the demands of curricular materials.

GOALS OF INTERMEDIATE-LEVEL INSTRUCTION

In addition to working with the skills introduced in the primary grades, the intermediate-level teacher must provide guidance in a large number of even more complicated reading tasks. The applica-

---

*In this context we will deal only with the developmental nature of these skills as Chapter 12 is devoted to teaching the study skills.

tion of skills previously taught also becomes more complex. For instance, visual discrimination taught in beginning reading involves perception of structural differences between whole word symbols. In grade four the child must perceive minute differences within words in order to use a dictionary. Also, getting meaning from context was relatively simple in beginning reading since the connotation of an unknown sight word was undoubtedly in the child's meaning vocabulary. In addition, the unknown sight word was probably the only new word on the page. In the intermediate grades a paragraph in a social science text may contain a number of new and difficult concepts as well as several unknown sight words.

The following objectives, while perhaps not including every facet of instruction, do provide a fairly representative picture of the breadth of the reading program in the intermediate grades.

1. Individual evaluation should take place to determine the capacity of students and the present level of achievement in all facets of reading including:
   a. sight word vocabulary
   b. word-attack skills
   c. level of silent reading
   d. meaning vocabulary and concepts
   e. ability to profit from listening situations including oral directions
   f. oral reading skills
   g. facility in finding information, use of reference materials
   h. work habits and attitudes
   i. rate at which curricular materials can be read
2. Following diagnosis, the teacher should devise a flexible reading program to take care of individual differences and needs revealed in the initial diagnosis.
3. Reading instruction must be deliberate and systematic. Inestimable damage to children can result from the philosophy that "children learn to read in the primary grades and read to learn at the intermediate level." They must do both at each level.
4. In addition to specific reading instruction per se, instruction must also be incorporated with the teaching of all subject matter. Children must be *taught to read* science, mathematics, health, and social science materials. It is

not intended that reading instruction be seen or treated as dichotomous, but rather that items 3 and 4 be complementary parts of a total program.

5. The child should be helped to expand his stock of concepts. This is essential in all content areas.
6. Practice should be provided in various types of functional reading—in newspapers, magazines, and books—to supplement basic texts in subject areas.
7. Guidance should be supplied in reading for recreation, pleasure, and personal growth.
8. The child's reading interests should be widened to build a sound foundation for life-long personal reading activities.
9. Appreciation should be developed for good literature, poetry and drama.
10. A wide selection of materials should be made available in all fields—science, literature, biography, current events, social studies, and the like.
11. A program should be devised for guiding the growth of intellectually gifted children.
12. Children should be helped to increase the rate at which they can comprehend printed word symbols in combination. This skill becomes increasingly important at this instructional level since the curriculum materials in the various content areas make ever-widening demands on readers.
13. Steps should be taken to improve critical reading skills such as:
    a. Coping with figurative or picturesque language
    b. Drawing inferences
    c. Classifying ideas and selecting those that are germane to the reader's purpose
    d. Evaluating ideas and arriving at the author's purpose or intent
    e. Detecting bias and differentiating between fact and opinion
14. The following reading-study skills should be developed and extended:
    a. Using books effectively—making maximum use of the index, table of contents, and appendix
    b. Acquiring facility in the use of a dictionary
    c. Using reference books effectively

d. Understanding graphs, maps, charts, and tables
e. Using library resources, card catalogue, and periodical indexes
f. Note-taking and outlining materials for a given purpose

15. Diagnosis should be continuous and ongoing throughout each instructional year. An initial diagnosis serves only for initial procedures.

SYSTEMATIC READING INSTRUCTION

The objectives listed above are illustrative of the broad reading program in the intermediate grades which has as its over-all goal the continuous growth of the child. Before such a wide array of goals can be achieved, all instructional activities must be well-planned and systematically carried out. There are several ways in which a given objective can be achieved, but regardless of a teacher's preference for particular techniques she must make certain that no important reading skill is slighted or ignored. Reading instruction in the intermediate grades should consist of the proper combination of:

1. Review or re-teaching of essential skills introduced at the primary level for those pupils who may not have mastered them there.
2. Introduction and systematic teaching of new reading skills characteristically emphasized in the intermediate grades.

A Period for Reading Instruction

A definite reading-instruction period should be incorporated into the program of the intermediate grades. Incidental teaching of reading in the subject areas, which is commendable in itself, will leave many children with inadequate instruction in fundamental reading skills. Using basic readers and the workbooks which are included in basal programs will assure systematic instruction in all skills and prevent serious instructional gaps which might occur in incidental teaching. A definite reading period does not imply that all pupils will be receiving the same instruction. As pointed out above, this practice is unjustifiably wasteful. Certainly in the use of workbooks, good readers will not need all types of drill included, and the poorer readers will need teacher guidance in this work, not merely the assignment of pages.

While the teacher works with a group of pupils who need review on word-attack skills, more advanced readers can be reading independently from supplementary sources. This reading can be influential in extending reading horizons and developing new reading interests. During some reading periods the teacher can work with the advanced group stressing appreciation or critical analysis of a poem or story while the skills group works independently on teacher-made or workbook skill-building exercises. At other times the teacher may not work with any particular group but will give hints on individual help. There will be some situations where instruction can involve the entire class. For example, the teacher may deal with the entire class when giving instruction in the use of the dictionary, in group planning of a unit, in word meaning sessions, when reading to the group, or when giving instruction in how to find materials. These instances of class-wide instruction would undoubtedly be followed by grouping techniques based on pupils' present achievement and individual needs.

Skills in Word-Attack

Word-attack skills must be both reviewed and extended in the intermediate grades. The specific tasks to be dealt with include all those which have been discussed at the beginning and primary levels. Since instruction in these tasks has taken place in previous grades, one of the real dangers at the intermediate level is the assumption that pupils are proficient in these skills. As a matter of fact many pupils will need review or reteaching of word-attack skills. Since it would be wasteful to teach these to the entire class, such instruction should take place on an individual or small group basis determined by pupil needs.

Experience indicates that lack of ability in phonic analysis will be a major stumbling block for many pupils at this level. Since most of the emphasis on teaching phonics falls in the primary grades, the curricular materials at the intermediate level may not contain enough practice for those pupils who are markedly deficient in this skill. Pupils in this category will have a variety of problems. Thus, to help all such individuals the teacher at the intermediate level should be familiar with the entire phonics program. So that the teacher may see the continuity of the total phonics program, Chapter 9 is devoted to this topic.

Prefixes and suffixes should be dealt with extensively at the intermediate level from the standpoint of both structural and meaning changes produced. (13) There is, of course, no limit to the prefixes or suffixes which should be taught at this level. The following prefixes should not be neglected: *dis, de, ex, in, ab, pre, re, sub, un, co, trans, in, be, con, mis, auto, al, semi, en.* Suffixes: *ment, tion, able, ous, ly, er, ful, ward, less, or, en, ence, ness, est, ible, ing, ist, ably, age, ed, ance.*

Syllabication is a dictionary skill which should be stressed in the intermediate grades. Breaking words into syllables is of considerable aid to the child in arriving at the pronunciation of words in reading and is also a real aid in spelling. Practice in breaking words into syllables is most helpful as a remedial technique (see Chapter 16).

Reading Instruction in Content Areas

It has been pointed out that the curriculum materials for the intermediate grades place major emphasis on the teaching of subject-matter content. At the same time the available data show conclusively that a great number of pupils at the intermediate level cannot cope with the content materials at their grade level because they lack the necessary reading skills. Thus, in the intermediate grades there is danger of a too literal acceptance of the old dictum that "a pupil learns to read by reading" or "nothing improves one's reading like more and more reading." This is true for readers who have mastered the necessary reading skills, but there is a fallacy in these statements when applied to any child who is deficient in reading skills. The more reading a pupil with poor reading habits does, the more he reinforces his poor habits. Reading with instruction and guidance aimed at improvement is the key. Learning in all content areas, from this point on in the grades, depends primarily on reading skill. The facts taught in science, geography, history, and mathematics are important, but the school's basic task is to teach each child the reading skills which will enable him to read independently in any of these content areas. Since many children still need instruction in reading skills, any reduction of emphasis on this facet of reading is a serious omission.

Spache (40) suggests a two-way reading program for the intermediate grades in which average and superior readers move rapidly through basal materials while reading instruction also is incorporated into the content areas. The nature of basal instructional materials precludes their being a total reading program. As a rule, author and publishers of basals point this out. While this is not a weakness of basals, any teacher or school which equates *reading instruction* with *basal instruction* inevitably ignores pupil needs in the content areas. Integrating reading and subject-learning is discussed more fully later in this chapter.

Reading skills advance learning in all content areas. For instance, reading about the world can be visually expressed and provides stimulation for further study. (Courtesy Cincinnati Public Schools.)

INSTRUCTIONAL PROBLEMS AT THE INTERMEDIATE LEVEL

The intermediate grades present a formidable challenge to the teacher of reading. The pitfalls are as numerous and as serious as those found at any instructional level. The most important challenge is achieving the proper balance between systematic instruction in reading and instruction in the subject areas of the curriculum. Academic failures and loss of interest in school occur in the intermediate grades because school practices, curricular materials, and educational goals tend to accentuate reading instruction problems.

A Transition Period

Teachers agree that ideally the process of learning to read progresses smoothly without perceptible breaks through a series of grade levels. There are certain factors in the total school framework, however, which cause many teachers to feel that an abrupt transition occurs between third and fourth grades. The end of the third grade and the beginning of the fourth is often designated as the period of "independent reading." There is evidence in classroom behaviors that some teachers do succumb to the philosophy that the intermediate grades should be characterized by a shift in emphasis from "learning to read" to "reading to learn" in the various subject-matter areas. The use of a number of non-integrated textbooks in various content areas tends to substantiate the idea that this is a transitional period.

These factors form the basis for the generalization that reading skills are taught in the primary grades and applied in the intermediate and later grades. A further generalization is that since reading skills are taught in the primary grades, children who have been through these grades have mastered the skills. It is true that once pupils reach the intermediate level they are expected to do more reading grade by grade while less time is devoted to the actual process of learning to read. A study of the relationship between reading ability and a language-factor intelligence test at all grade levels indicated, however, that the correlation between these measures was lowest at grade four. The authors posited a "fourth grade hump in reading" which may be accounted for by the increased difficulty of concepts, style of writing, and specialized vocabulary found in reading materials at this level. A second hypothesis was that this finding might reflect a decline in the systematic teaching of reading at the fourth grade level. (31)

Every instructional level in the school presents its own unique challenges to teachers. Undoubtedly it is not intentional that the intermediate grades constitute a break in the continuity of instruction in the elementary school. Nevertheless, the emphasis on separate textbooks in the various subject areas is one of the chief sources of instructional problems. These books call for a fairly high level of independent reading ability and special facility in a number of reading-study skills such as the ability to use the dictionary, reference materials, graphs, charts, and tables.

These curricular materials confront the reader with an ever-increasing number of unknown and relatively difficult concepts. (8) In addition, much more complex sentence structure and a variety of organizational patterns are found which frustrate many pupils. It is necessary to know many new and more difficult connotations for words met previously and to understand a large number of idiomatic and figurative expressions. The amount of reading which is required is suddenly increased, and pupils must develop the ability to read and comprehend at a more rapid rate. They must also develop flexibility in their reading to be able to adjust rate to both difficulty level and purpose. Instructional procedures for coping with these and other problems are discussed in the remainder of this chapter.

Variability Among Pupils

Individual differences in reading ability tend to increase with reading instruction. A given group of pupils will show greater individual differences at the end of four years of schooling than they did at the end of the first year. Good teaching aims at moving every child along at his maximum rate. The gifted child will move further in a given period of time than will the average child. Thus, the better the teaching, the greater will be the differences between children. By the time a group of children reach the intermediate grades, they are strung out over a considerable range of reading ability. Although different facets of the reading program receive varying degrees of emphasis at different grade levels, in the intermediate grades the emphasis almost has to be on what the individual child needs regardless of what is found in the curriculum guide of a particular grade. The need for individualized instruction in the intermediate grades grows out of the wide range of abilities found in children and their equally wide range of instructional needs.

Importance of Diagnosis. Diagnosis is essential to a successful reading program at the intermediate level. Principles of teaching reading do not vary with grade level or with the materials being used. The variability of pupils in the intermediate grades makes a number of principles, discussed previously, particularly appropriate to this period: (a) no child should be expected to deal with materials he cannot read; (b) instruction must be at the learner's present level; (c) a thorough diagnosis will single out the pupils needing special instruction and indicate the skills in which the student is deficient; (d) once weaknesses are discovered, instruction must be fitted to individual needs.

An illustration of the importance of following sound principles of instruction is provided by the pupil who has failed to master phonic-analysis skills. Experienced teachers know how unlikely it is that he will simply outgrow his inadequacy. The fact that the child has come this far without developing insights and techniques for overcoming his problem is in itself evidence that he is not likely to do so in the absence of skillful guidance and teaching. If a child has not developed the ability to hear the differences between the first syllables of words such as *dim*ple, *dem*onstrate, *dum*found, *dom*inoes, *dam*sel; or *mar*ble, *mor*tal, *mur*mur, *mer*cy, *mir*acle, it is useless to attempt to teach him a number of rules regarding short vowels, long vowels, or vowels followed by varying numbers of consonants. The child must be taught to make auditory discriminations, and the fact that this is ordinarily taught in first grade does not alter the fact that in this case it will have to be done now. Until the inability to discriminate between speech sounds is overcome, the student can make little real progress in gaining independence in sounding. The principle of going back to where the child is applies to every learning step in phonic analysis, such as learning initial consonant sounds, learning substitution of initial sounds, recognizing blends, distinguishing between long and short vowel sounds, and understanding syllabication.

Standardized tests and teacher-made informal reading tests appropriate for all of the elementary grades have been discussed in detail in Chapter 6. The reader may wish to refer to this discussion found on pages 181-193. A commendable practice in the intermediate grades is the use of teacher-prepared comprehension questions over the various subject materials covered. Such tests can serve two purposes. They are diagnostic from the teacher's standpoint, and they can provide excellent guidance for the reader. To devise tests which serve both these purposes is difficult and time-consuming. As a result, many attempts at preparing such tests tend to isolate facts and details. In this connection, it should be remembered that the pupil at the intermediate level needs practice in evaluating ideas, seeing relationships, and drawing inferences.

Differentiation of Instruction

Grouping pupils for instructional purposes is essential in the intermediate grades if the teacher is to deal successfully with the needs of all pupils. The philosophy and aims of intraclass grouping have been discussed in Chapter 5 and will not be repeated here. However, the range of reading ability among pupils at this level and the great variety of reading materials available make possible a number of grouping practices which can be used effectively. Highly structured groups become less practical in the intermediate grades. Yet all the virtues of grouping can be achieved if a variety of tasks at varying levels of difficulty are devised for use in a given classroom.

While a majority of the pupils in a social science class may profitably use the assigned textbook, there are numerous other materials available at all levels of difficulty. Some of these lend themselves to use by the entire class; other materials and tasks will be more appropriate for either accelerated or impaired readers.

1. A film may be shown to the entire class.
2. Pictures which illustrate a particular concept appropriate to the topic can be gathered and placed on the bulletin board. Perhaps this project can be carried out by some of the less competent readers.
3. A special vocabulary lesson can be worked out using new terms children are likely to meet in their reading.
4. Each child can also make his own "new word list" which grows out of his reading on the topic.
5. Newspaper and magazine articles may be read by some pupils in the class.
6. Models, charts, or other illustrations which clarify some facet of the project may be prepared and displayed. With some guidance from the teacher, this task may be made quite appealing to poorer readers.
7. Better readers may report to the class on material found in reference or other books.

In teaching or reviewing certain reading skills, the teacher can use many procedures parallel to those used at the primary level. Many pupils are now independent readers, and they can, if materials are available, do profitable supplementary reading while the teacher stresses the mechanics of reading with a group of less competent readers. At other times poorer readers can work independently on skill-building exercises while the teacher checks the progress of, and gives suggestions to, the group of advanced readers.

Individualized Reading. Discussed in Chapter 11 as a *method,* individualized reading might be mentioned here as an extension of traditional grouping practices. An individualized program can help teachers cope with pupil variability. The wider the range of abilities and the wider the range of pupil needs in reading, the more apparent it becomes that three or four reading groups will not be adequate to meet the needs of all pupils in a given classroom. Some pupils will not fit logically into any one of these groups. It is an educational paradox that as pupil abilities within the classroom become more diverse, the textbook approach becomes more widely used and the basic curricular materials become more rigid and inflexible. The aim of individualized reading is to have each child read the materials he is capable of reading and in which he is interested. When these two requirements are met, reading is likely to become purposeful and profitable. An individual reading program can be initiated at any grade level.

The unit approach discussed later in this chapter depends to a high degree on individualized reading even among children working in the same group or on the same facet of a given project. Independent readers must be permitted to read on their own and to pursue their immediate interests. Average readers may work alone or in small groups according to the nature of the project. Pupils with special problems may be worked with individually. Only good teaching and sound administrative practices can make it possible to meet the varied needs of all pupils.

DEVELOPING CONCEPTS

In an earlier chapter it was pointed out that because of the rigid control of vocabulary in beginning reading materials, teachers had a special problem of arousing and maintaining interest in these materials. Children's concepts and experiences extended far beyond this basal reader material. By the time the intermediate level is reached, the teacher's problem has traveled full circle. Difficult words and concepts are introduced in the content textbooks in such profusion that many pupils are frustrated and, in a sense, lost.

Meaningful reading at the intermediate level depends on the acquisition and continual extension of concepts. Here, pupils are confronted with more difficulties per reading unit than they met in their primary reading. One of the major reading problems is coping with the gap which tends to develop between the child's store of meanings and the demands made by the curricular materials he is expected to read.

Hildreth (21) writes, "The middle-grade pupil can now expect to meet new words he has never seen before in the proportion of about 1 in 10, even in material prepared for his age group and a still larger proportion of strange words in difficult texts." The problem of meaningful reading is complicated by the fact that in the intermediate grades, as well as at higher levels, there are found a great number of idiomatic expressions, abstract terms, figurative terms, and new connotations for words met earlier. In the primary grades, even though the occurrence of these is less frequent, teachers are alerted to them through the teaching manuals accompanying the basal reader series used. Also, deliberate instruction is provided in the workbooks which supplement the reader series. With the shift to separate textbooks in the content areas, there tends to be less emphasis on helping pupils with meaning difficulties precisely at the point where help is most needed. Examples of difficult concepts from fourth and fifth grade geography, science, and arithmetic books are cited below. Teachers found that many pupils did not understand these concepts even after the material had been assigned and covered in class.

Many years and great sums of money will be needed to *harness the river*.

It (blood) is carried through other *branching tubes* called veins.

When you are frightened, your *pupils get bigger*.

Check by doing each example again.

You bite and chew your food with the *crowns of your teeth*.

Ornithologists have examined the crops of many birds to find out what kind of food they eat.

Most of the *infections* and *contagious* diseases are caused by bacteria.

Birds help to keep the *balance of nature*.

We can use a *ruler* to subtract fractions.

Cloud formations make what is called a *mackerel sky.*

The *red corpuscles are racing through* the *capillaries.*

To solve problems like this, turn your *multiplication table of eights into a division table.*

The native city is *backward* and ugly.

The Mediterranean became a *melting pot* for surrounding civilization.

The people who lived in *fixed settlements* made far greater progress than the Nomads.

Now, as in ancient times, the Mediterranean is a great *connecting* highway.

There is plenty of *home-grown wool.*

Business and industry were *paralyzed.*

Science has *unlocked the greatest force in nature.*

China was not entirely *sealed off* from her neighbors.

A *belt of irrigated land* stretches almost all the way along the coast.

In time, *the front of Europe shifted* from the Mediterranean Coast to the Atlantic Coast.

As the *globe* shows, Europe and Asia really form one *land mass.*

The *shrinking world* and new inventions have made this possible.

If some day the river is controlled it will be a great *life-giver* instead of a *life-destroyer.*

Gradually the continent was opened up. Another "jewel" had *been added to the British crown.*

The top of the world will have a new meaning in the future.

Almost every farmer grows some *cash crop* besides food for his family.

Britain was busy for many years in getting *stepping stones* along the sea-ways.*

PRONUNCIATION AND MEANING PROBLEMS

Pronunciation and meaning problems can be dealt with in the context in which they are met, but there is nothing educationally unsound in reviewing or teaching a series of such words by means of either the chalkboard or a lesson sheet. One value of the latter procedure is that a given exercise can be used with only those pupils who reveal a need for it and may be used with them several times if needed. A list of words that are difficult to pronounce

---

*Unpublished data compiled by teachers in actual classroom situations.

might include: *aisle, fatigue, coyote, exit, plague, sieve, cache, posse, gauge, corps, beau, feign, nephew, antique, bouquet, isthmus, agile, chaos, ache, plateau, quay, bivouac, czar, recipe, stature, reign, viaduct, suede.* A number of exercises can be devised to teach the pronunciation and meaning of such words. A few are listed below:

1. In the first column the difficult words are listed and adjoining columns contain the dictionary pronunciation and meaning:

cache	cāsh	a hole in the ground, or a hiding place
feign	fān	to imagine; invent, hence, to form and relate as if true
quay	kē	a stretch of paved bank or a solid artificial landing place made beside navigable water, for convenience in loading and unloading vessels
bivouac	bĭv o͝o ăk	an encampment for a very short sojourn, under improvised shelter or none.

2. Use the difficult word and a synonym in the same sentence:

As they reached the *plateau* the guide said, "It will be easier walking on this *flat level* ground."

"Climbing mountains is hard work," said the guide. "We will rest when you feel *fatigued* so tell me when you get *tired.*"

3. Prepare a card for each word; one side of the card contains the difficult word and its pronunciation; the other side has a sentence using the word.

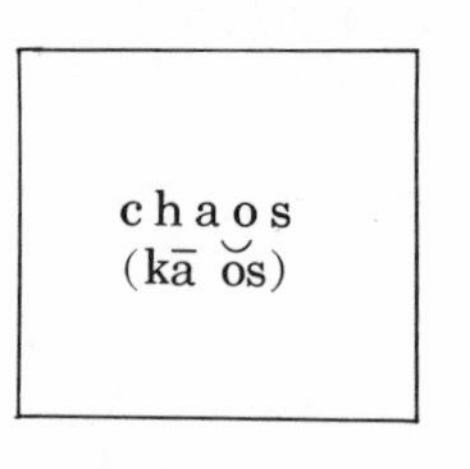

When a tornado strikes a community, *chaos* results. Houses are blown down, fires break out, fallen trees block the streets, telephone poles and wires are down, and the fire department cannot get through the streets.

4. Prepare a short paragraph in which the difficult word is used in several contexts.

From the aerial photographs it was difficult for him to *gauge* whether the railroad was narrow or regular *gauge.* He recalled that the day the picture was made the fuel *gauge* registered very nearly empty. He remembered attempting to *gauge* the effect of the tail wind on his chances of returning safely.

5. *Homographs* are words which are alike in form, but different in both sound and meaning. Words which fit these criteria present

considerable opportunity for confusion when standing alone, for pronunciation and meaning are not indicated. It should be pointed out that it is only through context or usage that the proper choices are indicated.

The announcer stated, "Thus we *close* the broadcast of this very *close* game."

The director was not *content* with the *content* of the scene.

The old man stated he would *refuse* to let the health department clear the *refuse* from his property.

The teacher said she would not *object* if each pupil brought an interesting *object* to school.

Some people would *rebel* at being called a *rebel.*

Truck farms *produce* a variety of *produce.*

Many a *minute* was spent in giving *minute* details.

When you make a *record* of your sales, be sure to *record* them carefully.

6. *Instant recognition of look-alike words:* There are a great number of words which, because they are very similar both in spelling and pronunciation, are often confused. If the reader has to carefully study such words, his reading is slowed considerably. If he miscalls the word, the meaning of the sentence is distorted or lost completely. Growth in reading implies instant recognition of words which have very similar appearance. Many students will need added practice in word recognition. A number of lists of similar appearing words can be prepared, and pupils may be permitted to choose lists for practice. The following series are illustrative.

decent	descent	descend
though	thorough	throw
tired	tried	trial
cease	crease	crash
mouth	month	moth
allow	alloy	allure
rogue	rouge	rough
board	broad	broth
chance	changes	chants
bother	brother	bather
hoarse	hearse	horse
daily	dairy	dairy
easiest	earliest	easterly
began	begin	begun
vary	very	every
advice	advise	adverse
crash	cash	clash

ballot	ballet	ballast
severe	several	sever
farther	father	further
crayon	canyon	cannon
quiet	quite	quit
with	which	width
depot	deport	despot
except	accept	expect
reflect	respect	relate
revere	reverse	revise
mental	metal	medial
easiest	earliest	earnest
brother	border	bother
device	devise	demise
scared	sacred	scarred
whether	weather	whither
thing	think	thank

7. *Confusion of Meanings:* Some words which look very much alike are often confused as to meaning. Wide reading, which insures meeting such words in many different contexts, is probably the most desirable method of expanding meanings. However, teacher-made exercises can also be useful and highly motivational. As a rule, children enjoy working with word meanings, particularly if the difficulty of the exercise material is geared to their needs. Figure 31 is an example of a teaching-testing exercise.

DEVELOPING PERMANENT READING INTERESTS

Developing permanent reading interests is closely related to pupils' motivation for reading. Maintaining interest in reading and healthy attitudes toward reading are special problems in the intermediate grades, particularly in schools which do not provide a wide range of reading materials in all areas. There are still too many instances where schools rely primarily on the one-textbook approach in the various subject-matter areas. The only justification for this practice would be a belief that all pupils in a given class read at the same level, that no children in the group lack the ability to read books at the designated grade level, and that no children are ready to move beyond these graded materials. In reality, a child who enjoyed a fair degree of success in primary reading may feel threatened by the much broader reading tasks demanded by the curricular materials of the middle grades. On this point Gates writes:

> There is evidence from various sources that children often need some help in breaking away from the primary reading habits to advance to the higher intermediate level. There are even cases in which perfection of the primary techniques presents a special danger, the danger that marked facility for reading at the primary level will induce a child to rest on his oars. (17)

When the child can read the words but meets many concepts he does not understand, his enjoyment of reading is curtailed. When the child senses that he is expected to read and understand, his inability to do so colors his attitude toward reading. Reading becomes a threat since he cannot attain arbitrary goals set by the teacher or cope with the questions provided by the text. No sense of fulfillment, achievement, or success accompanies the daily reading tasks which are then neither pleasant nor rewarding. When

FIGURE 31

Working With Words Whose Meaning is Often Confused

1. Some words which look very much alike are often confused as to *meaning*. Study the following words and then, in the sentences below, fill in the blanks with the proper word.

alter:	to change or modify	council:	a governing group
altar:	place used in worship	counsel:	to advise
medal:	a decoration awarded for service	affect:	to influence
meddle:	to interfere	effect:	a result produced by a cause
cite:	to quote, or use as illustration	pitcher:	container for water/a ball player
sight:	to see, act of seeing	carton:	a box or container
site:	location	cartoon:	a drawing, a caricature

meddle - medal:	1. It might be a good idea to give a ______ to people who never ______ in others affairs.
alter - altar:	2. In over 500 years, no attempt had been made to ______ the ______.
carton - cartoon:	3. You will find a humorous ______ on every ______ of breakfast food.
sight - site:	4. He hoped to catch ______ of the ______ where the new club was to be built.

2. The meanings of the pairs of words which follow are not given above. Place the proper word in the blanks in each sentence. Use a dictionary if you are doubtful about the meaning of any word.

miner - minor:	1. Most states have laws which prohibit a ______ from working as a ______.
course - coarse:	2. The fairways of the golf ______ were covered with ______ grass.
dairy - diary:	3. During the day Bill worked in a ______, but each night he would write in his ______.
descend - decent:	4. We should try to find a ______ trail if we hope to ______ the mountain before dark.
precede - proceed: cannon - canyon:	5. When an army is to p______ through a c______ surrounded by the enemy, it is the usual custom to have a barrage by c______ p______ the march.

reading does not fulfill these psychological needs which are so strong in children, interest in reading is likely to suffer.

Once the child discovers that reading is a satisfying experience, reading for many purposes should become a highly reinforced response. (2) The child should learn that he may read:

1. To gain information about countless interesting topics.
2. To realize a very important form of self-achievement.
3. To experience vicarious adventure and romance.
4. To better understand the world in which he lives.
5. To broaden that concept through understanding other people and other parts of the world (or universe).
6. To become familiar with and profit from the lives of great persons through the reading of biographies.
7. To keep informed about current advances in international relations, medicine, science, and new occupational opportunities.

All of the outcomes listed above depend on two factors: the child's ability to read, and the availability of interesting reading material.

Schools must assume the responsibility for making materials available including current publications such as newspapers, magazines, and brochures on special topics. In addition, of course, pupils must be encouraged to read. One of the best ways of doing this is to incorporate the use of supplementary materials into the daily curricular activities of the school. A daily newspaper which features national and international news is probably the most effective means of helping the student understand modern man's interdependence with others. The "news" is the most forceful illustration of this interdependence. An event which occurs any place in the world is read about or discussed freely that same day or hour anywhere in the world. Pupils should be led to appreciate our progress in communication, but they should also be taught to see and understand the cumulative effect of error, bias, or misunderstanding inherent in mass communication. The point here is that an event which is "reported" as having happened comes to be accepted as an event which happened. Further, the *way* it is "reported" may make it appear to have implications which do not necessarily follow.

This brings us to the point that building permanent reading interests can sometimes be obstructed by ignoring any topic which might be considered controversial. If the future allows us the luxury of retrospection, we may be forced someday to conclude that a most telling weakness of American education in the past has been the tendency of our schools to try to capture pupils' interests with watered down, expurgated versions of political, social, and economic issues. It has often been said that our schools have failed to teach the responsibility of good citizenship. Certainly schools have tried to teach abstract morality as it applies to citizenship, but often this teaching has been conducted in a sort of intellectual vacuum. Good citizenship in a free country rests on making choices. Free choice is an asset to society only where the issues are clearly seen and alternatives clearly understood. It is a tenable hypothesis that our schools from the intermediate to the college level have fostered immaturity among potential learners.

The school too must make choices. Units on topics such as the following are neither inherently good nor inherently poor:

"How the pioneers cleared the land, planted, and harvested crops."
"Agricultural advances in the U. S."
"A comparison of personal income in countries throughout the world."
"The effect of natural resources on the Westward movement in the U. S."

However, young citizens in the intermediate grades can also deal with:

"The effects on human health of chemical preservatives put in breads and the effects of poison insecticides used to control destructive pests."
"How poverty breeds political unrest."
"Is the waste of national resources an inevitable result of free enterprise?"
"Historical milestones in man's quest for personal (civil) liberties."
"The basic philosophical differences (aims) between various 'isms' or forms of government."

While it is true these topics might be controversial, error of opinion can be tolerated in the intermediate grades if reason (and reading) are left free to combat it. An excellent time and place for pupils to begin thinking on such topics is that point on the educational continuum where they are developing permanent reading interests and permanent attitudes toward reading.

Appreciation — A Developmental Process

Developing an appreciation for poetry and literature is not a function of chronological age, grade placement, or mere contact with good literature. One does not develop taste in literature as a result of one experience; taste evolves as a result of crossing numerous literary thresholds. Every teacher at every grade level should assume some responsibility for introducing her pupils to the world of good books.

The purpose of teaching is to provide experiences which facilitate personal growth. The ability to appreciate good literature assures one of a lifetime source of pleasure. In addition, the reading and understanding of literature will inevitably lead to insights relative to self and the world in which one lives. Literature is also a form of potential therapy for the alienated and those in flight from involvement. There are few human problems, fears, or aspirations which are not treated in literature.

Basic to helping children develop appreciation for literature is the recognition that appreciation comes only from actual participation. Reading is in essence a dialogue between reader and writer. Appreciation is personal, it cannot be standardized. Thus, appreciation may not result from such tactics as:

1. Urging students to read good literature.
2. Providing a list of acceptable authors or established literary classics.
3. Prescribing an inflexible agenda of reading materials for groups of students.
4. Assigning the same reading to all students in a given class.
5. Assuming that all students in a given class or school year have the readiness, and the skills needed, to "mine" a traditional reading list.
6. Relying on evaluative methods which imply that all students should arrive at the same interpretation of a story, analysis of a particular character, or insight into an author's purpose.

Unfortunately the above procedures, in modified and sometimes disguised form, are often followed in actual teaching situations. These practices, of course, negate what we know about reading, readers, the learning process, and finally, the development of taste in reading. There is a consensus that the schools' approach to teaching literature fails a great number of students who undertake the study of literature. (20)

Enjoying Poetry

In most instances the reading of poetry calls for a different reader-set than does narrative prose. While it is true that the poem is susceptible to more than one interpretation, the language of a poem must take precedence in determining the reading cadence. The poets chief concern is not with facts but with feelings. To enjoy poetry one must have or develop an ear for language. The reader, like the poet, must be receptive to the language as it comes to him.

The poem is designed to be heard. While one may of course hear the words and the language rhythms as he reads silently, there is no better introduction to poetry than to hear it read orally. The teacher who is skilled in reading poetry should read to students. If a teacher prefers, she may turn for help to expert readers who have recorded a wide array of great literature and poetry. A number of modern poets such as Robert Frost, Carl Sandburg, E. E. Cummings, Archibald MacLeisch have recorded portions of their own works. Dozens of highly competent artists including Julie Harris, Richard Burton, Jose Ferrer, Basil Rathbone, Sir Cedric Hardwicke and others have recorded a number of great classics.*

The poet is by definition and practice a word and concept craftsman. He uses imagery, allusion, analogy, symbolism; words are selected not for meaning alone but also for sound and rhythm. Emily Dickinson explains the process.

> "Shall I take thee?" the poet said
> To the propounded word
> Be stationed with the candidates
> Till I have further tried**

Thus, to paraphrase a poem is to destroy it. This does not imply that meaning is sacrificed in order to get other effects; nor does it preclude analysis or even group discussion for arriving at meaning.

The chief cause of the failure of the school to inculcate students with an appreciation for poetry lies in the language barrier. An

---

*One may secure a wide variety of recordings from the *National Council of Teachers of English.* These are completely catalogued in *Resources for The Teaching of English,* NCTE, 508 South Sixth Street, Champaign, Ill.

**Mabel Loomis Todd and Millicent Todd Bingham, ed., *Bolts of Melody—New Poems of Emily Dickinson* (New York: Harper & Row, Publishers, 1945), p. 228.

inadequate language background stalls the communicative process between poet and reader.

> Who goes to dine must take his feast
> or find the banquet mean;
> The table is not laid without
> till it is laid within*

While the reader must come to poetry prepared, he need not, as part of a planned curriculum, be continually exposed to that for which he is not prepared. Good poetry is distributed over a wide range of difficulty. The school's responsibility is to match the student's present ability with reading tasks of commensurate difficulty.

THE INTELLECTUALLY CAPABLE

The problem of arousing and maintaining interest in reading is not confined to the less than adequate reader. The excellent student also faces certain educational hazards in our schools. Since we teach great masses of children in large groups by textbook methods, it is almost inescapable that the more facile readers will not always be stimulated by our standardized methods and materials. The intermediate grades can become a very critical period for gifted students as far as maintaining interest in reading is concerned. The challenge of the intellectually able student is present at all grade levels but becomes more pronounced at the intermediate level because the child's abilities and interests are often beyond the standard curricular materials. When bright pupils are expected to "adjust" to this condition, they often become satisfied simply to get by or, worse, to become uncritical readers. They may plod through required text-reading which requires no mental exertion on their part.

It is true that there are marked differences in reading achievement and needs among pupils who are classed as intellectually capable. Some of this group will need instruction in the fundamental skills of reading. Their ability to deal with concepts may be far in advance of their reading level. A larger group of the extremely capable will be advanced both in the mechanical skills and in the ability to deal with concepts. For these pupils, graded materials

---

**Bolts of Melody, New Poems of Emily Dickinson*, op. cit., p. 229.

at their grade placement level will be mastered without as much drill repetition and guidance as is characteristically given to the class. The problem will not be alleviated by having these children do more work at this level, i.e., simply reading other textbooks. This solution will not extend the talented, who will acquire little additional information by spending time with other texts.

While stating that every child should be educated to his maximum ability to profit from instruction, our schools have been relatively unsuccessful in achieving this goal with the intellectually capable. Regardless of high ideals, our mass educational structure has in many cases led us to gear instruction to the "golden" mean. This is not to be construed as an expression of disaffection for universal free education but rather as a recognition of the need to effect a solution for one of its obvious shortcomings. If pupils are helped to develop study skills which lead to independence in reading and are provided easy access to interesting supplementary reading materials, the school has at least fulfilled its obvious obligations. However, there are many other instructional responsibilities which should be fulfilled for all children but which are particularly acute in the case of the intellectually capable.

The following procedures have been particularly successful in motivating the more able students.

1. If the school has a central library, pupils should be allowed to visit it whenever the need arises and not be restricted to specified library periods.
2. Pupils should be given systematic instruction in the use of library resources such as encyclopedias, *Readers Guide to Periodical Literature,* bulletins, newspapers, and current magazines.
3. Time should be provided for independent reading, and the reading done at such times should always be purposeful. The gifted child, or any child, should never be kept occupied with busy work.
4. As a child develops interest in a particular topic or field, he should be kept supplied with challenging materials which will extend his growth. He should be praised for all serious effort and accomplishment.
5. Children should be encouraged to make plans and carry them out independently after the initial planning with the teacher.

6. The teacher can afford to use more analysis of stories or literature with the more capable pupils. This might take place on an individual or small-group basis.
7. Those pupils capable of such work should be encouraged to participate in special creative activities such as:
   a. writing biographies of famous persons from material they have gathered from many sources.
   b. describing historical events based on wide reading about these happenings.
   c. writing plays or dialogue involving historical personages.
   d. making "resource maps" in social studies.
   e. giving oral reports based on outside reading which will be a contribution to the knowledge of the group.
8. Children should be encouraged to gather resource materials on a topic on which the class is working. These would include pictures, current magazines, bulletins, books which deal with any facet of the topic, and films. Such materials could be used in developing an "interest corner." (See Chapter 17, for further discussion of this procedure.)
9. Pupils should be given access to professional recordings of plays, poems, or prose. Such materials, as well as films and books, may be borrowed from libraries, curriculum centers, or the local state department of education depository.
10. Children should be encouraged to do research on topics which help them see the social forces which shape their society. This type of activity will make "learning for responsible leadership" more than an empty phrase.

INTEGRATING READING INSTRUCTION WITH SUBJECT MATTER

All reading instruction in the intermediate grades cannot logically be relegated exclusively to one scheduled period each day while the rest of the school day is devoted exclusively to teaching content subjects without concern for reading skills. The idea that various facets of reading must be taught concurrently with subject matter is constantly verbalized by teachers and educators. Even in schools which are departmentalized with one teacher responsible for social science, another for science, and so forth, a respect for the integration of reading and the content subjects emerges in the slogan "every teacher a teacher of reading." The nature of the reading materials and the great difference between pupils' instructional needs make it logical and even mandatory that some reading instruction be related to the social sciences, science, literature, arithmetic, and other subject areas.

Some discussions of this problem are couched in terms which suggest that the curriculum is seen as a series of separate tasks, one of which is instruction in reading. It is occasionally suggested that the duty of the school is to teach children to read as quickly as possible so that they can cope with other areas of the curriculum. In one sense, no one can disagree with this position, but in this setting, reading can easily become thought of as an assortment of mechanical skills which the reader applies to subject matter. Here we have more than a hint of compartmentalization, and this attitude is easily transferred to pupils who think they "read" reading one hour, "do" arithmetic another, and "study" social science, health, or science at other times.

The problem cannot be solved by assigning some degree of relative importance to reading and to subject matter, for once the school places subject matter in the curriculum the task of the school is to focus on pupil learning and effective teaching. Effective teaching-learning of all school subjects is highly dependent on students' ability to critically read subject-matter materials. Thus teachers cannot logically abdicate responsibility for teaching the reading of subject matter.

Acquiring facts, seeing relationships, drawing conclusions, finding pertinent information, expanding concepts, mastering new terms and special connotations of words in specific content areas are important parts of learning subject matter, and all involve the application of reading skills.

Working with Reading Skills in Different Content Areas

There are two points of view, which are probably not mutually exclusive, that relate to the issue of teaching reading skills while teaching subject matter. The first is that the various subject areas (social studies, science, arithmetic, health and the like) require radically different types of reading and, therefore, call for different types of reading instruction. (5) The point is sometimes made that certain skills are more identifiable with certain subjects than with others. "It seems reasonable to expect that the reading skills required for science material will differ from those required for materials of history, mathematics, or other content areas, each of which requires its peculiar combination of abilities." (37)

This point is carried further by some educators who list the various skills which they feel are most closely associated with each content area. The following skills are examples, each of which has been identified with reading in one of the areas — science, mathematics, social studies, or English:

adjust rate to purpose
attitude of the reader
drawing conclusions
word attack skills
getting main ideas
locating information
specialized vocabulary
read for main ideas
noting and weighing details
using contextual clues
organizing ideas
discriminating between relevant and irrelevant information

Most teachers of reading would find it difficult to associate each of the skills listed above with just one of the content areas.

This leads us to the second point of view which holds that while there are a great number of reading skills which go toward making up the total skill of reading, it is doubtful that these skills divide along content or subject-matter lines. Granted there are a few specifics which are more likely to be needed in one area than in another, but these do not constitute the essence of reading. A few specific skills would include map reading in history, graphs and tables in geography, abbreviations of elements in science, understanding scale drawings or blue prints in shop work. The basic premise of this point of view is that reading ability is a total process involving the total person and that a reader functions in *any* reading situation under a given set of attitudes, interests, and skills. There are not several sets of principles, one applicable to reading, one to science, one to geography. Reading weaknesses or inabilities inevitably operate in all reading situations.

It should be noted that there are not several sets of principles and practices in reading which divide along subject area lines. Whether the teacher is attemping to develop adequate concepts for *congruent*, *parallel*, *equivalent*, or *isosceles* in arithmetic or *plateau*, *pole*, *delta*, or *isthmus* in geography, the problem is working with word meanings. Drawing inferences should not be thought of as belonging exclusively to one area of the curriculum. A pupil may in the course of a day be asked to draw inferences as to what happens when a decimal point is inserted between digits in two-digit numbers; what effect mountains, located between the sea and the plains, have on rainfall on the plains; and what happens to the circumference of a balloon placed in the freezer compartment of a refrigerator.

A factor which may lead to the hypothesis that certain essential skills of reading are more appropriate to one content area than another is the fact that many pupils can read successfully from basal readers and yet do poorly in subject areas. The reasons for this have been discussed previously. The basal readers present a controlled vocabulary; teachers are alerted to new words and difficult concepts found in each lesson, and systematic instruction is provided to help the pupil over these potential difficulties. Since all reading skills are developmental, the real issue may well be the difficulty level of the material in subject-area textbooks. These materials call for a more extensive development of essential reading skills rather than a different configuration of skills for each content area. When one carefully analyzes the content of history, science, arithmetic, and geography books, he finds it difficult to isolate particular reading skills which are more characteristically needed in one area than in another.

What will inevitably be found is that the vocabulary and concepts met in each field are roadblocks for some pupils. Background or lack of background, interests, attitudes, ability to note details, grasp main ideas, and use context clues, word attack skills, and the reader's purpose, are factors which operate in all reading situations. Reading which children are expected to do in many content areas is farther removed from their actual experiences than is the material in basal reader series. Textbooks which may be excellent from the standpoint of accuracy and breadth of content may be relatively poor from the standpoint of the reader's present vocabulary and concepts.

The Unit Approach

A widely used method for integrating reading along with all language skills in the teaching of any subject is the unit approach. The unit has been discussed in educational sources under many different labels. Descriptive titles for this concept include *resource units*, *teaching units*, *activity units*, *core units*, and *survey units*.

The unit method is a classroom procedure which attempts to organize and integrate a number of learning activities around a particular theme. A unit may be devised for any subject area and can cover a time span of a few days during which pupils attempt to find the answer to a particular question or, as is usually the case, may extend over a period of weeks and culminate in some class project. The culmination might be a play, a school program, or a science fair consisting of many individual and committee projects, all related to the central theme. While the unit approach is not new, it is consistent with the aims of modern curriculum planning. Unit study can help avoid the tendency toward fragmentation of the curriculum into isolated, seemingly unrelated parts.

Special interest units integrate reading along with all language skills in the teaching of any subject. Such units arouse and sustain the interest of pupils as they assume responsibility for various facets of the theme. (Courtesy Bexley Schools, Bexley, Ohio; photographer: Arthur Burt, Inc.)

Units lend themselves to two types of major emphasis. The first type emphasizes pupil experiences built around a specific topic, such as *How We Get Our Food*. Experiences related to this topic might include visits to various types of farms, to a cannery, a cold storage plant, a meat packing plant, a dairy, or a bakery. Pupils may plant and care for a garden or a window box. The second major emphasis is on wide reading. It is likely that emphasis on the experience approach will come at the early elementary level, shifting to reading in the subject areas in the intermediate grades. These two methods are extremely compatible, and the proper combination of the two approaches undoubtedly makes for a better total learning situation.

The use of the unit approach that emphasizes wide reading is reserved for the intermediate grades because wide reading calls for pupils who have mastered the fundamentals of beginning reading. Also, it is difficult to secure a wide variety of interesting supplementary materials on a variety of topics at reading levels below the third grade. Finally, by the time they have reached the intermediate grades, pupils have had opportunities to learn to work both independently and co-operatively in small groups.

Advantages of the Unit Approach. The potential advantages of the unit approach are quite numerous. The actual benefits resulting from its use will vary with such factors as the teacher's skill, the reading ability and work habits of the pupils, and the amount of supplementary reading material available. Some of the more frequently mentioned advantages of the unit approach are summarized below.

1. The unit serves as the framework within which learning experiences are shaped into larger, more meaningful wholes. The unit permits more than the superficial study of a topic and encourages wide and varied reading.
2. Units can be used in any area of the curriculum.
3. The pupils learn that reading is the key to getting information on all subjects and not just an operation performed in the basal reader and accompanying workbooks.
4. The unit approach can and should include a great variety of experiences related to reading, such as excursions, field trips, and small group participation in working on various facets of the problem.
5. Units structure the learning situation to make reading more varied, more meaningful, and more interesting.
6. Units permit pupils of widely different reading abilities to work on different facets of the same project. Reading materials at many levels of difficulty can be used, and children need not be directly compared as readers.
7. The unit approach gives the teacher flexibility and freedom to work with a child or a group of children engaged in some reading activity at their own level. The retarded and

the accelerated reader can be working independently and successfully on something that is challenging.

8. Units aid independent reading and help to foster independence in research reading.

Examples of Units. A unit on weather designed for a fourth grade class may be used as an illustration. The teacher had aroused the interest of the class through an assignment of watching weather reports on television, finding interesting pictures of weather stations, and a class discussion of stories dealing with weather. Out of this grew the class decision to have a study unit on weather. Pupils worked co-operatively in identifying objectives, finding questions to be answered, and working on individual projects which fell within the limits of the unit. These are listed below:

1. Objectives of unit on weather:
   a. To learn ways in which weather helps or harms man.
   b. To learn what causes various types of weather and changes of seasons.
   c. To learn the causes and effects of rainfall, temperature, fog.
   d. To become familiar with the instruments used in measuring or predicting weather changes.
2. Questions to be answered:
   a. How is a thermometer constructed and how does it work?
   b. What is fog?
   c. What causes hail?
   d. What is lightning? Why is it followed by thunder?
   e. Why do we have seasons such as winter and summer?
   f. Why are some parts of the earth always hot and others always cold?
   g. Why is there very little rainfall in one part of a country and a great deal in another part?
   h. Why is it important for man to be able to predict weather?
   i. What is a barometer? How does it work?
   j. What is humidity?
3. Representative activities or projects, both individual and group:
   a. Keeping a daily record of temperatures. Securing temperatures registered in cities in different parts of the country.

b. Preparing charts and graphs which illustrate some aspect of weather.
   (1) Average rainfall for different states and countries.
   (2) The relationship between rainfall and the type of crops raised in a particular area.
   (3) The effect of rainfall on density of population.
   (4) Maps showing occurrence of tornadoes, hurricanes, or floods during past decade.

c. Explaining and demonstrating a thermometer and barometer.

d. Doing research on the work of the U.S. Weather Bureau in predicting weather — how it is done and why.

e. Studying the effects of weather on human dress, shelter, or diet.

f. Measuring rainfall during a rain.

g. Securing pictures which illustrate any facet of weather or the effect of weather, such as floods, erosion, storms on land and sea, barren deserts, and permanent snows.

4. Culminating activity:

   It was decided that at the end of the unit the class would have a Weather Fair. All individual and group projects would be displayed, including posters, graphs and charts, picture series, pupil-made instruments for measuring weather, and all written projects. Parents were invited to visit the class on a particular afternoon, and other classes in the school saw the display at certain times that day. Children explained their projects and received a great deal of ego satisfaction from this culminating activity.

Units Integrate Work in All Areas. A well-planned unit provides a variety of purposeful learning experiences, as illustrated below; the teacher had structured activities so that all facets of the curriculum received attention.

Spelling. Many words were learned incidentally as children printed them on their posters or charts. New words were assigned and studied as part of the unit (*weather, thermometer, mercury, rainfall, temperature, erosion, bureau*).

Health. One popular topic, *How Weather Affects Our Health,* almost became a unit within a unit. The entire class participated, and each pupil was asked to write a brief account of anything he had found in his reading that answered the question. The teacher had a few references for those children who needed help in finding material. What was ostensibly a health lesson also became a lesson in communication skills as the children worked on their written assignments. Practice in oral language usage also received attention as children discussed or reported their findings to the class.

Arithmetic. A lack of understanding of the problems to be solved is more of a stumbling block in arithmetic in the intermediate grades than is lack of computational skills. Failure to read problems critically will result in hazy concepts. In unit work the arithmetic problems which are met emerge from the immediate experience of the learner. Problems such as finding the average rainfall, average temperature, or total foodstuffs raised, are related to larger goals and become meaningful in the goal-directed activity. The need for accurate measurement becomes apparent in building a barometer or measuring a rainfall.

Science. Basically the unit was a science unit. One topic that received emphasis at this particular grade level was how science predicts and tracks weather and the scientific instruments used in the process. In studying the thermometer and barometer, many scientific principles and questions evolved, such as the principle of expansion, the principles of gravity and pressure, and the questions of whether mercury is a metal, why it is used in these instruments, what the function of heat is in causing a thermometer to work.

Social Science. The discussion above on health led into social science topics. A discussion of diet in relation to health led to questions and discussion on how weather affects diet or the production of foodstuffs. A discussion of the economic value of climate would logically follow. The relationship of climate to certain natural resources was discussed, i.e., to forestry, deposits of coal, and petroleum. The relationships between rainfall, temperature, winds, forests, and the types of crops were discussed. Methods of cultivation and crop rotation were studied in relation to erosion of the land.

Reading. Reading was the process which provided the raw material for all of the curricular activities mentioned above. The unit stressed, in the pupils' minds, that they were getting information for science, health, and geography. This reading was purposeful. Neither the reading nor the teaching of it were the compulsive "let's get this workbook page finished" approach. The teacher kept in mind all the principles of teaching reading. She had to be particularly careful not to expect all children to read the same materials and to provide a variety of supplementary materials at many grade levels. The following is a partial list of materials the teacher was able to assemble and make available.

Primary level (from basal readers)

"The Thermometer"
"Winter Is Coming"
"Under the Ice"
"Water into Ice"
"Rain-Sleet-Snow"
"Changing Weather"
"How Spring Came"
"Jack Frost"
"The Storm"
"The Magic Rain Cloud"
"Sing a Song of Seasons"
"Adventures in Science"
"The Wonderworld of Science"
"Little Wolf the Rain Dancer"
"The Thunderstorm"
"Spring Days"
"What Time of Year"

Trade Books

"Our Friend the Sun" (Polgreen; Holt, Rinehart & Winston, Inc., 1963)
"The Sun and Its Planets" (Hawkins; Holt, Rinehart & Winston, Inc., 1964)
"Air Is All Around You" (Branley; Crowell, Collier & Macmillan, Inc., 1962)
"Rain, Hail, Sleet and Snow" (Larrick, Garrard Publishing Co., 1961)
"How Weather Affects Us" (Provis; Benefic Press, 1963)
"Weather Experiments" (Feravolo; Garrard Publishing Co., 1963)
"What Is Air" (Pilty; Benefic Press, 1960)
"Poems for Weather Watching" (Riswall; Holt, Rinehart & Winston, Inc., 1963)

Intermediate Level

Life Magazine
National Geographic Magazine
U.S. Weather Bureau, *Collection of Weather Publications*
"Things You've Wondered About," Highlights Handbook (1962)
"What Is Weather" (Syrocki; Benefic Press, 1960)
"Science Experiments" (Keen, Zaffo, Wolf; Grosset & Dunlap, Inc., 1962)

In developing a unit, the teacher may find that her first important task is to secure materials at various levels. The references available will vary from school to school. Basal readers at all levels could serve for such a unit as well as selected reading from subject-matter texts. *My Weekly Reader* files would provide material on many topics, and a child is often pleased to bring to school his own books on some special topic.

Throughout the unit the reading skills of pupils must be dealt with; use of the unit method in no way restricts the teacher in developing the reading skills of her pupils. In fact, once the preliminary planning of a unit is taken care of, the creative teacher will find that she has as much time and opportunity to help individual pupils or small groups as she had when working with a conventional grouping arrangement. Most unit work introduces a fairly heavy vocabulary load. It follows that some time must be spent on sight word recognition problems. As the teacher has different children read for her and as pupils ask for help with unknown words, she can prepare several word lists of new words to be studied during the course of the unit. One such list might be taken from the more difficult sources and be used exclusively with the advanced reading group. Lists of easier words can be used in sight word exercises with average and poor readers. Many new and unknown words can be used for teaching phonic analysis and for stressing the importance of context clues in solving meaning difficulties.

CONCLUSION

The intermediate grades coincide with a period in child development during which learning should be a natural, pleasurable experience. Unfortunately this highly desirable outcome is not achieved by the large majority of pupils in these grades. It is true that children will have acquired enough reading ability and related language tools to permit them to read on many topics and to develop background in some areas of interest. It is not unreasonable to expect them to be able to move at a more accelerated pace than they did in the primary grades.

However, the school and the culture which supports it seem somewhat impatient with learners at this stage of their development. This is exemplified by two facts. First, the curricular materials provided by the school are often beyond the present reading ability of many pupils. Second, there is a diminished emphasis upon teaching the language tools which are needed for "mining" all subjects, and an air of urgency about having pupils accumulate facts in various subject areas.

The school has become a party to the utilitarian delusion that you can move children along the road to becoming scientists and mathematicians before they have acquired mastery of the language tools which are essential in these and all other academic areas. It is paradoxial that *reading instruction* in the intermediate grades suffers because of our inordinate respect for knowledge. It will be alleged that reading skills are also respected. Yet, no provision is made for assuring that pupils will have developed reading ability commensurate with the demands of the various content curriculums.

This, of course, is an example of false educational economy. Learning to read is a long-term developmental process. The curricular tasks found in the intermediate grades call for wide and extensive reading. To meet these demands successfully, pupils will need guidance in reading *curricular materials*. This means that skill in reading geography, science, and mathematics must be developed in the actual study of these subjects as well as in a period devoted to "reading."

A criticism of the secondary school, which is believed to have validity, is that it has abdicated this responsibility for teaching students "how to read subject matter." The same pressures which operate in the high school are presently being encountered in the elementary grades as content is "moved downward." There is little virtue in a strong academic curriculum unless the learner's reading ability is synchronized with the curriculum materials he is asked to read.

The intermediate-level teacher is faced with the formidable task of arriving at a meaningful differentiation of instruction which is geared to pupil differences. As stated in Chapter 11, American education is continually searching for formulas and formats which will achieve this goal. All classroom and administrative innovations are attempts to focus on this problem. The difficulty lies in the fact that differentiation of instruction must rest on meaningful on-going diagnosis of pupils' present abilities and instructional needs. Such diagnosis will reveal that no single textbook or other source will be equally good for all pupils in a grade. These are educational principles which, when waived, preclude meaningful differentiation of instruction.

YOUR POINT OF VIEW?

What is the basis for your agreement or disagreement with each of the following statements?

1. Prior to Sputnik American schools tended to "teach to the golden mean." The recent revolution in content curriculums tends to focus on the intellectually elite.
2. There is little evidence in either the curriculum materials or instructional objectives to indicate that there is an educationally significant transition between the primary and intermediate grades.
3. The unit approach relies too much on incidental learning and slights systematic instruction in reading.
4. The handicapped and gifted have sincere and articulate spokesmen among curriculum planners who have developed sound instructional programs for these groups. The average and near average pupil in the American school lacks an interested sympathetic lobby.
5. In reference to four above, the average teacher is very much concerned about the growth of the average pupil.
6. Variability among pupils in the intermediate grades could be reduced by improved teaching in earlier grades.

BIBLIOGRAPHY

1. Aaron, I. E., Frances Goodwin, and Vada Kent, "Fourth Grade Teachers Experiment with Cross-class Grouping for Reading Instruction," *Elementary English,* XXXVI (May 1959), 305-307.
2. Artley, A. Sterl, "Literature In The Language Arts Program," *Journal of Education,* CXXXVIII (October 1955), 9-13.
3. Bond, Guy L., and Eva Bond Wagner, *Teaching the Child to Read,* New York: The Macmillan Company, (4th ed.). Chapters 13, 14.
4. Braam, Leonard, "Developing and Measuring Flexibility in Reading," *Reading Teacher,* 16 (January 1963), 247-51.
5. Bracken, Dorothy Kendall, "Appraising Competence In Reading In Content Areas," *Evaluation of Reading,* Helen M. Robinson, (ed.), Supplementary Educational Monographs No. 88. Chicago: University of Chicago Press, 1958, pp. 56-60.

6. Burns, Paul C., "Instruction in Literature in Elementary School," *Reading Teacher,* 15 (September 1961), 38-42.

7. Carroll, John B., "Words, Meanings and Concepts," *Harvard Educational Review,* 34 (Spring 1964), 178-202.

8. Carver, Richard L., and William D. Sheldon, "Problems in the Development of Concepts through Reading," *Elementary School Journal,* LV (December 1954), 226-29.

9. Crosby, Muriel, "Concept Building: Human Relations," *Education,* 84 (September 1963), 36-39.

10. Dawson, Mildred A., and Henry A. Bamman, *Fundamentals of Basic Reading Instruction.* New York: Longmans, Green and Company, Inc., 1959, Chapters 8, 10 and 11.

11. Durrell, Donald D., and Walter J. McHugh, "Analysis of Reading Services in Intermediate Grades," *Reading Teacher,* 14 (September 1960), 26-29.

12. Endres, Raymond J., "Humor, Poetry, and Children," *Reading Teacher,* 19 (January 1966), 247-52.

13. Fitzgerald, James A., "Prefixes In Child Writing," *Elementary English,* XXXVI (December 1959), 576-80.

14. Freeland, Alma, "Intermediate Grade Reading and Needs," *Education,* 84 (April 1964), 466-71.

15. Furness, Edna Lue, "Pupils, Pedagogues and Prose," *Education,* 84 (March 1964), 402-10.

16. Gans, Roma, *Common Sense in Teaching Reading.* Indianapolis: The Bobbs-Merrill Co., Inc., 1963, Chapters 8, 9, and 11.

17. Gates, Arthur I., *The Improvement of Reading* (3rd ed.). New York: The Macmillan Company, 1947, 35.

18. Harrootunian, Berj., "Intellectual Abilities and Reading Achievement," *Elementary School Journal,* 66 (April 1966), 386-93.

19. Harris, Albert J., *How to Increase Reading Ability* (4th ed.). New York: David McKay Co., Inc., 1961.

20. Heilman, Arthur W., "Developing Reading Tastes In the Secondary School," *The High School Journal,* 49 (April 1966), 320-26.

21. Hildreth, Gertrude, *Teaching Reading.* New York: Holt, Rinehart, & Winston, Inc., 1958.

22. Hillenbrand, Robert, "The Appreciation of Picturesque Language in the Intermediate Grades," *Elementary English,* XXXVI (May 1959), 302-4.

23. Huus, Helen, "Libraries Bolster the Reading Program," *Reading Teacher,* 14 (March 1961), 236-40.

24. Jacobs, Leland B., "Books for the Gifted," *Reading Teacher,* 16 (May 1963), 429-34.

25. Johnson, Lois V., "Language Activities and the Study Trip," *Elementary English,* XXXV (February 1958), 108-11.

26. Juliea, Sister M., "The Magic of Words," *Catholic School Journal,* 64 (March 1964), 57-8.

27. Kline, Donald F., "Developing Resource Units," *Education,* 84 (December 1963), 221-25.

28. Larrick, Nancy, *A Teacher's Guide to Children's Books.* Columbus, O.: Charles E. Merrill Books, Inc., 1960.

29. Letson, Charles T., "Speed and Comprehension in Reading," *Journal of Educational Research,* LII (October 1958), 49-53.

30. McAulay, J. D., "Integrating the Social Studies," *Education,* LXXX (December 1959), 239-42.

31. Manolakes, George, and William D. Sheldon, "The Relation Between Reading-test Scores and Language-factors Intelligence Quotients," *Elementary School Journal,* LV (February 1955), 346-50.

32. O'Leary, Helen F., "Vocabulary Presentation and Enrichment," *Elementary English,* XXXXI (October 1964), 613-15.

33. Robinson, Helen M., and Helen K. Smith, "Rate Problems in the Reading Clinic," *Reading Teacher,* 15 (May 1962), 421-26.

34. Robinson, H. Alan., "Reading Skills Employed in Solving Social Studies Problems," *Reading Teacher,* 18 (January 1965), 263-70.

35. Root, Sheldon L., Jr., "Literary Understandings In the Reading Program of the Primary Grades," *Reading and Inquiry,* International Reading Association Proceedings, 10, 1965, 70-72.

36. Roswell, Florence G., "When Children's Textbooks Are Too Difficult," *Elementary School Journal,* LX (December 1959), 146-57.

37. Shores, J. Harlan, and J. L. Saupe, "Reading For Problem-Solving In Science," *Journal of Educational Psychology,* XLIV (March 1953), 149-58.

38. Sister M. Karen, "Poetry Comes to Life," *Catholic School Journal,* 65 (March 1965), 43.

39. Smith, Henry P., and Emerald V. Dechant, *Psychology In Teaching Reading*. Englewood Cliffs, N. J.: Prentice-Hall, Inc., 1961, Chapters 8 and 14.

40. Spache, George D., *Reading in the Elementary School*. Boston: Allyn & Bacon, Inc., 1964, pp. 199-200.

41. Stauffer, Russell G., "Concept Development and Reading," *Reading Teacher,* 19 (November 1965), 100-5.

42. Stewig, John Warren, "Metaphor and Children's Writing," *Elementary English,* XXXXIII (February 1966), 121-23.

43. Sutton, Rachel S., "Words Versus Concepts," *Education,* 83 (May 1963), 537-40.

44. Yandell, Maurine Dunn, and Miles V. Zintz, "Some Difficulties Which Indian Children Encounter with Idioms in Reading," *Reading Teacher,* 14 (March 1961), 256-59.

45. Zirbes, Laura, "The Developmental Approach in Reading," *Reading Teacher,* 16 (March 1963), 347-52.

Individualizing Reading Instruction

11

A history of American Education dealing primarily with classroom practices would be in essence a history of the attempts to deal with pupil differences. The first publicly supported schools in America were one-room rural schools which housed pupils of all ages and achievement levels. Out of necessity and logic, teachers in the one-room schools divided the total class into smaller groups of students; groupings being based roughly on reading ability, chronological age, or both. While the teacher taught one group, the remaining pupils worked at their desks in preparation for recitation.

As urbanization gained momentum, school enrollments grew larger. This necessitated establishing several classrooms within a school, each of which was presided over by one teacher. When multiple classroom-teacher units existed under one roof, pupils could be assigned to different classrooms on the basis of any one of a number of criteria.

Pupils entered school on the basis of chronological age, and it was easy to discern differences between pupils of widely divergent ages. This perception gave rise to questions such as, "When there are a number of classrooms in a building, why should each room contain pupils ranging from six to thirteen or fourteen years of age? Why not group pupils in such a way as to reduce the wide age and achievement differences?"

Thus, the graded system replaced the totally heterogeneous classroom. The theory on which the graded system rested was that pupils would move upward through the grades on the same basis as they entered school—chronological age. And further, that pupils exposed to the same instruction for a school year would be very similar in achievement at the end of that instructional period. Therefore, they would be equally ready to move to the next higher level of instruction.

With such an organizational pattern in the school, it was logical that learning tasks were arranged on an ascending scale of difficulty. The formal curriculum evolved into a "sequence of tasks" which were placed at particular levels or grades. Once there was a general agreement as to sequence and grade placement of tasks, graded instructional materials were developed so that over the years instruction became more and more dependent on such materials.

It was soon discovered that differences among pupils of a given chronological age were so great that a fixed curriculum was not effective for all pupils. As a solution to this problem, non-promotion was tried. Students who had not mastered necessary skills to do satisfactory work in the next grade were held back a year. It has been estimated that during one period of our history between 20 and 25 per cent of all students reaching the sixth grade had been retained in a grade at least once. Non-promoted pupils simply went through the same educational experience with the same teacher. This solution to the problem had little salutary effect upon the non-promoted child. It gradually became apparent that non-promotion was indefensible for it emphasized failure and made it visible to all. In this sense it was a form of punishment which could, and often did, effect the child's chance of returning to a normal growth pattern.

It was then reasoned that practically all children should continue through the graded system with their age-group peers. This practice was called "social promotion." This caused further confusion by moving a child to a higher grade in which mastery of prescribed learning tasks was dependent upon skills which he had not previously acquired. Inevitably this also dooms the child to failure.

Over the years a number of approaches have been inaugurated in an attempt to deal with pupil differences. In the past fifty years, instructional and administrative innovations have been numerous. These include the Dalton and Winnetka plans; activity-related programs; the experience approach utilizing experience derived materials; homogeneous and ability grouping; non-graded schools; the Joplin plan; the language experience approach; and programmed instructional materials.

Reports of the success of new approaches held out hope for reform. Once the initial enthusiasm began to wane, however, teaching tended to fall back on the old established order. Perhaps this occurs because *any* plan of individualizing instruction takes more skill and energy than simply treating a classroom of pupils as interchangeable parts. As Smith (29) noted, "It seems, however, that the seeds of these passing innovations lie dormant for a time and then spring up again in revised and better forms."

Each attempted reform started from sound premises and embraced commendable goals. No matter what plan was attempted, however, the school tended to gradually return to the graded system with its graded curricular materials. Treating a classroom of students as though all were alike in their instructional needs or present achievement inevitably results in poor teaching, simply because the premise is false.

Although the problem has remained unsolved, one favorable omen is the large number of reforms currently being proposed. Nevertheless there is danger that these proposals may be viewed as competing alternatives which must be either adopted in toto or rejected. Since schools, communities, and teachers differ radically, it is likely that no one plan would be equally good in all situations. Perhaps an *eclectic* approach (choosing practices and procedures from various approaches) would be best. The following discussion centers on the individualized reading movement which, to many observers, has over the years broadened its appeal by curbing early tendencies toward proscription of materials and practices.

THE INDIVIDUALIZED READING MOVEMENT

During the 1950's, frustration with the *status quo* in reading instruction reached a new high, and the climate for change seemed particularly good. A new emphasis on gearing reading instruction to individual pupil's needs and interests evolved through a movement which came to be called *individualized reading.*

Proponents of this reform movement had enthusiasm and fervor, both of which were essential if change were to be achieved. Two educational practices in particular, the use of basal readers and grouping by ability, came under fire.

There is little question that certain indefensible practices were to be found in the use of basals and grouping. Some teachers over-relied on basal texts to the exclusion of other materials. When this occurred, reading and learning to read could easily be reduced to deadly routines. Some pupils who had the ability to move through basals fairly rapidly were kept with the group with the result that their reading was severely rationed. These students were asked to complete tasks, such as workbook exercises, which added nothing to their growth in reading because they could do these things prior to the instructional period.

Children at the other end of the achievement continuum were kept reading the same primer and first reader for two or more years even though their progress through this material did not seem to match their potential. Overreliance on basals (or any other material) implies less than optimum use of other instructional techniques and materials.

The other area of concern, dividing a class into three groups, took on the characteristics of a mechanical ritual unrelated to caring for individual differences and meeting individual needs. In some classrooms, children did read "round-robin." Poorer readers were not only embarrassed, but they provided unacceptable models of oral reading for the remainder of the group. It was probably impossible to enjoy a story read under such adverse conditions. These practices were not inherent in the use of basals or grouping, but rather had grown as a result of teachers and school systems failing to use creativity in teaching. In an effort to bring about reform, some proponents of change made sweeping indictments against basal materials and grouping practices. It is generally agreed that it would have been more logical to focus on the actual abuses of basals and achievement grouping which were found in classrooms rather than to attempt to proscribe them altogether.

Although extreme positions have been abandoned by most advocates of individualized reading, a few examples are cited here for historical perspective:

> "Individualized reading requires the complete abandonment of the basal reader and the basal reader system."
>
> "One source of bias in many critics (of individualized reading), it should be recognized in advance, is the intellectual and emotional involvement in authorship of basal series."
>
> ". . . it is everywhere reported that children who have disliked reading change their minds. It is reported that maladjusted children change their attitudes and fit in with the group in other activities. Everywhere it is reported that the children do quantities of reading, not only the good readers but all of them."
>
> "Seldom are two children ready to be taught reading from the same materials at the same time."
>
> "First, we must admit that our group reading system is a rather dismal failure when it comes to teaching sounding."

Such generalizations raised more questions than they settled and caused some teachers to overlook the positive contributions offered by individualized reading. The potential dangers posed by such views have been mitigated as a result of moderation in the more recent criticism made by the very people who originally were most prescriptive. No sound educational purpose can be served by making such criticism the central issue for discussion.

INDIVIDUAL READING DEFINED

Like so many terms associated with reading instruction, there is no universally accepted definition of individualized reading. The term includes both instructional practices and classroom organization. If one thinks of a *method* as embracing a set of materials which provide for the systematic teaching of necessary reading skills over a relatively long period of time, individualized reading does not qualify as a method.

As Jacobs (11) states, "In the first place, 'individualized reading' is not a single method, with predetermined steps in procedure to be followed." Brogan and Fox (3) concur adding, ". . . the term refers to the variety of practices through which resourceful, sensitive teachers, working with and taking their clues from individual children, are helping each of them appropriately to move ahead in reading."

In one sense, individualized reading focuses on the child-as-reader more than the teacher-as-teacher. Reading is seen as an act of personal involvement which is synchronized with the child's growth and development. The emphasis on child growth is commendable, but many teachers who are favorable to this approach find the literature vague as to how one achieves reading goals. One frequently finds statements such as, "individualized reading is a state of mind"; "a new attitude"; "a philosophy or a way of thinking about reading instruction."

It would be difficult, if not impossible, to provide a blueprint for instruction which rested on such commendable but vague attributes. As a result, as Larrick (14) points out, much of what has been written about individualized reading has tended to deal with organizational mechanics, "how many minutes per child, how to keep records, how to sign up for the books, how to manage the class." These problems, she believes, teachers can work out for themselves once they view reading as a personal involvement of pupils and once teaching ceases to be dominated by the demand to cover a pre-stipulated content.

Individualized reading rejects the lock-step instruction which tended to become standardized within the framework of the graded system and traditional graded materials. However, with freedom from routine there comes the responsibility of replacing the routine with creative teaching. The success or failure of a given individualized program rests almost exclusively with the teacher. She is free to develop a program, utilize a wide array of materials, diagnose pupils' needs, and teach skills utilizing any number of approaches. Thus, freedom for teacher innovation is one of the strengths of this approach, but it is also one of the reasons why it is difficult both to define and evaluate individualized reading.

Over the years a number of practices have become associated with individualized reading. These include self-selection of materials by pupils, self-pacing in reading, individual pupil conferences with the teacher, and emphasis on record-keeping by teacher, pupil, or both. One other notable characteristic of individualized reading is the emphasis on the absolute need for a wide variety of reading material in each classroom. This becomes mandatory if each pupil is to select books in which he is interested and which he can read.

PRINCIPLES AND PRACTICES OF SELF-SELECTION

The self-pacing of reading and self-selection of reading materials are basic to the philosophy of individualized reading. Olson's (20-21) writing is frequently cited as the basis for the emphasis on seeking, self-selection, and self-pacing. While these concepts are not new to education, the individualized reading movement has given them a new emphasis focused on reading instruction.

The principle underlying the advocacy of self-selection is psychologically sound. Since there are tremendous individual differences among pupils in a given classroom, there is little justification for assuming that different pupils' needs and interests will be met equally well by one basal series or a single text.

The efficacy of the practice of self-selection of reading materials by pupils is influenced by several factors. First, the child must have some interests he wishes to explore further. This ties the ego to the reading situation. Second, there must be materials available which fit his interests and which he can read independently.

The theory is that when these conditions are met, the child will seek out the materials which fit his needs, interests, and present reading level. If he selects wisely, he grows. Much depends on pupil success, and some proponents of seeking, self-selection and self-pacing appear to have assumed that success is assured by this formula.

Carried to extremes, this idea of individualized reading can minimize the role of the teacher in guiding pupils to materials to the degree that self-selection almost becomes a fetish. There is some danger in attempting to close debate by re-asserting that "pupils, when permitted to do so, will select materials they can read." This may be true in a number of cases, but it is not an inevitable law of child behavior. As Spache (30) points out, a goodly number of pupils have no felt need for reading, do not seek reading, have not ascribed any personally relevant values to reading, and are not "sufficiently insightful into their personal or social needs either to recognize their needs or to find solutions through the medium of reading."

Self-selection on the part of pupils is to a degree limited a priori by the fact that the teacher or some authority has previously chosen the one or two hundred books found in the classroom from among thousands which are available. This infringement on the principle of self-selection is not decried simply because we accept the gathering of materials as part of the teacher's role. Individualized reading and self-selection do not preclude the teacher from recommending books or guiding pupils toward certain materials, but this type of guidance does call for a high level of teacher competency. She must know the child's interest, his reading ability, and the difficulty level of materials if her suggestions are to help her pupils grow.

The factor of economy in the teacher-learning situation must also be considered. If after a period of "seeking" a child has not made a selection and settled down to reading, his behavior may indicate that he is not yet ready for this approach. There is no evidence that a teacher praising a book or offering suggestions to pupils will result in undesirable psychological side effects. On the contrary, there is evidence that pupils respect teacher judgments and tend to be favorably disposed toward materials recommended by understanding teachers. With many pupils, self-selection can safely be tempered with guidance.

TEACHER-PUPIL CONFERENCE

The Teacher-Pupil Conference is one of the major identifying features of individualized reading and is potentially one of its great strengths. This potential is realized only when the teacher is skillful in achieving desirable goals. The conference is a brief session in which the teacher gives her whole attention to one pupil so that he may express himself on a story which he has selected and read prior to the conference. The primary goal of the conference is to assure the child he has an appreciative audience.

The chief value of the conference is that it ties ego-satisfaction to the reading process. For a student to share his feelings about a book with his teacher is an excellent ego-building experience. If the conference is to yield maximum pupil growth, however, the teacher must be more than a listener. If she is only a passive listener, the pupil will tend to standardize his role in the conference. The type of responses he makes the first time will tend to set the pattern for subsequent conferences. In addition to being an appreciative audience, the teacher must also assume some responsibility for helping the child develop a higher level of values and self-understanding. These goals are often best achieved through judicious questions.

The structure and prevalent practices of the present-day school are not conducive to close personal relations between teacher and pupils. Large classes, too many classes per day, and administrative and instructional busy work often stand as barriers between teacher and pupils. We extol creativity and yet teach to the "golden mean." We establish professional philosophy which stresses the importance of teaching to children's needs and interests, yet leave it possible for a student to complete his formal education without ever having had ten minutes of a teacher's undivided attention.

The teacher-pupil conference is worthy of further consideration because it also has possible therapeutic value. The conference serves as a catalyst which helps to produce teacher-pupil rapport, a factor which is highly underrated in its influence on learning. For some pupils, the teacher's positive response to their reading is a stronger motivation than the actual act of reading itself. The skillful sympathetic teacher can provide this extrinsic reward while slowly moving the child toward accepting reading as its own reward.

The conference provides the means by which the teacher can learn important facts about children's psychological needs and the means they have adopted for fulfilling these needs. With this knowledge, the alert teacher is in a position to become a party to sound bibliotherapeutic practices. Discussing their reading with a respectful adult will help children gain insights into their own problems and afford them examples of how others have met such difficulties.

Preparing for the Conference

The brief discussion which follows is not intended as a prescription for the only way to approach the teacher-pupil conference; rather, it is intended as a guide for forming one's own approach. Veatch has listed the factors which teachers may wish to consider in setting up conferences. (32)

1. As a general rule, the pupils inform the teacher when they feel ready to participate in a conference.
2. The teacher should be familiar with the book or story which a child plans to discuss.
3. Pupils are informed when and in what order they will be scheduled for the conference.

4. Provision must be made for all other pupils in the class to be engaged in some other meaningful activity. One suggestion is to have them selecting and reading books independently.
5. The teacher must be prepared to stimulate pupils through the use of questions. These should be questions that stimulate thought instead of asking only for factual information.
6. The class and teacher will have worked out some system for pupils to receive help pronouncing unknown words during their independent reading.

For helping students pronounce unknown words, a large number of possibilities exist. Some teachers permit the child to come to her and point out the troublesome word, and she whispers its pronunciation. If pupils do not abuse this privilege, it need not disrupt the teacher-pupil conference in progress. Other teachers feel that such interruptions detract from the intimate nature of the conference, and they appoint "helpers." These are the more proficient readers in the class who can usually help the other pupils.

Sperber (31) suggests that a seating arrangement be worked out so that the class falls into three groups, each containing one or more good readers. These better readers serve as resources for helping other pupils in the group with words they may not know as sight words.

On occasion an entire class may be involved in a writing assignment while the teacher is engaged in conferences. In one first grade classroom the children were observed to be writing a letter to a classmate in the hospital. The teacher printed a dozen words on the board explaining that these might be words the pupils would be using and that they could look at the board for help on spelling. The words were: *dear, Susan, hope, soon, well, sorry, you, love, sick, missed, get, school, from.* This selection of words anticipated a large percentage of the "spelling interruptions" which might have ordinarily occurred.

Another approach is to encourage pupils to "spell the words the way you think they are spelled." Such free writing exercises can have a diagnostic value for the teaching of spelling and the analysis of phonic skills.

Frequency and Length of Conferences

The related problems of length and frequency of conferences have received considerable attention. These matters are still the basis for questions from teachers. Although the individual conference is one of the key features of the movement which broke up the rigid stereotyped practices prevelant in reading instruction, there still has been a tendency for the thinking and writing about the conference to become somewhat fixed and formalized.

One of the problems has been that the length and frequency schedule will necessarily vary with the size of the class. A schedule which is logical for a classroom of 24 pupils will become unworkable with a class of 35 pupils. Furthermore, the length and frequency of the conference will also vary with different grade levels and different ability levels within the grade. A still further complicating factor is the difference found among readers themselves. The child who has read a story consisting of only several hundred words will probably not take as much sharing time with his teacher as the pupil who read *Charlotte's Web.*

Format of Conference

Since the conference is a technique for dealing with individual differences, it should not be permitted to acquire a "standardized format." There is always the possibility that teachers may develop the habit of treating the conference as a set ritual. They tend to make the same remarks, ask the same questions, and follow the same procedures with each pupil time after time.

The conference is in one sense a teaching tool that varies with individual pupil needs; a set formula for conferences is not desirable. In no sense is it necessary to think of all conferences as embracing the same procedures or lasting for the same duration. Some conferences might be exclusively a sharing time with the teacher; others might be devoted to helping the child get organized in the self-selection process. During a given week, a teacher may schedule nothing but 2-3 minute diagnostic conferences, planning on a minimum of two per pupil. Many teachers would be amazed at how much they can learn about a pupil's reading from such a practice.

In the case of a facile reader who needs little encouragement to read, a brief exchange between the teacher and pupil would suffice on some occasions. A word of praise, a question about whether there are still a number of books in the classroom that he wishes to read, and an offer of help when he needs it could be considered adequate, providing his previous conference was a full-fledged "sharing period."

Since the sharing-type conference is primarily an ego-building experience, it is obvious that some children will need more attention than will others. Some pupils continually avoid a conference because reading is a threat rather than a pleasure. Unlike the good reader who fulfills his ego-needs through the success and enjoyment derived from actual reading, these pupils need constant encouragement.

Expansion of the Role of the Conference

Up to this point, the discussion about the teacher-pupil conference has been restricted to the goal outlined above—providing a time for the child to share a favorite reading passage with a very appreciative audience, his teacher. Gradually questions were raised as to when and how other facets of instruction were to be provided. Specific examples include the diagnosis of the pupil's reading and the teaching of needed skills.

In much of the more recent writing on individualized reading, both of these vitally important aspects of reading instruction were eventually included as activities of the teacher-pupil conference. It is obvious that the inclusion of diagnosis and teaching of skills would change the nature of the conference. The original purpose of the conference would of necessity be diluted. However, it should be kept in mind that this expansion of the role of the conference is not mandatory simply because it is suggested in the descriptive literature. Teachers who evolve other solutions for including diagnosis and skill teaching can still preserve the original intent of the teacher-pupil conference.

Providing Meaningful Activities for the Class during Teacher-Pupil Conference

Individualized reading calls for a high degree of planning by the teacher, much of which will likely include pupil participation in outlining independent activities. Such activities are unlimited. The following brief listing is only illustrative. The tasks are not identified by grade level since many may be adapted to various levels. The listing includes class, group, and individual activities, covering skill development, recreational reading, reading in curricular areas, and creative activities.

1. Children select books or other reading materials. This will likely include browsing and sampling. Selection is followed by independent reading of materials.

2. Conducting library research for an individual or group report. Such activity may relate to a unit in some other subject.
3. Creative writing experiences might include writing original stories; poems; letters to a classmate in the hospital or one who has moved away; invitations to parents to visit school; a riddle composition to be read to the class during a period set aside for such activities.
4. Preparing art work such as:
   a. Drawing or pasting pictures in a picture dictionary.
   b. Drawing a picture to accompany a pupil-dictated, teacher-written story.
   c. Preparing posters or book covers to illustrate the high point in a book or story which the pupil has read.
5. Using workbook pages or teacher-prepared seatwork guides for the development of particular skills such as:
   a. A dictionary exercise which follows an introduction of a skill such as alphabetizing by initial letter, or by two or more letters, use of guide words, pronunciation guides, or syllabication.
   b. Word analysis skills (associating sounds with graphic symbols, noting compound words, abbreviations, and the like).
   c. Study skills involving effective use of parts of a book such as the index, table of contents, glossary, appendix, library card catalogue, reference materials.
6. Using an appropriate film strip with the entire class, a smaller group, or a pair of pupils. In each case, one pupil is appointed to move the frames.
7. Teaching and testing word meanings.
   a. Workbook pages or teacher-prepared seatwork may be provided.
   b. Children may work on "vocabulary building" cards or notebooks in which they write one or more common meanings for new or unknown words met in their reading.
   c. The teacher may place a list of words on the board. Pupils write as many sentences as possible, using a different connotation for the word in each sentence. Example: *Light*—light in weight; light as to color; light the fire; light on his feet; her eyes lighted up; light-hearted; etc.

8. Making a tape recording of a story. A group of 4-6 pupils may each read the part of one character. Practice reading and the actual recording may be done in the rear of the classroom or in any available space in the building.
9. Testing or diagnostic activities may be arranged. The entire class or any size group may take a standardized test (or reading subtest); tests which accompany basal series; *My Weekly Reader* tests; or informal, teacher-made tests. These will be scored and studied for the diagnostic information they yield.
10. Preparing interest corners, bulletin boards; devising choral reading activities for later presentation to the class.

These represent only a few of the reading-related activities which can be used. Teachers are limited only by their experience, creative ability, and the degree to which the pupils in their class have learned to function in independent activities.

Record-keeping receives considerable attention in the description of individualized reading programs. This term is not at all synonymous with diagnosis, although some aspects of diagnosis include record-keeping. For the most part, reports of record-keeping have dealt with such items as listing the title of the book read; author; type of book (biography, fiction, myth, science, etc.); number of pages in the book; some notation as to difficulty level of the book; and the date the pupil began and finished the book.

When records consisting primarily of factors such as these are kept, they have limited diagnostic value. The teacher may note that a particular child reads nothing but fairy tales or stories about horses, or that a pupil consistently chooses easy books. Such information must be supplemented by observations which focus on the process of reading. Most records contain a column for teacher's comments such as the following: "needs help on phonic analysis"; "needs to read more smoothly"; "word attack poor"; "weak on developing sequence of a story." Such observations, however, are only the first step in the diagnostic process. Each is an invitation to a further diagnosis to ascertain why these reading behaviors are present.

The type of records under discussion can be prepared by the teacher, the individual pupil, or both. One may find frequent mention that many pupils enjoy keeping a log of books read. There is ego-building potential in seeing one's list of books grow. A note of caution is necessary, however; sometimes the pupils' listing of books can become the primary motive for reading. Thus, that which started out as an extrinsic motivator becomes intrinsic, and the child reads just to be reading and misses the purpose of reading.

Also, if too much emphasis is placed on the number of books read, the competition of compiling a list may work to the detriment of slower readers. They cannot keep pace with the more facile readers in the group. Lists of books read will be compared and low output can become a psychological factor which turns some children away from reading.

Neither of these potential weaknesses should be thought of as an inevitable outcome of pupil record-keeping. However, since one of the positive strengths of self-selection and individualized reading is that competition and comparison between pupils is avoided, the teacher must be alert to see that this potential strength is not lost.

Jacobs (11) differentiates between record-keeping and evaluation procedures noting that "appraisal is integral with teaching." Many teachers supplement the child's reading records with check lists or cumulative accounts of observed reading behaviors. Check lists of difficulties can take many forms, but usually they make provision for teacher's responses to a large number of skills and reading habits ranging from knowledge of sight words and sounding ability to use of study skills and reading interests. Figures 32A and 32B, found on the following pages, are illustrative.

PROBLEMS RELATED TO INDIVIDUALIZED READING

Within the framework of individualized reading, some concepts are new and the procedures for achieving reading objectives are varied. This has given rise to a number of questions by teachers who are interested in this approach. It has been mentioned previously that despite the considerable amount of information available, there is no blueprint which outlines individualized reading as a total program.

In fact, divergent opinions and a multitude of procedures can be, and are, accommodated within the structure of individualized reading. The fact that the basic principles are so flexible has given rise to a number of questions such as: "What practices are included in individualized reading? How does one initiate an individualized program? What materials are needed? How does one take care of the remainder of the class during individual conferences? How and when is diagnosis of pupils' needs included? What are the provi-

FIGURE 32A

PUPIL CHECK LIST (SKILLS)

NAME:________ AGE:______ GRADE:______ DATE:______

I. *Basic Sight Vocabulary* Test Used:________________

No. of Words Tested________ No. of Words Missed________

Words Not Known____

____

II. *Difficulties Noted*

___ Reads Word by Word	___ Easily Distracted
___ Omits Words*	___ Guesses Words
___ Poor Phrasing	___ Word Analysis Poor**
___ Does Not Profit from Punctuation***	___ Errors Not Corrected
___ "Service Words" Missed****	___ Little Help From Context Clues
___ (Other)	

*Examples:
**Examples:
***Examples:
****Examples:

III. *Study Skills and Effective Use of Textbooks*

Understands and Effectively Uses:

	Yes	*No*	*Comments*
A. Index	______	______	
B. Table of Contents	______	______	
C. Glossary	______	______	
D. Appendix	______	______	
E. Card Catalogue	______	______	
F. (Other)	______	______	

sions for teaching needed skills?" These problems will be briefly explored with the understanding that the material presented is not a prescription to follow but a synthesis of the information available on these topics.

FIGURE 32B

COMPREHENSION CHECK LIST

NAME:______________ AGE:_____ GRADE:_____ DATE:______

Book Title and Author:____

____

Date Started:______ Finished:______ No. Pages:_____ Level:_____

Recall of Material Read

1. Level of Language Usage:
2. Following Sequence of Story:
3. Recall of Details: (unaided)________________________________
   with Questions:____
4. Knowledge of Word Meanings (special connotations, figurative language, etc.)
   Examples Tested:____
   ____
   ____
5. Examples of Pupil Responses:
   A. Describing Particular Character:
   B. Main Point of Story:
   C. Part Liked Best:
   D. Ability to Draw Inferences:
   E. Evaluation of Book (Does he recommend it highly — why or why not?):____
   ____
   F. Ideas Expressed by Pupil:
6. Pupil Interest in Reading (teacher judgment):
7. Does pupil need guidance in selection of material?

PRACTICES INCLUDED IN INDIVIDUALIZED READING

As mentioned earlier, individualized reading does not have a universally accepted definition, and as a result questions have arisen as to what practices are included and excluded. Fortunately, there is less of this type of questioning now than a decade ago. At that time the majority of descriptive articles focused on a limited number of practices such as self-selection, self-pacing, teacher-pupil conferences, record-keeping, and the like. While these practices have obvious merits, many teachers declined to accept them as a total reading program.

The fact that some articulate proponents of various approaches opposed the use of basals, grouping, and other practices probably added to the confusion. Such suggestions tended to divide teachers into two camps, pro- and anti-individualized reading. The tendency to proscribe classroom practices has subsided in favor of a much broader and more inclusive base. There has never been any sound educational basis for questioning the need for individualized instruction. There are obvious reasons why there should always be room for a wide array of different practices for achieving this goal.

The either-or phraseology of "individualized *vs* grouping" never has represented a true dichotomy since neither represents a methodological approach. It was gradually recognized that individualized practices and grouping practices complemented each other and that they did not necessarily represent mutually exclusive teaching philosophies. Indefensible practices can flourish under any label, and such practices should be eliminated without regard to philosophical or methodological loyalties. This tendency to move toward "middle ground" is based on the recognition that poor teaching is not inherent in any philosophy, set of materials, or administrative arrangements but rather in the manner in which they are utilized. By the same token, no combination of philosophy and materials by themselves can make a school or classroom immune to poor teaching.

The tremendous differences found among teachers strongly suggest that they cannot achieve equally successful results using a given set of procedures. This, plus the fact that teachers work under vastly different circumstances and attempt to cope with vastly different pupil needs, militates against any a priori exclusion of teaching techniques and materials.

Thus, teachers A and B in schools I and II, which house pupils of quite different cultural and socio-economic backgrounds, may have developed excellent but quite different individualized reading programs. One would not ask the question, "Well, which program, A or B, is individualized?" or "Which comes closest to being individualized?" Such questions could arise only if there existed an agreed definition of individualized reading and a standardized list of accepted procedures.

If teachers A and B exchanged classrooms, it is likely that their respective programs might be less effective than the programs in their previous classroom environments. Individualized reading practices will vary because differences among teachers precludes all teachers being equally successful with a given technique or procedure. A teacher who has strong reservations about pupils keeping records of books read might at the moment be incapable of making this practice work effectively in her class. Another may use basals extensively with a group of pupils slow in developing sight vocabulary and use trade books extensively with another group.

NEEDED MATERIALS

A reading program embracing self-selection and self-pacing and designed to meet individual pupil interests cannot function in a learning environment which does not include a wide array of reading materials. This should not be thought of as a special problem related only to the individualized reading. There is no justification for any classroom or school not meeting this criterion regardless of methodological approach or program. Therefore, the need for materials is not a unique feature of individualized reading but rather a factor which has been justifiably emphasized in this approach.

While there is little point in attempting to settle upon a fixed number of books which would be considered adequate, a minimum figure frequently mentioned is approximately one-hundred different trade-book titles per classroom. Assuming that the same hundred books should suffice throughout the year, a hundred books in a third grade would be totally inadequate.

Factors which must be considered include: grade level under discussion; range of interests and abilities of pupils; class size; whether books can be rotated with other classrooms; whether the school supports a central library; and whether the same materials are used extensively in other subject areas such as social studies and science in the preparation of units.

Materials should not be tightly equated with trade books alone, although these would likely be the major source. Classrooms should contain magazines, newspapers, various reading kits, *My Weekly Reader*, *Readers Digest* (Skill-Builder Materials), and most other reading materials children might choose to work with. Reading material would of necessity cover many areas such as biography, science, sports, exploration, hobbies, fairytales, medicine, space, poetry, humor, adventure, myths and travel.

STARTING A PROGRAM

All elementary teachers are likely to be doing some things which fit logically under the heading "individualization." Any of the formal aspects of individualized reading such as self-selection or individual conferences can be started with one pupil, a small group, or the class as a whole. Obviously, the latter approach would present the most problems; therefore, perhaps one should start with one of the other alternatives.

The first prerequisite is, of course, the availability of materials; and to this must be added the prerequisite that the child be able to read some of these materials. A reading vocabulary of 20 words is needed to handle a pre-primer, and with a few more words, a reader could make the transition to similar materials in different basal series. A sight vocabulary of 50 words and some ability at sounding out words would permit a reader to start his first trade book.

Within this ability range, a portion of the child's reading material might well be individual stories dictated by the pupil and printed by the teacher. This practice may be identified with the language-experience approach, but its practice is not precluded in individualized reading. Commercial picture dictionaries and teacher-pupil-prepared dictionaries would also be appropriate at this level.

Starting an individualized program by involving a small group of the more proficient readers in the class is another logical way to begin. This approach will present fewer organizational problems than involvement of the entire class. The teacher begins by calling together the students she has selected and explaining that she would like them to select their own books to read at their desks during the reading period.

Prior to this group conference, the teacher has gathered a number of books and placed them on the reading table. She has been careful to see that a goodly number of "new books" are included and has deliberately included books which she thinks will appeal to the five or six students in the group. There would be nothing wrong with calling the children's attention to certain books.

She concludes the group conference with, "When you have selected the book you wish to read, go to your desk and read it silently; you may keep the book at your desk until you finish it. For the rest of this week I am appointing Bill as a special helper. If you come to a word you cannot sound out, you may ask Bill; if he does not know the word, you should print it on one of these cards along with the number of the page on which it is found. Sometime during the morning I will come to your desks and help you read the sentences which have the hard words."

These directions and explanations have taken only a minute or two. The teacher now turns her attention to the remainder of the class, explains a seatwork assignment to a portion of the class, and conducts a planned session on work-analysis techniques with a selected group of students. She will observe how the pupils function in the newly organized individualized group. Do they find a book in a reasonable length of time? Is it at a level they can handle? How does the "helper" make out — do the other pupils bother him for help so often that it interferes with his own reading? This information may call for adjustments and further clarification.

Within a day or two the teacher will again briefly assemble the pupils in the individualized group and explain that she would like to have each student tell her something about the book he is reading and for him to read to her a part of the book he particularly likes. In order to do this, she will schedule an individual conference with each pupil. Pupils are to tell her when they are ready for their conference, and she will schedule the time.

PROVIDING FOR DIAGNOSIS

Individualized reading is an organizational-instructional approach which by its very nature calls for considerable diagnosis if children are to progress smoothly in reading growth. Achievement of individualization may soon be thwarted for some pupils in the absence of on-going diagnosis. It is doubtful that such potentially excellent procedures as self-selection and self-pacing were ever envisioned to operate independently of diagnosis and teacher guidance.

In the absence of teaching built on diagnosis, pupils tend to reinforce whatever poor reading habits they have at present. The same mistakes will be made time after time, and it may be weeks before "self-correction" is worked out. One example is the case of a child who consistently miscalled a word throughout the entire length of a story. "In one class a child read a story about an old man and a 'termite' for four days. On the fifth day during his conference he discovered the word was 'turnip.' No wonder he had missed comprehension and the humor." (22)

There are no diagnostic techniques which are associated exclusively with individualized reading, nor are there any which need be thought to be foreign to it. The individual teacher-pupil conference may in some instances be a major source of diagnostic information, but the conference cannot be the only time and place where diagnosis takes place. Diagnosis must be on-going, and every reading activity in the classroom should be viewed as serving some diagnostic purpose.

All seatwork, whether teacher-prepared or conventional workbook exercises, has diagnostic value. A student's spelling performance, both on formal weekly tests and in his creative writing, will give clues to his ability to associate letter sounds with letters and letter combinations. Brief informal tests may be developed for testing any facet of reading from recognition of words to understanding figurative language.

TEACHING READING SKILLS

The early individualized movement was in part a reaction against reading instruction which often stressed individual skills at the expense of the "total reading process." In some classrooms, all pupils received the same instruction, worked on the same skill-building exercises, and read the same materials. When these practices were prevalent, there was room for suspicion that instruction was predetermined rather than based on pupil needs and abilities. Such uniform practices inevitably resulted in some children becoming bored with reading instruction, and thus there existed a need for reform.

Unfortunately, the attack on uniform skills instruction for everyone tended to spread to the teaching of skills per se. Actually, skills-teaching was not explicitly rejected, but this facet of individualized reading instruction was neglected. In recent years the importance of skills-teaching has been accepted by practically all proponents of individualized reading. But the vagueness as to how and when the teaching is incorporated into the program still lingers.

Questions relative to teaching skills elicited two frequently repeated responses: 1. "Teach some skills in the teacher-pupil conference"; and 2. "Teach other skills as they are needed by the pupils."

The first answer suggests what is, on the whole, an uneconomical procedure, unless the child participating in the conference is the only one in the class who can profit from the instruction that is given. Any reading skill that can justifiably be taught to the entire class should be taught. Those students who learn with the first presentation should be doing something else when subsequent presentations are made to pupils who did not learn. Assume that eventually only one child in the class has need for further instruction; provision is now made for him to receive it individually. This may be done by the teacher; or a peer of the learner may function for a few minutes as a "helper"; or the material may be on a filmstrip and the learner may operate the projector himself; or he may work on a teacher-prepared worksheet; or with a commercially prepared programmed lesson. Where reading instruction is integrated school-wide, he may join five or six other pupils from other classes regardless of grade level, who have the same instructional need. This latter solution may fit under any one of a number of administrative titles such as "remedial reading," "modified joplin plan," "ungraded primary," etc. The actual instruction may be provided by a full-time remedial teacher, a one-day-a-week teacher, a teacher aid, or a student teacher working under supervision.

The second response, "teach skills when they are needed," cannot be faulted as to its face validity, but it can be argued that it is both vague and difficult to implement when each child in the class is reading a different book. Concern for providing differentiation of skills-instruction need not start from the premise that no two pupils, or larger groups in a class, cannot profit from the same instruction or drill. This extreme position is simply the antithesis of the practice which implies that all children in a class *could* profit from the same amount of time spent with the same book. Reliance on diagnosis, not slogans, is the only safe way to resolve what is appropriate instruction.

There are dozens of abilities and habits which may be listed under the heading *basic skills*. The three major areas with which the elementary teacher must be constantly concerned are *word recognition, ability to sound out or pronounce unknown words, and the knowledge of word meanings*. This is true regardless of the materials used, organization pattern followed, or one's philosophy of teaching.

CONCLUSION

In the absence of eternal vigilance and the search for creative responses to existing problems, reading instruction tends to lose vitality and become stereotyped. In American schools the tendency toward standardized teaching practices has been accentuated by two factors: the grade level system and the overreliance on graded instructional materials. Individualized reading represents a new emphasis on evolving classroom practices which fit individual pupil needs.

Seeking to find means of individualizing instruction is evidence of the awareness of pupil differences. Such awareness is absolutely essential to a sound reading program. However, what one does in actual practice as a result of this perception may or may not be sound.

In the early stages of the movement, lines were somewhat closely drawn as to what practices were included and which were proscribed. As Miel stated, "With any way of teaching which is hailed as promising there is always the danger that formalism will set in and that essential features of the proposal will be distorted in well-meant attempts to popularize the idea and secure wide-scale trial of it."*

An effective individualized reading program of necessity must rest on a rather broad base. It may include, but cannot be limited to, children selecting books; reading these at their own rate; and occasionally reporting to the teacher on their reading. Individualized reading does not exclude practices which may be thought of as integral parts of other instructional approaches.

Any instructional program must include the teaching of all facets of reading. A few examples are study skills, word-recognition techniques, library research techniques, integration of reading instruction with subject-matter teaching, expansion of meaning vocabulary and concepts, appreciation of poetry and literature. These are essential skills, and they should be taught. This position is not rejected by those who advocate individualized reading. But the details of how and when such essentials are to be taught have not been carefully delineated.

It also must be remembered that both the virtues and defects ascribed to individualized reading are potential and not inherent in

---

*Alice Miel, ed., *Individualizing Reading Practices,* Bureau of Publications, Teachers College, Columbia University, VI (1958).

the approach. The achieving of potentials and the avoidance of pitfalls is exclusively a function of individual teachers in specific classroom situations. This is not unique to individualized reading. Precisely the same conditions hold for *any* method or instructional framework.

Many authorities feel that individualized reading instruction calls for relatively high teacher competence. It is likely that this hypothesis is well-grounded. One reason for this would be that with the exception of self-selection, self-pacing, and the teacher-pupil conference, few concrete procedures have been spelled out in the system. Individualized reading lacks the structure that is found in the teacher's manuals of basal series.

Assuming this rationale is fairly accurate, it would appear we are faced with a paradox. The greatest potential weakness of individualized reading is that it lacks a blueprint for instruction, but blue-print-type structure leads to stereotyped unimaginative teaching, which was the chief factor in the rise of the individualized movement.

The implication is clear. Teachers who fit this analysis failed to recognize indefensible practices as poor instruction. Further, there is a suggestion that these teachers lack the training and insights necessary to function under the high degree of freedom and the resultant responsibility which is an integral feature of individualized reading. The conclusion seems warranted that training in reading instruction has not reached the degree of competency that our society should expect at this point in the twentieth century.

YOUR POINT OF VIEW?

Defend or attack the following statements.

1. Any practice which leads to children reading appropriate material would fit under the label individualized reading instruction.
2. Most of the individualized reading programs which have been described have more efficacy for better readers in a class than for poorer readers in the group.
3. It is impossible to establish and maintain an individualized reading program in the absence of individual teacher-pupil conferences.
4. Assume a teacher knew a great deal about a particular pupil (reading level, interests, instructional needs, etc.). Would pupil-self-selection of reading material be inherently superior to this teacher's suggestions relative to appropriate reading materials?
5. A. Assume you wish to set up an ideal individualized reading program. Which of the following materials would you feel free to use?

Trade books	Basal readers
Experience charts	Individual teacher-written stories
My Weekly Reader	Workbooks
Programmed reading materials	

B. Assume you are a first grade teacher and that you are free to use only three of the above types of material. Which three would you choose?

C. Assume you are a sixth grade teacher, would your choices remain the same as in B above?

BIBLIOGRAPHY

1. Allen, Roach Van, "Three Approaches to Teaching Reading," *Challenge and Experiment In Reading*. International Reading Association Proceedings 7, 1962, 153-56.
2. Blakely, W. Paul, and Beverly McKay, "Individualized Reading as Part of an Eclectic Reading Program," *Elementary English*, XLIII (March 1966), 214-20.

3. Brogan, Peggy, and Loren K. Fox, *Helping Children Read.* New York: Holt, Rinehart & Winston, Inc., 1961, 5.

4. Burton, William H., and Joseph Slika, "Some Arguments About Reading," *Education,* 84 (March 1964), 387-92.

5. Dolch, E. W., "Individualized Reading vs. Group Reading I," *Elementary English,* XXXVIII (December 1961), 566-75; Part II *Elementary English,* XXXIX (January 1962), 14-21.

6. Duker, Sam, "Needed Research on Individualized Reading," *Elementary English,* XLIII (March 1966), 220-26.

7. Evans, Robert, "Teacher Evaluations of Reading Skills and Individualized Reading," *Elementary English,* XXXXII (March 1965), 258-60.

8. Fay, Leo, "Basic Reading Skills," *Education,* 82 (September 1961), 10-12.

9. Frazier, Alexander, "The Individualized Reading Program," *Controversial Issues In Reading and Promising Solutions,* Helen M. Robinson (ed.), Supplementary Educational Monographs No. 91. Chicago: University of Chicago Press, 1961, pp. 57-74.

10. Gray, William S., "Role of Group and Individualized Teaching in a Sound Reading Program," *Reading Teacher,* 11 (December 1957), 99-104.

11. Jacobs, Leland B., "Individualized Reading Is Not a Thing," *Individualizing Reading Practices,* Alice Miel (ed.), Bureau of Publications, Teachers College, Columbia University, 1958.

12. Johnson, Rodney H., "Individualized and Basal Primary Reading Programs," *Elementary English,* XXXXII (December 1965), 902-04.

13. Karlin, Robert, "Some Reactions to Individualized Reading," *Reading Teacher,* 11 (December 1957), 95-98.

14. Larrick, Nancy, "Individualizing The Teaching of Reading," *Reading, Learning and The Curriculum.* Proceedings of the Twelfth Annual Reading Conference, Lehigh University, Bethlehem, Pa., 1963, 35-38.

15. Lazar, May, "Individualized Reading: A Dynamic Approach," *Reading Teacher,* 11 (December 1957), 75-83.

16. Lofthouse, Yvonne M., "Individualized Reading: Significant Research," *Reading Teacher,* 16 (September 1962), 35-37.

17. Metzler, Helen, "Providing for Individual Differences In Reading," *Improvement of Reading Through Classroom Practice.* International Reading Association Proceedings, 9, pp. 95-96.

18. Miller, Janet S., "Individualized Instruction," *Elementary School Journal,* 66 (April 1966), 393-96.

19. Morrison, Coleman, "Individualized Reading: Some Unanswered Questions," *Improvement of Reading Through Classroom Practice,* International Reading Association Proceedings, 9, 1964, 93-94.

20. Olson, Willard C., *Child Development.* Boston: D. C. Heath and Company, 1949.

21. ———, "Seeking Self-Selection and Pacing in the Use of Books by Children," *In Individualizing Your Reading Program,* Jeannette Veatch. New York: G. P. Putnam's Sons, 1959.

22. Putnam, Lillian R., "Controversial Aspects of Individualized Reading," *Improvement of Reading Through Classroom Practice.* International Reading Association Proceedings, 9, 1964, 99-100.

23. Russell, David H., *Children Learn to Read* (2nd ed.), Boston: Ginn and Company, 1961, Chapter 15.

24. Sartain, Harry W., "A Bibliography on Individualized Reading," *Reading Teacher,* 13 (April 1960), 262-65.

25. Schwartzberg, Herbert, "What Children Think Of Individualized Reading," *Reading Teacher,* 16 (November 1962), 86-89.

26. Sipay, Edward R., "Individualized Reading: Theory and Practice," *Children Can Learn To Read — But How?* Rhode Island College Reading Conference Proceedings, Providence, 1964, 82-93.

27. Sister Aloysius Clare Maher, "Individualizing The Teaching of Reading Through Tape Recordings," *Changing Concepts of Reading Instruction.* International Reading Association Proceedings, 6, 1961, 179-81.

28. Smith, Nila Banton, *Reading Instruction for Today's Children.* Englewood Cliffs, N. J.: Prentice-Hall, Inc., 1963, Chapter 7.

29. ———, *American Reading Instruction.* Newark, International Reading Association, 1965, 378.

30. Spache, George D., *Reading In The Elementary School.* Boston: Allyn and Bacon, Inc., 1964, p. 102, Chapters 4, 11.

31. Sperber, Robert, "An Individualized Reading Program In a Third Grade," *Individualizing Reading Practices.* Bureau of Publications, Teachers College, Columbia University, 1958, 44-54.

32. Veatch, Jeannette, "Self-Selection and the Individual Conference in Reading Instruction," *Improving Reading Instruction.* Joint Proceedings of Reading Conference and Summer Workshop, Vol. 1, The Pennsylvania State University, 1963, 19-25.

33. ———, "What Research Says About Individualized Reading," *Children Can Learn to Read — But How?* Rhode Island Reading Conference Proceedings, Providence, 1964, 94-101.

34. ———, *Reading in the Elementary School.* New York: The Ronald Press Company, 1966.

35. Vite, Irene W., "The Future of Individualized Reading Instruction: Bright and Promising," *Reading as an Intellectual Activity,* International Reading Association Proceedings, 8, 1963, 232-35.

36. Witty, Paul A., "Individualized Reading: A Postscript," *Elementary English,* XXXI (March 1964), 211-17.

Teaching Reading-Study Skills

12

Formal education has many goals, one of which is to help the child become increasingly independent within the framework of the school setting. To achieve such independence the learner must master a number of related language tools or skills. One important cluster of skills has been designated reading-study skills or work-type reading skills. In our reading dominated schools, these skills are of primary importance. Yet, in actual classroom practice, they are not always treated as though perceived as important. Obviously the need for these skills becomes more pronounced as students move upward through the grades. A review of the literature reveals general agreement about the major areas that have come to be designated as the reading-study skills. Included would be:

1. Locating Information
2. Evaluating Material
3. Organizing and Summarizing Data

4. Retaining Essentials of What is Read
5. Flexibility, or Adjusting Rate to Purpose

Any one of these major topics would probably include numerous specific skills; for instance, locating information would cover:

1. Effective use of books
    a. Table of Contents
    b. Use of Index
        (1) knowledge of alphabetical order
        (2) use of key words
        (3) cross-listings
        (4) following subtopics
        (5) significance of abbreviations and signals commonly used, e.g., "see also . . . ," or commas and hyphens in page listings
2. Use of Special References
    a. Encyclopedia
    b. Atlas
    c. Dictionary
        (1) extended knowledge of alphabetical order
        (2) selection of proper connotation of word
        (3) recognition of inflected and derived forms of words
        (4) use of diacritical marks
    d. Use of Library Aids
        (1) card catalogue
        (2) *Reader's Guide*
        (3) bound periodicals

The study skills are an excellent illustration of what is meant by the term developmental. It can be seen that any given skill is not taught exclusively, or once for all time, at a given grade level. Each skill can be thought of as being a continuum which represents both increasing difficulty of learning tasks and increasing potential usefulness to the learner. For instance, skill in using a table of contents is first taught systematically in grade one when the teacher calls attention to the list of stories found in a pre-primer. With this experience, no child will have mastered this skill to a degree required for effective use of the table of contents in a sixth-grade geography book. However, since teaching the use of a table of contents, index, or appendix is not seen as part of the content of either geography, health, or arithmetic; these and other related study skills may be neglected in all courses of study.

Brewer (2) states that if students are to be able to work effectively in content areas, ". . . the school must accept greater responsibility for initial teaching and provide guided practice in using the reading study skills. It is essential that these be interpreted as fundamental, and treated as such in order to progress in all curriculum subjects." While it is true that some children will learn study skills incidentally, the importance of these skills suggest that they should not be left to incidental learning.

LOCATING INFORMATION

As children become independent readers and attempt to find answers through wide and varied reading, they must understand and use all the hints and helps available in order to determine rapidly and accurately whether a particular book contains information in which they are interested. In other words, knowing how to use the book is a prerequisite for intelligent use of supplementary reading in the subject areas and in any unit work. In the intermediate grades, the increased need for study skills stems from the nature of the materials used, the need for wide reading, and the fact that supervision is not always readily available. Reading ability is a prerequisite for the development of study skills, but this ability in itself does not assure that a pupil has mastered these skills. Extensive reading may not result in mastery of study skills. When a pupil fails to develop adequate study skills, the educational process may become dull and unpleasant. Therefore, guidance and specific instruction must be provided to help children develop these skills.

During the past few years, we have witnessed a tremendous expansion of the availability of books, professional journals, and other printed matter in practically every area of man's experience. This advance in knowledge in the past two decades, even when compared with previous centuries, has been so dramatic that the period since 1945 has been labeled the era of the "knowledge explosion." Educational methods, of necessity, will have to change radically to adapt to this new challenge. Competency in any given field takes on a new meaning in the face of the mass of information presently available.

The contents of any subject area cannot be encompassed within the framework of a single textbook or even a series of texts. The time lag between research and publication, and the adoption of textbooks in the various content areas, causes the most recent texts to be somewhat inadequate. Good teachers have always attempted to provide supplementary reading materials, but achieving this goal has not always been easy. Today, providing a wide array of supplementary materials is not just a matter to be recommended, it is an absolute necessity.

Thus, with a need to cover much more material in many different sources, the study skills have rather abruptly increased in value to the learner while the school's respect for these skills and its ability to effectively teach them has lagged. The following discussion deals with facets of instruction that relate to locating information.

EFFECTIVE USE OF BOOKS

In teaching any of the study skills, the teacher at each grade level starts from, and builds on, what the student presently knows. To do this, the present ability level of each student must be determined. A good place to begin is with the textbook adopted for use in a given course. Teachers have learned from experience that many students are not particularly adept at "mining" a book. Learning situations should lead to the development of facility in this area.

It is easy to develop exercises that foster such growth. Some teachers do not particularly like the exercise approach, but it should be kept in mind that any learning situation is, in essence, an exercise. The issue is how exercise materials and specific teachings are used in relation to the goals to be achieved. Some very important learnings deal with the mechanics of learning — *how* to use a card catalogue, *where* to look in an encyclopedia, *when* an appendix or glossary might be useful, *what* is likely to be found in an appendix or glossary, and the like.

Workbook exercises are often provided to help pupils understand the function of an index, table of contents, or appendix. It is not uncommon to find pupils who can work out correct solutions to workbook problems which consist of sample lines from an index but who still do not know how to get help from a real index. One of the best ways to teach children how to use a book effectively is to design a learning situation around a textbook which they will be using throughout the year. A social science, health, or other text would provide ample opportunities for teaching the functions of the table of contents, charts, indexes, or appendixes. The use of the child's actual text will give him something concrete to return to when he is in doubt. Skills learned in using one text should transfer to books in other areas.

Student deficiencies in using a table of contents, index, glossary, and appendix are frequently not detected by teachers. When this is the case, provisions may not be made for teaching these skills. Too often it is assumed these basic skills have been taught or are being taught elsewhere. For example, as an outcome of an in-service program, a group of teachers agreed to build a one-page testing-teaching exercise consisting of fifteen to twenty questions which would measure students' skill in using these parts of a book. The exercise was to be specifically applicable to the textbook students were using in one of their courses. Although the books had been in use for nearly three months, few students were able to complete the exercise without error. Teachers discovered glaring deficiencies and tremendous individual differences in students' ability to use these reader aids. In one class, the time students took to do the "book mining" exercise was noted. The range was from six to twenty-two minutes (a range of 400 per cent), with some students unable to complete the task. An exercise similar to that under discussion is shown in Figure 33 on the following page.

An exercise of this nature might be used initially with an entire class. For the proficient student, this will be a justifiable review. For other students, this experience will serve as a diagnostic instrument. The observant teacher will note which students have difficulty and what their problems are. Teaching small groups and individual students the skills they need should be an outgrowth of the teacher's findings. General concepts will also be taught in the process. This particular experience was constructed for use with a sixth-grade social studies text.*

The exercise, based on a textbook in use, teaches a number of facts about the book. Question one takes the reader to the table of contents and requires that he be able to associate his home state as a part of a larger geographical region of the United States. Question two calls attention to a sixteen-page atlas; and question three focuses on a second highly specialized table of contents which deals exclusively with maps.

Questions 4–8 deal with ways in which the index may be helpful. The reader must locate pictures through the use of key words and be prepared to look under different headings. (Grand Coulie Dam

---

*Norman Carls, Phillip Baron and Frank E. Sorenson, *Knowing Our Neighbors In The United States* (New York: Holt, Rinehart & Winston, Inc., 1966).

FIGURE 33

How to Use a Book

1. The region in which we live is discussed under the heading ______________________________.
2. The last 16 pages in the book are called an Atlas. Looking at these pages can you define "atlas"? ______________
3. On what page can you find a listing of all maps, graphs and diagrams found in the book? ______________
4. Does the book contain a picture of Wonder Lake? _____ How did you go about answering this question? ______________ ______________________________
5. Is there a picture of the Grand Coulie Dam in the text? _____
6. Under what heading must you look to find it? ______________ ______________________________
7. In the index there is a main heading *Exploration.* What six subheadings are found under it? ______________ ______________________________
8. The book contains a double page map called Main Air Routes in the U.S. There is no heading "Main Air Routes" in the index. How can you find this map? ______________ ______________________________
9. There are two sections of the book which provide the pronunciation of difficult words, these are ______________ and ______________.
10. The pronunciation of the following words is provided in the ______________. In the blank spaces show the pronunciation and page number where found:
    SHOSHONE ______________ Page______
    COMANCHE ______________ Page______
    FORT DUQUESNE ______________ Page______
11. A particular page contains the *definition* of difficult words used throughout the book. That page is called the ______________ and is page number ______.

---

is found under Grand Coulie *Project.*) Topics may be listed as subheads under a more general heading. Thus, Dutch, English, Spanish and other explorations are all listed under *Exploration.* Questions

9–11 deal with information about pronunciation and meanings of more difficult words, and call attention that these aids are divided between the index and glossary.

Profiting from Reader-Aids Provided in Books

Students sometimes fail to realize that a number of reader-aids are incorporated in most reference books and textbooks. Unfamiliarity with, or disinclination to use, these aids will inhibit students from "mining" books with maximum efficiency. The student, although he has a need for this skill, does not recognize the need since he is not aware of the value of these aids or how they might improve his learning.

It will be noted that, for one purpose, the table of contents might be skimmed. With other goals in mind, it must be read critically. A comparison of different books would disclose that a table of contents may consist exclusively of chapter titles. This is similar to an outline composed of nothing but major topics. In some books, chapter titles are followed by a number of topics in the order in which they are discussed. Students may note that this, in essence, is a modified index containing only major headings in *chronological* order. The index, on the other hand, is in *alphabetical* order, dealing with smaller topics, and cutting across chapters.

The major learnings are: (1) that parts of the book are deliberately designed as aids for the reader; (2) these are valuable aids and are used with profit by the efficient reader; (3) each of the different parts of a book has a definite purpose. The efficient reader must make instant decisions as to where to go for specific types of help. In other words, he learns what type of information is contained in each section, where the various aids are located, and how each may be used effectively. Once learned, this knowledge can be transferred and applied to any book. The following is an abbreviated treatment of what the reader might expect to gain from the various helps found in most books:

As "Aids" for the Reader	*Information the Reader Might Expect to Find*
Title Page	Main title and subtitle. (The latter may set forth the limitations and narrow the topic.) Name of author, date published.

Table of Contents	Chapter titles followed by major topics discussed in each chapter. Is book divided into major parts (I, II, III)? What are these? Length of chapters give hint as to thoroughness of treatment.
Preface	To whom or to what group does the author address the book? What is his stated purpose? What new features does he stress? What unique features does he believe are found in the book?
Illustrations	Title, item and page where found.
Index	Major topics in alphabetical order; minor topics under each heading; key phrases, cross listings, photographs, drawings, charts, tables.
Glossary	Difficult or specialized terms presented in alphabetical order, with a definition.
Appendix	Organized body of facts related to subject under consideration. For example, in a geography book the appendix may give the areas of states or nations, population, state and national capitals, extent of manufacturing exports, imports, mineral deposits, etc.

USE OF LIBRARY

Effective use of library resources may well be one of the most underrated and undertaught skills in the entire school program. The library is *basic* to the school's reading program. It is a place where children read and receive guidance in both the use of books and in research techniques. Children at all grade levels need the experience of frequent contacts with a good school library.

Some teachers use the library effectively themselves but do not assume responsibility for teaching students to do so. On the other hand, there are a number of teachers who would score low on any evaluation of their personal use of library facilities. To illustrate, one school librarian and principal were convinced that a substantial number of the teaching staff were somewhat derelict in their per-

Some important study skills deal with the effective use of books; others deal with locating books and materials which contain desired information. Knowledge of how to use the card catalogue and other reference materials effectively is a valuable asset of the independent reader. (Courtesy Bexley Schools, Bexley, Ohio; photographer: Arthur Burt, Inc.)

sonal use of the library. Further, student use of the library for these teachers' courses seemed to be less than optimum. A one-hour library unit was incorporated into the total in-service program. Each teacher was relieved of his regularly scheduled duties for a one-hour period, and this time was spent in conference with the librarian. The librarian assumed responsibility for discussing and pointing out resources which related directly to the various subjects taught by each teacher. Pamphlets, bound volumes, pertinent books, government documents, current magazines, and the like were located, and suggestions were made as to how the librarian might help the faculty member and the students in his classes.

Records disclosed that the attitude of a number of the teaching staff changed markedly after this experience. Some teachers visited the library more frequently, spent more time in the library, and checked out more materials. In addition, the students in these teachers' courses were channeled into the library much more effectively.

It is generally conceded that it is difficult to teach library usage in a classroom setting removed from the library materials themselves. However, certain facts related to the library can be discussed prior to a visit to the library.

Several teachers in one school built a model card catalogue drawer using a three-by-five index-card box and constructing approximately 100 author cards ranging from *A* through *G*. This model was used by teachers in their various classrooms and was particularly useful in working with individual students who were not yet competent in the use of the card catalogue.

Another useful teaching device consisted of a library check list devised by teachers and the librarian. The list consisted of eight or ten specific tasks which the student was to perform in the library such as:

1. Find the book *King of the Wind* by Marguerite Henry.
2. A. Who is the author of the book *A Child's History of Art?* ______.
   B. What is the call number of this book?______.
   C. Fill out a library card for this book______.
3. Where are the bound volumes of *My Weekly Reader* located? ______.

These items provide guided practice in the use of title and author cards, location of books and journals on the shelves, and the proper filling out of library cards. Other tasks cover specific learnings related to the library.

To use this technique effectively, small groups or individual students go to the library at specific times. The librarian may give a brief explanation of how to use certain facilities in the library. Then each child may be handed a check list of tasks. The problems may vary according to grade level and individual student needs. In some cases a student monitor may work one hour a week in the library helping other students with the check list and other problems.

There are numerous ways in which teachers and the librarian may work together in teaching study skills. One account of such a co-operative endeavor describes a joint teaching venture in which one teacher and the librarian conducted a weekly library usage period. Topics covered included search techniques, organizing a paper, constructing the bibliography, outlining, and notetaking. (17)

At some stage of the library-skills program the *Dewey decimal system* might be explained. A duplicated sheet containing information may be studied in class or in a library visit. The amount of details included would be determined by teacher objectives and student readiness. Material such as the following might be included: All books are divided into ten major groups and each group is numbered as follows:

000 - 099	general works, bibliographies, encyclopedias, periodicals
100 - 199	philosophy, psychology
200 - 299	religion
300 - 399	education, government, law, sociology
400 - 499	language
500 - 599	physical science, mathematics
600 - 699	medicine, engineering, agriculture
700 - 799	fine arts (painting, architecture, music)
800 - 899	literature
900 - 999	history, travel, biography

Reference Materials

Using reference materials is an important study skill which, as a general rule, is not thoroughly taught in our schools. Many students reach high school or even college with only a hazy idea of how to make a systematic search of available materials. The child, both in and out of school, is constantly faced with the problem of locating material and deciding whether it is relevant to his purpose. (20) Although a few children in the upper primary level are ready for limited use of instruction in the use of reference materials, it is in the intermediate grades that teachers have a major responsibility to teach these skills.

The Encyclopedia

The use of encyclopedias and other reference books should be deliberately taught. If a set is located in the room, different children or groups can be taught facility in their use at various times. Instruction here will parallel points already covered above, i.e., topics are arranged in alphabetical order, books are numbered in series, the alphabetical range covered is indicated on the cover, and cross listings and key words will have to be used. The teacher can make a set of card exercises, each card containing a question: "What book and what page tell about coal?" "About the Suez Canal?" "About Iron Deposits?"

Teaching any given unit in any content area can provide the framework for teaching efficient use of the encyclopedia to those students who need this instruction. Assume a health class is developing the topic *The Advance of Medicine.* Students might be asked to list all of the possible headings under which they might list data which relates to *The Advance of Medicine.* The responses might range from one suggestion to "look under medicine" to a half page of suggestions which might include medicine, surgery, disease, medical research, drugs, germ theory, space medicine, and public health. Other headings might include particular diseases such as cancer, tuberculosis, yellow fever, diabetes, poliomyelitis; or the names of individuals who made significant medical discoveries such as Walter Reed, Jonas Salk, Louis Pasteur.

INTERPRETING AND EVALUATING MATERIAL

Locating information is an important part of the learning process, but this step is only a prelude to the ultimate goal of assimilation of material. The ability to locate information will have little impact on personal or academic growth if the student is unable to read the material he has located.

Teaching students how to read critically is undoubtedly the most difficult task attempted in our schools. In fact, if the matter is pressed beyond the usual textbook definitions, asking a group of teachers to *define* critical reading is more likely to result in chaos than in unanimity. Practically all of their definitions are abstractions, simply because critical reading involves so many variables.

Interpreting and evaluating material is probably as close a synonym for *critical reading* as can be found. Illustrations of the analytical abilities involved include:

1. Knowing what the author has said
2. Grasping the validity of statements and knowing when and how to check validity with other sources
3. Differentiating between fact and opinion

4. Noting when inferences are being drawn and drawing them when they are not stated
5. Detecting author bias as well as inaccuracies which might not be traceable to bias
6. Understanding one's own biases as these relate to what is being read
7. Taking into consideration an author's use of allusions, satire, humor, irony and the like
8. Developing some criteria for judging an author's competency in the area in which he writes

Undoubtedly this list could be extended. Each of the above abilities is developmental in nature and should be taught at all grade levels. The reading tasks found in the intermediate grades are characterized by an increasing difficulty that requires a high degree of competency if the reader is to grow increasingly perceptive. This point holds even as we move into the high school and beyond. How many adults are immune to propaganda, know both sides of controversial issues, and do not let their emotions color interpretations while reading? Parke (23) suggests that students read for much the same reasons as do adults; namely, to keep informed, secure answers to questions, solve problems, follow directions, and share with others. It is likely that students do more reading that calls for interpretation and evaluation than do adults simply because this is the nature of being a student.

The test of critical reading often applied in our schools is the students' demonstration of the ability to restate or write what an author has said. The inability to discern what the author is saying may well be evidence of inability to read the material critically, but paraphrasing, by itself, is not evidence of critical reading either. Restating the gist of a passage but failing to detect author bias will result in a transfer of author bias to the reader's own thought. Knowing what the author is saying without seeing that some statements are contrary to fact will inhibit critical reading, as will reciting strongly expressed opinions as if these were statements of verifiable facts.

Interpreting and evaluating calls for the application of a number of the mechanical reading skills and higher level abilities listed above. Students need both guidance and systematic practice in developing work habits and study techniques, a number of which are dealt with in the following discussion.

RETENTION OF MATERIAL READ

The organization of our schools and the curricular materials used to make learning very dependent upon reading. Once the mechanical process of recognizing printed words is fairly well-established, the most frequently cited weakness of students at *all* educational levels relates to inefficient retention of what is read. Remembering what is read is synonymous with "learning from reading." Of most reading that students are expected to do, this is the primary goal.

When we subject students to an examination of materials read, we are in essence sampling the knowledge they have gleaned and retained. We often find that reading is relatively ineffective when judged by what students retain. Approximately the same degree of efficiency (or inefficiency) in retention is found when the material is presented orally via lecture. Some loss in the communicative process is inevitable. Since the role of the teacher is to guide and direct learning activities, we should seek to examine every approach or technique that will further that purpose.

Retention of material read is influenced by many factors, one of which is the reader's "set." *Set* is a psychological term which refers to a reader's perception of the task. This is often discussed under the general heading of the "reader's purpose." It is probably true that, as teachers, we sometimes fail in helping students develop a meaningful purpose for reading. Sometimes more stress is placed on the ritual of covering material than on assimilation. This misemphasis is seen, for example, when a teacher gives a reading assignment just as a class period ends; or when there is no further elaboration than "your assignment for our next meeting is chapter 8—read chapter 8 for Friday."

Many students will follow these instructions with no appreciable learning taking place. It is also unlikely they will make contributions if the material is discussed in class. When the reader's only purpose is to fulfill an assignment, he will read chapter 8, or any other chapter, without conscious interaction with the material. If, as he finishes the reading, his teacher were suddenly to appear and ask, "What have you just read?" the answer would be, "I don't know, I was just trying to finish the assignment."

Use of Questioning to Inculcate a Learning Set

Studies indicate that questions that are considered prior to the actual reading, have a salutory effect on both learning and retention. (13) Questions provide a purpose for reading and alert the reader to important issues to be covered. In this sense, questions provide a preview of what will be met in the reading situation. This technique is one of the highly justifiable procedures of most "study programs." (3, 7)

The use of questions should not be limited to preparing students for assignments. A greater value for questions results from helping the student formulate concepts. Yet, as Smith (29) points out, questions per se have no inherent value. In any teaching situation, questions can be used most unimaginatively. The efficacy of questioning lies in the interaction which may take place between teacher and student as together they explore the *meaning* of what is being taught and learned. "The artful teacher initiates and sustains the kind of thoughtful discourse that helps students ruminate and organize ideas."

USING THE DICTIONARY

The use of the dictionary is another important study skill associated with reading instruction at the intermediate level. The three major tasks in learning dictionary usage are (1) learning to find a particular word, (2) learning to determine its pronunciation, and (3) learning to select the correct meaning of the word in the context in which it is used. Teaching dictionary skills is often neglected by teachers even when they acknowledge the value of these skills. This neglect might stem from a teacher's feeling of inadequacy about certain relatively difficult facets of dictionary usage such as diacritical markings or pronunciation keys. On the other hand, teaching may fall short of maximum efficiency when dictionary skills are taught as something extra rather than as an intrinsic part of the regular reading instruction. The use of the dictionary should always be seen by both teacher and pupil as a means of getting meaning, not as a form of rote drill or a penalty for making certain errors.

There are certain prerequisites which are essential for successful use of the dictionary. A few of these skills or understandings are:

1. The knowledge of alphabetical order
2. The understanding that a word can have many different meanings
3. The knowledge of root words and the various inflected and derived forms of root words

4. The understanding that letters and combinations of letters have different sound values in different situations and that some letters are silent
5. The knowledge that *y* on the end of some words is changed to *i* before adding *es* for plurals

Facility in the use of the dictionary paves the way for a number of potential breakthroughs in the struggle for independence in reading.

1. Unlocks the sound or pronunciation of words
2. Discloses new meanings of words which may be known in only one or a limited number of connotations
3. Confirms the spelling of a word when one can approximate its correct spelling
4. Expands vocabulary through mastery of inflected and derived forms of known root words

These skills are developmental in nature and must be refined and extended as the child moves upward through the grades. The alphabetizing ability which is adequate for successful fourth-grade work will be inadequate for junior high or high school. The brunt of teaching dictionary skills falls on the intermediate grades simply because most of those skills are introduced during these years of instruction. The success the child feels and the utility he sees in dictionary usage can be most important factors in how he reacts to the dictionary as a tool for helping him in all facets of communication. Pupils must be shown that dictionary skills are permanently needed skills. Failure to master these skills can color the attitudes of pupils for many years to come.

A number of developmental tasks are associated with dictionary usage and there is a general agreement among educators on what these tasks are and the order in which they should be presented.

Developmental Tasks in Dictionary Mastery

1. Recognize and differentiate between letters
2. Associate letter names with letter symbols
3. Learn the letters of the alphabet in order
4. Arrange a number of words by alphabetical order of their initial letter
5. Extend above skill to second and third letters of words, eventually working through all letters of a word if necessary

6. Develop facility in rapid, effective use of dictionary, i.e., where does H, P, V come in the dictionary; open dictionary as near as possible to word being studied
7. Develop the ability to use accent marks in arriving at the pronunciation of words
8. Learn to interpret phonetic spelling used in dictionary
9. Use pronunciation key given somewhere on each double page of most dictionaries
10. Work out different pronunciations and meanings of words which are spelled alike
11. Determine which is the preferred pronunciation when several are given
12. Select the meaning which fits the context
13. Profit from guide words found at the top of each page to tell at a glance if the page contains the word being sought
14. Use intelligently special sections of a dictionary: geographical terms and names, biographical data, foreign words and phrases

Although particular skills are characteristically taught at a given grade level, what the individual child has learned or not learned should determine what is taught. Fortunately, dictionaries are available at all levels of difficulty from simple picture dictionaries to massive unabridged editions. The needs of the child and the goals of the teacher should determine how these differences in dictionaries will be utilized in the classroom. A child who is expected to use a dictionary which calls for skills far beyond what he has mastered will profit little from the experience. Any classroom practice which puts the child in such a position has little if any educational justification.

RATE OF READING

The rate at which one can assimilate meaning from printed symbols becomes a reading problem when students are expected to understand curricular materials for which their reading skills, habits, and abilities are inadequate. The intermediate grades are probably the first level at which a concern for rate of reading is justified since at this point emphasis begins to be placed on the various content areas. In recent years there has been considerable emphasis on the need for improving rate of reading. The impetus for this concern with rate undoubtedly came first at the college level, where, for the past several decades, considerable attention has been given to the improvement of reading ability with emphasis on rate. College reading improvement programs grew out of the conviction that many college students have the capacity to meet the demands of the college curriculum but that their reading habits make them poor academic risks. It is undoubtedly true that many teachers, ranging from high school to the intermediate levels, are convinced that this is also the case with many of their students.

Over the years the term *rate of reading* has been widely but not always wisely used. It has been a popular practice to speak of the rate of reading of the average high school senior, college freshman, or adult. The impression was often left that the figure quoted, such as 325 or 375 words per minute, had some real significance. The implication was that once an individual's rate for reading a given passage was established, this figure could be cited as though it were a constant for any reading situation. The emphasis on rate led some individuals to confuse the entire reading process with the number of words one could allegedly cover in a specified period of time. In an effort to lessen this tendency, it became popular to talk about "rate of comprehension," a term which emphasized that reading is getting meaning. But this term was also subject to semantic confusion since several factors are always at work in determining one's rate of comprehension. There are a number of variables which influence the rate at which different reading materials can be assimilated:

1. The reader's knowledge of the general subject matter
2. The vocabulary load, difficulty level of words and concepts
3. The reader's degree of motivation
4. The reader's purpose for reading the material
5. The physiological state of the reader, whether fatigued, etc.
6. The length of the reading period
7. Mechanical factors such as size of print and length of line
8. The readability of the material as determined by such factors as style of writing, sentence structure, and sentence length
9. The reader's mastery of the mechanical skills of reading, such as number of words known as sight words, ability to sound unknown words, ability to profit from punctuation, and freedom from the habit of inserting, omitting, or repeating words or phrases
10. The number of figures, illustrations, cross-references, and footnotes the material contains

Consideration of these factors reveals that no one sample of reading behavior can provide a valid basis for establishing a person's rate of comprehension. Any figure arrived at would be valid only for the particular material read under the precise conditions which prevailed while it was being read. Regardless of the fact that the term *rate of reading* is vague and may lead to confusion, there is little question that the rate at which pupils read curricular materials is an instructional problem which tends to become more acute as they move through the grades.

Varying Rate According to Material and Purpose for Reading

A facile reader must develop several different rates for reading different types of printed matter. (4) This fact merits careful attention in the intermediate grades because here the pupil must read a great variety of materials in various content areas. The child should learn to adjust his reading behavior to the material and to the objectives he has for reading it. A magazine article may be read with good comprehension at several hundred words per minute while the same reader may have to spend several minutes in reading a mathematical problem stated in forty words. Or assume that a pupil, having read a particular passage, is attempting to recall the five largest cities of the United States. He has tentatively settled for New York, Chicago, and San Francisco but the other two city names do not come to mind. As he rereads, it would be a slow and possibly wasteful effort to read carefully every word and sentence of the entire section which contains the desired information. If the pupil had mastered the technique of scanning material, it would be a speedy process to find the one or two sentences that contain the desired data; these could then be read carefully. Many readers find that they can read long descriptive passages in a novel much more rapidly than dialogue.

Developing Flexibility

The term flexibility, as applied to reading, refers to the ability to read different materials at different rates. An analogy might be traced between reading and walking. Just as most individuals have settled into a particular characteristic gait in walking, they have also developed a favorite reading pace. However, all individuals can walk faster when circumstance demands it. Examples would include the threat of rain, noting one is late for an appointment, or the likelihood of missing a bus. In the absence of such motivators, the individual settles back into his characteristic gait.

It should be obvious to anyone who reads widely that there is little justification for reading all material at the same rate. Such a habit will be wasteful in many situations. The flexible reader is one who has developed the ability to "adjust to the terrain." He has developed the ability to discern where more rapid reading is appropriate, and he has developed the ability to read more rapidly in such situations.

Initial training in learning to read concentrates heavily on word recognition. It is obvious that the individual who fails continually to increase his sight vocabulary can hardly be expected to learn to read more rapidly or more efficiently. The need for growth in rate of reading is an excellent example of the developmental nature of reading. Unfortunately, formal instruction in reading makes little provision for helping students develop this skill.

Improving Rate Through Improving Reading Skills

The problem of improving rate can be oversimplified unless one keeps in mind that rate is influenced by the reader's skills, habits, and attitudes toward the material being read. It would be unrealistic to attempt to improve slow rate of reading without dealing with those factors which are the basis for the slow reading. When slow reading is simply a habitual response stemming from a lack of basic reading skills, it can be dealt with by practice in those skills. Lack of skills, or the development of habits such as guessing, substituting or omitting words, adding words to salvage meaning, or ignoring punctuation, inevitably contribute to slow reading. Inadequate word-attack skills may prevent the child from arriving at the pronunciation of words or cause him to arrive at the pronunciation very slowly. Word-by-word reading is usually related to these problems.

Reading in phrases is a skill which relates to rate of reading on two scores. Word-by-word reading is time-consuming and also tends to interfere with getting the meaning. A child who has been taught to read for meaning will have to repeat sentences and parts of sentences when he loses the thought because he has been so slow in piecing the various work units into a meaningful whole. When word-by-word reading is habitual—that is, when it has been reinforced by many thousands of reading experiences—it is sometimes advisable to give the reader practice on reading easy phrases. Gradually, more difficult reading material can be used. The teacher can make up drill exercises which use phrases in isolation, exercises which show logical phrases underlined, or short passages where the student underlines logical phrases. These three procedures are illustrated in Figure 34 below. Figure 35, on the following page, presents a sustained reading passage arranged in phrases.

FIGURE 34

A. The following phrases or short sentences are designed to give practice in reading a number of words as one thought unit. Some pupils read one word at a time — that is, they pause after each word: up, the, mountain. *Since this is a logical thought unit it should be read:* up the mountain. *Read the phrases from left to right across the page.*

In the car   down the hill   at the farm   from the house
had to leave soon   in the big house   he will be   has gone away
the white horse   eat some cake   ran to the house   the show
can see it   the pretty dress   will look good   we can see
much too much   the tiny boat   on the paper   to the fair

B. In the following paragraph logical thought units have been separated. Be sure to read each phrase as a whole. There are many different ways we could read the same passage. The following is only one example.

Billy saw the car   coming down the road.   He said to himself,
I hope I can get a ride   to town.   He began to wonder
if he should   accept a ride   if he didn't know   the driver.
The car pulled up   and slowed down.   He saw a man
and two boys   about his age.   The boys shouted,   "Hi, Billy."
He recognized the twins.

C. Underline phrases which could be read as one unit. Remember that there may be several different ways to arrange words in thought units. Underline the way you think is best.

The twins, Roger and Sandy, had moved to town several weeks ago. "Hop in the car," said Sandy. "Have you met my dad?" asked Roger. Billy shook hands with Mr. Farrell. As they neared town, Mr. Farrell said, "Can you come and play with the boys at our house or must you go straight home?"

FIGURE 35

The passage below tells something about the reading process. The material has been arranged in short phrases to provide practice in phrase reading. The ability to read in phrases is learned through practice. After reading this material several times, you should be reading it both faster and more smoothly. Try to apply this skill when you read other materials which have not been phrased.
(Read down the columns, reading each line as a unit.)

This exercise
is arranged
in columns
of phrases
to help you
in developing
the habit of
reading phrases.
Try to read
each line
"as one unit."
That is —
do not read
each/word/
as/a/unit/.
With practice,
you will find
you can read
several words
as units.
As you read
other materials
which have not
been phrased,
let your eyes
and your mind
cooperate
in selecting
several words
which are
"logical thoughts."
This will help you
to read
more rapidly,
more smoothly,
and with good
comprehension.
Your eyes
and your mind
are capable
of dealing
with several
smaller words
or with a
very large one.
For instance —
Mississippi
Rhode Island
cheerfulness
peppermint
in olden days
cold and rainy.
The examples
cited above
are relatively
long units.
They were easy
for you to read
because they are
familiar.
You have seen
each of them
many times
and you know
their meanings.
These phrases
were not related
to each other.
Other phrases
on this page
are related.
This is a bit
more difficult
to read smoothly.
First because
the thought units
vary in length.
Secondly,
some readers
might select
different
phrasing patterns
than shown here.

CONCLUSION

Study skills, which include locating information, organizing and evaluating material, effective use of library resources, and adjusting reading rate to purpose and material, are a most important cluster of reading skills. Their importance to the learner is not always paralleled by the effectiveness with which they are taught. One of the reasons for this is that these particular skills cut across all subject areas, while responsibility for teaching them is left vague.

Ideally, helping children develop efficient study skills should be an integrated part of the *teaching* in all content areas. Ironically, in actual practice in many classrooms the "content" itself takes precedence over the process of developing effective skills in locating, evaluating and organizing this material.

When study skills are neglected, teaching often becomes ritualistic. All pupils read the same material and are given no guidance or even opportunity to explore the world of books. An example is provided by an observation of a study hall in which row after row of students were listlessly attempting to answer questions found at the end of a particular chapter in their history text. These children had read exclusively from this textbook, and were now required to respond to stimuli such as:

1. List three rulers of Persia.
2. Name three great conquerors.
3. Who is noted for asking questions? (Socrates—and the textbook authors had learned little from him.)

The time wasted in such busy work is a serious indictment of teaching and a sure way to stiffle interest in learning. To hold a child to reading only from a text which gives a larger treatment to the Roman Baths than to Roman Law (because the former can be illustrated with a half page of bad art), is totally indefensible. Here there can be no growth, no development of interest. What results is a reaction against Rome, Greece, and history in general, none of which are solid educational objectives.

Some important study skills do appear to deal primarily with mechanics. Examples include dictionary usage; profiting from reader aids such as a glossary, index, appendix; use of the card catalogue and other library aids. However, these need not be taught mechanically. They are best learned as part of larger educational activities such as unit work which will call for ascertaining definitions and pronunciation of unusual terms, deciding upon the specific connotation of a word; and finding related materials in a wide variety of sources. These and other opportunities for learning are on-going—they occur daily. Thus, one need not resort to lengthy drill on dictionary or reference material skills. The study skills are developmental in nature and are best taught and learned as part of a total growth process.

YOUR POINT OF VIEW?

What are your reactions to the following statements?

1. While study skills are important, pupils who progress through the grades will master these skills through incidental learning.
2. Rate of reading or rate of comprehension is determined by such factors as intellectual level, background experience, and concepts held. Therefore, working directly on "speeding reading" will be ineffective unless these factors are dealt with.
3. As a general rule the questions found in intermediate and junior high school level textbooks deal with isolated facts and do not help the child to organize information and see relationships. (Why not destroy the opposing point of view by citing questions from two or three geography, health, history, or science texts?)
4. One of the strengths of American schools is their thoroughness and effectiveness in helping pupils develop study skills.
5. In regard to dictionary usage, there are few if any new skills introduced beyond fifth or sixth grade. Thus, learning dictionary skills is not developmental beyond this level.

BIBLIOGRAPHY

1. Bond, Guy L., and Eva Bond Wagner, *Teaching the Child to Read* (4th ed.). New York: The Macmillan Company, 1966, Chapters 10 and 11.
2. Brewer, A. Madison, "The Reading Study Skills," *Improving Reading Instruction.* Joint Proceedings of the Twenty-fifth Reading Conference and First Intensive Summer Workshop, Vol. I. The Pennsylvania State University, University Park, Pa., 1964, 25-30.
3. Carner, Richard L., "Levels of Questioning," *Education,* 83 (May 1963), 546-50.
4. Carrillo, Lawrence W., and William D. Sheldon, "The Flexibility of Reading Rate," *Journal of Educational Psychology,* XLIII, 1952, 299-305.

5. Cheyney, Arnold B., "A City-wide Effort Improves Study Skills," *Clearing House,* 36 (February 1962), 330-32.

6. Coleman, Mary Elizabeth, "How To Teach Dictionary - Index Skills," *Explorations In Reading.* Eleventh Annual Reading Conference Proceedings, Lehigh University, Vol. 2, Bethlehem, Pa., 1962, 51-56.

7. Daniels, Hazel, "Questioning — A Most Important Tool In The Teaching of Reading," *Education For Tomorrow-Reading.* Joint Proceedings of the Twenty-sixth Reading Conference and the Second Intensive Summer Workshop, Vol. II, The Pennsylvania State University, University Park, Pa., 1965, 61-65.

8. Dawson, Mildred A., "Learning To Use Books Effectively," *Education,* 83 (September 1962), 20-22.

9. Dechant, Emerald V., *Improving The Teaching of Reading.* Englewood Cliffs, N.J.: Prentice-Hall, Inc., 1964, Chapter 13.

10. *Elementary English* (April 1964), Theme of Issue: *The Dictionary In the Elementary School.*

11. Heilman, Arthur, "Teaching The Study-Reading Skills at The Elementary Level," *Reading, Learning and The Curriculum.* Proceedings of the Twelfth Annual Reading Conference, Lehigh University, Vol. 3, Bethlehem, Pa., 1963, 41-46.

12. Hester, Kathleen B., *Teaching Every Child to Read* (2nd ed.). New York: Harper & Row, Publishers, 1964, Chapters 13-17.

13. Holmes, E., "Reading Guided By Questions Versus Careful Reading and Rereading Without Questions," *School Review,* XXXXIX, 1931, 101-06.

14. Holmes, Jack A., "Speed, Comprehension, and Power in Reading," *Challenge and Experiment In Reading.* International Reading Association Proceedings, 7, 1962, 143-49.

15. Huus, Helen, "Antidote for Apathy — Acquiring Reading Skills for Social Studies," *Challenge and Experiment In Reading.* International Reading Association Proceedings, 7, 1962, 81-88.

16. Jenkins, William A., "Reading Skills In Teaching Literature In The Elementary School," *Elementary English,* XXXXI (November 1964), 778-82.

17. Lauck, Mary Ruth, "Every Teacher a Reading Teacher," *Reading, Learning and The Curriculum.* Proceedings Twelfth Annual Reading Conference, Vol. 3, Lehigh University, Bethlehem, Pa., 1963, 18-21.

18. Mahoney, Sally, "Basic Study Skills and Tools," *Elementary English,* XXXXII (December 1965), 905-15.

19. Massey, Will J., "Critical Reading In The Content Areas," *Reading as an Intellectual Activity.* International Reading Association Proceedings, 8, 1963, 104-07.

20. McKee, Paul, *Reading—A Program of Instruction for The Elementary School.* Boston: Houghton Mifflin Company, 1966, Chapters 9, 11.

21. McKim, Margaret G., and Helen Caskey, *Guiding Growth in Reading* (2nd ed.). New York: The Macmillan Company, 1963, Chapter 12.

22. Miel, Alice, "How to Make a Student," *Reading Teacher,* 15 (September 1961), 8-13.

23. Parke, Margaret B., "Reading For Specific Purposes," *Elementary English,* XXXXI (March 1964), 242-45.

24. Patterson, Charles W., "Pilot Project in Reading and Study Habits," *Reading Teacher,* 17 (April 1964), 531-35.

25. Pauk, Walter, "Study Skills and Scholastic Achievement," *Reading Teacher,* 19 (December 1965), 180-82.

26. Robinson, H. Alan, "Reading Skills Employed In Solving Social Studies Problems," *Reading Teacher,* 18 (January 1965), 263-69.

27. Robinson, Helen M., "Development of Reading Skills," *Elementary School Journal,* LVIII, 1958, 268-74.

28. Schubert, Delwyn G., and Theodore L. Torgerson, *Improving Reading In The Elementary School.* Dubuque, Iowa: William C. Brown Company, Publishers, 1963, Chapters 6-7.

29. Smith, Nila Banton, *Reading Instruction for Today's Children.* Englewood Cliffs, N.J.: Prentice-Hall, Inc., 1963, Chapters 10, 11, 23, 24.

30. Tinker, Miles A., and Constance M. McCullough, *Teaching Elementary Reading.* New York: Appleton-Century-Crofts, Inc., 1962, Chapters 8-9.

31. Whipple, Gertrude, "Essential Types of Reading In The Content Fields," *Improvement of Reading Through Classroom Practice.* International Reading Association Proceedings, 9, 1964, 31-33.

Sex Differences in Learning to Read

Even though there are many studies which purport to throw light on the question of whether boys and girls differ in their ability to master the process of reading, this issue has remained somewhat clouded. One of the complicating factors is that the culture, and the school as part of the culture, may have unconsciously assumed that there is no difference between the sexes. This preconception could stem from the following factors:

1. Standardized achievement tests are built and used on the basis that the "norms" are equally adequate for both sexes. Reading readiness tests use the same problems and the same norms for both sexes. This is also true of reading tests and achievement tests used throughout the grades.
2. American schools in their actual practice have rejected the idea of any sex difference in learning to read, since both boys and girls enter school at the same chronological age.

3. Since the American schools recognize no sex differences, it is a simple matter to assume that there are none.

It is often alleged that the studies on sex differences in reading ability are not in agreement in their reported findings. In other words, the data are said to be inconclusive on this subject. In part, the inconclusiveness of the data stems from the fact that studies which are not actually comparable are sometimes treated as if they were.

Whether two studies are comparable depends on the answers to the following questions:

1. Do the studies deal with the same age group?
2. Are the sexes equated on M.A., I.Q., past experiences, etc.?
3. When grade level is the criterion, is C.A. equated within the grade level?
4. Are the measuring instruments comparable?
5. Are the statistical procedures in both studies comparable?

Assume that Study A, testing six- and seven-year-olds, finds girls superior to boys in reading, and Study B, testing ten- and eleven-year-olds, finds no statistical difference between the sexes. These studies should not be thought of as comparable, and contrary findings should not be viewed as canceling each other. The point here is that, if the issue is to discover sex differences in learning to read, we should be most interested in the early elementary age levels.

Assume that one study tested four facets of achievement customarily measured at a given grade level. Girls were superior on X subtest, and boys were superior on Y subtest, while no statistically significant differences were found on subtests W and Z. Now, if subtests W-X-Y-Z are lumped together under the heading Achievement, the conclusion may emerge that there is no sex difference. However, if X is considered alone, girls were found superior; if Y is considered alone, boys were found superior. The question is whether each of the subtests W-X-Y-Z is equally related to learning reading. Unfortunately, many studies are based on the cancellation process, and conclusions that there are no sex differences are often advanced in situations similar to the illustration above.

Another problem which clouds the issue is whether disparities reported in different studies are actually statistically significant—that is, are the differences real, or does the difference stem merely from chance factors? Four methodological practices bear on this problem: (1) Some experimenters have reported differences but have not tested their results for significance; (2) different studies employ different statistical procedures for arriving at conclusions of statistical significance; (3) different experimenters use different criteria for establishing statistical significance;* (4) conclusions advanced by experimenters are not always completely supported by their data.

Despite the fact that our schools operate from a premise of no sex differences in reading, and that standardized readiness and reading tests also seem to embrace this hypothesis, many teachers and educators do feel that there are real differences between boys as a group and girls as a group in the way they respond to the learning situation labeled "learning to read."

The more one delves into the literature on reading (and non-reading), the harder it becomes to believe that there are no differences between the sexes in mastering the beginning stages of reading. It would be extremely difficult, if not impossible, to find a sizeable group of experienced teachers in the primary grades who, on the basis of their experience, could say that boys as a group and girls as a group are equally inept at mastering the reading process during the first few years of formal instruction.

The purpose of this discussion is to focus attention on sex differences in learning to read. The period dealt with is arbitrarily limited to the elementary years, with emphasis on the primary grades.

DATA RELATED TO SEX DIFFERENCES IN LEARNING READING

As studies are reviewed the cautions mentioned above must be kept in mind. The problem is not a simple process of counting so many studies reporting differences and so many reporting no differences. The effect of a study reporting differences between seven-year-old boys and girls is not cancelled or refuted by a study reporting no differences between high school boys and girls.

The sources of data on this topic fall into three main categories:

1. Data from school situations where the two sexes are compared on reading achievement. *Reading achievement* may include many different subheadings.

---

*One experimenter may insist that a real difference is established only if he could expect to find a difference, as large as he found, once in one hundred times. Another might accept five chances out of one hundred as significant.

2. Data reported from clinical sources, child-guidance clinics, and reading laboratories and clinics.

Representative studies from each of the categories listed above will be cited, starting with data from school situations. The question we are dealing with is, do boys as a group differ from girls as a group in their response to a particular situation called "learning the fundamentals of reading?"

Ayres (7) was one of the first to call attention to sex differences in school achievement. His book *Laggards in Our Schools* does not deal with differences in reading per se. However, he pointed out that 12.8 per cent more boys than girls repeated grades; that 17.2 per cent more girls than boys completed "common school" (eighth grade); and that there was 13 per cent more retardation among boys.

St. John (45) reported no significant difference in the measured intelligence of approximately one thousand pupils in grades one through four, but stated that girls very distinctly excel boys in reading at grade levels one through four. The study covered a four-year period and reported that boys showed 7 per cent more repeating of grades or non-promotions than did girls.

Wilson, et al., (51) report a study covering three years at Horace Mann School. Boys and girls in first grade showed no differences on mental tests, but the authors state ". . . the difference between girls and boys in paragraph reading in this grade was statistically reliable." In reading at second grade level, "the average of chances was 88 in 100 that the girls would be superior." At third grade level, girls surpassed the boys but not significantly. It should be pointed out that the intelligence level of the pupils in this study was considerably above the mean for all children their age.

Alden, et al., (1) report data from children in grades two through six who were tested with the *Durrell Sullivan Reading Capacity Test.** Over six thousand children were tested, and the number of boys who were one or more years retarded in reading was double that of girls in each of the first five grades. Table 3 gives the data on these sex differences.

One of the most significant studies on sex differences was reported by Stroud and Lindquist (46) in 1942. Over three hundred schools with 50,000 pupils were the source of data. The data compiled covered a number of years of testing in the Iowa schools, using the Iowa Every-Pupil Basic Skills Test. In this program,

*Harcourt, Brace and World, Inc., New York.

TABLE 3

Sex Differences Between Boys and Girls in Reading Retardation Measuring One Year or More Retardation

Grade	*Per cent Boys Retarded*	*Per cent Girls Retarded*
2	9.7	4.2
3	14.7	7.1
4	23.6	12.0
5	25.5	11.6
6	13.7	9.9

grades three through eight are tested on reading comprehension, vocabulary, word study skills, basic language skills, and arithmetic skills. The authors state, "Girls have maintained a consistent, and on the whole, significant superiority over boys in the subjects tested, save in arithmetic, where small insignificant differences favor boys." Table 4 shows the mean difference in reading comprehension scores between boys and girls for grades three through eight. It should be noted that the largest differences occur at grades three and four and decline significantly at grade six.

TABLE 4

Sex Differences in Reading Comprehension as Measured by the Iowa Every-Pupil Test of Basic Skills

Grade	*Mean Differences (all favoring girls)*	*Significance Ratios*
3	2.12	2.57
4	2.75	3.38
5	1.29	1.77
6	.30	.39
7	.10	.14
8	.47	.50

Jackson (22) wished to ascertain whether advanced readers and retarded readers could be differentiated on the basis of psychological, social, or environmental factors. He selected 300 advanced readers and 300 retarded readers in grades two through six. The criterion for selection was that pupils fall in either the upper quarter or the lower quarter of their grade in reading ability. The significant fact is that Jackson found a disproportionate number of girls (59 per cent) among the advanced readers and a disproportionate number of boys (63.3 per cent) among the retarded readers. He states, "The data reveal a statistically significant difference between the sexes in relation to reading ability."

Hughes, (21) using the total comprehension scores from the Chicago Reading Tests, measured reading achievement of boys and girls in grades three through eight. She found that the greatest difference was at grade three where the girls achieved more than a half-school-year above the boys. This difference favoring girls was significant at the 1 per cent level. At grade four the difference favoring girls was significant at only the 5 per cent level, while in grades five through eight girls made higher reading scores than did boys, but the differences were not statistically significant.

Nila, (30) during the first weeks of school, tested three hundred first graders on a number of individual and group readiness tests. She reports that on the basis of these test scores, the boys as a group and the girls as a group were equally ready to read. These pupils were tested at the end of the school year for reading achievement. Seventy-two were designated as reading failures; forty-five, or 63 per cent of the failures, were boys, and 37 per cent were girls.

Gates (18) tested over thirteen thousand children in grades two through eight and compared girls and boys mean scores on three reading subtests at each grade level. He states, "In each of the twenty-one comparisons the mean raw score for girls is higher than the mean raw scores for boys, and most of the differences are significant."

Prescott (34) tested over 7,000 boys and 7,000 girls beginning first grade on the Metropolitan Readiness Test to determine whether this test showed sex differences. He reports that when chronological age is equated the performance of girls is superior to that of boys (difference favoring girls significant at the 5 per cent level). Carroll (12) also found sex differences in reading readiness at first-grade level. These differences were in favor of girls and were large enough to be satistically significant.

Data from Cooperative First Grade Studies

During the school year 1964-65, twenty-seven first-grade reading studies were supported by grants from U. S. Office of Education.

A large per cent of these compared the efficacy of different methodologies and materials. Some of the studies did not directly compare scores of boys and girls. Others sought only to determine if one particular instructional approach was more effective with either boys or girls than were other approaches. However, a number of these studies do provide data on sex differences in reading achievement in grade one.

Each of the studies used a number of common pre- and post-treatment measures. The Stanford Achievement Primary Battery Form X was administered to subjects in all studies at the end of grade one. The five reading subtests on this battery are Word Reading, Paragraph Reading, Vocabulary, Spelling and Word Study.* Results from studies which compared the achievement of boys and girls are cited in the following discussion.

Tanyzer and Alpert, (47) comparing mean scores achieved through the use of three basal approaches (Lippincott; ITA; and Scott, Foresman), report, "In each of the three basal reader systems, the girls achieved higher mean scores than the boys. Significant differences favoring girls occurred on the spelling and paragraph meaning subtests" (p. 105). Hahn (19) reports comparative data only for the Word Study test, the mean for girls being significantly higher than that for boys (p. 45).

Fry, (17) using three methods groups (ITA, Diacritical Marking System, and regular basal materials), compared the mean scores of all boys with those of all girls. He reported a significant difference in reading achievement favoring the girls. None of the methods proved to be more advantageous for boys as a group. Heilman (20) found girls' mean scores higher on all reading subtests. The differences being significant on each of the subtests except vocabulary.

Wyatt (53) found significant differences favoring girls on Paragraph Reading, Spelling and Word Study. Boys were superior, but not significantly so, on vocabulary; and girls were superior, but not significantly so, on word reading. Murphy (29) reports, "There were significant differences between the mean scores of the boys and girls on the Stanford Achievement Tests in April, all favoring girls" (p. 69). Specifically, there were three reading approaches used in the study which resulted in 15 separate comparisons of boys and girls mean scores. Six of these comparisons yielded significant differences, all in favor of girls.

*Administration of the Arithmetic subtest was omitted in some studies, and no references to scores on this subject are made in this discussion.

Spache (41) reports, "There were significant differences between the means earned by girls and boys" (p. 288). All the differences found favor girls. Schneyer, et al., (38) report significant differences favoring girls on Paragraph Reading, Spelling and Word Study Skills.

Not all of the studies which note sex differences found the differences to be significant. Spencer and Moquin, (42) using an individualized and basal approach, found girls' mean scores superior to boys on four of the five subtests. The differences were reported as not being significant. Stauffer and Hammond, (44) report data separately for two treatment groups. In each treatment group, girls were superior to boys on all five subtests of the Stanford Achievement test. However, no test of significance of these differences was applied.

Sheldon and Lashinger (39) report higher means for girls on all of the Stanford Achievement reading subtests except vocabulary. They report, "no test of significance of means was carried out for these reported scores but by inspection it appears that the mean differences were consistently small" (p. 56).

Chall and Feldmann's study (13) dealt primarily with teacher implementation of given methodological approaches. In reporting no significant sex differences on achievement on any of the subtests they state, "This lack may be in part a function of the generally depressed scores earned on all of the tests in the sample. On the other hand, the lack of sex differences has been noted in other samples of socially disadvantaged children" (p. 100).

Manning, (23) as a result of his study, states, "The assumption that girls are superior to boys in first-grade reading abilities is held invalid by the results of this investigation." In this study three instructional approaches were compared:

Approach A	Use of Basal Series following Teacher Guide
Approach B	Basal Series plus Intensive Skills program with emphasis on mastering of letter names and sounds
Approach C	Same as B, plus emphasis on children's writing

While agreeing with Manning's observation that boys profited more from treatments B and C, one may still have reservations as to whether the data conclusively refutes the assumptions that girls and boys differ in early reading achievement.

Each treatment group was subdivided into four I.Q. levels. In the B and C treatment groups girls achieved higher means than boys on 7 out of 8 I.Q. comparisons on both Paragraph Meaning and Spelling, and higher means on 5 of 8 comparisons on Word Study. Boys made superior mean scores on Vocabulary and no differences were noted on Word Reading. When data for all treatments were combined, girls were superior on Word Reading and Spelling, and significantly superior on Paragraph Meaning and Word Study.

Clinical Data

The second source of data on sex differences in reading is found in reports from clinical sources, such as child-guidance clinics and remedial reading clinics. Rarely do the data from these sources deal primarily with sex differences. As a rule, the titles of reported research do not indicate that sex differences are discussed, but, almost without exception, these studies reveal a disproportionate number of referrals of boys as compared with girls and, also, an even more disproportionate percentage of seriously retarded readers among boys. The range of percentages is from approximately 65 per cent boys and 35 per cent girls to 90 per cent boys and 10 per cent girls. Monroe (28) reported an exhaustive study of over 400 children who had been referred to the Chicago Institute for Juvenile Research for various problems, including impaired reading. One group of 155 children was referred specifically for reading problems; in this group 86 per cent were boys and 14 per cent were girls.

Blanchard, (10) in discussing seventy-three consecutive cases seen at the Philadelphia Child Guidance Clinic, in which reading was given as one reason for referral or where a reading problem was found to exist, reports that sixty-three of these cases were boys, and ten cases were girls.

Young, (52) investigating forty-one cases diagnosed as retarded in reading and referred to the Psycho-Educational Clinic, Harvard University, reports that thirty-seven of the cases were boys and four cases were girls. He further reports that over a period of years this same ratio held for all children referred who were retarded in reading but had at least average intelligence.

Preston (35) studied the effects of security-insecurity in the home, the school, and the social situation of retarded readers. In a sample of 100 reading failures possessing normal intelligence and no physical defects, there were seventy-two boys and twenty-eight girls.

Missildine, (27) studying the emotional adjustment of thirty retarded readers picked at random from clinic files, reported twenty-five of the thirty were boys. All but two of the children in this study were below ten years of age.

McCollum, (24) discussing forty severe reading disability cases referred to a reading clinic during one year, reports that 78 per cent were boys. Axline (6) reported a study of thirty-seven second graders selected on the basis of reading retardation or non-reading. Twenty-eight, or 76 per cent of the retarded readers, were boys. Vorhaus (50) described 225 reading disability cases seen at the New York University Reading Institute. One hundred and seventy-eight, or 80 per cent of these cases, were boys. All cases were reported as having average or better intelligence.

Fabian (15) reports on a group of 279 children given diagnostic tests at the Brooklyn Juvenile Guidance Center. Ninety-nine of these children were at least eight years of age, had I.Q.'s of eighty or above, and showed reading achievement at least 25 per cent below expectation based on mental age. Of these ninety-nine children, sixty-seven were boys, and thirty-two were girls.

Many other clinical and remedial studies, particularly those of a "case study" nature, also report a preponderance of boys as remedial reading cases. However, these reports are not cited here because the number of cases they discuss is too small for evaluation.

The evidence seems to indicate that there are differences between boys as a group and girls as a group in learning the fundamental skills of reading in the primary grades, but it is not clear what causes these differences. A number of hypotheses have appeared in the literature which attempt to explain the data discussed in this chapter. Some of the more frequently mentioned hypotheses are listed and discussed below. The aim is not to attempt to prove or disprove these various points of view, but rather to present them for critical consideration.

1. *Boys and girls at certain ages differ in "intelligence."* This issue will probably have to go unresolved at the present because, as Terman points out, contemporary tests of intelligence are not constructed to point up differences. And if boys surpass girls on some items and girls surpass boys on other items, who is to say which items are the more valid indicators of general mental ability. (48)

2. *Boys and girls mature at different rates and some phases of growth are closely related to reading.* Since the data are conclusive that girls develop more rapidly than boys, this hypothesis is sometimes seen as the key to the problem under discussion. In skeletal development, girls as a group are superior to boys throughout the

pre-school period, and by the age of six years they are at least a full year in advance of boys. Since boys are less physiologically mature, eye muscles and visual acuity may not be equal to the task of beginning reading, and their attention span may not be developed enough to allow for lengthy concentration on teacher guidance. Maturation cannot be hastened through stress or training. The results of a large number of different experiments in language development present, practically without exception, data showing girls to be statistically superior in language usage and facility throughout the pre-school and primary periods.*

A long-term study carried out at the University of Michigan compares the chronological age at which boys and girls begin to read and the "rate of progress" made after each has mastered a certain level of reading ability. The authors report a significant difference favoring girls in the age of learning to read. However, once children achieved a reading age of eighty-four months on the Gates Primary Reading Test, no difference between boys' and girls' rate of advancement was found. (4)

The champions of the organismic age concept attempt to show a relationship between rate of development in many phases of growth, both physical and mental, and reading ability. Organismic age is the average of age scores on height, weight, mental age, dentition, grip, and the like. Thus, organismic age is weighted quite heavily with physical growth factors. For an explanation of the organismic age concept see Olson (31) and Olson and Hughes (32). For a critical analysis of this concept see Blommers, et al , (11) and Tyler (49).

Balow, (8) in a study of first-grade children, found that mean scores of girls were significantly higher than those of boys on subtests of the *Gates Reading Readiness Test*. Girls had a significantly higher mean on a Paragraph Reading test administered in February. When readiness scores were held constant, the sex differences in achievement disappeared or became too small to be significant. The author concluded that "the ability to see similarities and differences in words accounts for the differences between the sexes in reading achievement." Since this skill is amenable to teaching, Balow suggests that sex differences in reading are more related to educational than maturational factors.

---

*Dorothea McCarthy, "Language Development in Children," *Manual of Child Psychology*, ed. Leonard Carmichael (New York: John Wiley & Sons, Inc. 1954).

3. *The school environment and curriculum at the primary level are more frustrating to boys than to girls.* This hypothesis is very closely related to the preceding one. For instance, if boys and girls mature at different rates it is logical to suppose that participating in the same classroom activity is not the same experience for each group. One group is more mature than the other, but each group is equally expected to do close work, make fine discriminations, sit quietly for extended periods of time, pay attention, co-operate, finish tasks, and inhibit aggression. Many educators think that these are the factors which frustrate boys as a group more than girls.

A study of over seven-hundred children in grades one through five who, due to academic retardation, were selected for special classes, showed boys outnumbering girls by a ratio of more than two to one. Yet the mental age of the boys was slightly, but not significantly, higher than that of the girls. It was concluded that boys were more interested in concrete things and in problem-solving in areas other than those which are purely linguistic. In other words, boys were more interested in unacademic things, as measured by the actual school curriculum, and were penalized for this. Noting that there was more instability among the boys, the author asked, "Is the instability of retarded boys an essential trait or one produced by a school environment that is not altogether fitting?" (14)

During the primary and early elementary years, the emotional, personality, and behavioral problems which schools refer to various agencies include a disproportionate number of boys as compared with girls. Since boys are the poorer achievers, it follows that in our culture the school, the teacher, and the home (automatically but perhaps unconsciously) put more pressure on boys at this age level. Frustration results and is reflected in poor or inadequate responses in any stress situation, such as learning a very complicated symbol system. The disproportionate number of boys found as referrals to guidance clinics and reading clinics may be related to this cultural tendency.

Robinson (37) is convinced that research supports a hypothesis of a sex difference in reading achievement during the first few years of formal schooling, but she states: "At present it is not clear whether just being a girl gives a young child a better chance for early reading success or whether something inherent in the school situation or the social setting militates against the progress of boys." After pointing out that boys as a group produce more remedial reading problems, get lower school marks, have a higher incidence of non-promotion, and produce more "behavior problems" than do girls as a group, Smith and Jenson (40) conclude, "all these findings emphasize the fact that the school functions less effectively for boys than for girls."

Preston's (36) study of reading achievement of German children reports sex differences favoring boys. In addition, he reports more variability among scores made by girls, which is at variance with most findings of American studies. These data strongly suggest cultural influence as being important factors in learning the reading process.

4. *Basal reader materials are less motivating and satisfying to boys than to girls.* This idea is an extension of the preceding hypothesis, three, since the reading materials are naturally part of the curriculum. The rationale behind this hypothesis is that the rather sterile, repetitious "look, oh, look; see baby play" vocabulary and the rigid conformist mood, tone, and atmosphere contained in and conveyed by the pre-primers, primers, and early readers are considerably less challenging to boys than to girls. It is often alleged that the "content" is a far cry from what the culture has taught to and expects from boys. Therefore, beginning reading, which should be an exciting, challenging new adventure, is actually a dull, regressive sort of experience unless the teacher can project a great deal into the material.

Data from Manning's (23) study, discussed earlier, indicates that significant differences favoring girls were found in a regular basal program. A basal program supplemented by other approaches resulted in significantly higher achievement on the part of both boys and girls.

5. *Most primary teachers are women.* Allen (2) states: "Social environments for males and females are not and never have been the same or equal," and points out that from this fact may stem differences in interests, values, and achievement. Bell (9) holds that the difference in reading success between boys and girls is related to their emotional relationships with their teachers. It is his opinion that it is easier for girls to identify with women teachers and that boys are not provided with enough opportunities for the expression of aggression. The various studies all agree that boys show more aggression and aggressive tendencies than do girls. Of course, the school frowns on aggressive behavior and no doubt influences some teachers to react toward boys in a manner different from that

manifested toward girls who, as a group, may have a reputation for being docile, quiet, and co-operative. Terman (48) states that there is ample indication that some sort of "halo" effect operates in the classroom to give girls higher teacher ratings or grades than would be merited on the basis of objective achievement test results. St. John (45) does not question the fact that in grades one through four girls "distinctly" excel boys in reading and general school achievement, but he states: "They (girls) excel *less* when achievement is measured by standard tests than when it is measured by *teacher marks*." (Emphasis added.)

McNeil and Keislar (25) found kindergarten boys' achievement superior to that of girls when beginning instruction relied exclusively on the use of programmed materials. When this instruction was followed by four months of teacher instruction (all women teachers), girls' achievement was superior to that of boys. The authors state, "The fact that the superiority in reading of boys was not maintained under teacher direction indicates that there are variables within the classroom which militate against the maximum performance of young male learners."

Heilman (20) conducted an intensive in-service program in which participating teachers studied and discussed research data relevant to sex differences in learning to read. These teachers did make a number of classroom and teaching adjustments. Boys taught by these teachers had higher mean scores on each of the subtests of the Stanford Achievement Test at the end of grade one, than did boys taught by control-teachers in the same community. "In-service training which resulted in teacher awareness of sex differences in learning to read appears to have evoked classroom practices which tended to enhance the performance of boys."

6. *Boys are less motivated to learn to read.* This hypothesis is closely related to certain others that have previously been mentioned, but it is advanced often enough in the literature on reading to be considered independently. Nila (30) is of the opinion that girls are more likely to work up to the capacity of their abilities than are boys. She states: "The writer believes that the reason boys and girls who are equally ready to read do not make the same progress lies in the factor of motivation." Wilson, et al., (51) state: "It would seem probable that the reasons for more rapid progress by girls are related to learning interests and dispositions, rather than to more subtle sex differences such as mental qualities or characteristics of femininity."

SUGGESTIONS FOR ALLEVIATION OF THE PROBLEM

Coping with the problem of sex differences is a difficult problem, since, as stated previously, our schools tend to operate from the premise that in the early grades there are no significant sex differences in learning to read. Although evidence from primary classrooms does not support this premise, established use is often accepted as the best of evidence that that practice is correct. Any of the factors mentioned above may be present in the case of an impaired reader without justifying the conclusion that the factors in question cause the impaired reading. On the other hand, rejecting all hypotheses would not reduce the ratio of failure among boys as compared with those among girls. Since reading is such an important achievement in our culture, educators should not think of sex differences in learning to read as just another statistic. If there is anything the school can do to prevent the present number of failures in learning to read, it should be done. The following suggestions attempt to focus on school practices which might alleviate this problem.

1. *Staggered school entrance* based on the demonstration of a maturity level (social, emotional, intellectual) which would assume readiness for reading tasks. A genuine pre-school or readiness program, with children moving into grade one at any time during the academic year, would likely be an outgrowth of following this practice. This proposal has several advantages: (1) De-emphasizing chronological age as the criterion for school entrance; (2) The initial number of pupils that first-grade teachers have to deal with would be smaller, giving the teacher a chance to know each child better. As other pupils come in, she could spend more time getting to know them; (3) This practice would destroy the myth that all pupils in a given classroom should be doing the same tasks. The great disadvantage of the proposal is that it is too wide of a departure from present practice to be acceptable to schools and parents. The ungraded primary holds more promise at the moment.

2. *The ungraded primary,* functioning ideally, would encompass all the advantages listed above, since the child moves through the curriculum at his own rate. The concept of promotion is discarded for the primary grades, as is an arbitrary achievement schedule. Thus, the ungraded primary could permit the less mature, the less ready, to have a longer period of time to adjust to reading tasks without risking the stigma of failure. This plan is not a panacea,

and the administrative framework alone will accomplish nothing. It is the philosophy and the practice in the classroom which give the plan value.*

3. *An educational program for adults* which would explain the fact that children of a given chronological age are all not equally ready for the same tasks. In fact, before an ungraded primary plan could possibly be successful, parents and teachers would have to understand and accept this truth. Further, the fact should be accepted that a child's growth is not uniform and that there will be plateaus as well as normal and rapid growth periods.

4. *Less pressure* on children in learning to read would be a natural outcome if the preceding suggestion were acted upon in our schools and communities. This would have a salutary effect in reducing reading problems, particularly among those children who react adversely to pressure. Certainly, it is evident to observant teachers and clinicians that extreme pressure brought to bear in learning as complicated a symbolic process as reading often inhibits learning. Since boys as a group appear to suffer most from school and home pressures during the primary years, they would gain the most from a lessening of school and social pressures.

5. *More emphasis on psychological assessment* than we now have in the primary grades is essential if all children are to be taught effectively in the classroom. Five times as many boys as girls are referred to clinics after academic or behavioral problems are noted by the school. It seems likely that boys as a group would profit considerably from earlier diagnosis and guidance.

6. *Research on reading interests* of boys and girls, together with research on the nature and the content of required reading materials in the schools, might suggest changes which would be favorable to boys. This research would have to go far beyond the questionnaire method and would actually involve the use of quite varied materials.

CONCLUSION

Over a period of several decades, data from American schools have been reported which indicate that girls as a group measure higher in reading achievement in the early grades than do boys. Furthermore, in the population of "reading failures," boys constitute a significantly higher percentage of the total than do girls.

---

*The ungraded primary plan is discussed in Chapter 5.

A number of factors have been advanced as possible explanations of this difference in reading achievement. These include general maturational factors, the school environment, reading materials used, a preponderance of women teachers in the primary grades, and differences of motivational level between the sexes. Of these, the one hypothesis that seemed most tenable was the differential in maturation which, based on numerous studies, definitely favored girls.

Several recent studies* have contributed data which suggests that the cultural mileau of the school, *including instruction*, may play a significant role in producing sex differences in early reading performance. The important implication here is that there are variables within the learning environment which, when taken into consideration in instruction, tend to enhance the performance of boys. Two such variables are the teacher (her attitude and behavior patterns) and teaching materials.

---

*See studies by Preston, Manning, McNeil and Keislar, and Heilman cited in this chapter.

YOUR POINT OF VIEW?

Defend or attack the statements below.

1. A thoroughly differentiated instructional program in grade one which is based on sound on-going diagnosis would materially reduce the difference between the reading achievement scores of boys *vs* girls.
2. The "halo effect" favoring girls is less likely to be found among experienced teachers than among beginning teachers.
3. Since research data tend to indicate that sex difference in reading are not significant at the end of the elementary school period, sex differences in learning to read are of little educational importance.
4. The teacher is not a causal factor in the disproportionate number of reading failures among boys as compared with girls.
5. Assume a forced choice item on a test required you to select one of the following broad categories as being the most influential causal factor in the production of sex differences in beginning reading. Which would you choose? Why?
   a. Physiological — maturational factors.
   b. Social — cultural — environmental factors.

BIBLIOGRAPHY

1. Alden, Clara, Helen B. Sullivan, and Donald Durrell, "The Frequency of Special Reading Disabilities," *Education,* LXII (1942), 32-36.
2. Allen, C. N., "Recent Research on Sex Differences," *Psychological Bulletin,* XXXII (1935), 343-54.
3. Ames, Louise B., and Frances L. Ilg, "Sex Differences In Test Performance of Matched Girl-Boy Pairs In the 5 to 9 Year-old Age Range," *Genetic Psychology,* 104 (1964), 25-34.
4. Anderson, Irving H., Byron O. Hughes, and Robert W. Dixon, "Age of Learning to Read and Its Relation to Sex, Intelligence, and Reading Achievement in Sixth Grade," *Journal of Educational Research,* XLIX (February 1956), 447-53.

5. ———, "The Rate of Reading Development and Its Relation to Age of Learning to Read, Sex, and Intelligence," *Journal of Educational Research,* (March 1957), 481-94.

6. Axline, Virginia, "Nondirective Therapy for Poor Readers," *Journal of Consulting Psychology,* XI (1947), 61-69.

7. Ayres, Leonard, *Laggards in Our Schools.* New York, Russell Sage Foundation, 1909.

8. Balow, Irving, "Differences in First Grade Reading," *Elementary* English, XL (March 1963), 303-06.

9. Bell, John E., "Emotional Factors in the Treatment of Reading Difficulties," *Journal of Consulting Psychology,* IX (1945), 125-31.

10. Blanchard, Phyllis, "Reading Difficulties in Relation to Difficulties of Personality and Emotional Development," *Mental Hygiene,* XX (1936), 384-413.

11. Blommers, P., L. Knief, and J. B. Stroud, "The Organismic Age Concept," *Journal of Educational Psychology,* XLVI (1955), 142-50.

12. Carroll, Marjorie W., "Sex Differences in Reading Readiness at the First Grade Level," *Elementary English,* XXV (October 1948), 370-75.

13. Chall, Jeanne S., and Shirley C. Feldmann, *A Study In Depth of First Grade Reading.* Cooperative Research Project No. 2728, USOE, 1966.

14. Cornell, Ethel, "Why Are More Boys than Girls Retarded in School?" *Elementary School Journal,* XXIX, 213-26.

15. Fabian, A. A., "Reading Disability: An Index of Pathology," *American Journal of Orthopsychiatry,* XXV (April 1955), 319-29.

16. Freeman, Frank, and Catherine Miles, *Encyclopedia of Educational Research,* Walter S. Monroe (ed.). New York: The Macmillan Company, 1952, 1205.

17. Fry, Edward Bernard, *First Grade Reading Instruction Using A Diacritical Marking System, The Initial Teaching Alphabet and a Basal Reading System.* Cooperative Research Project No. 2745, USOE, 1965.

18. Gates, Arthur I., "Sex Differences in Reading Ability," *Elementary School Journal,* LXI (May 1961), 431-34.

19. Hahn, Harry T., *A Study of the Relative Effectiveness of Three Methods of Teaching Reading In Grade One.* Cooperative Research Project No. 2687, USOE, 1965.

20. Heilman, Arthur W., *Effects of an Intensive In-Service Program on Teacher's Classroom Behavior and Pupil's Reading Achievement.* Cooperative Research Project No. 2709, USOE, 1965, p. 53.

21. Hughes, Mildred C., "Sex Differences in Reading Achievement in the Elementary Grades," *Clinical Studies in Reading II,* Supplementary Educational Monographs. Chicago: University of Chicago Press, No. 77, 102-6.

22. Jackson, Joseph, "A Survey of Psychological, Social, and Environmental Differences between Advanced and Retarded Readers," *Journal of Genetic Psychology,* LXV (1944), 113-31.

23. Manning, John C., *Evaluation of Level Designed Visual-Auditory and Related Writing Methods of Reading Instruction In Grade One.* Cooperative Research Project No. 2650, USOE, 1966.

24. McCollum, Mary E., and Jary J. Shapiro, "An Approach to the Remediation of Severe Reading Disabilities," *Education,* LXVII (March 1947), 488-93.

25. McNeil, John D., and Evan R. Keislar, *Oral and Non-oral Methods of Teaching Reading By an Auto-Instructional Device.* Cooperative Research Project No. 1413, USOE, 1963.

26. Means, Chalmers, "Sex Differences in Reading Achievement," *Improving Reading Through Classroom Practices.* Joint Proceedings of the Twenty-seventh Reading Conference and the Third Intensive Summer Workshop. Pennsylvania State University, 1966.

27. Missildine, W. H., "The Emotional Background of Thirty Children with Reading Disabilities with Emphasis on Its Coercive Elements," *Nervous Child,* (July 1946), 263-72.

28. Monroe, Marion, *Children Who Cannot Read.* Chicago: University of Chicago Press, 1932.

29. Murphy, Helen A., *Reading Achievements In Relation to Growth in Perception of Word Elements In Three Types of Beginning Reading Instruction.* Cooperative Research Project No. 2675, USOE, 1965.

30. Nila, Sister Mary, "Foundations of a Successful Reading Program," *Education,* LXXIII (May 1953), 543-55.

31. Olson, W. C., "How Children Grow," *NEA Journal,* XXVI (September 1947), 436-37.

32. ______, and B. O. Hughes, "The Concept of Organismic Age," *Journal of Educational Research,* XXV (March 1942).

33. Pauley, Frank R., "Sex Differences and Legal School Entrance Age," *Journal of Educational Research,* XXXV (1951), 1-9.

34. Prescott, George A., "Sex Differences in Metropolitan Readiness Test Results," *Journal of Educational Research,* XLVIII (April 1955), 605-10.

35. Preston, Mary J., "Reading Failure and the Child's Security," *American Journal of Orthopsychiatry,* X (1940), 239-52.

36. Preston, Ralph, "Reading Achievement of German and American Children," *School and Society,* XC (1962), 350-54.

37. Robinson, Helen M., "Factors which Affect Success in Reading," *Elementary School Journal,* LV (January 1955), 266.

38. Schneyer, J. Wesley, Charles B. Schultz, and Sheila Cowen, "*Comparison of Reading Achievement of First-Grade Children Taught by a Linguistic Approach and a Basal Reader Approach.* Cooperative Research Project No. 2666, USOE, 1966.

39. Sheldon, William D., and Donald R. Lashinger, *Effect of First Grade Instruction Using Basal Readers, Modified Linguistic Materials and Linguistic Readers.* Cooperative Research Project No. 2683, USOE, 1966.

40. Smith, C. A., and M. R. Jenson, "Educational, Psychological and Physiological Factors in Reading Readiness," *Elementary School Journal,* XXXVI (April 1936), 689.

41. Spache, George D., Michaela C. Andres, H. A. Curtis, Minnie Lee Rowland, and Minnie Hall Fields, *A Study of a Longitudinal First Grade Reading Readiness Program.* Cooperative Research Project No. 2742, USOE, 1965.

42. Spencer, Doris U., and L. Doris Moquin, *Individualized Reading Versus a Basal Reader Program at First Grade Level, In Rural Communities.* Cooperative Research Project No. 2673, USOE, 1965.

43. Stanchfield, Jo M., "Boys' Reading Interests As Revealed Through Personal Conferences," *Reading Teacher,* 16 (September 1962), 41-44.

44. Stauffer, Russell G., and W. Dorsey Hammond, *Effectiveness of a Language Arts and Basic Reader Approach to First Grade Reading Instruction.* Cooperative Research Project No. 2679, USOE, 1965.

45. St. John, Charles W., "The Maladjustment of Boys in Certain Elementary Grades," *Educational Administration and Supervision,* XVIII (1932), 659-72.

46. Stroud, J. B., and E. F. Lindquist, "Sex Differences in Achievement in the Elementary and Secondary School," *Journal of Educational Psychology,* XXXIII (1942), 657-67.

47. Tanyzer, Harold J., and Harvey Alpert, *Effectiveness of Three Different Basal Reading Systems on First Grade Reading Achievement.* Cooperative Research Project No. 2720, USOE, 1965.

48. Terman, Lewis M., and Leona E. Tyler, "Psychological Sex Differences," *Manual of Child Psychology* (2nd ed.), L. Carmichael (ed.). New York: John Wiley & Sons, Inc., 1954, Chapter 17.

49. Tyler, F. T., "Concepts of Organismic Growth: A Critique," *Journal of Educational Psychology,* XLIV (1953), 321-42.

50. Vorhaus, Pauline G., "Rorschach Configurations Associated with Reading Disability," *Projective Techniques,* XVI (1952), 3-19.

51. Wilson, Frank T., Agnes Burke, and C. W. Flemming, "Sex Differences in Beginning Reading in a Progressive School," *Journal of Educational Research,* XXXII (April 1939), 570-82.

52. Young, Robert A., "Case Studies in Reading Disability," *American Journal of Orthopsychiatry,* VIII (1938), 230-54.

53. Wyatt, Nita M., *Reading Achievements of First Grade Boys Versus First Grade Girls Using Two Approaches: A Linguistic Approach and a Basal Reader Approach with Boys and Girls Grouped Separately.* Cooperative Research Project No. 2735, USOE, 1965.

Critical Reading

14

EXPLORING THE CONCEPT OF CRITICAL READING

One of the basic difficulties in attempting a definition of critical reading is the fact that this concept has no fixed boundaries. Kerfoot, (21) while granting the complexity of reading comprehension, notes a high degree of ambiguity in various discussions of the term. Critical reading can take place on many levels. A high school senior, a college sophomore, and a doctoral candidate in English, may all critically read *Macbeth,* though the performance of the high school student would be considered inadequate at the higher educational levels. Reading matter is distributed over a wide range of difficulty and complexity. Very few people explore the more difficult end of the continuum, yet the goal of formal education is to guide and direct each student to "explore to the maximum of his ability."

At a given moment a reader can comprehend at a level commensurate with his academic background, experience, and intellectual level. In the final analysis, the catalyst between writer and reader is the manner in which the latter uses his past experiences in the reading situation. Thus, it is fruitless to talk about getting *the* meaning of a passage, since most serious writing lends itself to a number of interpretations. As Triggs (39) points out, the meaning which is attributed to written symbols in any reading situation is not intrinsic within the passage but is actually supplied by the reader.

Critical reading is developmental in nature. It is an on-going process. Some second graders may merit the designation *critical readers,* but no one would suggest that their interpretation of the Constitution is adequate for our society. Nevertheless, if children are to become adept at critical reading, they must be guided toward this goal from the beginning of their experience with reading. Helping the child develop ability to read critically is a problem and a challenge for teachers at all grade levels. Reading for meaning is emphasized by the authors of practically all basal reader series, and the emphasis is particularly noticeable at the beginning reading level. Pre-primers and primers contain instructions on building meanings around the few lines of print found in these books. Pictures are widely used to aid the child in extending concepts encountered at this level. One study of the degree of emphasis on critical skills found in a number of basal reader series lists thirty-three skills being stressed in the first six grades. (42)

As the child progresses in reading ability, the materials he reads increase in difficulty. The teacher's task becomes that of keeping children's concepts abreast of the material they are reading. This is easier in the prepared basal reading materials than it is in the content areas where more words and concepts are likely to be new to the child. In the stories children read there are many opportunities to sharpen critical reading powers if the teacher is able to take advantage of them. Children must develop the ability to interpret stories, determine whether places and characters are real or imaginary, discern moods of character, relate the sequence of events, and give plausible explanations of why persons felt and spoke as they did.

In the content fields the analysis is much the same, but the events perhaps deal with natural phenomena rather than with story-book characters. (1) "What factors make it necessary for country X to import considerable food-stuffs?" (2) "There are a number of substances called minerals; each has a different boiling point. What does this statement mean? What is its significance to man? Give examples." If the information necessary to answer these questions is gleaned through reading, critical reading has taken place.

Critical reading is not simply getting answers. Some exercises may get at certain facts but help very little in developing critical reading. Other types of questions are characteristically asked about material similar to that alluded to in the previous paragraph: "What are the main imports of country X?" "List the minerals discussed in this chapter." "What is the melting point of lead?" "Who discovered a process for making steel?" and the like. Correctly answering these questions may not be evidence of critical reading. Seatwork or questions accompanying reading assignments are often dull. Some of these call for merely repeating sentences or words which answer questions or for scanning the entire article to find a synonym. Examples:

1. A story is read and a task is assigned. Fifteen statements, in jumbled order, are to be numbered to coincide with the order in which they appeared in the story.
2. Write a word that is used in this story for the word *large*.
3. Write the word which means a place where ships unload.
4. Copy the sentence that tells the number of lakes in Minnesota.

The appetite for critical reading is often dulled by thoughtless, time-consuming tasks such as these. Yet these and similar questions are referred to as aids to measuring or developing comprehension. Unfortunately, this type of busy-work is often encountered about the same time that the child is ready to do independent reading.

PREREQUISITES TO CRITICAL READING

A number of abilities must be dealt with in teaching for critical reading. When the student develops these abilities, his reading skill is enhanced; when they are neglected, the result is likely to be inept and uncritical reading. Jenkins (18) raises and answers a question relative to the identity of these skills, "What are vital reading skills that must be considered when teaching literature in the elementary school? I think the list is as comprehensive as our knowledge of reading." A few of the frequently listed abilities are:*

*For an excellent summary of factors related to comprehension, see Frederick Davis, "Fundamental Factors in Comprehension in Reading," *Psychometrika,* IX (1944), 185-97.

1. The ability to recognize the meanings of words
2. The ability to select the one appropriate meaning of a word which may have many meanings
3. The ability to deal with figurative language, not insisting on literal meanings when the author does not intend literal interpretation
4. The ability to determine the author's main ideas
5. The ability to paraphrase, or restate, what the author has written
6. The ability to see the relationship between one part and another and of all parts to the whole
7. The ability to adjust to the author's organizational pattern
8. The ability to determine the author's purpose, his intent in writing, his point of view, his biases, or whom the author is addressing and with what goal in mind
9. The ability to draw inferences which are not specifically stated in the data
10. The ability to recognize literary devices such as humor, satire, or irony, and to detect mood or tone

Recognizing Words

An example of a form of word paralysis is provided by the fourth-grade boy who was quite adept at arithmetical computation, including division. He came to a page in his workbook in which the directions read, "Write the quotients for the following problems." The boy did not attempt to solve a single problem on the page because the word *quotient* baffled him. The problems looked very much like the ones he had done previously, but surely this strange word instructed him to do something new and unknown. The teacher had assumed that everyone in the class knew the word, since it had been discussed at length. The concept had not been mastered, at least by this student.

The content areas, such as science, mathematics, health, and social studies, use hundreds of words which can inhibit learning if not fully understood. Examples are *ratio, proportion, respiration, longitude, exponent, photosynthesis, plateau, congruent, catalyst, inertia, delta,* and *contagious.*

Cole (6) tells of a student in a chemistry class who asked his instructor for help in understanding the law: "The volume of a gas is inversely proportional to its density." The instructor tried without success to explain the concept embodied in the law. Finally, he asked the boy to define volume, volume of a gas, density, and inversely proportional. The boy had only one concept for *volume* — a book; *gas* was what is used in a stove; *density* meant thickness; he had no concept to go with *inversely proportional.* The boy had actually "memorized" the law, a fact which emphasizes the futility of such effort in the absence of understanding.

The child's need for learning new words and concepts never abates, but sometimes the great mass of material to be taught may interfere with the effective teaching of meanings. In earlier chapters a number of procedures have been suggested for helping children master unknown words. Some of these procedures have merit for use in the upper grades and should be used when appropriate. A technique used with success by some teachers is the *word meaning period.* Ten- to fifteen-minute periods are used in which pupils present and discuss words whose meanings they had not known when they met them in their reading. A number of variations can be introduced to keep the period interesting. A pupil reads the sentence containing the word he has just learned and tells its meaning in that context. Other pupils can volunteer to use the word in different contexts, supply synonyms, or give other words which have the same root.

Another variation is a teacher-planned period devoted to learning important word roots and to demonstrating the possibilities of word building through the addition of prefixes, suffixes, and other roots. For example, *dict* is a root meaning "to say." To *pre*dict is to say in advance, and implies that an event is pre *dict* able. This same root permits one to say that if one is to *dic*tate, his *dic*tion in *dic*tating should be clear and that his pronunciation should not contra*dict* the *dic*tionary. The study of word meanings can be a fascinating and rewarding experience.

On the other hand, an assignment to learn a number of roots listed in one column, and the common words made from each of these roots listed in an adjacent column, may not be highly motivating because the drill is detached from a meaningful learning situation. In science, geography, or social science, however, words and concepts are met which need clarification. This provides an excellent opportunity for the integration of teaching meanings with teaching subjects. Terms and concepts, such as *photosynthesis, extracting minerals, geology, biology, plywood,* and *perspective,* can be used as a starting point for a study of word derivations.

The teacher might use the following exercise for teaching how some of our common words were built from words borrowed from other languages. *Auto* is a Greek word meaning *self; graph* is also

Greek and means to *write;* when we put these two roots together we have our English word *autograph.* Do you see how the meaning of this word is related to the Greek word from which it is built?

Root		Root		
photo	= light;	*graph*	= to write:	photograph (to write with light)
tele	= far;	*graph*	= to write:	telegraph
phono	= sound;	*graph*	= to write:	phonograph
geo	= earth;	*graphy*	= to write:	geography
bio	= life;	*logy*	= to study:	biology
geo	= earth;	*logy*	= to study:	geology

Word meanings can be further explained by studying roots and prefixes, and roots and suffixes.

Prefix		Root		
con	= with, together;	*tract*	= to draw:	contract
re	= back;	*tract*	= to draw:	retract
ex	= out of;	*tract*	= to draw:	extract
im	= into;	*port*	= to carry:	import
trans	= across;	*port*	= to carry:	transport
re	= back;	*port*	= to carry:	report

Root		Suffix		
port	= to carry;	*able*	= capable of:	portable
dict	= to say;	*tion*	= act of:	diction
grat	= thanks;	*full*	= full of:	grateful

When pupils evince interest in word building (roots, prefixes, suffixes), the teacher can make available teacher-constructed exercises similar to the examples above. Knowledge of roots and prefixes will help a child work out the meaning of many words that at first glance may appear strange and difficult.

Selecting the Appropriate Meaning

Teachers in one school tested the children in all grade levels, first through high school, on a few common words like *set, run, stick,* and *mine.* The word *set* elicited approximately ten different meanings in the first-grade class. The number of different meanings associated with this word increased through the grades and reached twenty-eight correct usages in a third-year high school class. Yet the word *set* is considered a rather simple word.

The ability to select the appropriate meaning of a particular word which has many meanings is essential for critical reading. The word *base* has many meanings: third base, the base of a triangle, the base line of a graph, a naval base, base motives, and a number of others. *Dividend* does not have the same meaning in mathematics that it does when used as an increment from investments in stocks and bonds. The literal definition of *island* as "a body of land entirely surrounded by water" is not the meaning implied by John Donne when he states, "no man is an island entire unto himself — each is a piece of the continent, a part of the whole." Nevertheless, this conventional meaning would have to be known in order to understand the author's intended meaning. The child's learning of various connotations of words is complicated by the widespread use of figures of speech. Although these expressions may increase the difficulty of a passage, they also add to its beauty or forcefulness.

Dealing with Figurative Language

Figurative language is a potential barrier to readers if they have a predilection for concrete meanings. Our language contains many colorful words which suggest vivid images, but, more important, our language is extremely flexible. Mutual agreement between persons using the language permits picturesque comparisons between things which are unlike. Cyrano De Bergerac, sword in hand but mortally wounded, describes the approach of death, "I stand — *clothed with marble, gloved with lead*." Overstatements or gross exaggeration emphasize particular qualities—"He's as patient as Job," "strong as Hercules," "tall as a mountain." Likenesses are suggested through implied functions — "The ship *plowed* the waves," "The arrow *parted* his hair." Sometimes, in fact, words are used in such a way as to mean just their opposite. Obviously, understanding material containing such expressions depends on the reader's realization of the intended meanings.

As early as second and third grade, numerous figures of speech and idiomatic expressions appear in basal reader series. The following passage is filled with expressions which probably would pose no problem for adults but which might mystify a child who reads slowly or literally.

> Joe, *flying down the stairs, rested his eye* on the hawk. Grandfather *buried his nose in a book* and acted as if he were *completely in the dark*. Grandmother and Sue *put their heads together* and tried to figure out *which way the wind was blowing*. Joe *tipped his hand* by carrying the gun. On the *spur of the moment* Grandmother *hit the nail on the head*. *Cool as*

a cucumber, she called to Joe, *"Freeze in your tracks* and put that gun back upstairs!" Joe's *spirits fell* as his grandmother's words *took the wind out of his sail.* He *flew off the handle* and told about the hawk. *"That's a horse of a different color,"* said Grandmother, satisfied that she had *dug up the facts.* "Let the boy alone," said Grandfather. "He will *keep the wolf from the door."* Outside, Joe thought, "I'd better *make hay while the sun shines,"* as he *drew a bead* on the hawk.

Although these expressions may not bother most children, more difficult figures of speech will constantly confront them. The children who are baffled by such expressions need more experience with them. For these pupils, the teacher should devise exercises over and above those which are found in workbooks at their grade level. If the reader is *thinking while reading,* he will probably develop the flexibility necessary to deal with this type of language.

Identifying Main Ideas

The ability to arrive at the author's main ideas is often considered virtually synonymous with critical reading. Getting the main ideas from a passage is not an isolated skill that can be developed out of context with all other reading skills. This skill depends on the reader's mastery of the mechanics of reading, breadth of vocabulary and concepts, background, and attitudes. While the importance to the reader of getting main ideas is obvious, the reasons for the extreme difficulty of teaching this skill are not so self-evident.

Workbook exercises in the elementary grades attempt to deal with this problem. There are lessons in which the child reads a paragraph, and is asked to select the best title for the passage from among three suggested titles; or, after reading a paragraph, he is to select the best summary sentence from among the three listed. These exercises are designed to make the child conscious of reading for meaning or reading critically. Evidently, not enough of this type of drill is provided or such techniques are not sufficient for cultivating habits of reading critically. Many pupils do not become proficient in grasping main ideas or the author's purpose.

A pupil who can read every word and who knows the meanings of the words in a passage can fail miserably in identifying the important facts. Such occurrences emphasize what was pointed out previously, that reading is more than the sum of its parts. Always, there is the interaction between the reader (meaning such psychological factors as adjustment, attitudes, past experience) and the material to be read. A reader who may get the significant points while reading a science unit may be quite inadequate in his interpretation of a story or a unit on geography. Such performance can usually be traced to lack of interest, background, or failure to discern the purpose for reading. The critical reader is one who has attained smoothness and facility in reading skills and who does not let his previous experiences or attitudes interfere with the analysis and evaluation of what he reads.

One can understand why the pupil who lacks reading skills, word knowledge, or background, may fail to grasp important meanings. In the intermediate grades and above, getting the author's main ideas can be complicated by the special vocabularies of various subject areas, such as health, science, mathematics, and geography. Another problem is the increasing complexity of sentence structure met in materials at these levels. Difficulties are compounded in many instances because systematic instruction in reading has ceased in many schools by the sixth grade or junior high level, although, in reality, many pupils have considerable need for further systematic instruction in reading.

Paraphrasing

The ability to paraphrase, or restate in one's own words, the author's main ideas is usually the criterion by which the pupil's critical reading ability or comprehension is judged. The inability to paraphrase often implies one of two things: either the pupil did not fathom what the author was trying to tell him, or he lacks the language facility to restate what he read. Paraphrasing is one of the most effective and, at the same time, one of the least used techniques available to teachers at all levels. Walpole (41) states, "Paraphrasing provides a simple classroom technique which not only commits the pupil to a specific task of interpretation, but also enables him to study other versions and see how people interpret the same passage in widely varying ways." Paraphrasing exercises provide an almost ideal example of a means of integrating all of the language arts. First, the student gets experience in interpretive reading. Second, by writing he gains experience in all facets of composition, such as sentence and paragraph construction, organization of material, and grammatical usage. This technique can be highly motivating to students if care is exercised in the selection of reading passages.

In order to paraphrase accurately or restate the essence of what an author has written, one must be able to grasp the meaning as he reads. Paraphrasing demands that one see the relationships between various parts of a passage and see how these parts are related to the total effect sought by an author. As a rule, good readers have developed the ability to read in "thought units." Thus, their reading habits lead them naturally into logical and meaningful phrasing. They have learned to see the relationships between words and how the author builds a pattern of thought units into a large whole. The point under discussion cuts across several factors which have been listed as related to critical reading: main ideas, paraphrasing, adjusting to author's organization, and seeing the relationship between a part and the whole.

The following illustrations have been used with high school groups. In each case, passage A was read by the student who was then asked to write a sentence or two restating what the author said. Immediately following this, each pupil was given passage B which was the same passage but was divided into meaningful thought units. All of the students stated that it was easier to get meaning from passage B. The point of the exercise was to help students see that in their reading for meaning they must do what was done for them in passage B, i.e., read in meaningful thought units. Such an exercise can be developed for use at practically any reading level.

Passage A

> A man rises, sometimes, and stands not, because he doth not, or is not believed to fill his place; and sometimes he stands not, because he overfills his place: He may bring so much virtue, so much justice, so much integrity to the position, as to be a libel upon his predecessor, and cast infamy upon him, and a burden upon his successor.*

Passage B

> A man rises, sometimes,
> and stands not,
> because he does not,
> or is not believed to fill his place;
> And sometimes he stands not,
> because he overfills his place:
> He may bring
> so much virtue,
> so much justice,
> so much integrity to the position,
> as to be a libel upon his predecessor,
> and cast infamy upon him,
> and burden upon his successor.

---

*Paraphrased from John Donne, *Complete Poetry and Prose of John Donne* (New York: The Modern Library, 1946), 338.

Passage A

Man, of whom David had said (as the lowest diminution that he could put upon him), 'I am a worm and no man' — he might have gone lower, and said, I am a man and no worm.*

Passage B

Man,
of whom David had said,
(as the lowest diminution that he could put upon him)
'I am a worm and no man' —
He might have gone lower,
and said,
I am a man and no worm.

Discerning Relationships and Organizational Patterns

Factors six and seven, seeing relationships between the parts and the whole and adjusting to the author's organizational pattern, are, to some degree, dealt with in any paraphrasing exercise. These skills should be deliberately taught; as a rule, they cannot be taught through a mere discussion of critical reading. The child needs concrete experiences and illustrations. These should be provided in all areas of the curriculum, since each subject matter calls for meaningful reading.

Many educators are of the opinion that pupils in American schools, at all levels, do not have enough experience in writing, and, as a result, lack opportunities to learn good habits of organization of paragraphs and larger units. Most of the practice pupils receive in analysis and organization in the elementary grades is found in reading and language arts. In the upper grades the responsibility for such instruction is usually associated with the teaching of English. Many exercises which aim at helping the pupil see how larger meaningful language units are built and logically held together fail because they can be solved or completed without critical thinking.

Keeping one narrow question in mind and rereading the passage as often as necessary will lead to the correct response on exercises, such as underlining key words or topic sentences, selecting the best of several suggested titles for a story, rearranging the jumbled steps in an outline, striking out sentences which do not belong in a

---

*Ibid., 369.

paragraph, or discovering paragraphs which interrupt the thread of narrative. Each of these exercises attempts to teach something about organization and analysis which is useful in critical reading. But taken individually or together, these often fail if they are synthetic or artificial. One can master the tasks called for in these drills and still not be able to transfer any appreciable learning to other reading situations. Many pupils do not see the relationship between working on these exercises and reading textbooks in geography, history, or science. To see such parallels, the purpose must be clear.

It should be pointed out that the type of exercise mentioned above is not inherently poor. Pupils should be taught the significance of key words and phrases which authors use to indicate contrasts, comparisons and transitions. Critical readers profit from clues, such as "There are *three* main points" — "First," "Next," "And in conclusion," "while on the other hand," "provided that," "differ in some respects," "as well as," and the like. One author has aptly labeled such clues as *signal words.* (24)

Further Prerequisites to Critical Reading

The last three factors can be discussed as a group. These include the ability to determine the author's purpose, to draw inferences, and to recognize literary devices such as humor, satire, and irony. In dealing with stories or literature, teachers are more likely to attempt to deal with these factors consciously and deliberately. Most literature teachers place more emphasis on analyzing the plot and the characters and on studying the author's style and organization. In fact, it is possible to have too much analysis of literature. An author of children's literature, Adele De Leeuw, has a word on this point: "As an author, I have a plea. Do not spoil reading by too much classroom analysis. Let the interpretation come of itself. . . . The sacred trust of teachers is to keep upon that path to broader understanding, and not to close it by the insurmountable block of too much analysis."* This author's plea is no doubt warranted, but nevertheless children need a degree of guidance so that they can gradually become proficient in the interpretation and analysis of what they read.

---

*Adele De Leeuw, "Nobody's Doll," "With a High Heart," and "Linda Marsh," *Promoting Growth Toward Maturity in Interpreting What Is Read* W. S. Gray, ed. (Chicago: University of Chicago Press, 1951), pp. 49-53. Copyright 1951 by the University of Chicago.

Almost all the prerequisites for, and obstacles to, critical reading are related to the two skills of discerning a writer's purpose and of drawing inferences. The presence or absence of bias, a lack of background, the habit of accepting that which is in print or that which is allegedly backed by authority, and the lack of experience in dealing with controversial topics, all help to determine whether critical reading can take place. College students too have trouble discerning an author's purpose. Students in a reading improvement course, after reading and discussing several serious paragraphs, were given the following passage by Mark Twain. Each student was to read the passage silently and to write a sentence or two answering these questions: "What is the author's purpose? How does he achieve it? What is the author's mood?"

> It was a crisp and spicy morning in early October. The lilacs and laburnums, lit with the glory fires of autumn, hung burning and flashing in the upper air; a fairy bridge provided by kind Nature for the wingless wild things, that have their home in the tree-tops and would visit together; the larch and the pomegranate flung their purple and yellow flames in brilliant broad splashes along the slanting sweep of the woodland; the sensuous fragrance of innumerable deciduous flowers rose upon the swooning atmosphere; far in the empty sky a solitary oesophagus slept upon motionless wing; everywhere brooded stillness, serenity, and the peace of God.*

Hundreds of students, and a smaller number of teachers and adults, have responded in essence: "It is a beautiful fall day. He describes nature, the beautiful colors, and the peace and quiet one finds in nature." Despite the first line a number of readers move the day into spring. Occasionally a reader says, "I wondered about the oesophagus, but thought it might be a tropical bird." However, once adults are shown the ridiculous nature of the passage, they seriously doubt that others would be so easily taken in by it.

The ten abilities related to critical reading operate in all reading situations, not just in those that occur during the clock-hour devoted to formal instruction in reading. They operate whenever reading is used in the pursuit of knowledge, whether in history, geography, economics, health, mathematics, science, or literature. The reader must know the meaning of the words used and the different shades of meaning words have in different contexts. He must separate main thoughts or ideas from qualifications; he

---

*Mark Twain, "A Detective Story," from *The Man That Corrupted Hadleyburg* (New York: Harper & Row, Publishers), 304.

must detect the author's purpose, bias, and intent. From the first grade through college, the teacher has a major responsibility to structure reading situations so that these factors and many others are kept in proper focus.

KNOWLEDGE AND BACKGROUND

The absence of the skills discussed above is a major stumbling block to critical reading, but such factors as how long, how thoroughly, and how extensively they have been practiced also will have a bearing on one's level of critical reading. As Durrell (9) points out, "The efficiency of transferring ideas from one person to another is seldom high," and there is an unavoidable loss for the reader in this process. Eller (11) lists a number of obstacles to critical reading found in the school, in society, or in both. Some of them follow:

1. Pupils form the opinion that anything in print is true.
2. Children are conditioned to accept authority blindly.
3. Schools have relied on single texts in the various content areas, and the teacher stresses "what the book says." Thus, children do not learn to look for differences of opinion or for interpretations.
4. Schools avoid controversial topics and emphasize uniformity.

Each of these points is inevitably tied in with experience, and is thus affected by a person's background and knowledge. It is likely that the greatest barrier to critical reading is the reader's lack of background and experience. The teacher has to deal with this problem regardless of the level or the curriculum area in which she teaches. In reality, we are dealing with two questions. First, what does the reader bring to the reading situation in the way of experience and understanding? And second, what does he need in order to understand the particular reading he is attempting? Both of these points are related to one of Herbart's five steps in the learning process — the preparation of the learner for that which is to be learned. (37) As noted earlier, it is in beginning reading instruction that the teacher often does the best job of preparing the learner. The higher one goes through the grades, the more need there is for this type of preparation because the reading materials deal with concepts which are often beyond the present stock of concepts held by some students in the room.

A third-grade class is reading a story about bees storing honey in a hollow tree. The facts that the bees "belonged to a farmer," worked for him in a hive he provided, and yet one day swarmed and left the hive, may call for a good deal of explanation by the teacher, or by bee experts in the class, before all aspects of this story are meaningful to every member of that third-grade class.

A high school or college student reading *John Brown's Plea to the Court* can hardly be expected to arrive at a sound critical analysis of this passage unless some background facts are also known: who was John Brown?; when did he live?; what political-social issue was involved?; what experiences did John Brown have in Kansas prior to the Harper's Ferry episode?; was John Brown's attitude shared by a large number of people living at that time?; how would one describe John Brown's emotional maturity?; is the real issue here the question of whether the end justifies the means?

Critical reading has neither disappeared nor is it widely practiced. There is so much to read on so many important topics that no one can hope to read everything available on any topic. As a result, many people are content to settle for digests of magazine articles and condensations of books. This type of reading matter flourishes because so many people feel a need for at least a thin veneer of culture, but not a coating thick enough that it would require critical reading or thinking. Jenkinson (19) sees reading as a type of thinking which is susceptible to training and which invariably draws upon acquired information and established responses.

College students' and adults' reactions to the Mark Twain passage cited previously are illustrative of behavior which would naturally occur in a society which has not been perturbed by the obstacles to critical reading and thinking which have gradually accumulated in its mass educational system. It is a rare day when millions of people are not taken in by some form of advertising which in the final analysis is as divorced from meaning as is the Twain passage. Also, on numerous occasions, people are faced with political arguments which are equally meaningless. Whether or not our schools will produce more critical readers is an issue which has great significance for a democracy's future. Probably the most devastating criticism of the schools, which bears on this point, is that "the schools reflect the culture around them."

A goal of formal education is to guide students to fully explore a wide range of reading matter. Critical reading provides the means for developing the background and impetus upon which a good education is based. (Courtesy Los Angeles City School Districts.)

DEVELOPING INTERESTS THROUGH PURPOSEFUL READING

We make much of the fact that the child's reading must be purposeful, yet much of our actual reading instruction must appear to the child to be related only to *learning* to read! Children need guidance in discovering the values inherent in meaningful reading. While a large number of values could be cited, the one we are concerned with at the moment is the pleasure and growth potential to be found in this activity. There is no denying that pleasurable and purposeful reading is dependent upon the development of mechanical and comprehension skills. Yet millions of individuals attain satisfactory proficiency in these skills without ever finding a deep personal satisfaction in reading. Persons who love to read find this fact difficult to believe. However, studies of the reading interests and activities of a great number of high school and college graduates demonstrate its truth.

No doubt the school shares the responsibility for this outcome. Perhaps the degree of emphasis that is placed on *learning* to read leads pupils to see this accomplishment as an end in itself rather than the means of many desirable ends. Whatever the cause, too many children experience an uncritical, unimaginative growth in reading. Reading should never deteriorate into a ritual but should serve as a means of awakening the senses and stirring the imagination and the emotions. Whether the child is exploring one of the man-made wonders of the world or one of nature's wonders, such as the functioning of an ant colony or the metamorphosis of the monarch butterfly, reading can feed the senses with raw material for building concepts. Feelings and images aroused by reading can also stimulate emotions. A poet speaks to his love:

"I never think of you
but what some new virtue
is born in me."

A leader in the American Revolution, having been chided for a long absence from America, writes a friend a few observations in 1789:

> A thousand years hence, perhaps in less . . . the ruins of that liberty which thousands fought for, or suffered to obtain, may just furnish materials for a village tale. . . .
>
> When we contemplate the fall of empires and the extinction of nations of the ancient world, we see but little to excite our regret. . . . But when America shall fall, the subject for contemplative sorrow will be infinitely greater than crumbling brass or marble can inspire. It will not then be said, here stood a temple of vast antiquity, here rose a Babel of invisible height, or there a palace of sumptuous extravagance, but here, oh painful thought! The noblest work of human wisdom, the grandest scene of human glory, the fair cause of freedom rose and fell. Read this and then ask if I forget America.*

It is true that children in the primary grades do not read Cyrano De Bergerac or the letters of Thomas Paine. But the point is that they may never read these authors or Blake, Milton, Oliver Wendell Holmes, Hawthorne, Mark Twain, Dostoievsky, Whitman, or Lincoln if they do not learn to read for pleasure and develop an appreciation for reading. The primary grades are not too early to awaken the senses and emotions through reading.

**The Complete Writings of Thomas Paine,* Philip S. Foner, ed. (New York: The Citadel Press, 1945), II, 1274.

There are many ways in which a creative teacher's enthusiasm becomes contagious. Such a teacher is a good storyteller, with the ability to become completely engrossed in the stories she tells or reads to children. She will understand children's capacity to be drawn out of their immediate environment by becoming involved in a story. For instance, the story of the first day in school of a child from another land can arouse a strong feeling of empathy. Children sense the feeling of loneliness, strangeness, and fear. They see that the children in the story also sense this and accept the newcomer and help in various ways to make him feel accepted and at home.

DEVELOPING A QUESTIONING ATTITUDE

Teachers use newspapers and other mass media for both the teaching of critical analysis and mechanical skills which relate to such analysis. The potential values in the use of such materials are numerous. There are also barriers to significant learning, two of which are inadequate planning and the tendency to avoid discussion of issues which might prove to be controversial. Children should be permitted and encouraged to interpret and analyze advertisements, political cartoons, editorials and syndicated columns.

"Clues to use while reading the news" can be developed by noting and discussing details such as the following:

1. Newspapers from widely separated areas will carry identical word-for-word news stories. How does this come about?
2. The same "news" story in different newspapers may be found under vastly different headlines. That is, the different headlines may imply almost opposite conclusions based on the same facts. Why?
3. Editorials on the same topic (legislation, foreign policy, education) may present diametrically opposed conclusions. How might this be accounted for?
4. The same editorial may appear in papers which have no mutual connections. Is this a coincidence? Who prepared the editorial? How did it get in dozens of different newspapers the same day or during the same week?

In addition to the above approaches which deal with communication as an industry, there can be classroom experiences which focus on critical analysis and interpretation such as:

A. *Compare the editorials* found in four or five metropolitan papers which deal with a particular current issue. Assume there are apparent differences of opinion; what might account for these differences? 1) Political orientation of editor or publisher; or 2) does a particular newspaper have somewhat of a standing policy on certain issues (labor-management, foreign aid).

B. *The political cartoon:* Gather cartoons, from different papers and drawn by different artists, which deal with the same topic. Ask students to analyze and put into words what the cartoon is attempting to say. Student interpretation of any given stimulus will vary considerably. This will facilitate discussion and help students to see the importance of "the reader's background" which includes bias, emotional attachments, and the like. Such factors always function in any interpretation of a cartoon, editorial, feature article, or news story.

C. *Detecting propaganda techniques:* The teacher or a committee of students might prepare and duplicate an editorial which by design contains biased statements, factual errors, and various propaganda techniques. Each student has a copy of the material and independently edits or rewrites the editorial. Next, have class discussion of the original material and substitutions, deletions and corrections made by members of the group. Differences between student reactions will in many cases be marked, particularly if the topic is chosen wisely. In the discussion, students will be exposed to points they missed and points of view different from their own.

D. *Study a current issue longitudinally:*

1. Compare different newspaper and news magazine treatment of this problem.
2. Attempt to account for differences in editorial points of view.
3. Study several columnists or news analysts interpretations.
4. Analyze the day-to-day statements of the decision-makers or those spokesmen attempting to mold public opinion. Based on the issue being studied, these might be legislative leaders, State Department officials, labor leaders, candidates for high office, the President or White House Staff, etc.

WHAT THE SCHOOL CAN DO

There are a number of practices which, if followed, will have some impact on improving instruction. The following list of procedures can serve as a summary on critical reading.

1. Do not violate the principles of teaching reading, which apply particularly to critical reading.

    a. Diagnosis is essential in order to discover weaknesses before the child has a reaction formation against reading.
    b. Instruction should be based on pupil's needs.
    c. Reading is getting meaning.
    d. Many approaches and techniques are needed.
    e. Do not ask the child to read over his head. Asking a child to read something he cannot read is unjustifiable and asking him to read it critically is expecting the impossible.

2. Pre-teach difficult, new, or unknown words as they are encountered in any reading — particularly in subject areas. Work on both pronunciation and meaning.

3. Get rid of the idea that reading and the teaching of reading take place during the "reading period" and that during other periods subjects are taught.

4. There should be a deliberate effort to study the organization of sentences, paragraphs, and larger units.

    a. Stress the function of pronunciation for students needing this type of drill.
    b. Explain and analyze difficult sentence structure, dependent clauses, complex sentences, and inverted order.

5. Teach and expect orderliness, organization, and logic in written work.

6. Use all audio-visual aids available. Concepts are built through sensory experiences. And experience with word symbols alone is an ineffective way to broaden concepts. The concept of land erosion might be taught with words, i.e., "erosion is the wearing away of land by rain or the action of water." However, a single good picture of badly eroded land might fix this concept and make it much more meaningful. A film showing the cutting of forests, plowing, and lack of cover grass, will broaden the concept even more.

7. Use purposeful study questions in advance of pupil reading. Questions given prior to reading can be most effective in structuring any reading situation. Eventually the student should get in the habit of asking the proper questions for himself, but this takes time and experience. In order to master this technique the child needs guidance and direction. This is an excellent method for giving the student a motive or goal in his reading. Too often this technique is neglected or not used as a means of implementing critical reading.

8. Wide reading on fewer topics, rather than superficial reading on many topics, will permit students more practice in organizing, analyzing, seeing relationships, comparing sources, and determining whether information belongs or is related to the topic under discussion.

9. Teach interpretation of graphs, charts, tables, figures, wherever they occur in any subject area.

10. Explain and teach analogies and how the reader must always make sure the analogy applies.

11. Provide practice in recognizing bias, distortion, and various propaganda techniques. A recent study indicates that sixth-grade children can be taught to detect some propaganda used in materials they read. (26) This does not mean they can become immune but that they can detect certain propaganda devices after periods of instruction aimed at helping them identify these techniques.

12. Help children develop a questioning attitude so that they will differentiate between fact and opinion, see cause and effect relationships, and use clues in evaluating the merit of a work. These clues might include the origin or context of the article (reputation of the magazine or publisher); the writing or publication date (have significant advances taken place since publication?) and the reputation of the author (is he objective, is he selling a point of view?).

CONCLUSION

Without question, the most important task of the school is helping children develop critical reading ability. All facets of the curriculum demand this skill of students. Good teaching in any of the various subject areas will contribute to the child's ability to read materials in that area. Poor teaching assumes that students have the prerequisite skills for critical reading and tends to focus on learning facts rather than on the *process of mining* content materials.

Critical reading is not a skill that is acquired once and for all time. It is a developmental process that might be thought of as a continuum. To become and remain a critical reader requires continuous growth. Each successive grade level makes higher demands on the reader. If pupil growth does not keep pace with the demands of the curricular materials, learning is inhibited. Furthermore, the gap between reading ability and the demands of the school tends to widen once it is permitted to develop.

Comprehension of reading material cannot be taught in isolation. Acquiring this skill is dependent upon mastery of a wide variety of other reading and language skills. These range from sounding letters, using punctuation, and recognizing whole words to knowing multiple meanings of words, drawing inferences and detecting propaganda devices. A breakdown or lapse in the application of any reading skill can thwart critical reading. A combination of weaknesses reduces the possibility of critical reading.

There are no short cuts to critical reading. Every given piece of writing demands the simultaneous application of numerous skills. When pupils lack these skills, the first task of the school should be to teach them.

YOUR POINT OF VIEW?

Be sure to read the following statements critically before giving your analysis of them.

1. If we agree that we cannot talk in terms of *the meaning* of a passage, we must conclude that it is impossible either to evaluate or to teach critical reading.
2. Since critical reading depends on the application of numerous reading skills, early reading instruction should focus less on critical reading and more on skill development.
3. In most classroom situations critical reading is equated with supplying responses which have arbitrarily been decided upon as being correct. Creative reading which might lead to divergent interpretations is not encouraged.
4. A person with no training or background in physics or genetics could not read critically a series of conflicting reports on the effect of "atomic fallout."
5. A high school student could not arrive at a sound critical analysis of the effect of tariffs on American industrialization by critically reading only high school textbooks on American history.
6. Honest judges with equal ability in critical reading of statutes will agree on the constitutionality of a particular law. (Assuming, of course, that they have read the constitution critically.)
7. America's free public education system is the world's foremost example of "socialized education."

BIBLIOGRAPHY

1. Arbuthnot, May Hill, "Developing Life Values Through Reading," *Elementary English,* XXXXIII (January 1966), 10-16.
2. Artley, A. Sterl, "Critical Reading in the Content Areas," *Elementary English,* XXXXI (February 1959), 122-30.
3. Barbe, Walter B., and Thelma E. Williams, "Developing Creative Thinking in Gifted Children through the Reading Program," *Reading Teacher,* IX (April 1956), 200-3.
4. Carter, Homer L. J., Dorothy J. McGinnis, *Teaching Individuals to Read.* Boston: D. C. Heath & Company, 1962, Chapter 9.

5. Carver, Richard L., and William D. Sheldon, "Problems in the Development of Concepts through Reading," *Elementary School Journal,* LV (December 1954), 226-29.

6. Cole, Louella, *The Improvement of Reading.* New York: Farrar and Rinehart, Inc., 1938.

7. Cook, Luella B., "Language Factors Involved in Interpretation," *Reading Teacher,* XII (February 1959), 152-57.

8. Davis, Frederick B., "Fundamental Factors in Comprehension in Reading," *Psychometrika,* IX (September 1944), 185-97.

9. Durrell, Donald D., "Development of Comprehension and Interpretation," *Reading in the Elementary School.* Forty-eighth Yearbook, Part II, National Society for the Study of Education. Chicago: University of Chicago Press, 1949.

10. Eisenman, Sister M. Victoria, "The Situation In Literature," *Elementary English,* XXXXII (October 1965), 644-45.

11. Eller, William, "Fundamentals of Critical Reading," *The Reading Teachers' Reader,* Oscar S. Causey (ed.). New York: The Ronald Press Company, 1958, 30-34.

12. Gainsburg, Joseph C., "Critical Reading is Creative Reading and Needs Creative Teaching," *Reading Teacher,* 15 (December 1961), 185-92.

13. Gray, William S., "New Approaches to the Study of Interpretation in Reading," *Journal of Educational Research,* LII (October 1958), 65-67.

14. Greene, Harry A., and Walter T. Petty, *Developing Language Skills in the Elementary School.* Boston: Allyn & Bacon, Inc., 1959.

15. Hanna, Paul R., "Generalizations and Universal Values: Their Implications for the Social-Studies Program," *Social Studies in the Elementary School.* The Fifty-sixth Yearbook, Part II, National Society for the Study of Education. Chicago: University of Chicago Press, 1957, 24-27.

16. Hillenbrand, Robert, "The Appreciation of Picturesque Language in the Intermediate Grades," *Elementary English,* XXXVI (May 1959), 302-4.

17. Homze, Alma, "Interpersonal Relations in Children's Literature 1920-1960," *Elementary English,* XXXXIII (January 1966), 26-28.

18. Jenkins, William A., "Reading Skills in Teaching Literature in the Elementary School," *Improvement of Reading Through Classroom Practice.* International Reading Association. (June 1964), 324-25.

19. Jenkinson, Marion E. D., "Reading—Developing the Mind," *Changing Concepts of Reading Instruction.* International Reading Association Proceedings, (June 1961), 170-73.

20. Karlin, Robert, "Critical Reading is Critical Thinking," *Education,* 84 (September 1963), 8-11.

21. Kerfoot, James F., "Problems and Research Considerations in Reading Comprehension," *Reading Teacher,* 18 (January 1965), 250-57.

22. Langman, Muriel Potter, "Teaching Reading as Thinking," *Education,* 82 (September 1961), 19-25.

23. McKee, Paul, *Reading — A Program of Instruction for the Elementary School.* Boston: Houghton Mifflin Company, 1966, Chapter 10.

24. Macrorie, Ken, *The Perceptive Writer, Reader, and Speaker.* New York: Harcourt, Brace & World, 1959.

25. McCullough, Constance, "Implications of Research on Children's Concepts," *Reading Teacher,* XIII (December 1959), 100-7.

26. Nardelli, Robert R., "Some Aspects of Creative Reading," *Journal of Educational Research,* L (March 1957), 495-508.

27. Nordberg, Robert B., "Levels of Communication in Reading," *Catholic Educational Review,* LIV (February 1956), 92-100.

28. Petty, Walter T., "Critical Reading in the Primary Grades," *Elementary English,* XXXIII (May 1956), 298-302.

29. Russell, David H., *Children Learn to Read.* Boston: Ginn and Company, 1961, Chapters 13 and 14.

30. Schneyer, J. Wesley, "Use of the Cloze Procedure for Improving Reading Comprehension," *Reading Teacher,* 19 (December 1966), 174-79.

31. Serra, Mary C., "A Study of Fourth Grade Children's Comprehension of Certain Verbal Abstractions," *Journal of Experimental Education,* XXII (December 1953), 103-18.

32. Sister M. Baptist R. S. M., "The Promise That is Poetry," *Catholic School Journal,* 65 (May 1965), 45.

33. Smith, Nila Banton, "The Good Reader Thinks Critically," *Reading Teacher,* 15 (December 1961), 162-71.

34. Smith, Philip G., "The Art of Asking Questions," *Reading Teacher,* 15 (September 1961), 37.

35. Sochor, E. Elona, "The Nature of Critical Reading," *Elementary English,* XXXVI (January 1959), 47-58.

36. Strang, Ruth, and Dorothy Kendall Bracken, *Making Better Readers.* Boston: D. C. Heath & Co., 1957.

37. Stroud, J. B., *Psychology in Education.* New York: Longmans, Green and Co., Inc., 1957.

38. Taba, Hilda, "The Teaching of Thinking," *Elementary English,* XXXXII (May 1965), 534-42.

39. Triggs, Frances O., "Promoting Growth in Critical Reading," *Reading Teacher,* XII (February 1959), 158-64.

40. Usery, Mary Lou, "Critical Thinking Through Children's Literature," *Elementary English,* XXXXIII (February 1966), 115-18.

41. Walpole, Hugh R., "Promoting Development in Interpreting What Is Read in the Middle and Upper Grades," Supplementary Educational Monographs, University of Chicago. Chicago: University of Chicago Press, No. 61, 162-67.

42. Williams, Gertrude, "Provisions for Critical Reading in Basic Readers," *Elementary English,* XXXVI (May 1959), 323-31.

Remedial Reading

15

Americans assign an extremely high value to literacy. For years it was taken for granted that the mere process of attending school would result in acquiring this prized asset, except in cases in which the individual was too dull or simply refused to learn. Individuals who were alleged to fit either of these categories usually dropped out of school, and there were numerous niches for them to fill in our society.

Gradually laws were passed which forbade dropping out of school prior to reaching a designated age, usually 16 to 18 years. "School" became much more of a threat to the twentieth-century severely impaired reader than hell was to his Puritan ancestors. But as soon as an individual fulfilled the requirements of the law, he could leave school and still find a niche in adult society.

Automation emerged as the most significant socio-economic factor since the industrial revolution and changed the picture drastically. Now the impaired reader could elect to stay in school until he reached the legal age minimum; get expelled from school for anti-social behavior; or drop out of high school (with the tacit approval of the authorities). Regardless of which option he elected *there was no niche for him to fill in our complex society*. During the mid-sixties, as unemployment figures for the population as a whole dropped to unprecedented lows, the figures for the not-in-school age group 18 to 22 hit new highs with no encouraging signs of a better tomorrow.

The fervor of the fifties was expended on the "great talent search." The upgrading of the curriculum in mathematics, science, and languages was now focused on the more basic educational problem of how to equip students with the necessary reading skills demanded by the established curriculum in our schools.

The failure of large numbers of children to learn to read at a level commensurate with their intellectual ability may well be our number one educational problem. Marksheffel (9) estimates that between 2.5 and 5 million school-age youths are "so severely retarded in reading that they require immediate specialized help." The serious nature of this problem has been known for years, but education at the local level could never muster the finances and trained personnel in such quantities as to be able to even slow down the growing number of impaired readers.

As the severity of this problem was grasped by citizens and government alike, the needs of American youths in this area yielded its "local" status and became a matter of national interest. Education of youth and the goals and survival of society were re-affirmed as being inseparable.

The long years of neglect behind this problem made its solution more difficult. When federal funds were made available in abundance, the first fact learned was that money alone could not produce a solution. Education is a process not a commodity. Education as a creative process had been stiffled too long, and creative ideas could not be conjured up with the same rapidity with which congress voted appropriations. A number of practices which were supported by federal funds turned out to be rather unimaginative. One of these was the hastily assembled in-service program which paralleled course work and which failed to involve teachers in sharing activities and intensive study of research and other professional materials related to reading instruction. A second was the tendency of local schools to acquire a large supply of gadgets such as pacing devices and other mechanistic paraphernalia which had little relevancy to elementary reading instruction.

REMEDIAL READING DEFINED

Unfortunately there is no universal agreement as to the meaning of the terms remedial reading instruction and remedial readers. In its broadest sense the term remedial reading covers special instruction for those individuals whose reading achievement is X amount lower than their expected achievement based on measured intellectual capacity for learning. There is also no universal agreement as to the value of X. Figures cited in some research suggest that this criterion might be a range of from six months to two years difference between achievement and capacity.

It should be noted that such a broad definition of remedial reading does not differentiate pupils on the basis of what might have caused their lack of growth in reading. Some specialists in the field would prefer that "remedial" be reserved for those cases in which there is evidence that the major cause is a neurological condition. Instruction involving other cases might then be labeled "corrective instruction."

There is general agreement that remedial reading instruction aims at removing the barriers to learning which inhibited this learning in the past. It is not concerned with poor reading per se, but rather with bringing children's achievement closer to their actual ability. Remedial reading instruction is not concerned with providing special attention for all pupils who are reading below grade level or chronological age norms. To illustrate this point one might think of two third-grade pupils of the same age who read at the same level as noted below:

Child A	C. A. 8-4	M. A. 9-2	I. Q. 110	Reads 1^2
Child B	C. A. 8-4	M. A. 7-0	I. Q. 84	Reads 1^2

Although both pupils are in the same grade and are reading at the same level, only pupil A should be thought of as a remedial reader. He has above-average intelligence, but he is learning at a rate far below his capacity. Child B, although in the third grade, is achieving as well as could be expected on the basis of his ability, and, according to the preceding definition, would not be a logical candidate for remedial reading. He is now learning about as rapidly and as thoroughly as can be expected. Should we decide to give him remedial instruction aimed at bringing him up to his grade level (or chronological age level), we would be implying that methodology or technique in instruction can actually compensate for a lack of ability in academic achievement. Since we do not believe this, it would be irrational to attempt to practice it. However, it is important to realize that when we take this position, we assume that our assessment of his ability is accurate. Pupil A, who is reading slowly in view of his ability, might profit from a change in technique and from individual instruction in certain mechanics of reading. These practices might help him to move forward at a rate commensurate with his ability. This in essence is the philosophy behind remedial instruction.

It has been pointed out previously that reading ability is held in very high esteem in our culture and that children are expected to achieve up to an arbitrary grade-level standard. The fact that at least a third of all pupils in a given grade fall below this standard is well-known to educators. Schools which are geared to mass education, a rigid grade-level structure, and promotion without regard to mastery of skills will continue to produce remedial readers.

Remedial reading, as it is usually understood, puts the onus of failure on the child who needs the remedy. Some authorities have suggested that the term should be *remedial teaching* to intimate that the teaching, not the pupil, is at fault. Neither position is always fair to either pupil or teacher when all factors in reading failures are considered.

It is easy for a teacher to blame the child who develops habits of laziness, inattention, disinterest, withdrawal, or aggression. It is just as easy for parents and critics of schools to blame schools and teaching methods or for teachers to blame parents and home environments. Fixing blame, unless the blame is clear-cut, is dangerous.

DEGREE OF IMPAIRMENT AS A CRITERION FOR REMEDIAL INSTRUCTION

Within the framework of remedial instruction, each school system is free to set its own criteria for pupil participation in the program. Rarely is special attention provided for pupils unless the gulf between ability and present achievement measures at least a year, and a more common figure would be a minimum of two years.

It should not be inferred that such a criterion will, as a general rule, result in an impaired reader receiving special help in reading. Usually there are long histories of failure and frustration. Working with remedial readers is often accompanied by the dual tragedy of unnecessary suffering by children who fail and educational energy expended in remedial rather than preventive efforts. In general, when our schools observe the maladjustment stemming from failure to learn, and when this maladjustment is expressed in behavior which the school does not condone, a remedy is advocated. All too often remedial reading is a form of educational penance in which schools and teachers practice the principles they believe in, but which they either failed to follow or found it impossible to follow, in the regular process of teaching reading.

COMMON MISCONCEPTIONS ABOUT REMEDIAL READING

Despite the widespread use of the term remedial reading, there is some degree of confusion regarding what it is, what practices it embodies, and who its practitioners are. Vague concepts often give rise to misconceptions. Some of these are discussed below.

The most widely held misconception is that remedial reading instruction is based on a set of principles which differ appreciably from those principles which are the basis for the school's regular developmental reading instruction. It is easy to see how such a misconception might develop. Virtually every college or university which prepares teachers for the elementary schools has one or more courses entitled "Remedial Reading," "Practices in Remedial Reading," or "Methods and Techniques in Remedial Reading." Many textbooks bear similar titles. Remedial reading clinics are found on almost every university campus. Schools hire "Remedial Reading Teachers." Workshops devoted to remedial reading are commonplace. With this much evidence it is easy to conclude that remedial reading is a subject matter different from the teaching of reading. It is sometimes difficult to convince teachers that all of the principles and most of the practices which are characteristic of remedial reading are also applicable to developmental reading.

An illustration of this point is found in the behavior and the attitudes of two groups of teachers enrolled in different sections of a course entitled "Remedial Techniques in Reading." In the first section the instructor stated that there were not two distinct approaches, one regular and the other remedial, to teaching reading. Some teachers seemed skeptical and were quite reluctant to accept this point of view. In the second class a different approach was tried. Each student was handed a sheet of paper and was asked to list all of the principles of teaching which she identified with remedial reading. The major points mentioned included:

1. Go back to the child's present reading level.
2. Do not expect the child to read material which forces him to experience failure, i.e., he must have developed readiness for the task.
3. Help the child build self-confidence—use abundant praise. Undue pressure in the learning situation may interfere with learning.
4. Use a variety of approaches.
5. Base instruction on a thorough diagnosis.
6. Build interest in reading—have a large stock of supplementary reading materials.

As each point was mentioned, the group noted that it applied equally well to any good classroom program. It was conceded that no principles had been listed which applied exclusively to remedial reading.

A second misconception centers around the practices and the procedures believed to be reserved to remedial reading instruction. Remedial reading is sometimes thought of as consisting of a bag of tricks which includes, among other items, a vast number of games and motivators. When experienced teachers attempt to list methods and procedures which might be identified as "remedial," it is obvious that these methods and procedures are equally justifiable for use during the months in which the pupil is becoming a remedial reader. It might be conceded that in remedial teaching there is more emphasis on devising unique ways of approaching a particular learning task. This emphasis is justified because the remedial reader usually needs more motivation for reading than does the successful reader. It should be pointed out that games and motivators are used to arouse the pupil's interest and to hold his attention in the hope that this attention and energy can be directed toward reading. These "crutches" must be replaced with more effective and less time-consuming procedures as soon as the child can make the transition. Therefore, to make the use of motivators the identifying badge of remedial reading is misleading.

Experienced teachers often think of remedial reading as being composed of a number of highly specialized techniques which only the initiated can practice. For example, a group of teachers, as part of a course in remedial reading, were to tutor a child whose reading achievement was considerably below his ability. There was a file available for each child which contained intelligence test results, parent interviews, and a summary of the child's reading level and reading weaknesses. Later, several of these experienced teachers admitted that they "felt completely lost" during the first few sessions because they were not sure that they knew enough about remedial reading to work with the case. In a discussion, they admitted having had children in their regular classes with problems at least as serious as those found in the assigned case. They also indicated that they expected something special or extraordinary to be imparted to them in the area of remedial reading before they could work with an impaired reader. Once this notion had been dispelled, they taught successfully and with much creativity and insight.

A third misconception is that remedial reading is something that must be done outside of the regular classroom. It is true that in some school systems the remedial program develops as a sort of appendage to the regular structure, but remedial reading must of necessity be conducted in the classrooms of those schools which have no such special provision. Inevitably there are pupils in these classrooms who must be considered remedial readers. (4)

DIFFERENCES BETWEEN REMEDIAL AND REGULAR READING INSTRUCTION

The position has been taken that there may be little if any difference between the principles or the practices followed in remedial reading and the everyday instructional activities of a conscientious, creative classroom teacher. Nevertheless, when remedial programs supplement the regular reading instruction there are probably some real differences between the two. The chief cause of the differences has already been implied: in remedial reading we conscientiously adhere to the principles that we often only verbalize in the regular classroom instruction. Thus, when differences exist they probably stem from two sources:

1. *The attitudes and philosophy of administrators and teachers*

a. In the remedial program, as a rule, there is no immediate conscious endeavor to get the child up to "grade level" or some other arbitrary standard. He will read materials which he can read with some degree of success regardless of his grade placement.

b. The teaching-learning atmosphere will probably be more permissive. The child will not be labeled a failure, and he will be accepted as a person. Even though the objective is to read, pressure on the child to read will be lessened. As a result, he will be less threatened by the reading situation.

c. In the remedial program more attention might be focused on the reasons for failure, thus revealing certain other factors which may have to be dealt with concurrently with the actual reading problem. Considerable emphasis will be placed on how to interest the child in reading; as a result, senseless drill is likely to be held to a minimum.

d. There will be conferences with parents, if it appears that the child is under pressure and tension at home.

e. A great variety of reading materials will be available, and children will be permitted to choose what they wish to read. They will be encouraged to read books they *can* read, not necessarily books at their grade level.

f. The teacher will know a great deal about the child, and she will know exactly his reading achievement as well as his instructional needs.

g. There will be time for individual instruction as needed, and each child in the group will require such instruction.

h. In the remedial program, there may be more emphasis on the use of "motivators." In the regular classroom only a few pupils need this type of instruction in order to learn.

i. In remedial reading, the psychological needs of the child are considered to be very important. He is encouraged to set goals he can achieve and is praised for any accomplishment.

j. In remedial reading, children never feel as if they are in reading competition with others. They may compete with their own previous performance, but they do not have to measure up to some arbitrary standard.

These attitudes and goals undoubtedly differentiate between remedial and regular instruction, yet the regular classroom teacher probably subscribes to all of them. They are universally advocated as sound classroom procedure. How, then, do these factors become more characteristic of remedial reading than of the regular classroom instruction? The answer is found in the second source of difference between regular and remedial instruction.

2. *The conditions under which teachers function*

These conditions have been briefly discussed in Chapter 1 under the heading, "School Practices Affecting Instruction." Included were: too many pupils per teacher to permit individual instruction; universal promotion in a grade-level system; non-teaching activities of teachers; the schools' and the communities' disinclination to wait for readiness; school entrance based on C. A.; and others. Some teachers in the first grade have admitted to attempting to teach as many as forty children how to read. Fortunately, this would never happen in a remedial class. In the remedial class there is time for diagnosis, time for building a program to fit individual needs as disclosed by the diagnosis, and time to give individual attention where it is needed. Supplementary materials are available and competitive pressures are removed from the learning task. These steps are taken because educators know that this is the way to get the job done, and they see to it that it is done this way. They also say that these are the principles and the practices to follow in the teaching of reading prior to the child's becoming a severely handicapped learner, but they somehow do not insist that conditions prevail which will permit these principles and practices to be followed.

It is a sad commentary on American education that sound principles of teaching a skill as important as reading can be followed only after so many children have suffered so much due to the inadequacy of the instruction. Teachers regret this terrible waste and the attendant risks of producing maladjustment and antisocial behavior. They have guilt feelings because teaching as a profession has not as yet evolved the procedures which would prevent teaching under conditions that threaten the mental health of their pupils.

CAUSES OF READING IMPAIRMENT

A survey of the literature on reading reveals a number of factors reported as possible causes of reading problems. Those which seem to be universally agreed upon are:

1. Physical handicaps
2. Intellectual capacity
3. Educational factors
4. Emotional involvement
5. Home environment

These topics are discussed in other chapters of this book. However, it should be noted that each of the topics covers an extensive range of causal factors, as illustrated below under the major headings of physical and educational factors.

1. Physical handicaps:
   a. Impaired vision
   b. Hearing loss, or a lack of facility in auditory discrimination
   c. Low vitality, lack of energy to apply to the learning task
   d. Inadequate attention span
   e. Absence from school due to illness at crucial instructional periods
   f. Specific language disability stemming from physiological impairment

2. Educational factors:
   a. The child, having moved from school to school, has encountered different methods of teaching which may have produced confusion
   b. Lack of individual instruction when needed
   c. Failure of the school to detect reading weaknesses
   d. Universal promotion not related to the mastery of basic skills
   e. Inadequacy of the instruction stemming from poor teacher preparation
   f. Lack of an adequate supply of interesting reading materials at the pupil's reading level

In a majority of the reading problems it is unlikely that severe impairment can be traced to one and only one factor. If it is true that there are innumerable factors which affect learning to read, it is logical to surmise that these factors can work together in hundreds of different combinations. This makes diagnosis, particularly from the psychological standpoint, extremely difficult and complicated. Figure 36 attempts to illustrate the complexity of factors which may influence the development of good reading habits. While any one of these is sufficient to cause trouble in learning to read, it is unlikely that any one operates alone for any great length of time. Unresolved problems seem to hasten the growth of other problems.

When faced by a complex problem, most people prefer simple explanations and simple remedies. This is true of the complex problem of explaining how and why such a large number of school children with adequate intellectual endowment become seriously impaired readers. Earlier it was pointed out that at different times simple explanations and remedies for this problem enjoyed wide-

FIGURE 36

SOME FACTORS INFLUENCING THE ACQUISITION OF READING ABILITY.

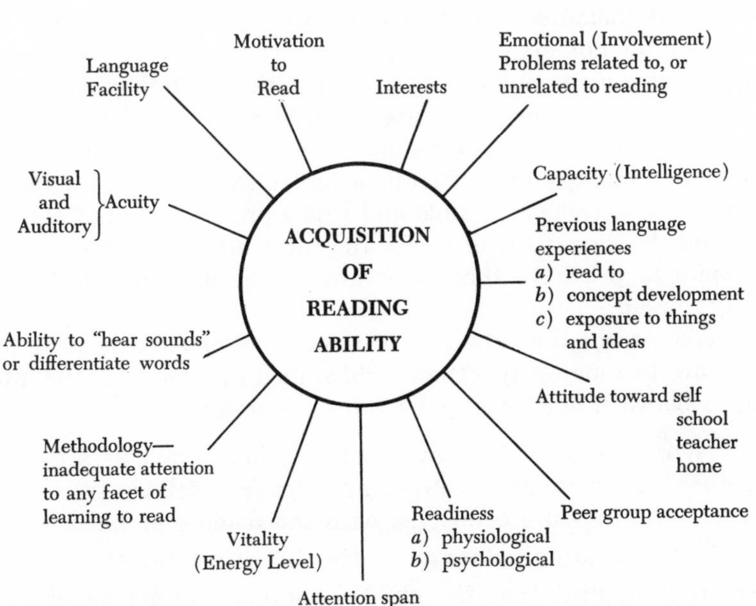

spread acceptance. Inadequate intelligence, special disabilities, and the schools' lessened emphasis on the synthetic method of teaching phonics have at one time or another been advanced as the chief cause of reading problems. Certain of these theories have been downgraded as explanations of reading failures. Nevertheless, there is still the tendency to advance hypotheses which in the final analysis may be over-simplifications in that they neglect to take into consideration the interaction of various factors.

EMOTIONS AND READING

Whether or not the school and the teacher are aware of it, the school experiences that children have are a most important factor in determining the kinds of persons they will become. The school may take partial credit when children learn at a level approximating their capacity or when they exhibit social and emotional behavior that society recognizes as acceptable and healthy. Yet few of us, as teachers, like to admit that the schools must also share the credit (or guilt) for pupil maladjustment. If reading disabilities are to be curbed, the school must seek out and attempt to mitigate its own contributions to pupil maladjustment.

Psychologists and psychiatrists as well as informed teachers know that maladjustments in the learning process (reading disabilities) do not stem from any one academic practice or malpractice as some popular writers seem to think. Methodology alone is not responsible for producing the host of impaired readers and non-readers that plague our schools, homes, and guidance clinics. While methodology may often be a contributory factor, the human organism is extremely flexible and it is a proven fact that children can and do learn to read under the most adverse methodological procedures, provided that they are physically and emotionally ready to read.

It is apparent from the literature on emotions and reading that there are two major hypotheses which might account for the interaction between emotions and reading disability.

1. Where emotional behavior and reading problems are found together, the emotional involvement stems from failure, frustration, tension, and pressure connected with the reading problem.

Reading failure ⟶ Emotional reactions

Here it is implied that the child's emotions become involved in reading through success or failure. While competition may not be new to the child, the type of competition he encounters in the reading situation *is* new to him. Never before has so much been expected from him by his parents and his teacher. Reading ability is very highly prized in our society, and pressures on the child from parents, teacher, and peers all seem to focus on this one front. He has not sensed this type of pressure in his drawing and coloring activities, in rhythm activities, in listening to stories the teacher has read, or in other activities found in the curriculum.

The child's frustrations mount as a result of failure and also as a result of his inability to please the figures of authority—parents and teachers. His attitudes toward himself are influenced by attitudes around him. Feelings of inferiority and personal inadequacy result. When one's ego is threatened, tension and emotional conflict are inevitable. Under these circumstances, the child resorts to some behavior which, irrational as it may appear to adults, seems to the child to be a means of escape from an untenable position.

It is amazing how varied the responses of different children are to frustration and ego-threatening situations. The same classroom stimulus will not produce like responses among different children.

The teacher's remark, "now let's open our reading workbooks—we should be on page thirty-nine," may elicit responses varying from elation to nausea among the various pupils in the class. The individual child's past experiences both at home and school, and the impact these experiences have had on the child's attitudes toward himself, toward the teacher, and toward parents and peers, will all determine the response which this stimulus evokes. One child may give the appearance of functional deafness—he didn't hear the request; one may request to leave the room; another child may respond with the ultimate of conformity, and open his book to page 39, even though he has never worked successfully on any of the preceding pages or any preceding workbooks.

2. Unresolved emotional problems, which originally need not have been related to reading, may prevent the child from applying his energies to the learning task. The non-reading behavior is simply a symptom of the emotional problem.

Unresolved emotional problem ⟶ Reading problem

When reading problems and emotional involvements are found together, there may also be other factors contributing to the reading problem (i.e., physical factors, educational procedures used, learned responses to frustration).

Several principles of teaching reading discussed earlier are related to emotional problems and reading. In Chapter 1 it was pointed out that learning to read is a very complicated process and that language functions are among the most sensitive indicators of maladjustment. Unrelenting pressure brought to bear on a child to make him read will not always achieve desirable results. Further, it was suggested that sometime in the future it is likely that children with emotional problems severe enough to prevent learning will receive treatment before being expected to harness their energies to learning tasks.

The Teacher's Role in Dealing with Emotionally Involved Reading Problems

What should the teacher do for children with reading problems who also show evidence that there is an emotional factor involved? Several factors make this question difficult to answer.

1. Some teachers, parents, school boards, and critics of education do not yet admit that in many cases non-learning and emotional problems are inextricably knit together. After several years of in-

struction in reading and special tutoring, Johnny, who has adequate intelligence, is still a non-reader. Some factor other than lack of intelligence or poor methodology must be contributing to Johnny's problem. However, if it is ruled out before the search is begun, emotional maladjustment will not be unearthed as the culprit.

The belief that the schools have a tremendous impact on ego-development or ego-starvation of pupils is gaining wider acceptance, and teachers are coming to realize that they are necessarily involved in the process of dealing with social and emotional maladjustments. Yet there are many critics of American education who think that the school's concern with the social and emotional development of children is a tender-minded, do-gooder escape mechanism thrown up as a rearguard action by confused teachers engaged in a retreat from teaching.

It must be admitted that some teachers who verbally embrace the principle that the school should be concerned with the pupil's emotional health are hazy as to *why*. To some teachers the reason may appear to be more closely allied to public relations than to learning. These teachers may not be aware of the fact that the learning process is very sensitive to emotional and social disturbances and in the final analysis is affected by maladjustment in these areas. "Meeting the child's needs and interests" may have, through constant usage, been reduced to jargon, but it once was meaningful. "Educating the whole child" may share the same present-day reputation, but this too once had meaning. Both of these principles involved the recognition that all school experiences are related to learning. The school cannot meet the needs of children if it ignores psychological needs such as the need for success, self-realization, creativity, and an acceptable concept of self. Failure in school is the most important factor in thwarting the fulfillment of the child's needs.

2. The teacher's ego needs can contribute to the child's insecurity and pose threats to his adjustment and concept of self. The fact that some children fail to make progress commensurate with grade-level norms may become a threat to the teacher. This threat is often met with more pressure and sometimes with unconscious hostility.

3. Another important factor is the conviction on the part of teachers that they are not prepared to deal with emotional problems. This lack of preparation is undoubtedly the case with some

teachers, some parents, some clinicians, and quite a few detention homes. Also, it is probably true that most of the maladjusted are not equipped to help themselves. There are some children who have emotional problems which teachers cannot hope to alleviate, just as there are some pupil maladjustments produced by the school which could have been prevented.

Teachers as Therapists. In recent years, however, there has been an awareness on the part of many clinicians in child-guidance clinics as well as remedial clinics that the school—or, more correctly, the teacher—is in a therapeutic relationship to children because of the very nature of the school and the activities which are carried on in the school. This is not to imply that teachers should consider themselves trained therapists when they are not, but rather that, try as they may, they cannot escape the fact that much of the activity in the classroom is ego-involved activity and how teachers handle everyday situations in the classroom has an impact on the mental health of pupils. (19)

Woodruff, (22) in his book *The Psychology of Teaching* states, "Every teacher is of necessity a psychologist in *function,* with or *without training.*" (Emphasis added.) He does not say that teachers are psychologists, but rather implies that their daily tasks in the classroom require them to deal with, understand, and influence human behavior (learning). This they do with or without training in understanding or influencing behavior. Actually, the average teacher is not without training for this part of her job, and the better the teacher the more she understands her limitations. But with or without limitations, she must find ways to help children grow, to help children face frustration, to help children accept reality, and to help children drain off tension so they can apply energy to learning tasks instead of burning it up in behavior not related to learning.

The issue is that, if teachers see themselves as exclusively concerned with methodological procedures or techniques, they are likely to find that some of their pupils do not seem to profit from any of the procedures or techniques used.

When classroom procedures fail, certain pupils may be referred to a reading or child-guidance clinic for help. If, as a result, they receive the right combination of attention to their psychological needs and attention to techniques aimed at the mechanics of reading, all may turn out well. In many cases there are no such facilities available, at least not until the child's behavior becomes so deviant that something *has to be done.* Can teachers themselves provide this right combination? Many teachers do practice a certain amount of therapy, and they rarely see it as something extraneous to the learning situation. It is simply part of the job of guiding the learning activities of children.

To illustrate, an elementary school arranged for a thorough diagnosis of a number of children with severe reading problems. One third-grade girl, Mary, was a non-reader. She had intelligence adequate for learning and was attractive but shy and retiring. When asked about friends, she had only one friend, Miss Blank (her teacher). In answer to other questions, Whom do you like to play with? walk home with? visit? Miss Blank was the only human being mentioned. At noon, this child and teacher were observed in the cafeteria. All the children in the third grade sat around one long table, the teacher at one end. Mary sat next to her and was most possessive. She put her hand in the teacher's, looked at her most of the time, talked to her (not shy here). In fact, before the meal was over, she had managed to slip her chair up very close to the teacher and place her head on the teacher's lap. The teacher stroked her head and shoulder all the while talking to others around her and keeping in touch with all that was going on around the large table. As the group left, Mary and the teacher left hand-in-hand.

Later, Mary's problem was discussed. Her teacher brought up the matter of the child's complete dependence on her and stated that she had to be very careful that Mary's possessiveness did not arouse antagonism among the other children. (There had been absolutely no resentment shown in the cafeteria although this type of behavior was a daily occurrence.) The teacher knew these facts: Mary lived with grandparents; her parents were divorced, and the father worked in another state. The child created fantasies of her father coming to see her; he never came. Several months earlier the mother had taken employment as a waitress in a large city several hundred miles away and had not been home to visit the daughter during this period. The grandparents fulfilled the child's physical needs, and she was fairly well-dressed and clean. They completely failed to help the child in her emotional problem, which stemmed from feelings of rejection and attendant guilt feelings about her own contribution to parental rejection.

While all of this history was known to everyone in the small community, including Mary's two previous teachers, none had sensed the child's loneliness or great need for someone to tie to, until Miss

Blank. The important point is that Miss Blank did not feel that she was doing something "nice" for Mary. She did not think of what she was doing as therapy. Her problem, as she saw it, was to protect Mary by concealing from the other children the fact that Mary was monopolizing the teacher. No change had yet occurred in Mary's reading behavior, but gradually she was able to bring some energy to bear on learning. Meeting the needs of children is therapy, and the more flexible and creative the reading teacher is in discerning the child's real needs, the more likely it is that she will alleviate present reading problems and forestall the appearance of others.

EXPERIENCE DETERMINES POINT OF VIEW TOWARD CAUSES

Educators and clinicians who deal extensively with reading problems undoubtedly have vastly different experiences with readers. There are significant differences in the role of each group and in the work climate in which each group operates. The community expects different types of behavior from educators and clinicians. Therefore, it should not be considered unusual when divergent views emerge as to the cause and cure of reading problems. It should be kept in mind, however, that one's original premises as to the cause of reading problems will influence the procedures advocated for working with impaired readers.

When blind men feel different parts of an elephant, each man forms a disparate hypothesis on the nature and structure of elephants, even though all the men had a common experience labeled "elephant feeling." This is demonstrated by the story of the five blind men, each of whom felt only a part of the elephant, such as the trunk, tail, leg, ear, and side. They variously described an elephant as being like a snake, a rope, a tree, a fan, and a wall. The reasons for their varied conclusions are quite evident to the person who entertains the total picture of an elephant. It is also quite obvious that, on the basis of their individual experiences, their deductions were quite plausible, despite the fact that not one of them emerged with a good concept of an elephant.

All people who work with impaired or disabled readers do not work from the same side of the elephant. Educators differ among themselves regarding the origin and the cure of reading problems, as do psychologists, clinicians, and therapists. This divergence of opinion may have arisen from differences in training which lead to dissimilarity in the relative emphasis placed on learning factors.

Most educators have reasoned that when a child has been exposed to reading instruction which has not "taken," it is obvious that the instruction was not adequate for this particular child. The proper approach to such failure was to vary the method of teaching and to introduce new techniques which might prove effective. Experiments were designed to test or establish this premise. Groups of retarded readers were subjected to specific types of instruction for varying periods of time. Strangely enough, almost any technique advocated and reported had a degree of efficacy with some cases. The data for a group of retarded readers are given on reading tests in the form of pre-test and end-test means, and the group gain reported is often significant. In most cases, the data show that some individuals made no gain or even appeared to decline in reading ability, as measured by the tests used. The important conclusion of such studies, however, is that the group made a mean gain of so many months' reading when compared with a control group of retarded readers who were not exposed to these particular methods and techniques. The methods used to effect these changes gain widespread appeal among teachers having in their classes children who have failed in reading.

In our society the educator's duties include responsibility for methodology and for techniques of teaching. It is only natural that educators have tended to concentrate on experimentation in the area of method. Figure 37 attempts to illustrate the behavior most likely to result when one starts from the premise that methodology is the key to all reading problems.

If all children who failed to learn to read did learn to read as a result of varying techniques and methodology, the only necessary premise would be the one discussed above. Unfortunately, this is not the case. We know that some children have had several different teachers who used different approaches to teaching reading, but the children still failed to learn to read. Neither pressure, punishment, nor variation in procedures proved effective with these children. Quite often they developed behavioral problems and showed evidence of maladjustment. If the behavior problems were of the overt aggressive type, the child was probably referred to a child-guidance clinic, a reading laboratory, or psychiatric help if it were obtainable. Referrals undoubtedly included children with high intelligence who had not, over a period of years, profited from instruction.

FIGURE 37

ILLUSTRATION OF HOW THE ATTITUDE IS REINFORCED THAT FAILURE IN READING CAN BE REMEDIED BY CHANGE IN METHOD

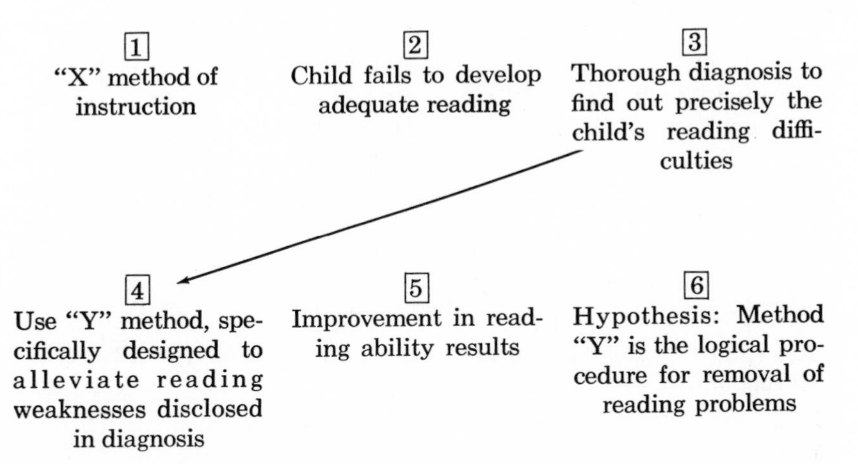

The psychologist-clinician finds that most cases of referral for reading failures are not, at the time of referral, simple uncomplicated learning problems amenable to solution by methodology alone. The evidence already at hand makes it obvious that more work on the reading problems alone will probably not be any more effective than it has been in the classroom. The clinician may tend to see all reading problems in the light of his own experiences. His role, and the type of cases he is likely to see, may lead him to the premise that impaired reading ability and emotional problems are inseparable. Usually, prior to or along with any work on reading, some form of therapy is introduced. Regardless of the therapeutic approach, the goals of this therapy are likely to include:

1. Reduction of the tension connected with reading
2. Change of the child's attitude toward self (ego-rehabilitation, self-confidence, etc.)
3. Change of the child's attitudes toward authority (school and parents)
4. Building interest in reading

Figure 38 is an attempt to illustrate this concept.

The best informed opinion today seems to be that reading behavior is a part of one's total development. The reading process

FIGURE 38

(Methodology and techniques cannot always remove reading failures and concomitant behavior problems. Some reading problems have their roots outside the reading situation and a frontal attack on reading will not solve the problem.)

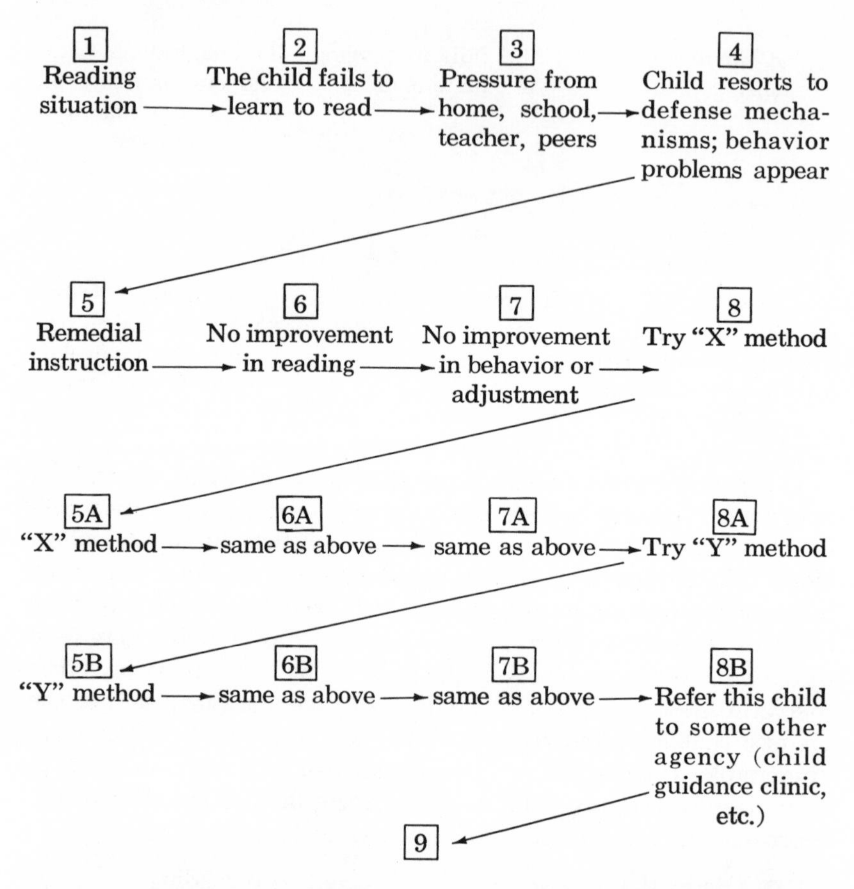

Hypothesis: Some emotional problem (possibly originally not related to reading) is still unresolved. The problem must be attacked and alleviated before the child can concentrate on the learning task.

---

and the reader interact at all times. While one may be primarily interested in a child's reading behavior, this behavior is but one facet of the individual's total growth process. It is generally conceded that both conscious and unconscious motivations are involved in reading difficulties.

Reading difficulties stem from many causes; but, no matter what the cause, any child having difficulty with reading needs special help. Perhaps the child is socially immature or lacks experience. He may not have mastered a vocabulary sufficient to express his own ideas or to understand the ideas of others. Perhaps he comes from an underprivileged family and poverty has affected his health, leaving him undernourished or undersized. Perhaps his mind is undernourished, too, because his parents read very little or speak English imperfectly. He may lack security because his father keeps moving from job to job, thus interrupting his school work. It may be that his parents neglect him or favor a brighter child in the family. Or he may lack emotional maturity and cannot concentrate on a difficult abstract skill such as reading because he is anxious, unhappy, hostile, or depressed. (15)

ADMINISTRATIVE PROCEDURES

Many schools and communities have inaugurated reading programs designed to help those children who have failed or who are not progressing at a rate commensurate with their ability. The administration and operation of programs differ, sometimes because of the belief that one administrative setup has certain inherent superiorities over all others, and in other cases because at the moment other approaches are not possible because of financial or other limiting factors. One of the most common or widely followed procedures is remedial reading carried on by the regular classroom teachers. (11) (23) (24) Most teachers group pupils on the basis of their reading ability. Whether or not this practice qualifies as remedial is determined by what goes on in the classroom. While grouping may be the first step toward providing remedial instruction, it is obvious that provision must be made for some individual instruction, or else the grouping will result in structure without substance. In a school which has no other method of dealing with impaired readers, the only remedial teaching which will be done will be provided by the regular classroom teachers. However, the fact that reading problems are not dealt with in a special setting is not prima facie evidence that they are being dealt with in the classroom.

A second approach is the use of a reading specialist or a remedial reading teacher. In some instances, such a teacher's duties consist exclusively of remedial work; she teaches no regular classes. In other situations, one or more teachers may divide their time between a regular assignment and remedial teaching. An interesting variation of this is the practice of the Dearborn schools, as reported by Jackson. (6) Elementary teachers spend five weeks in the Dearborn Reading Center working with cases and building materials. They then return to their regular classrooms with new insights in reading problems.

Another issue is whether to work with impaired readers as individuals or in small groups. Often the reading problems involved dictate the answer to this question. Group instruction probably should be used wherever it is feasible. This is done not only for the sake of economy, but also because grouping provides a social setting for the instruction. Small groups of five or six are sometimes superior to a group of two children. Two pupils often get involved in competing for the attention of the tutor. If one of the two is, or feels, inferior to the other in reading, the problem is accentuated by the direct comparison. Children will feel less singled out and possibly less threatened in a slightly larger group situation. Small group instruction in no way precludes individual work and individual help within the group. In any case, the size of the group should be adjusted to the instructional problems to be solved.

There are certain other administrative practices which do not fit the traditional framework of classroom instruction. One of these is the use of part of the summer period as a make-up term. This practice, while not widespread, has in recent years found its way into a number of schools. In some instances, instruction is provided during the summer for children reading far below their ability level. This instruction might be for one or two hours per day, in small groups, one or more teachers from the school being hired for a specified number of weeks. In other cases such instruction is provided on a tuition basis. The latter practice can raise serious problems unless it is possible to enroll children who need instruction but who are unable to participate for financial reasons.

Summer programs are usually voluntary on the part of the student, but some schools use the subtle pressure of tentative non-promotion or of probationary promotion as a means of motivating the poor readers and the under-achievers to participate in the summer program. Usually such pressures are not needed if an interesting program is developed and explained to children and parents.

Several such programs are described in recent publications. An article by Still (20) reports that a four-week summer remedial program, which enrolled 72 pupils ranging in age from 6 to 17 years, resulted in a mean gain of 10 months in reading achievement.

Googins (5) describes a six-week summer program which featured the use of materials entirely different from those used by the pupils during the regular school year. This feature was instrumental in developing wider interests and more positive attitudes toward reading.

The scheduling of summer remedial reading programs has increased as a result of Title II and III funds available to local school districts. A number of the initial projects funded by NDEA and ESEA may have erred in their emphasis on mechanical devices and gadgets. In some instances where this occurred, one of the objectives was to secure this relatively high-priced equipment for use in the school's regular reading program. Widespread use of such materials could result in deleterious side effects if schools substitute gadgetry for sound developmental instruction.

General Administrative Considerations

Regardless of what administrative procedure is followed, the resultant program can be successful. On the other hand, following any particular method will not in itself assure a successful program. Any administrative plan or organization is at best only the bare framework upon which a program can be built. The principles and practices which are followed determine the degree of success any remedial program will enjoy. Thus, the administrative details may vary without hindering a program as long as teachers follow sound practices. There are a number of general considerations which are very important in determining the success or failure of a special reading program. Some of these are listed below.

1. *In inaugurating a new program the administrator should be certain to involve the teaching staff, since the teachers are ultimately responsible for making the program work.* A new program or a program change should evolve out of a co-operative effort of both administrators and teachers. Both have areas of responsibility, of training, and of competency, which will help them in foreseeing and solving the problems which are sure to arise.

2. *As new personnel come into the school, they must be thoroughly briefed on all phases of the program — its goals, how referrals are made, and each teacher's role and responsibility in the total effort.*

3. *All teachers should be totally familiar with both the goals and the limitations of the program.* It would be psychologically bad for teachers to expect more from the program than it is designed to

deliver. For instance, remedial instruction outside of the classroom cannot be expected to relieve the regular classroom of pupil variability. Neither should such a program be permitted to become a dumping ground for all reading cases which merit some individual attention.

4. *The remedial instruction must not be an ego threat to the pupil.* It might be construed as a punishment if it is tacked on the end of the school day or if it takes the place of play, recess periods, or any other activity which the child values.

5. *The instruction should have regular curriculum status and should be integrated with all school goals in the teaching of reading.* If the remedial instruction is done outside of the classroom and is not integrated with the regular classroom instruction, the child may possibly be exposed to poor educational practices. In one situation he is expected and encouraged to read materials considerably below his grade level, while in the other situation he may be expected to cope with workbook exercises and textbooks at his grade level even though these materials are too difficult for him. Methods of approaching the same goal, such as phonic analysis or sight word study, may vary considerably or even be contradictory. One reading situation may be permissive, and the other may be rigidly structured.

6. *Releasing a teacher for remedial work at the expense of increasing the class size of other teachers may result in unconscious resentments against the program.* If teachers feel that they are forced to work under more difficult conditions, they may feel justified in attempting to shift any and all problem cases to the remedial reading teacher.

7. *If a special program is inaugurated, it is important to "take parents along."* An interview may help explain what the school is attempting to do — and that it is being done for the child's good.

8. *The basic criterion as to whether there* is *a program is whether the teacher or teachers have time to prepare lessons and materials.* If this important factor is missing, one can conclude that at the most there is only a "paper program."

9. *Where a special program or out-of-class teaching exists, there should be a clearly understood method of referral.* Most schools have a testing program, and test results coupled with teacher judgment are probably the most widely practiced referral procedure. Where reading, intelligence, and academic achievement scores are available, all should be used as criteria for referral.

SPECIAL PROBLEMS

Need for Prevention

In addition to these administrative considerations, there are several special problems which are extremely important and which are both administrative and procedural in nature. The first of these is the recognition and referral of first-stage remedial cases, or emphasis on prevention rather than cure. The longer reading failures go uncorrected, the more complicated and severe they are likely to become. As a rule, reading problems become interwoven with social, emotional, and behavioral problems.

Ordinarily, children are not referred to a reading or child-guidance clinic until some time after the problem has developed. Also, it is undoubtedly true that many schools which attempt to provide some formal program of help for retarded readers fail to get the children and the special help together until poor habits and poor attitudes have had a chance to become solidified. Children who are experiencing difficulty in reading, often develop symptoms which are then advanced as the cause of the reading problem. Dawson (3) expresses the belief that, "many pupils learn to be poor readers, that bad habits and negative attitudes are learned, that many so-called remedial readers could have been effective and confident readers under a program of preventive teaching."

An analogy might be drawn between working with reading problems and the prevention and cure of tuberculosis. If the medical profession and our society had continued to attempt to cope with tuberculosis the way we still try to deal with reading problems, today we would undoubtedly be a nation of consumptives. Fortunately, medical practice and concern shifted from emphasis on "cure" to emphasis on prevention. Slum clearance, diet, sunlight, mobile X-ray units, health education, and stress on early detection — all practices evolving from sound principles — have, to a considerable extent, controlled this malady. Even if American education achieves a mushrooming of good reading sanatoriums aimed only at cure, we will never be able to cope with our reading problems because our educational system is geared to mass production. Unfortunately, it becomes very apparent that remedial reading is not thought of as concerned with prevention of reading problems but rather with their cure.

Perhaps one reason why teachers and schools do not get to reading cases earlier is the belief that these problems will disappear with passing time. Some problems perhaps do solve themselves. Others, when ignored, become stubborn, severe, complicated problems. When children with adequate ability fail to learn to read when exposed to the usual classroom procedures, they need help quickly. The school's failure to put emphasis on early detection and immediate help for children failing in reading is undoubtedly a factor in producing some reading difficulties which, once the process of cure is undertaken, are slow to improve.

Need for a Variety of Materials

Supplying a variety of materials is a second special administrative and instructional problem. According to Whipple, (21) one of the first steps necessary to improve reading instruction in most schools is to secure a wide variety of supplementary reading material. She states, "Teachers have indicated that they need much more reading material in order to satisfy pupils' needs, especially supplementary material and less difficult reading material for retarded pupils." There are some obvious reasons why a great variety of materials are needed when working with seriously impaired readers. Each reading failure case in the elementary grades has failed while using the conventional classroom materials, composed of basal readers, workbook-type materials, and textbooks in the various curricular areas. Thus, in many instances, they develop an aversion for these materials.

Since these children are reading at a level below their grade placement, their experience level is often far in advance of their reading level. The content of basal reader materials which can be read successfully may be quite elementary. Poor readers of average or superior intellect have a special need for materials which are easy to read, from the standpoint of mechanics, and yet have a high interest potential. (17) As a general rule, a seriously impaired reader does not volunteer a multitude of topics that he is interested in exploring through reading. Anyone who has worked at length with such cases will recall those youngsters who maintained that they wanted to read only stories about horses, jets, fairy tales, cowboys, space travel, or some other specific topic. Such an interest is the most important lever available to the teacher, provided that she has accessible materials on the topic at the child's reading level.

The more reading ability the child has, the easier it is to find supplementary material on any given subject. During recent years, more and more supplementary materials at the easier levels have been published. Teachers should be familiar with a number of books and series of books which are available and of particular interest to poor readers. In addition, teachers should be conversant with guides, reviews, and bibliographies which can be used as resources for finding new materials as they are published. A representative list of reading materials and of sources of information about materials is found at the end of this chapter.

Parental Reactions to Reading Problems

Parents' reaction to poor reading is a third special problem. A parent who has worked with a child daily and week-ends, who has drilled him on sight words, such as *them-then; when-where; these-those; but-buy;* etc., only to have the child miss these same words day after day usually displays some hostility, either overt or unconscious, toward the child. Parental reactions can take many forms, but some variation of one of the following is very common. Shifting all blame to the child, the parents come to believe that he is lazy, obstinate, and deliberately trying to exasperate adults, or that he is just dull. Even when parents entertain the latter hypothesis, they usually continue to drill, pressure, or shame the child, evidently supposing that he can somehow be sharpened by this procedure.

Another reaction is to posit that the reading failure stems from some special defect other than lack of intelligence, such as poor vision. This assumption is a form of rationalization; the physical factor in question is not the real cause. The disability hypothesis is not destroyed by hearing or visual examinations which result in negative findings, because it can be reasoned that the diagnosis may be in error.

A third solution is to shift the blame outside the child-home orbit, and then the most obvious recipient is the school. In a case where the reading problem has existed for several years, the present teacher is often excused, but some previous teacher, usually the first, is seen as the source of the trouble. This analysis, of course, can be correct. However, in many cases it is not. Many parents vacillate between the three positions, emphasizing different ones at different times.

Rarely are parents able to see how the home and patterns of overprotection, psychological rejection, excessively high standards, perfectionism, or unfilled psychological needs stemming from the family configuration, are related to reading failures. There is no doubt among clinicians who work with remedial cases that an emotionally unstable home environment is a factor in many such cases. Self-confidence, or the lack of it, is conditioned by home, as well as school, experiences. Initiative, self-direction, and social adequacy are determined by attitudes found in the home. Some parents have little insight into how their own expectations and responses to children's failures are related to reading difficulties.

If the reading problem is to a large degree a symptom of maladjustment in the home, working with reading alone is not going to the root of the problem. In cases where a child is referred to an outside agency, such as a child-guidance clinic or reading laboratory, parents are often counselled and worked with prior to, or concurrently with, reading instruction for the child. This, of course, is one of the most difficult problems facing the schools. At the present time, schools lack the authority and the facilities for dealing with home conditions which are closely related to school learning situations. Thus, the school is often handicapped in that it is forced to deal only with a symptom — poor reading — rather than with the basic cause of the poor reading. Parents are not likely to be aware of the fact that their attitudes and behavior are related to their child's poor reading and attempts on the part of the school to probe this very sensitive area are likely to arouse strong resentment and hostility.

BOOKS OF HIGH INTEREST LEVEL AND EASY OR MODERATE DIFFICULTY LEVEL

Cowboy Sam Series. Eight titles, easy reading primer through primary grade level, illustrations. Subject matter: Indians, rodeos, rustlers, and other cowboy adventures. Benefic Press, Chicago.

The American Adventure Series. More than a dozen books chiefly biography and adventure, dealing with the lives and exploits of such figures as Daniel Boone, John Paul Jones, Kit Carson, Chief Black Hawk, etc. Third grade level and above. Wheeler Publishing Co., Chicago.

Allabout Books. Intermediate grades; weather, whales, chemistry, stars, dinosaurs, volcanoes, etc. Excellent drawings, indexed. Random House, Inc., New York.

Pleasure Reading Series. Eight books. Greek stories, Aesop's stories, Bible stories, Anderson stories, etc. Controlled vocabulary, illustrated. Garrard Publishing Co., Champaign, Illinois.

The Every Reader Library and *Junior Every Readers.* Intermediate grades, simplified classics. *A Tale of Two Cities, Sherlock Holmes, Ivanhoe, The Trojan War,* Greek and Roman myths, etc. Webster Publishing, Manchester, Missouri.

Childhood of Famous Americans Series. Can be handled with third grade reading ability; more than 50 titles. Biographies of American presidents, writers, inventors, scientists, including George Washington Carver, Alexander Bell, Luther Burbank, Jane Addams, Clara Barton, Lou Gehrig, etc., The Bobbs-Merrill Co., Inc., Indianapolis.

Landmark Books. Biography, history, exploration; nearly a hundred titles on a great variety of topics from the voyages of the Vikings to the story of the F.B.I.; upper intermediate grades. Interest level ranges much higher. Random House, Inc., New York.

Real Books. Supplementary reading on a vast variety of topics. Real Books about stars, space travel, baseball, camping, pirates, explorers, inventors, famous Americans, etc. Intermediate grade level, indexed, illustrated. Garden City Books, Garden City, New York.

The Basic Vocabulary Series. Ten titles. Folk stories, animal stories, circus stories, "why" stories, etc. Books composed of basic words, plus 95 of the most common nouns and a controlled vocabulary of not more than one new word per page. Garrard Publishing Co., Champaign, Illinois.

The New Reading Skilltext Series consists of workbooks with difficulty range of kindergarten through grade six, illustrated titles, *Bibs, Nicky, Uncle Funny Bunny, Uncle Ben, Tom Trott, Pat the Pilot.* Charles E. Merrill Books, Inc., Columbus, Ohio.

Easy To Read Series. Trade Books for beginning readers which practice some degree of vocabulary control, minimum number of different words approximately 75; range upwards to 300 different words.

Early I Can Read Books	(Harper and Row, Publishers)
I Can Read Books	(Harper and Row, Publishers)
Beginner Books	(Random House, Inc.)
Beginning to Read Books	(Follett Publishing Company)

Sailor Jack Series; Dan Frontier Series. Hardback books ranging in difficulty level from pre-primer through grade three. Benefic Press, Chicago.

Reader's Digest Reading Skill Builders. Children's magazines, elementary reading level covers first through sixth grade with several books at each grade level, Reader's Digest Association, Pleasantville, New York.

True Books, I Want To Be Books, About Books. Covers wide array of topics, animals, occupations, American Indians, science, exploration. Grade Level 1-5. Childrens Press, Inc., Chicago.

Programmed Reading. Workbook-type materials grade one through three, stresses early writing and letter-sound analysis. Webster Publishing, Manchester, Missouri.

My Weekly Reader. Weekly newspapers with separate editions, grade one through six. Also *Read-Study Practice Books;* and *Phonics and Word Power* consisting of three workbooks at each grade level 1-3. American Education Publications, Inc., Columbus, Ohio.

Gates-Peardon Reading Exercises. Introductory levels A-B, Grades 1-2; Preparatory levels A-B, Grades 2-4.

Little Owl Books. (Reading Time Library) Consists of forty books and accompanying Teacher's Guide. Content includes prose, poetry, fiction, science. Grade level K-2; *Young Owl Books.* Forty books, grade level 2-4; *Wise Owl Books.* Twenty books, grade level 4-6. Holt, Rinehart & Winston, Inc., New York.

Signature Books. Biographies of "names that made history." Dozens of books about American presidents, world-famous authors, inventors, explorers, scientists, etc. Intermediate grade level, interest level of teens and adult. Grosset & Dunlap, Inc., New York.

The Reading Laboratory. Sets of boxed material; short complete stories, ranging in difficulty from primary level through high school. Questions and answer keys provided and teacher's handbook available as well as individual student record books. Science Research Associates, Inc., Chicago.

Building Reading Power, Loretan, Umans, et al. Programmed kit covers context clues, structural analysis, and comprehension skills; booklets, response sheets, masking sheets, and teacher's manual available. For those reading on or about fifth grade level. Charles E. Merrill Books, Inc., Columbus, Ohio.

CONCLUSION

Reading instruction has emerged as the number one problem of American education because seriously impaired readers cannot find a niche in our society. We have developed a highly complex society which, in turn, has created a greater need for communication skills. In recent years, as federal funds became available to local school districts for special projects, the number of proposals for remedial and other reading instructional programs exceeded all other areas of the curriculum combined.

Individuals who have followed a normal pattern in learning to read may find it difficult to accept the fact that large numbers of youth experience difficulty in mastering the reading process. Accepting the facts as they are still leaves the problem of rationalizing *why* this problem persists.

There will probably always be a number of children who fail to learn to read because of physiological and other clinical causes not yet fully understood. On the other hand, there are many children whose failure to learn could have been prevented by practices which are presently within the power of schools to apply and follow. If schools in a given community should embark on programs which aim at preventing failure in reading, there will be less need in those communities for remedial reading programs.

YOUR POINT OF VIEW?

Evaluate the following statements.

1. Due to automation and the knowledge explosion in recent years, reading ability is more important today than it was twenty-five or fifty years ago.
2. Emotional factors are no more important in the learning of reading than in any learning situation.
3. Many students who are academically in the top 15 per cent of their class or age group are reading well below their potential.
4. Inadequate reading ability, or failure to learn to read well enough to meet the demands of the school curriculum, is a factor in producing anti-social behavior and delinquency.
5. Instructional practices associated with remedial reading do not differ markedly from practices which should be found in the regular classroom.
6. In most remedial reading situations methodology is less important in changing reading behavior than is the type of relationship established between teacher and child.

BIBLIOGRAPHY

1. Bardon, Jack I., and Virginia D. C. Bennett, "When Teaching Does Not Take," *Elementary School Journal,* 66 (May 1966), 426-32.
2. Bliesmer, Emery P., "Evaluating Progress in Remedial Reading Programs," *Reading Teacher,* 15 (March 1962), 344-50.
3. Dawson, Mildred A., "Prevention Before Remediation," *Reading and Inquiry*. International Reading Association Proceedings, 10, 171-73.
4. Frostig, Marianne, "Corrective Reading In the Classroom," *Reading Teacher,* 18 (April 1965), 573-80.
5. Googins, Duwane G., "Helping Retarded Readers within a Small School District," *Reading and Inquiry*. International Reading Association Proceedings, 10, 178-79.

6. Jackson, Joseph, "A Reading Center Approach within the Classroom," *Journal of Educational Psychology,* XLVII (1956), 213-22.

7. Johnson, Marjorie Seddon, "Reading Instruction in the Clinic," *Reading Teacher,* 15 (May 1962), 415-20.

8. Kasbohm, Mary Crowley, "Remedial Reading Materials," *Elementary English,* XLIII (March 1966), 209-14.

9. Marksheffel, Ned D., "Therapy: An Interdisciplinary Approach," *Reading and Inquiry.* International Reading Association Proceedings, 10, 1965, 197-200.

10. Money, John (ed.), *Reading Disability Progress and Research Needs In Dyslexia.* Baltimore: The Johns Hopkins Press, 1962.

11. Otto, Wayne, and Richard A. McMenemy, *Corrective and Remedial Teaching.* Boston: Houghton Mifflin Company, 1966.

12. Plessas, Gus P., "Reading Abilities of High and Low Auders," *Elementary School Journal,* 63 (January 1963), 223-26.

13. Pollack, M. F. W., and Josephine A. Piekarz, *Reading Problems and Problem Readers.* New York: David McKay Co., Inc., 1963.

14. Rasmussen, Glen R., and Hope W. Dunne, "A Longitudinal Evaluation of a Junior High School Corrective Reading Program," *Reading Teacher,* 16 (November 1962), 95-101.

15. Reich, Riva R., "More Than Remedial Reading," *Elementary English,* XXXIX (March 1962), 216-19.

16. Sellin, Donald, "Using a Basic Reading Series with Educable Mentally Retarded Children," *Reading Teacher,* 19 (March 1966), 442-45.

17. Sister Mary Julitta, "A List of Books for Retarded Readers," *Elementary English,* XXXVIII (February 1961), 79-87.

18. Sister Mary Xavier, O. S. U., "Fostering Security of Youth through Guidance Programs," *Catholic Educational Review,* LVIII (January 1960), 34-43.

19. Spache, George D., "Clinical Diagnosis in the Classroom," *Reading Teacher,* 14 (September 1960), 14-18.

20. Still, Jane S., "Evaluation of a Community Sponsored Summer Remedial Reading Program," *Elementary English,* XXXVIII (May 1961), 342-43.

21. Whipple, Gertrude, "Desirable Materials, Facilities and Resources for Reading," *Reading In The Elementary School.* Forty-eighth Yearbook, N.S.S.E. Part II, 147-71.

22. Woodruff, Asahel D., *The Psychology of Teaching* (3rd ed.). New York: Longmans, Green and Company, Inc. 1951, 8.

23. Zentgraf, Faith M., "Promoting Independent Reading by Retarded Readers," *Reading Teacher,* 17 (November 1963), 100-101.

24. Zintz, Miles V., *Corrective Reading.* Dubuque, Iowa: William C. Brown Company, 1966.

16 Working with Remedial Readers

When teachers read books, attend workshops, or enroll in courses in order to improve their teaching of reading, they are apt to become impatient with materials on "the theory of reading." They want instead concrete techniques to help Johnny, who is having difficulty in learning to read. Johnny is ten years old, is in the fifth grade, and has adequate intelligence, but he reads at first grade level. Lately he has become a behavior problem. The teacher wants to know: "What can I do with Johnny? I've tried everything. What would you do?" Johnny comes in all sizes, ages, grade levels, and degrees of impairment.

Frequently the college teacher who works with teachers of reading is frustrated with the repetition of "What would you do with Johnny?" If he evades the question, he invites the suspicion of gross ignorance. On the other hand, attempting to give an answer to the question in the context in which it is asked does not come to grips with the real problem of improving the teaching of reading. The instructor in teacher-training courses wants to go back step by step along the trail of reading failure, searching for all clues to the cause of Johnny's present difficulties. The classroom teacher pleads: "What do I do now?"

This difference in approach is the outgrowth of three factors. First, the classroom teacher's role is defined by society and the educational institution in which she functions. Her task is to teach all children assigned to her classroom. If the number of children is large, she has less time to concern herself with institutional practices which produce maladjusted learners. Furthermore, she is likely to regard the analysis of these institutional practices as beyond the scope of her authority. As the number of reading casualties mounts, she often turns to "newer practices" in the vain search for a solution.

Second, the university professor enjoys the luxury of being able to remain aloof from the immediate problems of the individual classroom. Although not unsympathetic with Johnny's problem or the teacher's problem, he knows that the "Johnnies" are legion and their number is growing. Hence he prefers that the teacher phrase her question in such a way as to lead to a long-range solution for the whole problem. As he tries to come to grips with the larger problem, he inevitably deals with theory, or "principles."

Third, most teachers feel that there is a vast body of "newer" practices available on college campuses, in the latest books on reading, or just across the border in the next state. These teachers might be happily surprised to learn that what they have known for years about teaching reading is substantially the same as the practices recommended in the more recent books on techniques of reading. The truth is that improvements in teaching the mechanics of reading evolve slowly. One premise of this book is that reading problems in American schools are due less to the teachers' lack of knowledge than to their disinclination or inability to follow the sound principles of teaching which they already know.

CHARACTERISTICS OF A SOUND REMEDIAL PROGRAM

Previous discussion has suggested that techniques for remedial reading instruction do not differ radically from the instructional practices already found in the regular reading program. However, teaching a severely retarded reader may be complicated by his previous failure experiences and his reactions to them. For this reason the process of learning is more complex for remedial readers than for normal readers.

The following discussion of practices in remedial reading focuses on those problems which it is believed can be handled in the school. The extreme cases of non-reading stem from genetic defect and call for diagnostic techniques and treatment which in most cases lie beyond the competence of the school to provide. In no case is it implied that there is a one best way to deal with slow-learning readers. There are a number of practices, however, which should be common to most programs because they can be accommodated within any framework designed for working with remedial readers. The topics discussed below are important because they relate to the teacher's daily contact with children and influence the degree of success her program will enjoy.

Thorough Diagnosis — the First Step

In diagnosing the reading problems of children in a given class, a teacher must determine each child's full academic potential, as well as his present skills, weaknesses, and habits. (A diagnostic check list dealing only with reading behavior is illustrated in Figure 16, Chapter 6.) When the etiology of a reading failure is not a simple one, a teacher needs a comprehensive set of data in order to work intelligently with the child. The diagnosis should extend not only to the reading but also to the reader, and should be concerned with all educational, emotional, and environmental factors. Knowing her pupils' psychological needs and observing their social behavior can help a teacher detect many signs of maladjustment which are, or may become, related to reading behavior. Figure 39 is a personal inventory containing items which focus the teacher's attention on social-emotional behavior and which may reveal the presence of unresolved problems.

If the school makes psychological assessments of pupils, a teacher should refer problem children as soon as possible after she detects behavior patterns which indicate poor adjustment. Even when there are no clinical facilities available, a teacher aware of the fact that a particular child is under strain and tension may permit her relationships with this child to be more therapeutic than usual. The experienced teacher knows she must discover why non-learning or poor learning takes place. If the answer is simply poor teaching rather than emotional reactions that have become

FIGURE 39

Personal Adjustment Inventory for Retarded Readers

Name: ______________________
Address: ______________________
Age: ______________________
Grade: ______________________
Father: Living ( ) Deceased ( ) Occupation: ______________
Mother: Living ( ) Deceased ( ) Occupation: ______________

	Above Average			Average			Below Average		
Feeling of security	( )	( )	( )	( )	( )	( )	( )	( )	( )
Acceptance by peer group	( )	( )	( )	( )	( )	( )	( )	( )	( )
Attitude toward school	( )	( )	( )	( )	( )	( )	( )	( )	( )
Degree of self-confidence	( )	( )	( )	( )	( )	( )	( )	( )	( )
Reaction to frustration	( )	( )	( )	( )	( )	( )	( )	( )	( )
Language facility	( )	( )	( )	( )	( )	( )	( )	( )	( )
Ability to follow directions	( )	( )	( )	( )	( )	( )	( )	( )	( )
Independent work habits	( )	( )	( )	( )	( )	( )	( )	( )	( )
Concentration span	( )	( )	( )	( )	( )	( )	( )	( )	( )
Background and experiences which relate to reading	( )	( )	( )	( )	( )	( )	( )	( )	( )
Parents' attitude toward child's reading	( )	( )	( )	( )	( )	( )	( )	( )	( )
Parents' acceptance of child	( )	( )	( )	( )	( )	( )	( )	( )	( )
Estimate of home:									
(Socio-economic status)	( )	( )	( )	( )	( )	( )	( )	( )	( )
(Emotional climate)	( )	( )	( )	( )	( )	( )	( )	( )	( )

Observed behavior which is related to judgments on above items:
____
____
____
____

attached to the reading problem, remedial reading instruction is much different and much easier. Therefore, one of the objectives of remedial reading instruction is that the program must take into account both the individual's reading problems and why he has failed in his overall school efforts. In many cases it would be useless, if not unwise, to proceed without concern for the reasons why an individual has developed as he has.

The assessment of reading ability has been discussed in Chapter 6. The discussion of standardized and informal reading tests found there is equally applicable to remedial reading and will not be repeated here; however, one point should be reviewed. Although standardized tests may differ in merit, the best available test is almost useless without a careful evaluation of its conclusions in the light of the testee's individual characteristics. When emphasis is placed more on administering tests than on their instructional implications, it is easy to acquire the feeling that testing is an automatically desirable academic rite.

A group test, which yields a score that in turn is translated into grade-level or age norms, may not tell much about why a child reads poorly. Most standardized tests which are administered individually at the various grade levels are composed of relatively short reading passages. These tests tend to overestimate readers, placing their reading ability level somewhat higher than the level they can actually handle in sustained reading. Reading tests are designed to measure the same skills that a child is using in his daily reading activities. Therefore, it should be kept in mind that teachers have a number of procedures available in the classroom for discovering a child's strengths and needs in reading. These include:

Standardized group and individual tests and informal teacher-made tests.

Basal reader material. Reading orally for a few minutes from any graded basal reader series will disclose whether a child can read successfully the material he is attempting.

Various word lists for sight-recognition tests.

Worktype assignments such as workbook exercises for evaluating particular skills.

Group participation situations in the classroom, which are the culmination of a reading assignment.

Classroom achievements in spelling, writing, and unit work.

Cumulative records which show the child's achievements and how he handled tasks over a period of time. These point up both the progress made and the skills yet to be mastered.

Diagnosis Is Continuous

The alert teacher guards against thinking of a standardized test or any testing situation as if it were terminal. No child reveals all there is to know about his reading in any one given sample of his reading behavior. When diagnosis is continuous, "patterns of errors" become more apparent. An isolated observation may in itself be valid, but it is the sum of many observations and their relationship to each other which gives a total picture of the remedial reader. Something is learned each time a child reads aloud to the teacher, each time he attempts seatwork or exercises. Group discussion may reveal clues like vocabulary weakness or misconceptions about words. Diagnosis must be seen as part of the whole remedial process, not just the prelude to remedial instruction.

Keeping a record of each remedial session is an important and closely related part of continuous diagnosis and the use of varied techniques. A record of what was done and the apparent success or usefulness of each procedure can serve as a guide to future preparations. Out of such a record will emerge a series of immediate goals.

Stress Evidence of Progress

The impaired reader has usually had a long history of failure and frustration associated with reading. These experiences have colored his attitude toward reading and toward himself as a reader. He expects to fail in reading. Since his level of aspiration is low, he needs experiences which will break the "I can try—and you can teach—but I'll fail" syndrome.

A thorough diagnosis will reveal certain mechanics of reading in which the child is weak. Using the results of such a diagnosis, it is a good policy to work on some phase of reading which will yield objective evidence of progress. Lack of confidence and aversion to reading must be overcome, and one of the best ways to do this is to dramatize progress. If the lack of a particular skill is an obstacle to further progress in reading, working on that specific skill is a highly justifiable procedure. A child with an inadequate sight vocabulary is likely to develop a number of other reading weaknesses which are related to this deficiency (see Figure 40). Therefore, an appreciable success in extending a child's stock of sight words may be instrumental in reducing other weaknesses.

One of the major differences between poor and expert readers can be traced to word-recognition abilities. It is often said that a superior reader can omit a number of words and still salvage meaning from what he is reading. To do this, he must omit only those words which are expendable. The following sentence serves as an example:

Many writers have on occasion demonstrated that you can omit or strike out as high as one fifth or one sixth of the running words in a paragraph or on a page and still not distort or destroy the author's intended meaning.

In the following version, 40 per cent of the words are removed without any appreciable distortion of meaning:

________ writers have ________ demonstrated ______ you can omit ________ ________ ________ as high as one fifth or ________ sixth of the ________ words ________ ________ ________ ________ on a page and ______ not distort ________ ________ the ________ intended meaning.

On the other hand, one or two substitutions may completely destroy the intended meaning. Assume the reader substitutes *hit* for *omit* and *runners* for *running* in the illustrative sentence above. We now have:

> Many writers have on occasion demonstrated that you can hit or strike out as high as one fifth or one sixth of the runners . . .

With this much of an erroneous start the reader will probably conclude he is reading about baseball. To salvage the meaning, he must change following words. Eventually he will have to begin again, thus introducing another reading fault—repetition. Moving his eyes

FIGURE 40

(How low sight vocabulary becomes a contributing factor in other poor reading habits or mechanical weaknesses — which in turn are related to comprehension.)

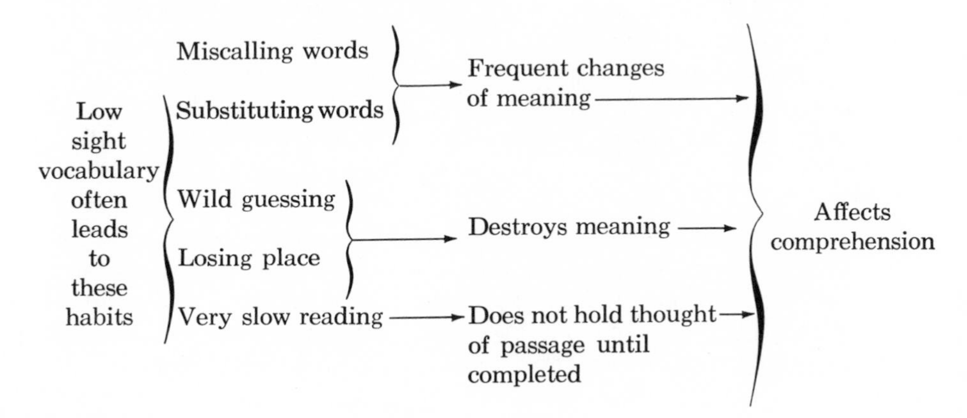

back over words may cause him to make reversals (*was* for *saw; on* for *no; won* for *now; pot* for *top.*) He may change, omit or transpose letters in his search for familiar words, leading to miscalling smaller words such as *sack, lacks; them, then; thin, than.* He may lose his place, skip lines, or reread passages, exhibiting the numerous habitual responses of the slow reader.

This illustration has dealt exclusively with the errors which fall under the general heading, mechanics of reading. It is apparent that all the weaknesses cited can also handicap the reader's comprehension. Figure 40 attempts to show the relationship between inadequate sight vocabulary and other reading defects.

Help Child Gain Insight

The attitudes toward self and reading which a child has formed while failing in reading are often inhibiting factors in remedial situations. Most remedial readers have been conditioned to suspect and dislike reading. If instruction is to be successful, the child must go through another conditioning process in which he finds reading pleasant and rewarding. Since his previous reading situations produced tension and threatened the child, a climate which he can tolerate must be developed.

Establishing rapport is primarily the responsibility of the teacher. In many cases the child conceals his real attitude toward reading, authority, and books. A teacher may think she is working with a docile, co-operative child, but she may be working with one who has learned it is best to conceal resentment and hostility and to feign interest. Such a child is probably burning up energy which might well be channeled into the learning situation. His reading progress depends upon his perceiving and accepting the fact that he actually can succeed at reading, which in turn may depend on his gaining insight into the causes which have contributed to his poor reading. A remedial program should help the child gain such insights. This insight provides him with direction and motivation, and helps him obtain a degree of objectivity about himself and his capabilities.

Once he has gained insight, the child should be helped to set his own goals. Attainment of this objective can be the basis for a healthy teacher-pupil relationship. If the child is resentful of authority, his setting his own goals will have therapeutic value, especially if, with guidance, he can make these goals realistic.

Realistic goal-setting and insight into the causes of his reading problems should help the child overcome whatever poor work habits he may have developed. Many children have experienced difficulty in completing workbook assignments. They have learned to omit questions or problems which they do not understand because their asking for help calls attention to their inadequacy. They may develop the habits of guessing when in doubt, wasting time, or seeking ways of evading tasks which are distasteful. It may be a long road back to good work habits, but traveling this road is an important function of remedial instruction.

BIBLIOTHERAPY

Another type of therapy available to classroom teachers is found in reading materials themselves. Reading provides vicarious experiences, and it is through experience that children work out their problems. Whether these solutions are inadequate, unrealistic, or desirable depends on the experiences and the person's reaction to them. Russell and Shrodes (16) state: "*Bibliotherapy* may be defined as a process of dynamic interaction between the personality of the reader and literature—interaction which may be utilized for personality assessment, adjustment and growth."

In order to see how literature affects individuals, we might start with a discussion of the pre-school child. Children are enthralled by stories read to them. If you are a parent, you probably recall certain favorite stories which never seemed to lose their appeal for your child, regardless of how often the stories were heard. In fact, long after you felt that the child could not possibly be interested in hearing that story again, he would insist on hearing it. Maybe on some occasion you attempted to skip a page or two only to have him stop you and point out the omission. Perhaps you noticed that each time you went through a certain passage the child would ask the same question or make the same statement.

On the other hand, there would be certain stories which, after having heard once, the child never selected again. Some stories you might start only to have him select another one. It is doubtful that you attempted to determine the reasons for these choices. It was common sense to conclude that he liked some stories better than others. Also, at this age you could expect no help if you asked him why he liked this story. It would be hard to deny that something other than the literary tastes of two- or three-year-olds enters into these choices. The following is an excerpt from a case history, which, although a very small sample of behavior, is quite suggestive of a child's needs in relation to literature.

> A boy (age approximately 3 years), both parents living and together, social-economic status high. Child read to quite a good deal, has many children's books. The mother relates the following: "He likes for me to read to him before he goes to bed and I do just about every night. His favorite story just now is the *Three Little Kittens.* He likes that to be the last story, but he will not go to bed until he has been assured several times that 'the naughty kittens are okay now.' "
>
> "Did they find their mittens?" he asks.
>
> "Yes, they found their mittens."
>
> "Kittens okay now?"
>
> "Yes, kittens are all right now."
>
> The mother states that the boy dislikes the poem "Dapple Grey." She thinks it is because the woman in the poem whipped the pony. The child has never been subjected to any corporal punishment with the exception of an occasional light slap on the hand accompanied by "no-no!"
>
> A tenable hypothesis is that the child identified with the three little kittens whose behavior displeased their mother. The kittens were in fact rejected for their behavior, but they were able to reinstate themselves in their mother's affection and they were fed pie, a most demonstrative form of affection and reward. Having identified with the kittens, reassurance that all was well with them was necessary before the child felt entirely secure. Thus, the insistence on the happy ending. Even the wisest parent is sometimes unaware of the innumerable times each day a child of two or three years engages in behavior which results in reproof, scolding, and disapproval. The child, like the kittens, has much to learn about property and propriety, and while he cannot understand the terms which we have used to describe the situation, he does grasp the dynamics of the authority-child, affection-rejection situation.

The aim of the discussion above is to point up the fact that children use stories and literature as a means of finding parallels to their own problems and needs even before they can read themselves. The possibility of using bibliotherapy, of course, increases with age, understanding, and the acquisition of mental age and insight in dealing with concepts.

In an analysis of the bibliotherapeutic value of a series of books by Clara Ingalls Wilder, it is suggested that this author's writings help children with the solution to problems in such areas as gaining maturity, fears and misunderstandings, and physical, intellectual, and moral achievement, as well as dealing with the growing-up process which reflects the child's need for material and emotional security. Wenzel states: "There are many people who know a great deal about books and many others who are thoroughly familiar with children. It is only in the last few years, however, that attempts have been made to bring books and children together."* It is encouraging that an increasing number of teachers are becoming interested in the value of books and literature as a means of helping children help themselves in dealing with their personal problems.

The Use of Bibliotherapy

There are many suggested helps in the literature for teachers desiring to use bibliotherapy in their classroom. Russell discusses procedures appropriate for use in guidance programs and lists books dealing with topics such as adoption and foster homes, belonging to the group, family relations, working with others, and the like.** Shrodes (19) stresses the value of using literature as a means of providing vicarious experiences, stating: "Bibliotherapy is made possible by the shock of recognition the reader experiences when he beholds himself, or those close to him, in a story or some other piece of literature."

Bibliotherapy, while particularly well-suited for children showing symptoms of maladjustment, should also be considered as a method of presenting challenging ideas, promoting growth in concepts, and developing insight into one's own behavior, for all children, whether maladjusted or not. Reading literature or viewing drama provides many psychological outlets. Any adult who can recall his own growing-up process can probably also recall some emotional experiences stemming from reading or seeing plays or movies. Reading lends itself to practically all of the mechanisms of adjustment: compensation for weaknesses and failures; identification with heroes, and, in the same process, the identification of qualities and behaviors which the society respects and rewards; a haven for withdrawal; a substitute for overt aggression.

---

*Evelyn Wenzel, "Little House" and "Books of Laura Ingalls Wilder," *Elementary English,* XXIX (1952), pp. 65-74.

**David H. Russell, "Adventuring in Literature with Children," *Association for Childhood Education,* Washington, D. C., Leaflet No. 5.

One of the virtues of using reading as a form of therapy is that the reader remains in control of the degree to which he becomes involved in identifications. His discoveries of self will usually not be traumatic. He can gain insight into his own problems (and behaviors) at a pace which he can tolerate. Therapeutic values may be inherent in reading materials anywhere on the literary continuum from the *Three Little Kittens* to Dostoevsky's *Notes from the Underground.*

The teacher's task is to perceive the child's needs, bring the child and the right book together, draw out meanings from the book by questioning, and help the child develop confidence and self-assurance as insight permits him to see himself and his problems mirrored in what he reads.

DEVELOPING AND MAINTAINING INTEREST IN READING

Building rapport between teacher and pupil helps the child tolerate the reading situation, but success in reading provides the drive which will keep him at the task. Following a change in attitude toward reading, the next logical step is to help create within the child a desire to want to read. This can best be accomplished if the child's reading materials parallel his interests. Remedial readers, as a rule, do not respond helpfully to questions such as "What are you interested in?" or "What do you want to read today?" The answer is likely to be "nothing," said more or less politely. A number of techniques can be used either to discover or to arouse a remedial reader's interest:

1. Books with colorful jackets, or books opened to interesting pictures, may be left where they will be noticed. The teacher can observe the child's reactions to see which books he rejects and which ones hold his attention. The teacher might discuss or read from one that captured the pupil's attention in order to whet his appetite for reading.
2. Thorough preparation of lesson plans is of great importance; the problems of motivation, interest, attitudes, work habits, and attention span are more acute with a remedial reader. Lesson plans should always include alternate tasks in case a particular task fails to motivate the remedial reader or hold his interest.
3. The child can be asked to participate in a sentence completion task wherein he supplies information:

a. "When I grow up, if I am able to do the type of work I like to do best, I will be a ______."

b. "The person I would like best to meet and talk with is ______."

c. "If I could travel anywhere in the world, the place I would like most to visit is ______."

These and other items can be used to discover areas of the child's interest such as science, exploration, athletics, aviation, or medicine.

4. One teacher used this technique successfully: a child found her reading a book when he arrived for his session of individual instruction. The book was at his reading level, and was one she believed he would enjoy. The boy, noting that it was not an adult book, looked at the picture and read the text beneath it. "I can read that," he said. The teacher replied, "Good, someday you can read this book, but today we are going to review sight words, work on prefixes, read a story . . ." The boy then interrupted with "I'd like to read that story." The fact that the teacher was reading and enjoying the book, plus the fact that the boy had demonstrated to himself he could read it, were factors in producing his reaction. The teacher was wise not to suggest immediately that the boy read the book. His own decision to do so made his reading "ego-involved," and he eventually asked to read other books in the series.

5. Another approach that proved successful in working with a child, who seemingly could not get interested in any reading matter, was leaving a tape recorder and microphone in a conspicuous place. The child walked in and immediately inquired, "What's that?" "Oh, that's a tape recorder—someone else was using it today." "Can I use it—can I record something?" "Sure, you can use it sometime." "How about today?" "Well, I don't know—if you can find something you want to read, I guess we can record it today." The boy went at once to the shelf containing books at his reading level, looked at two books, put them back, and selected a third. It was a book about flying and airplanes which the teacher had unsuccessfully tried to get the child to choose and take home at a previous session. The novelty of recording interfered with reading for a few minutes, but then served as a highly motivational device for many succeeding sessions. Eventually the child was able to listen to the playback, correct his own errors, and point out the types of improvement he should work for.

This suggestion will not prove effective with every child. In one case, that of a boy of ten reading at the first grade level, the recorder was tried unsuccessfully. The slow, halty, error-ridden reading on the playback was too much for him. He volunteered that he did not want to use the recorder any more.

Rapport between pupil and teacher is vital in the remedial program. A proper blend of instruction and activity encourages the pupil to bring reading into the proper focus as he begins to accept himself as a person and as a reader. (Courtesy of Cincinnati Public Schools.)

TYPES OF REMEDIAL READING CASES

It is quite likely that the individual differences among remedial cases being taught at a given level are much greater than those among normal readers who are being taught at that level. The immediate reading problems of remedial readers are often quite varied. Page two of the Durrell Analysis-of-Reading-Difficulty Test* lists ninety-eight different problems the test administrator is alerted to look for in administering this test. These problems fall under fourteen different headings and cover skills in the mechanics of reading and the habits which make for facile or poor reading. Such a check list indicates the tremendous differences among children who are experiencing difficulty in reading. What

*Published by World Book Co. (Tarrytown-on-Hudson, New York: 1955).

it does not show is that equivalent failure, as measured by achievement tests, does not evoke equivalent behavior.

In teaching remedial reading, there is no one procedure which can be recommended as having universal efficacy in dealing with different cases, nor is there one procedure which is necessarily best for eliminating what might appear to be the same problem found in different cases. Because of the vast differences found among remedial readers, it is important for the teacher to look for some means of identifying or classifying these cases. It would be extremely helpful if such a classification could be done on the basis of some specific characteristic or criterion, if that characteristic is of fundamental importance in dealing with the child.

In the discussion which follows, an attempt is made to identify several types of remedial reading cases on the basis of one important criterion which then becomes the key to how the remedial instruction should be approached. More specifically, the classification is for the purpose of suggesting whether a diagnosis indicates that the teacher can hope for success in *working directly with the reading problem;* whether the reading problem is tied to *emotional or other problems* which need to be worked with simultaneously; or whether the solution of the problem *involves more than the usually prescribed educational procedures.* Identifying these types does not imply that all cases which fall under a given type are alike or that specific teaching techniques and methods should be associated with a particular type of case. However, it is undoubtedly true that cases falling generally into one or another of these types are more alike than are cases taken at random from the total population of remedial readers.

First Type

Type I embraces those cases where the reading problem is fairly uncomplicated as far as the pupil-learning situation is concerned. The criterion for placing a case under Type I is that the child has failed to master important steps or skills in the reading process and systematic work on those weaknesses is the most logical approach to the removal of the reading difficulty. The root of the child's problem may have been non-readiness to read, poor educational practices, or absence from school at critical periods. However, antecedent conditions or experiences are not the important factors when dealing with these cases because, by definition of

Type I, these antecedent conditions have little relationship to what we do now.

Don was a second grader of average intelligence, seven years and eight months old. The family lived on a farm; Don attended a rural school and was doing poorly in reading. At a parent-teacher conference his teacher stated that he was not reading up to his ability and that she would not be able to give him the individual help he needed. His mother had neither the training nor the time to help Don, but she did make arrangements to have him receive individual instruction outside the school three evenings a week. Some of the more important conclusions abstracted from the diagnosis were that Don was weak in sight word recognition; often ignored or failed to profit from punctuation; substituted, added, and omitted words; and, as a consequence, read very slowly. His reading level was primer level, although he could slowly work his way through material in a first reader. Don was not defensive about his poor reading. Neither his teacher nor the home had caused him to feel like a failure, and he did not feel that he was letting his parents down. He quite frankly admitted that he needed help in reading and was able to work effectively on reading problems from the very first individual meeting. In a few weeks Don could actually see that he was improving. He kept 48 consecutive appointments over a sixteen-week period. His teacher wisely used a variety of approaches and attacked several different problems in each hour session. Thus, fatigue and loss of interest were avoided. This, coupled with much praise, helped Don to build self-confidence in his ability as a reader.

Second Type

Type II cases are similar to those of Type I in that a straight forward attack on reading is the logical approach; but they differ in that the antecedent conditions or experiences which produced the reading problem should be considered when attempting remedial work. In these cases, to ignore these antecedent conditions in working with the problem may be wasteful or even harmful. The following example does not attempt to answer the question why two boys in the same classroom, diagnosed as having the same problem, learned differently, but rather to point out that two children reading at the same level and having much the same reading weakness may have acquired it under different circumstances; therefore, each one may need different remedial help.

Two fourth-grade boys who had failed to make adequate progress in reading after a relatively successful beginning were diagnosed as being handicapped by very poor phonic analysis skill. Their patterns of reading were very similar. The first boy attempted to sound words as a whole. He would not follow through on a word nor divide unknown words with syllables. When he came to an unknown word, he would size it up as a unit and make a hurried guess. When he guessed wrong, he remained loyal to his response and, if necessary, would change, add, or omit words which followed, in order to salvage meaning from the passage. It was surprising to discover that he could correctly sound syllables if words were divided for him.

In the early stages of reading, he had been put under pressure by his parents not to hesitate or stall in pronouncing words, particularly words he had previously pronounced correctly. As a result, he learned the habit of "saying something" instead of relying on the slower method of analyzing the sound components of the word. Many of his rapid responses were correct and the habit became reinforced. As the material he read became more difficult, his percentage of correct guesses declined, but the habit continued. Other poor reading habits were natural outgrowths of his attempts to *make* meaning from his reading.

The other fourth grader knew a considerable number of sight words, but, in contrast to the first boy, he was completely incapable of sounding syllables or letters in combination, even in words he knew by sight. Also, recognizing meaning did not seem to be an objective of his reading. He also miscalled, substituted, and omitted words, but not in an effort to invent meaning. He did well in spelling on weekly tests, but, a short time after each test, he could not spell a fourth of the words he had previously spelled correctly. Spelling was a rote memory process.

The first boy overcame his word-attack problem in approximately twelve hourly sessions of instruction, much of it on syllabication. The second boy required a number of months to help him overcome his difficulty. He needed hours of drill on distinguishing speech sounds in words, including extensive work on such elementary phonic skills as initial consonants and consonant blends. Progress in mastering vowel sounds was slow, and it was necessary to give him constant praise for even the smallest accomplishments. At the time of diagnosis, both boys showed much the same reading behavior, with a crucial weakness in phonic analysis. However, the way in which each boy's problem had developed called for different approaches or solutions.

Third Type

Type III includes those reading cases where the child's reaction to his failure in reading is a significant factor. It would be quite helpful if most reading cases in our schools fell under Type I, but we would be ignoring a great deal of research data and going contrary to the experience of most elementary teachers if we believed this to be the case. Under Type III we are assuming that no matter how obvious the reading problem may be, it is difficult to come directly to grips with it through instructional techniques alone. We must deal with the child's reaction or attitude toward himself and toward reading. In other words, he is not emotionally ready to face the reality of his reading problem. As a rule, a program of therapy must be inaugurated in conjunction with any work on reading.

The objective is to produce a reading situation which is uncomplicated and which will lend itself to a successful attack on the reading problem. In short, cases which fall in Type III must have tensions reduced and attitudes changed in such a manner and to such an extent that the case logically becomes ready for inclusion in Type I. All pressure, judgments, and threats of failure or inadequacy must be removed before the child can make progress in reading. The real difference between Type I and Type III cases is that in the former we can safely work on the reading problem, but in Type III this may be useless or harmful until the intermediate step, reducing tension and changing attitudes, has taken place.

An illustrative case of Type III is that of Robert, a third-grade child of above-average intelligence who had difficulty reading at primer level. At home, he had been drilled on reading by both parents, neither of whom had the patience that was needed to help Robert overcome his difficulty. His self-confidence had been destroyed and, as pressure in the reading situation mounted, his effectiveness as a reader decreased. He was an extremely frustrated child and was showing definite signs of withdrawal in the reading situation. His teacher was annoyed at some of the odd mistakes he made when reading or attempting to work independently in a workbook. The first step in helping Robert deal with his problem was a series of conferences with his parents. It was agreed that they would give up all their efforts to teach him reading themselves. This was not an easy decision for the parents to make since they naturally did not see the relationship between their behavior and his reading problem. The next few months Robert showed very little measurable growth in reading ability. However, in this situation, Robert was accepted by his teacher in spite of his reading failure. As the pressures at home diminished, he was gradually able to concentrate his energy on the reading task, and he did begin to learn.

Emotional problems which were not originally related to reading can become contributing factors in severe disability cases. Here, the unresolved emotional problems are such strong barriers to learning that the child is at the moment uneducable (as far as learning to read is concerned). And yet, the lack of reading ability is only a symptom of some larger problem. Results cannot be expected from working with the symptoms alone. In most instances of this nature, it is necessary to inaugurate a program of therapy prior to attempting to work directly with the reading problem. A brief description of such a case follows:

Edward was a second-grader, seven and one-half years old, whose father was successful in business; both parents were well-educated. He had a younger sister four and a half years old. Even though Edward was beginning the second grade, he was virtually a non-reader. His mother was quite concerned about his lack of academic success. Diagnosis showed that Edward was a very bright boy (a Stanford-Binet I.Q. of 140) but on a reading test he knew practically no words. The examiner reported that he was very polite and co-operative and did everything that he was requested to do.

Edward's apparent willingness to work held out high hopes that through individual help he would learn to read. Here are brief descriptive passages abstracted from his tutor's daily reports (emphasis has been added):

> *Second meeting:* Edward stares hard at the words for a long time and *gives the appearance* of trying very hard.
> *Third meeting:* We took a trip to the museum and Edward dictated a story about what he saw and did. He enjoyed the trip very much. *He seemed panicky when I suggested he read our story about the trip.*
> *Fourth meeting:* An unsuccessful attempt was made to teach Edward words by the kinesthetic method. He writes the words mechanically and does not *remember* the pronunciation *immediately* after he has finished tracing a word.
> *Fifth meeting:* Edward appears to be testing the limits. Sometimes he is co-operative and appears to be trying his best; at

> others he appears to be trying to see what the tutor's reaction will be to things he says and does *which he probably considers bad and unacceptable*
> *Seventh meeting:* I definitely have the feeling that Edward is *trying not to learn to read* and at the same time leaves the impression that he is trying very hard.

At this point it became obvious that continued work on reading alone would not be advisable or profitable. This conclusion should have been arrived at sooner; however, too much emphasis was attached to high intelligence and seeming willingness to work cooperatively. From this time on, as each session was devoted more to therapy than to instruction, these facts emerged. Edward had strong feelings of hostility toward his younger sister and also toward his mother. He felt his sister was favored in the home, "[he] was punished more," "she could get by with more," "[he] was picked on," all symptoms of a feeling on his part of psychological rejection at home.

It was hypothesized that Edward was using non-reading as a means of getting revenge on his mother. He was asked who would be made most happy if he became a good reader. Without hesitation he replied, "My mother." Edward and the teacher discussed why a baby sister "could get by with more" than an older brother, how people sometimes got mad at their parents even though they loved them, and how almost everyone tried to "get even." Finally the teacher said to Edward, "I know you can learn to read whenever you want to, but you don't have to learn to read here if you don't want to; however, we would be happy if you did decide to learn to read." Edward could accept this because he had developed guilt feelings, but he had not been able, by himself, to find a way out. Being told "you will learn to read when you want to" and not being judged for his behavior gave him a chance to work out a solution. He seemed to make very little progress in reading in the tutoring sessions, but at school his behavior changed quite radically. He ceased being passive and retiring in the group, and his reading improved greatly. His need for non-reading was disappearing.

Fourth Type

The most severe cases of impaired reading and non-reading are classified as Type IV. While there is general agreement as to the nature of the identifying symptoms found in these cases, the terminology used in discussing these severe reading problems is most confusing. There are more or less fixed meanings for the terms *alexia,* a cerebral disorder which leads to the loss of ability to read; and *dyslexia,* a genetic defect that interferes with learning the reading process.

Branching out from these, we find *strephosymbolia* (meaning "mixed symbols" (14)), congenital word blindness, neurological dysfunctioning, specific reading disability, symbolic confusion, brain damage, specific language disability, genetic defect, minimal brain damage, unilateral cerebral dominance. All refer to extreme cases of non-learning-to-read in spite of formal instruction and exposure to the usual classroom procedures.

The lack of definitive terms and variations in diagnostic approaches makes it difficult to estimate what per cent of reading problems belong in Type IV. Shedd (18) asserts that "approximately half of all those with reading difficulties suffer from a disorder with a specific symptom syndrome." This disorder he calls *symbolic confusion,* pointing out that other writers have used the term *specific language disability*. The symptoms listed are:

1. Confusion in right-left discrimination accompanied by each of right-left dominance
2. Problems in discriminating details (field-background)
3. Impaired rhythmic speech patterns
4. General awkwardness
5. Poor writing and spelling

Bryant (3-4-5) and Stuart (22) posit much the same pattern of symptoms among severe reading cases in which the problem stems from neurological dysfunction. Additional symptoms frequently cited include poor visual perception in general; impaired memory of words; and inconsistency, i.e., recognizing a word in one sentence but not in the following one.

Senz, (17) noting the renewed interest in the role of neurological dysfunction, states "our measurements of brain function are crude and open to more than one interpretation." Further, since there are a large number of children who do not learn to read as a result of their school experiences, it is becoming increasingly popular to diagnose such children as being brain injured or neurologically handicapped. Senz concludes "that the diagnosis of 'minimal brain damage' is more often an act of faith than an act of reason."

We have not made appreciable progress during the past few decades in a number of crucial areas such as: (1) evolving reliable diagnostic techniques which establish neurological dysfunction as a concrete clinical entity, (2) determining the approximate number of pupils affected by specific language disorders, (3) discovering the relative effectiveness of various treatments, and (4) expanding our knowledge as to the interaction of genetic and other factors in these severe cases of impaired learning.

The varied terminology which has been developed has resulted in little significant progress since the early twenties when "congenital word blindness" was the blanket diagnosis used to cover the more stubborn cases of reading difficulty.

Another important issue upon which there seems to be general agreement, but no unanimity, is the role of the school in dealing with these severe reading problems. It seems safe to say that the majority of investigators conclude that teaching these children to read is a most difficult and time-consuming task. Silver and Hagin (20) see working with perceptual-motor problems as calling for a long-range, well-planned program. "Planning based upon careful diagnostic formulations utilizing the skills of psychiatry, neurology, education and psychology is needed so that appropriate training experiences are offered when the child can best assimilate them."

Bryant (3-4-5) holds that the reading specialist (a somewhat vague term) can work with the problem cases under discussion. However, he points out that many reading specialists are "inclined to consider a case diagnosed as neurological dysfunctioning as beyond their help—and probably hopeless. This is not the case." He further suggests that the usual classroom instructional techniques will likely not prove effective. Although the remainder of this chapter deals with instructional techniques, the outlining of a remedial program applicable to Type IV cases is beyond the scope of this discussion.

Limitation in Classifying Remedial Cases

In this attempt to identify types of remedial cases, the aim has been to provide a framework for leading teachers to a better understanding of reading problem cases. The aim has also been to suggest that different approaches are indicated in attempting to deal successfully with different types of readers, even though their reading problems may appear on the surface to be very similar. Teachers should guard against the several pitfalls in this process of classifying.

1. The boundaries between types should not be considered as rigid.

2. The correct diagnosis of a child as one problem type or another is not a permanent classification analogous to blood-type or fingerprints. As children have new experiences, their needs, attitude toward self, others, and learning will change.

3. A teacher working with children may develop an unconscious bias which supports one particular hypothesis. This will, of course, interfere with accurate diagnosis, and an accurate diagnosis is the basis for all good remedial instruction.

TECHNIQUES AND PROCEDURES

Several children who had been referred to a reading laboratory for diagnosis and remedial instruction are discussed here. The objctive is to illustrate both the different problems and the teaching procedures used in an attempt to alleviate these problems. The diagnosis of the first case is discussed in detail and several lesson plans are presented. The other cases are treated in less detail.

Study 1: William

William was a nine-year-old boy with above average intelligence who had been referred because of very poor reading ability. For some time he had made no noticeable progress in reading and had been held in the third grade for a second year. The initial testing in reading included a standardized reading test, a recognition test of sight words in isolation, and an informal reading test using materials from basic readers. On the standardized test he failed the second grade level (a passage of fifty-one running words) because he was unable to recognize the words *began, rain, wanted,* and *know,* miscalled the words *by, little, took,* and *take,* added the word *it,* and omitted one word. The major weaknesses revealed by the diagnosis included:

1. Very slow and labored reading — many hesitations
2. Words omitted
3. Miscalling of many easy words, with occasional self-correction
4. Lip movements in silent reading
5. Poor or inadequate phrasing

TABLE 5

DIAGNOSIS OF READING PROBLEM CASE SHOWING TESTS USED AND TYPES OF ERRORS FOUND
(BOY, AGE 9: I.Q. 110; THIRD GRADE; READING LEVEL 1^1-1^2)

Test Used	Grade Level	Errors and Weaknesses Noted: Sight Words Not Known	Words Miscalled	Repetitions	Words Omitted or Added	Rate
Durrell Analysis of Reading Difficulty	1st	Could not pronounce: *drink* (21 running words in passage)	*chair* → *couch*	2 repetitions in 21 running words	*is* (omitted)	21 running words 32 secs.
	2nd	Could not pronounce: *began, rain, wanted, know* (51 running words)	*big* → *little* *took* → *take*	3 repetitions	*it* — added; *away* — omitted	51 running words 80 secs. (scored middle first grade on rate)
Informal Reading Test	First Grade Reader	missed 6 words in 103 running words: *once, only, they, under, could*	*must* → *much* *cross* → *across* *then* → *when* *raised* → *rushed* *think* → *like* *point* → *plant*	5 repetitions	omitted: *far, any, my*	Very slow
Dolch Basic Sight Word Test	1st to 3rd	missed 1 out of 4 words — miscalled and then corrected a number of words	examples of words missed: *by, drink, any, kind, just, both, found, grow, first, away, cold, best, light, gave, hurt, red, try, only, there, woman, chose*			Very slow

6. Missing one fourth of the 220 words on the Dolch Sight-Word Test*
7. Repetitions
8. Poor posture — pointing at words

Table 5 summarizes the child's reading behavior and illustrates a one-page form which might be utilized to record the results of diagnostic testing.

Results of any diagnosis, shown in a concrete manner, would alert a teacher to specific problems which need attention. Poor habits and the absence of needed skills become more obvious when precise errors are noted. As one studies this table, he sees that a small stock of sight words and lack of ability to sound words are major obstacles to reading progress. However, there is evidence that the boy did pay attention to initial consonants, but did not "follow through" the entire word. For example, he called chair *c*ouch; took, *ta*ke; raised, *ru*shed; must, *mu*ch. He also appeared to have considerable trouble with the initial blends *th*, *wh*, *ch*, and others. His very slow rate suggested that he may not have developed instantaneous recognition of small service words, although, after study, he may have named them correctly.

The Remedial Program for William. One of the first entries made by the tutor included the following:

William's interest span is quite short, and motivating him for an hour is a problem. However, he is not a behavior problem and is very cooperative. He likes to talk and does talk quite fluently. His comprehension of what he reads is extremely good. This is surprising in view of his many poor reading habits and very slow reading. In addition to working on sight words and word analysis, the boy's attitude toward reading must be changed. Work on these objectives can go on simultaneously.

Illustrative Lessons Used with William. A few sample lessons taken from the tutor's files are cited along with illustrations of actual materials used.

(Lesson 3)

We talked for a few minutes about things Bill has been doing at school. I told him he has an interesting way of expressing himself — I think he would have enjoyed talking

*Edward W. Dolch, *The Basic Sight Word Test* (Champaign, Ill.: Garrard Publishing Company, 1942).

for the full hour, but when I suggested we go to work he was quite co-operative and worked very well this period.

1. We worked with a film strip, *Vowel Sounds Help You** (10 minutes).

2. [We] worked on "hearing vowel sounds." I would drop the initial consonant from three-letter words and sound the remaining two letters. Bill was to:

a. tell which vowel was sounded.

b. say the letters which made the sound heard (i.e., um, et, at, im, en, un, ug, ap, ip, etc.)

c. give a word which used this sound (i.e., hum, met, hat, him, pen, sun, rug, cap, sip, etc.) (5 minutes).

3. We read from *Young Reader's Animal Stories* (12 minutes).

a. [We had] blackboard work on the words Bill missed during his reading (3-4 minutes).

During the reading I praised Bill for things he did well and tried to point out concretely how he was making progress in his reading. [I] also pointed out things we had to work on. He could supply some of these goals himself, which indicates he is gaining insight into reading problems.

4. [We] worked on syllabication (5 minutes). Stimulus words were presented in one column and the words were to be broken into syllables in an adjoining column (see Figure 41).

FIGURE 41

Divide each word into syllables. See sample on first line.

locomotive	lo-co-mo-tive	vacation	va-ca-tion
window		together	
yesterday		picture	
afternoon		valentine	
nothing		tomorrow	
pencil		halloween	
children		hundred	
another		grandmother	
stockings		arithmetic	

*"Vowel Sounds Help You," "Your Eyes and Ears Are Good Helpers," "Test Yourself on Sounds," "The Vowel," "Backbone of a Syllable," are some filmstrips on phonics available from The Society for Visual Education, Inc., Chicago, Illinois.

"Hearing Sounds in Words," "Letters Which Work Together," "Long Vowel Sounds," and others are available from Popular Science Publishing Co., Audio Visual Division, New York.

5. Billy read silently to get the answers to five questions given him prior to the reading. ([We] finished out the hour with discussion.)

(Lesson 5)

1. [We] worked (5 minutes) on attacking longer words — names of famous people, cities, states, and compound words (Figure 42).

FIGURE 42

Fold the paper on the dotted line. Pronounce the words in Column A. If you need help, see Column B where words are broken into syllables.

COLUMN A	COLUMN B
Steinmetz	Stein metz
blacksmith	black smith
George Washington	George Wash ing ton
Andrew Jackson	An drew Jack son
themselves	them selves
fisherman	fish er man
wonderful	won der ful
Benjamin Franklin	Ben ja min Frank lin
Canada	Can a da
President Cleveland	Pres i dent Cleve land
holiday	hol i day
fireplace	fire place
fairyland	fair y land

2. [We] used the tape recorder as Bill read from the book *Let's Look Around.* When we played the story back I noticed that Bill could fill in the words quite easily where he paused or was helped during the recording (20 minutes).

3. I read to Bill in the area of science. Afterward I asked him several questions over the material and he demonstrated good comprehension (10 minutes).

4. [We] worked on initial blends *br, fl, pl, tr, dr,* [and] used [a] separate card for each blend. [We] used cards containing easier words utilizing each initial blend (8 minutes) (see Figure 43).

FIGURE 43

Illustration of Cards Prepared to Facilitate Drill on Initial Consonant Blends

Card 1	Card 4	Card 8	Card 10	Card 3
brag	flag	plan	trip	drop
braid	flood	play	track	drink
brick	fled	plain	trap	dress
broke	flat	plant	train	drug
broom	flock	plug	tree	dream
bread	flash	plenty	trim	drive
brave	flame	plot	trust	draw
brain	flee	plum	tribe	drank
break	fleet	planned	trade	dry

5. Bill finished out the hour reading silently from *Let's Look Around.*

(Lesson 8)

1. [We] played "word-war" [with] 50 cards.*
2. Bill related a story which I took down verbatum.
3. Bill read silently from *Cowboy Sam and the Fair.*

While Bill read, I typed the story he had just dictated.

4. [We had a] brief discussion of material read silently.
5. [We] worked on a special "sounding page," whose aim is to help Bill "go on through a word" when he is attempting to sound words. Longer phonetic words are in a column on the left. To the right are the same words with one syllable added on each new line. The column on the right is covered with a card until a word on the left is missed, then the pupil looks at the word in its syllabic units. Of all the techniques for teaching sounding, this was the most successful with Bill (see Figure 44).

---

*A competitive game which permits drill on sight words. This game calls for two players, teacher and child, and an even number of cards. On one side each card bears a word which the child is in the process of learning. The back of the cards are blank. Cards are shuffled like dominoes in the middle of the table and each player draws 10 cards at a time. Players alternate in "leading" a card, which is then played on by opponent. However, the pupil *always* attempts to call or name both cards. If successful, he takes both cards for his "army stack." If he fails on either, both cards go to opponent's army. The largest army at the end of the game wins. This game is extremely successful since the tutor can control the game by the way he plays his "difficult" and "easy" cards, and also by the words he includes in the game.

FIGURE 44

Pronounce the words in Column A. When you meet a word you cannot pronounce, go to Column B for help.

A	B	A	B
November	No Novem November	Washington	Wash Washing Washington
inventor	in inven inventor	senator	sen sena senator
elephant	el ele elephant	holiday	hol holi holiday
locomotive	lo loco locomo locomotive	Wisconsin	Wis Wiscon Wisconsin
remember	re remem remember	important	im import important
		continent	con contin continent

6. Bill read [the] typed story he had dictated earlier. We then worked on the words he missed.
7. Bill selected the book *Riding the Pony Express* to take home.

From the sample lessons cited, note that a good balance was maintained between sustained reading and drill on mechanics. The reading program was designed to include a variety of interesting activities. ("William's interest span is quite short and motivating him for an hour is a problem.")

Study 2: Martha

Martha was a ten-year-old girl in the fifth grade. She was a good student, had never repeated a grade, and was very personable and apparently well-liked by other children. She volunteered that she liked the subjects health, spelling, physical education, and music. She disliked science, reading, and social studies. Martha had developed a few bad reading habits which prevented her reading from being pleasurable. She had been referred to the reading laboratory, at least in part, because she did not like to read and, as a result, read very little. Without going into detail, the relevant findings disclosed by the diagnosis could be summarized as follows:

1. Martha ignored or failed to profit from punctuation.
2. She miscalled many words which she actually *could* get correctly.
3. She was not concerned by the fact that her frequent substitutions of words and ignoring of punctuation destroyed meaning.

In one brief reading session Martha made the following errors and did not correct any of them on her own initiative.

leading	(called)	leaning	lessons	(called)	classes
pleasant	"	present	grin	"	gleam
searching	"	seeking	quickly	"	quietly
long	"	large	echoed	"	shouted
called	"	said	beamed	"	because
problem	"	program	admiringly	"	approval
shaping	"	shaking	Hale	(proper name)	Hall

A majority of the errors indicate no effort at maintaining the sense of the passage. Context was simply ignored. Following the reading, Martha was asked to identify the words she missed, and she was able to do so in 80 per cent of the cases.

Martha did admit to being interested in fairy tales and myths. Fortunately this was an area in which material at a reading level which held her interest was plentiful. It was pointed out from the very beginning that a change in two or three reading habits would make a noticeable improvement in her reading ("use punctuation"; "do not guess at or substitute words"; "be sure what you read makes sense").

Following are some of the procedures used in working with Martha.

1. If she ignored or missed punctuation, her teacher would read the same paragraph, asking Martha to listen. This served as a good model which Martha could hear as she followed the passage with her eyes.
2. A tape recorder was used for a few minutes each session. Martha was asked to criticize her own reading as she

listened to the playback. She was able to point out errors, thus demonstrating that she understood the problem and that she was capable of a better performance.

3. It was agreed that when Martha miscalled a word and went on, her attention was to be called to the error. This emphasized reading for meaning, and gradually Martha was able to catch some of her errors without being prompted.
4. A limited amount of drill was provided each day on words that look alike, start alike, or sound alike. Martha was to pronounce each word, and, when asked, use it in a sentence. This type of drill emphasized that minute differences in words must be noticed, and that paying heed to the initial letter or blend is not enough to assure reading accuracy if the reader guesses from that point on (see Figure 45).
5. As Martha paid more attention to the total word and made fewer errors and substitutions, her reading became more "meaning-centered." Reading became more interesting and challenging, and she was gradually guided into reading materials other than fairy tales and fables.

FIGURE 45

Below are columns of three words which look alike or sound alike. Pronounce each word carefully.

tired	tried	trial	farther	father	further
cease	crease	crash	crayon	canyon	canteen
mouth	month	moth	quiet	quite	guilt
flash	flush	flesh	with	which	width
board	broad	broth	except	accept	expect
adopt	adapt	adept	reflect	respect	relate
dairy	diary	daily	whether	weather	whither
seize	seige	size	thing	think	thank
desert	disturb	dessert	vary	very	every
easiest	earliest	earnest	advice	advise	adverse
brother	broth	bother	crash	cash	clash

6. Thought questions were prepared on sustained reading materials, and these questions were given to Martha prior to having her read the passage.
7. Two-part plays and poems were occasionally used, the teacher reading one part, Martha the other. This type of

exercise helped stress accurate reading, attention to punctuation, and reading for meaning.

Martha may have had more reading ability than many remedial cases in that she knew many sight words and could sound out words. Nevertheless, she had reached the stage where she apparently could not resolve her reading problem by herself. In reality she had quite a serious reading problem, since her attitude toward reading made it a distasteful chore and a meaningless ritual. Fortunately, with guidance and individual help, she was able to overcome her poor reading habits. When her reading became meaningful, it also became pleasant and rewarding.

Study 3: Jerry

Jerry was a nine-year-old fourth-grader and an only child. His father was successful in business and his mother was active in community and social affairs, but not to the point of neglecting her role as a homemaker. Following an interview with Jerry's mother, an experienced clinician characterized her as "not being rejecting, but somewhat cold and reserved." The mother made the following comments about Jerry's reading: "Jerry is concerned with his reading ability; in fact, he has been, even from the first grade. He seems nervous when he reads and he doesn't like to try reading situations. He lacks confidence and will not attack new words or words he doesn't know. He is very poor in spelling, too."

The examiner made the following comments about Jerry: "Jerry is a very bright boy; he loves to talk, and he has had many experiences about which he talks quite intelligently. However, he talks most about his father, whom he reveres. In his reading Jerry shows signs of insecurity, reading with more volume than necessary, seems to go to pieces when attempting to read material that is difficult for him — will bite his nails during such a reading session."

Jerry's behavior in reading is summarized in the following findings from the diagnostic tests:

1. Moves lips excessively in silent reading.
2. Reads slowly and seems threatened by this habit — tries to speed up and then miscalls words he knows; then he reads very choppy, missing punctuation, losing place, says "just a minute" — rereads, etc.
3. Missed only 14 of 220 words on Dolch Sight Word Test and corrected all but four of these errors on second trial. Yet,

in sustained reading situations, Jerry miscalls a number of these same words.
4. Repeats words and groups of words even when he knows all the words involved. This was a habit Jerry developed as a means of giving himself time to probe ahead into the remainder of the sentence; also this sometimes occurred when he was deliberately attempting to speed up his reading.
5. Phrasing is inadequate.
6. Occasionally ignores punctuation.
7. Not consistent in word attack or sounding.

Following are some conclusions which grew out of the testing and interview with the mother.

1. The parents had high aspirations for Jerry.
2. Jerry was very much aware that his father was successful, and he seemed to be attempting to measure up to his father.
3. Father and son got along fine, but the father apparently did not have enough time to spend with Jerry — at least not enough to meet Jerry's needs at the moment.
4. Jerry needed a tremendous amount of reassurance because he sensed he was not measuring up to his parent's academic standards and expectations.
5. Unconsciously, his parents had, and were, putting pressure on him to improve in his reading. Feeling that his relationship with his parents (love, respect, affection) was dependent on his performance in reading, he put pressure on himself to succeed.

Many of the procedures mentioned previously were used with Jerry. No opportunity was missed by the teacher to praise Jerry for his improvement in reading and his excellent attitude in the reading situation. His reading problems were played down. Speed of reading, which seemed to be very important to Jerry, was ignored during sustained reading. Eventually he stopped pushing for speed, and his mechanical errors declined in frequency. Speed was touched on indirectly in an exercise designed to help Jerry read in phrases or thought units. Jerry would read a series of phrases and the teacher would record the time and the number of errors. Then, later in the hour or at the next session, Jerry would attempt to improve his scores. Before long he wanted to manipulate the stop watch himself, mostly to prove beyond doubt that his improved scores were on the level. Columns of phrases are illustrated in Figure 46.

Jerry enjoyed role-playing. He pretended that he was a radio announcer when using the tape recorder. He became very ego-involved in this procedure, and the purely mechanical defects of his reading (repetitions, substituting smaller words, phrasing, and ignoring punctuation) were often present to a smaller degree than at other times. Since he played back these recorded sessions, it was easy to demonstrate improvement in his reading. He enjoyed working with jigsaw maps of the United States and of countries making up other continents. He would sound out the name of the state or

FIGURE 46

near an old well	would swing very high
still on the ground	liked to count
mud on the fence	caught in the act
forgot to get up	then and there
saw the other neighbors	right in the middle
by the side	beat the drum
winked his eye	wanting to fly
gave him some	into the garden
plenty of cakes	funny little man
under the tree	book on the table
see the surprise	left them behind
when he looked	came over the hill
just what is	was very fine
eggs for breakfast	light as a feather
fishing near by	how much money
waved from the door	bother the robber
where the corn grew	a ride in the forest
must be something	tied in a knot

country as he placed it and, when asked, would attempt to spell the names by syllables. Occasionally the teacher would print a state name on paper or the blackboard, and they would sound it together.

CONCLUSION

Earlier chapters have emphasized the importance of a good start in reading while at the same time stressing that reading is a developmental process. Since reading is a developmental process, it is inevitable that barriers to successful reading will be found at all levels of instruction. This problem is accentuated by the fact that our schools operate on a grade level structure which permits pupils to move upward through the grades without having mastered the skills which are prerequisite for dealing with the planned curriculum. As a result, the reading abilities of some pupils and the curricular aims and the materials used to achieve them are not always synchronized.

There are an unlimited number of factors which can contribute to poor reading. Rarely, however, does one factor stand alone as the sole cause. The interaction of various factors makes it difficult to accurately evaluate causation of impairment in reading ability. This, in turn, makes it imperative that all available data be used in discovering causes, as well as any tentative prognosis as to what programs will lead to cure. Thorough and continuing diagnosis is essential in working with seriously impaired readers. The experience of failure in reading produces a complex teaching-learning situation. The longer the process of failure has operated, the more complex the problem is likely to be.

There is no dichotomy between remedial and regular classroom teaching, at least as far as principles and instructional practices are concerned. The most perceptible difference is that remedial programs are more likely to permit teachers to follow sound principles of teaching. Remedial reading has not been treated as a separate type of instruction, since it is believed that most regular classroom teachers will also be called upon to function as remedial teachers. This is true because they will most certainly have remedial readers in their classes. No particular administrative pattern for remedial programs has been singled out as superior. Factors in the local school system undoubtedly determine which of several approaches would be most productive. The mechanical details of operation are not the essence of a program; what each individual child does *is* the program.

Motivating the reader is the key to the success of any remedial program. After years of instruction, failure and drill, impaired readers are likely to resist all reading situations. It would be difficult to list all the factors which might conceivably be useful in motivating poor readers. Those factors, which have been discussed in some detail, include the necessity of having a variety of reading materials at the difficulty level the reader can handle; working on factors which will make the most difference in the child's reading, and which help to emphasize progress; helping the child to develop insight into his reading and allied problems; seeing that reading is always purposeful; helping the child regain self-confidence and accept the fact that he can learn to read. All of these are instrumental in reducing tension in the reading situation.

A good remedial program must consist of the proper blend of instruction and a degree of rapport between teacher and child which can lead to the child's acceptance of himself as a person and as a reader. If this is interpreted as therapy, then good teachers are therapists. Reading is a major part of an individual's total educational development.

YOUR POINT OF VIEW?

Defend or attack the following statements.

1. When a school system makes provisions for remedial reading instruction, it is likely that this instruction will follow sounder principles of teaching than does the regular instructional program.
2. Because of the nature of the teaching tasks in all elementary grades, teachers are inevitably remedial reading teachers if they teach all children in their respective classrooms.
3. The effectiveness of remedial instruction in reading is largely determined by the degree to which it meets the child's psychological needs.
4. Assume that you are assigned the task of materially reducing the number of remedial readers normally found in a given school system. Would your recommendations deal primarily with teaching methods, school practices other than methodology, or both? Would you also have to deal with parents' attitudes?
5. Points *A* and *B* are advanced as facts. If the reader accepts them as facts, the problem is to deal with the premise which follows.

   A. Classroom data indicates beyond doubt that individual differences of considerable magnitude in reading ability will occur among children of comparable capacity or ability.

   B. Equal amounts of expert instruction given to all of these children will actually result in extending the range of differences in reading ability.

   Premise: "The degree of emphasis placed on remedial reading in the past fifteen years indicates a lack of willingness to accept the premise of individual differences in learning to read and applies special instruction where it will have the least impact on achievement."

BIBLIOGRAPHY

1. Balow, Bruce, "The Long-Term Effect of Remedial Reading Instruction," *Reading Teacher,* 18 (April 1965), 581-86.
2. Bliesmer, Emery P., "A Comparison of Results of Various Capacity Tests Used with Retarded Readers," *Elementary School Journal,* LVI (May 1956), 400-402.

3. Bryant, N. Dale, "Reading Disability: Part of a Syndrome of Neurological Dysfunctioning," *Challenge and Experiment In Reading*. International Reading Association Proceedings, 7, 1962, 139-43.

4. ______, "Learning Disabilities in Reading," *Reading as an Intellectual Activity*. International Reading Association Proceedings, 8, 1963, 142-46.

5. ______, "Some Principles of Remedial Instruction for Dyslexia," *Reading Teacher,* 18 (April 1965), 567-72.

6. Durr, William K., and Robert R. Schmatz, "Personality Differences Between High-Achieving and Low-Achieving Gifted Children," *Reading Teacher,* 17 (January 1964), 251-54.

7. Ginolt, Haim G., *Group Psychotherapy with Children.* New York: McGraw-Hill Book Company, 1961.

8. Graff, Virginia A., "Testing and Reporting Procedures for an Intensive Tutoring Program," *Reading Teacher,* 19 (January 1966), 288-91.

9. Henderson, Edmund H., et al., "Self-Social Constructs of Achieving and Nonachieving Readers," *Reading Teacher,* 19 (November 1965), 114-18.

10. Kephart, Newell C., *The Slow Learner In The Classroom.* Columbus, Ohio: Charles E. Merrill Books, Inc., 1960.

11. Krich, Percy, "A Newspaper for Remedial Reading," *Education,* 84 (March 1964), 418-21.

12. Martin, John, "Reading Attitudes — Whose Headache?" *Elementary School Journal,* LIX (April 1959), 386-87.

13. Mingoia, Edwin M., "A Program for Immature Readers," *Elementary English,* XXXXI (October 1964), 616-21.

14. Orton, Samuel T., *Reading, Writing and Speech Problems In Children.* New York: W. W. Norton & Company, Inc., 1937.

15. Robinson, Helen M. (ed.), *Corrective Reading in Classroom and Clinic.* Supplementary Educational Monographs, No. 79. Chicago: University of Chicago Press, 1953.

16. Russell, D. H., and C. Shrodes, "Contributions of Research In Bibliotherapy To the Language Arts Program," *School Review,* LVIII (1950), 335-42.

17. Senz, Edward H., "Neurologic Correlates In The Reading Progress," *Challenge and Experiment in Reading.* International Reading Association Proceedings, 7, 1962, 217-18.

18. Shedd, Charles L., "The Diagnosis and Treatment of Symbolic Confusion," *Changing Concepts of Reading Instruction.* International Reading Association Proceedings, 6, 1961, 97-102.

19. Shrodes, Caroline, "Bibliotherapy," *Reading Teacher,* IX (1955), 24-29.

20. Silver, Archie A., and Rosa A. Hagin, "Maturation of Perceptual Functions in Children with Specific Reading Disability," *Reading Teacher,* 19 (January 1966), 253-59.

21. Strom, Robert D., *Teaching in the Slum School.* Columbus, Ohio: Charles E. Merrill Books, Inc., 1965.

22. Stuart, Marion Fenwick, *Neurophysiological Insights Into Teaching.* Palo Alto, Calif.: Pacific Books, 1963.

23. Zintz, Miles V., *Corrective Reading.* Dubuque, Iowa: William C. Brown Company, 1966.

man is blue
man is red.
T O
Write these names correct
1 miss lowden
2 mr emens
4 miss turner
6 puff

17 Improving Teaching

One of the virtues of American education is that its practitioners have never been entirely satisfied with their practices or the result of their efforts. Educators have realized that if education is to fulfill the role assigned to it, teachers can never feel that they have reached the point where their professional growth is adequate for the task. The concept and practice of in-service education is not new but grew out of obvious necessity during the last half of the nineteenth century. It is a matter of fact that during those years teachers were not well-prepared. There were almost no standards for teachers or for teacher preparation and little professional incentive to create standards. The first decade of the twentieth century had ended before a single state required a high school education as a requirement for teaching.

In years past the administrative officers of a school system had the responsibility of personally helping teachers who needed guidance in teaching techniques and procedures. Eventually the positions of superintendent and principal became more administrative and less involved with teaching practice and classroom activities per se. The concept of the supervisory teacher evolved. This person, by training and experience, qualified as an expert in methods and materials. The improvements which came about in a school system depended on the special abilities and knowledge of the supervisor and the degree to which teachers perceived this person as a potential help. Today, most progressive administrators attempt to organize the total school program so that teachers have the freedom and the facilities to participate in any program which they might plan co-operatively.

As the quality of the formal training of teachers improved, the complexity of problems faced by teachers and the amount of data on methods and materials also expanded rapidly. Although the reasons are different from those of a half century ago, the need for in-service education is undoubtedly as great today as ever before. This is due, at least in part, to the following factors:

1. In recent years more teachers have been needed than there are qualified applicants. Therefore, special dispensations in the form of temporary certificates were granted to persons with less training than the legal minimum. Many of these individuals stay in teaching and work toward meeting state certification requirements. In-service training for this group can be of considerable help in solving particular instructional problems.

2. The recent past has been a period of high mobility among teachers. In a given one- or two-year period as many as a third of a teaching staff of some schools may be new teachers, either beginning teachers or new to that particular school.

3. American schools have accepted more responsibilities while at the same time accepting working conditions which make it tremendously difficult for these responsibilities to be successfully met. Co-operative planning of all school personnel is required to keep schools as effective as they were yesterday because the energies of teachers are dissipated in non-teaching activities.*

4. Cultural, social, and technological changes of a magnitude never experienced in any previous decade have caused demands for radical curriculum and methodological changes in American schools. There is always a degree of inertia in education, as well as

---

*Some schools have alleviated this problem to some degree through the use of Teacher Aids supported both by local funds and NDEA Title I and Title II Projects.

other institutions, which can be overcome only by providing teachers with new tools and concepts for dealing with more complex problems. It is becoming obvious that a qualified teacher may remain qualified only in the legal sense of that term unless she continues to grow professionally while on the job.

PROFESSIONAL COMPETENCE — THROUGH IN-SERVICE PROGRAMS

One of the most thorough discussions of the concept of in-service preparation of teachers is in the 57th Yearbook of the National Society for the Study of Education. (32) Portions of this book are theoretical and attempt to chart courses of action based on research in the social sciences. These sections deal with motivation, social change, and perceived roles of individuals in any co-operative endeavor leading to change. The role and function of the teacher, the supervisor, and the administrator is explored at length as is the role of the teacher-training institution.

The changes taking place in society and the problems facing schools made it mandatory that in-service programs meet today's needs. The old practice of dealing with just the basic minimum competencies needed in teaching is no longer identified with in-service programs. The later practice of equating in-service with acquiring college credits, although still strong, is being questioned today. The following discussion outlines the major types of programs and cites a few illustrations which have proven successful. In-service programs for improving reading might be classified under the following headings:

1. Consultant — group participation
2. Local group participation
3. Special training for instructional personnel*

While a great number of different approaches would fit under the headings listed above, there would also be programs which would logically cut across more than one of the classifications.

*Marvin L. Berge, Harris E. Russell, and Charles B. Walden, "In-Service Education Programs of Local School Systems," *N.S.S.E. Yearbook*, LVII, Part I, Chap. ix. These authors suggest a different type of classification in which they describe three *patterns* of in-service education: centralized, decentralized, and centrally co-ordinated approaches. The criterion for these designations is who, or what segment of the school, assumes the chief responsibility for inaugurating the in-service program.

Consultant — Group Participation

The essence of this approach is that an educational unit such as elementary teachers, secondary teachers, or a total school faculty, arranges to meet with some individual from outside the group either to isolate problems or to work toward solutions of problems already identified. The consultant is usually thought of as a resource person and is chosen on the basis of having skills, competencies, and knowledge which will be useful to the group. The consultant-group relationship can function under a great variety of plans and can cover time intervals ranging from a one-day workshop to a series of planned meetings which cover a span of a semester or a year. A number of approaches under the consultant-group category are listed below, followed in some cases by a brief discussion of an illustrative example.

Workshops. There are several types of workshops which can result from the co-operation of a group and a consultant. These programs for improving the teaching of reading can be held on a college campus or in any community which arranges to have a consultant meet with the school personnel. An in-service workshop which varied somewhat from the more common practices is described here. This was a community-supported effort to improve instruction, for the school board offered to underwrite the expense of any in-service program in which the teachers elected to participate. After discussing the instructional needs of the system, the teachers chose a program aimed at improving reading instruction. A consultant was selected, and after preliminary planning between the teachers, the administration, and the consultant, a program of six half-day meetings spaced throughout the fall semester was agreed upon. From noon until three in the afternoon, the consultant visited various classrooms and talked briefly with teachers about facets of reading instruction. Late afternoon and evening sessions, which included teachers, administrators, and the consultant, were held on each of the six days. At the close of each meeting, topics for the next session were selected. Children from the school were used in demonstrating various facets of informal diagnosis. Remedial procedures were explained and demonstrated. Teachers then used these practices, when appropriate, in their own classrooms. Many teachers modified the procedures or used them as a basis for the preparation of other teacher-made materials.

Certain school practices including grading, reporting of grades, promotion, heterogeneous grouping, and the library period were discussed, and group recommendations resulted. Since the administration and teachers worked their way through these problems jointly, the possibility for change was extremely good.

Pre-School Orientation Conferences. Workshops devoted to reading and curriculum improvement are popular in-service practices today. An example of such a workshop which proved very successful occurred in a school system which had become concerned with its pupil-promotion policies and problems. The decision was made to shift from the conventional grade-level primary to a modified ungraded primary system. It was envisioned that a series of levels-of-competency would replace the rigid grades-one-two-three framework and that a number of levels would be defined for each year of instruction. Since the new procedures would be quite a departure from current practices, it was agreed that teachers would return one week early to attend and participate in a full week's workshop-conference on the new program. This was done on a contractual basis, the teachers being paid for the week at the same rate as their regular salary.

A consultant from a large city school system which had established this type of program several years earlier was secured as a resource person for the week's conference. He was to work with the teachers and administrators to explain the criteria for the various levels of competency and answer questions about the plan. An evaluation of this in-service technique revealed very positive reactions on the part of teachers. They particularly appreciated the fact that the conference permitted them to become familiar with the basic principles of the new program before they attempted to make it work in the classroom. They did not feel imposed upon by the school system since the training program was not assigned as an extra duty but was a separate contractual agreement. Teachers felt secure in that they were alerted to the type of questions parents were likely to ask as the school moved into the program.

Post-School Programs. Post-school workshops in reading improvement are frequently offered as part of a summer school program on a college campus or as a project of some local school district. When such a workshop is held in the community, it must be desired by the teachers participating in it. There are several potential threats to the success of such a program, the chief of which is that teachers have just finished a school year and are likely to be in a physical and psychological slump. This can also be true if they attend summer school or a workshop on campus, but sometimes the change has a salutary effect. Some systems require that teachers take a prescribed number of professional courses or credits in a given time period and the post-school workshop is a method of fulfilling such a requirement.

An experience shared by the writer in a post-term in-service program is described here because it appeared to be successful and because it illustrates an attempt to strike a proper balance between lecture-discussion, growth through the study of literature on teaching reading, and actual laboratory experience.

Twenty-three elementary teachers in one city system enrolled for college credit in a two-week reading improvement workshop. All sessions were held in a large elementary school building in their community during the first two weeks of June.

The extension division of the university which offered the workshop loaned approximately ninety volumes of texts and references on reading which included over forty different titles. More than a hundred issues of professional journals were provided including *Elementary English, The Reading Teacher, Childhood Education,* special issues of *Education* devoted entirely to reading, and selected issues of *The Elementary School Journal.* Teachers brought their professional books and journals which dealt with any phase of reading. Films, filmstrips, and sources of supplementary reading materials were available for use during the entire workshop. Tutoring materials were made available by the school. These included basal reader series, workbooks, subject area texts and supplementary reading materials at all grade levels.

Lecture-discussion-demonstration sessions were scheduled each morning and from one to two in the afternoon. These group meetings were held throughout the entire two-week period. The room used was furnished with a portable blackboard, screen, projector, and film strip projector. Tutoring sessions, as noted below, were held in individual classrooms, one teacher and child per room. Topics dealt with in the lecture-discussion periods covered a wide range and included the following:

1. Informal diagnosis of reading problems — including demonstrations
2. Methods of helping children master sight words
3. Procedures for helping pupils extend meanings and concepts
4. Choral reading (participation)
5. Demonstrations of materials, including motivators such as games, exercises, and other teacher-made materials

6. Brief progress reports on selected cases being tutored
7. Word analysis with emphasis on phonic analysis
8. The relationship between emotional problems and reading problems
9. Teacher demonstration of remedial techniques
10. Factors related to critical reading

Laboratory experiences were an integral part of the workshop as each teacher worked one hour each day with a child from the local school who was experiencing difficulty in reading. These children were volunteers and were tutored on a non-fee basis. The twenty-three teachers were divided into two groups for the tutoring experience. From two to three in the afternoon the twelve teachers in group I worked on library assignment (using materials described above) and on preparation of materials and lesson plans for the next tutoring session. Group II spent this hour in tutoring a child. From three to four in the afternoon, the two groups reversed activities and group I now tutored readers. This arrangement permitted each tutor and reading case to have exclusive use of a classroom during the teaching hour and made a more than adequate supply of reading material available for the library groups.

Local Group Participation

All of the previous procedures involved local group participation but much of the responsibility for the program was centered in the consultant. The concept advanced here is that the local school personnel provide the initiative for identifying areas in which change is needed and for designing and carrying through the projects which will achieve desired changes. This emphasis on local group participation does not imply that the group may not at some time seek the advice of a consultant. The point is that there is a great wealth of potential for change and improvement residing in the personnel of most school systems. A second point is that this resource is often neglected. Teachers may come to feel that they have little to offer their colleagues in the art of teaching. But unless there are no individual differences among teachers in skill, knowledge, and technique, it is obvious that in any school system teachers can profit from sharing and co-operative endeavors. Teachers are not likely to suggest they have something to offer fellow teachers because this could be interpreted as immodest or egocentric behavior.

The initiative should be taken by the administration to structure a program in which teachers come to rely on local action for improvement. Many schools which hold regular teacher meetings have let these meetings deteriorate into announcement-making, minute-approving, policy-stating, rule-explaining sessions which leave little place for actual study of instructional problems such as improving the school's reading program.

Two examples of schools which evolved solutions to reading problems through the co-operative effort of their own staffs and resources are briefly discussed here. The first deals with a problem that is often felt, rarely expressed, and even more rarely dealt with in a concrete and constructive manner; namely, the fact that some upper intermediate and many junior high and high school teachers are not well-versed in what has gone on before in teaching reading. That is, there are many teachers at these levels who have not taught at the various lower levels and who are not conversant with the goals, objectives, and techniques which are characteristic of grades other than those they teach. This handicaps teachers in attempting to help those students who did not master certain skills of reading.

The teachers in one school, who had adopted a one-year school-wide program of improving reading instruction, decided upon the plan of having a teacher from each grade level discuss and demonstrate what she did in teaching phonic analysis. The rationale for the procedures used was given, followed by the steps taught at each grade level. Since this was done grade by grade, all teachers received a more unified picture of the total developmental process, as well as specific techniques which they could use with pupils who had failed to master certain needed skills. This technique proved so helpful that it was decided to use the same procedure with other reading problems such as teaching of word analysis, emphasis on developing meaning, teaching study skills, and developing vocabulary and concepts.

Several intermediate-level teachers in a small school system were frustrated in their attempts to find reading materials for the slow or impaired readers in their grades. When this situation was discussed by the teachers, it became apparent that the problem was equally acute in all grades. A co-operative study was planned by the teachers and administration which confirmed the suspicion that their school had a totally inadequate supply of supplementary reading material not only for slow readers but for facile readers also. Committees were formed and teachers visited other schools to secure comparative data. A list of publishers of children's books was compiled and a number were requested to send brochures. The administration subscribed to three professional journals which carried reviews of current books for children. The P. T. A. voted a sum of money for books, and the teachers were requested to select the titles. The school board voted a small fixed sum for each classroom which could be spent for this purpose. While these accomplishments may appear to be a rather minor breakthrough on the educational front, it was a most noteworthy achievement from the standpoint of the teachers involved.

Special Training Provided by the School System

There are many instances of a school system underwriting some special training for teachers with the goal in mind that the competencies acquired in this practice will result in improvement in the school program. Those individuals receiving the training can use it in their classroom and can also act as a leavening agent for the entire school. An excellent example of clinical training provided teachers in a large school system is found in Jackson's (24) account of the Dearborn Public School Reading Center which handles severely impaired reading classes in that community. The purpose of the training "is to provide a remedial internship for teachers on the assumption that this practice will spread the techniques of teaching reading throughout the system and will materially reduce the number of reading problems within the classroom." A number of teachers from the elementary schools are assigned to the reading center for a period of several weeks, during which time their regular classes are handled by full-time teachers who rotate from school to school, thus permitting many teachers to have the clinical experience. At the reading center, the teachers tutor children who have been referred to the center, build materials which they can use both at the center and in their regular classroom, and learn diagnostic techniques and teaching procedures practiced at the center.

Any of the in-service practices described above can be successful when certain conditions are met. The psychological climate of the school must be conducive to experimentation and change. Human motivation and behavior suggests that any in-service program which results in change will have to be a program that deals with matters which the participating teachers perceive as problems. In other words, a program which results in improvement must evolve out of a shared conviction on the part of the local teachers that problems exist and that something can be done to alleviate them.

Because of the authority structure of the schools, another condition essential for change is that the teachers and the administration work co-operatively on any in-service improvement project. Proposals which evolve out of an in-service program and are handed to an administrator who is not aware of the step-by-step analysis of the problem and the proposed solution are likely to be laid aside. This outcome is frustrating to the teachers and is wasteful of time and energy. Proposals growing out of group study should have excellent prospects of being carried out or there is little justification for the expenditure of effort which produced them. This emphasis on the interdependence of teachers and administration in bringing about desirable change leads us to the next point which merits attention in any effort to improve the teaching of reading.

Good learning environments don't just happen! The hours spent behind the scenes are critical — outstanding instructional programs are built on the right combination of creative teaching coupled with appropriate materials and methodology. (Courtesy Columbus, Ohio, Board of Education.)

CREATIVE USE OF RESOURCES

Educators are quite disdainful of an educational practice of a few decades ago known as the reading circle or round-robin reading. Pupils sat in a half circle as poor readers, good readers, and non-readers, each attempting to read a paragraph while the rest of the group practiced "following the place" and, in some cases, listening. There were so many weaknesses in such an approach that today it is difficult to believe that this practice was so prevalent such a short time ago. It is even more difficult to understand it still being used today. Undoubtedly in another decade some of the widely used current practices will seem equally difficult to justify. This is already true if we evaluate some of the present practices (or omissions) in the light of the best practices and facilities and resources available. In essence, we have not come too far from the reading circle.

Creative Teaching is Not Dominated by Materials

Creative teaching is not likely to emerge as a result of placing undue faith in new instructional materials or "newer approaches" to reading. Recent reading instruction has been characterized by a rather naive hope that our problem might be solved by reliance on innovations such as modified alphabets, non-graded schools functioning within a grade-level framework, talking typewriters, literature in boxes, programmed workbooks, projecting materials on screens, over-emphasis on phonics, taking pictures out of basal readers (while giving awards for excellence of pictures in trade books), restricting beginning reading vocabularies to regular spellings (the *at cat fat rat* syndrome). As a result, much of our energy has been dissipated either in jumping on bandwagons or abandoning sinking ships whose cargoes are yesterday's hoped for "breakthroughs." These are examples of educational rituals which have little impact on achieving sound programs in reading.

No materials, whether they be basals, text books, packaged programs, or subject area textbooks, can in themselves assure against stereotyped, unimaginative use. Good instruction is not achieved simply because a certain set of materials is adopted. In fact the same materials will be found in both good and poor programs. In many of the latter cases it will be found that teachers tend to be dominated by materials or methodological loyalties.

Outstanding instructional programs are built on the right combination of creative teaching coupled with appropriate materials and methodology. Each of these factors has considerable influence on achieving a proper climate for learning. Superior teachers will probably not see themselves as partisans of one methodological approach to the total exclusion of others. They will not debate the superiority of language experience, basal, individualized or programmed reading but will use concepts, procedures, and materials from these and other instructional approaches. They know that *teaching* is the most highly weighted of all of the factors involved in creative instruction.

Supplementary Materials Important. On the other hand, materials play an important role in effective teaching. The past few years has witnessed a tremendous increase in reading materials dealing with a vast array of topics and available at all reading levels. In addition there has been a proliferation of basal materials which now provide schools with a variety of approaches to reading instruction. Becoming conversant with all of these materials is in itself a challenge, but more important to instructional programs is the creative and intelligent use of those materials which happen to be in use in a particular school or classroom.

Supplementary reading materials and their importance in improving reading instruction have been discussed in earlier chapters. Some teachers, when books have not been readily available in the school, have used ingenuity in securing them from city, state, or mobile libraries. Materials can be used to stock interest corners for various subject areas such as science or social studies, or for particular units such as the "March of Medicine" or "Man In Space." Books, pamphlets, film strips, pictures, and magazine articles can be gathered which relate to a specific topic. These interest corners can be changed as often as desired or when units are completed. Teachers will find that they do not need to be personally responsible for gathering all this data if they do assume responsibility for arousing students' interest in specific topics.

The Teacher as a Resource. Every teacher is an educational resource in the community in which she serves. But teaching constitutes a resource which has been neglected by teacher-training institutions, local communities, and by teachers themselves. The fact that the professional training of elementary teachers is grossly inadequate in the teaching of reading was documented in the recent Harvard-Carnegie Study by Austin, et al. (2) Data indicated that the professional training of some teachers did not include a single course in the teaching of reading; many other training programs included a limited amount of reading methodology as a part of other methods courses; and that reading instruction in the intermediate grades received little attention in training programs which included reading methodology.

While shocking, this data should not have come as a surprise to teacher-training institutions. Practices related to the training of teachers of reading at each teacher-training institution were well-known to that institution's staff. With few exceptions, the course of study and related experiences found in various training programs were remarkably similar. Unfortunately, few programs have been materially strengthened since the publication of this study.

The need for knowledge in one's field is not questioned in other areas of teaching such as history, mathematics, literature, or science. However, providing the training which would result in extensive knowledge of the reading process seems to have been waived both in pre-teaching training and in in-service programs. No one would argue for a moment that training institutions or local school systems *want* inadequately trained teachers of reading. But both apparently would accept this outcome rather than radically change the *status quo* in training programs.

The Teacher as Reader. The resource value of reading teachers is enhanced as they become avid readers. Too few teachers distinguish themselves as "readers" of research reports and professional materials related to reading instruction. It is no exaggeration to state that a large per cent of elementary teachers are unfamiliar with much of the pertinent research in reading. Their training did not equip them to interpret research or transfer research findings into classroom practice. Until this deficit in training and its concomitant depressant effect on professional growth is remedied, outstanding instructional programs will continue to be limited in number.

Growth through individual study is differentiated here from more structured activities such as in-service programs and enrollment in college courses. Every teacher of reading should keep informed of the research developments and other writing in this area. To be so informed is a prerequisite of professional competency. No teacher can read all of the research and related writing since there is more available each year on reading than on any other educational topic. However, if teaching as a profession were judged by this one criterion — amount of professional reading teachers do in their field — it is probable that teachers as a group would not distinguish themselves in comparison with other professional groups.

Both the amount of reading done and the amount of professional materials available will vary greatly among individual teachers and school staffs. To illustrate, extremes encountered during the operation of in-service programs in two communities might be cited. In one community more than twenty elementary teachers enrolled in a reading improvement workshop agreed to pool all of their professional books, journals, pamphlets, articles, and materials which dealt with any facet of reading. Subsequently it was found that not one teacher owned a single professional book or subscribed to a journal other than the magazine issued by their State Educational Association. By the time of the second meeting one professional book had been borrowed from a teacher not in the group.

At the other extreme a similar workshop in another community was scheduled by the administration in that school system's curriculum center. Here, available to all teachers in the community were copies of practically every professional book on reading, all basal reader series, and a number of professional journals which together would contain at least 80 per cent of all research done in reading. The teachers in this group owned and subscribed to a creditable amount of professional material. There were quite noticeable differences between the two groups of teachers as to knowledge about teaching reading, attitudes toward reading, and flexibility of method in teaching.

Most teachers do not have access to professional libraries such as those found in colleges and universities, and there are limits on the number of books and materials each teacher can acquire personally. There are methods by which teachers and schools can work cooperatively in solving such problems.

1. Teachers in a given school can work out a plan whereby each interested teacher subscribes to a different journal (*Elementary English, Reading Teacher, Childhood Education, Elementary School Journal*, etc.). These materials are then made available to each teacher.

2. The school administration may subscribe to several professional journals and purchase a number of professional books, indexes, and reference materials for use by all teachers. These can be placed in the library or in a central location in the building.

3. Books, pamphlets, films, and other materials may be secured on a loan basis from the State Office of Public Education or from an extension division of a university.

Reading To Pupils. The second facet of the reading teacher as reader relates to reading to students. It is important that pupils see and understand that their reading teacher is an avid reader. Not only does she love to read, but she wishes to share reading experiences with them.

Obviously, when a teacher reads to students, she will make sure that she provides them with a good model of oral reading. As she reads with expression and feeling, pupils will learn much about how to interpret poetry and good literature. As the teacher reads, she is teaching appreciation and providing motivation for students to extend their own reading horizons.

Teachers have a tremendous influence on children's reading. Studies indicate that pupils show a preference for materials which teachers praise or recommend. Thus, an important criterion for judging the school's reading program is the classroom behavior of teachers. Those who love to read will want to share with students those stories and literary passages which they love. Teaching reading without a feeling for, and appreciation of, good literature reduces reading instruction to an educational ritual for both teacher and pupil.

Developing Creativity Among Pupils. Closely related to the creative use of materials is developing creativity among pupils. (42) A teacher may fulfill her contractual obligation if she "teaches children to read," but she is not going too far if she inculcates them with the idea that all reading should be purposeful. Children must read for something — pleasure, specific information, personal growth, understanding their world, problem-solving, or recreation. Perhaps teaching for these outcomes has always been the mark of good teaching, but unfortunately it has not been the identifying feature of most teaching. It is possible for a student to finish his formal education (at any level) without ever having thoroughly learned this lesson. Perhaps this is the key to the studies which report that formal education does not permanently affect the amount of reading or reading tastes of individuals after they have concluded their formal schooling.

Using reading ability for creative activity does not automatically follow the mastery of basic skills although these skills are a prerequisite, nor in the final analysis is creative teaching exclusively what the teacher does. The measure of creative teaching is what the pupils *experience.* Both materials and the way they are used can inhibit or enhance the possibility of creative experience. There is always the danger that formal instruction, which is essential, may become too formalistic. Creativity is an *emergent* quality. It is not taught. The conditions under which it will emerge or develop must exist or be provided. Achieving this condition is creative teaching.

Teacher-Sharing — A Creative Use of Resources

Good educational practice should provide for teachers to continue their professional growth in ways that will result in increased teacher effectiveness. Once the newness of beginning teaching has worn off, the mere experience of teaching per se appears to have no salutary effect on teaching effectiveness. Fattu (14) states, "It appears that a teacher's rated effectiveness at first increases rather rapidly with experience and then levels off—the teacher may show little change in rated performance for the next 20 to 30 years."

The totally inadequate preparation of teachers for the difficult task of teaching reading would seem to make it mandatory that highly effective in-service training programs would be developed to fill this need. However, the common format of in-service training has proven to be totally inadequate to meet the need of teachers and school systems. Short-term reading conferences and highly standardized "field courses in reading" have had little impact on the serious problem of reading instruction in American schools.

The lack of concern for teacher training and professional growth through local school in-service activities has been accompanied by a heavy emphasis on research which compares various methods and different "instructional materials." The thousands of studies which compare methods-materials have not resulted in any clear instructional mandate. Perhaps the inconclusive research findings resulted from the fact that *what* the teacher does in the classroom has more impact on pupil growth in reading than the instructional materials she uses.

Today, as in the past, elementary teachers have tended to be professional isolates, each an island unto herself. As a result, teaching tends to become stagnated and uncreative with teachers repeating the same approaches year after year. Despite the grossly inadequate in-service training of teachers, few communities have worked out meaningful in-service programs in which teachers meet together as professionals to share ideas and teaching techniques or discuss research and professional materials.

The inability or disinclination to establish such an in-service format and climate for growth is the cause of great waste in

American education. It is a truism that significant differences exist among teachers, and it would be illogical to assume that teachers cannot learn from each other. Many teachers are not aware of effective techniques used by other colleagues in the same school system. This is true because there is little professional communication between teachers.

While it is possible that individual teachers might evolve methods of sharing, comparing, and growing, this is not likely to occur on any large scale. Professional isolation has become a deeply ingrained characteristic of elementary teaching. There is little likelihood that teachers operating "on their own" can significantly reduce the waste of resources in their community. What is needed is a plan worked out co-operatively by teachers and the administration. Participating teachers should be volunteers rather than prisoners of an edict. A few teachers who care about professional growth constitute a much more powerful leavening agent than does an assembly of 100 per cent of the teachers, some of whom fear change to such a degree that they will consciously or unconsciously scuttle any attempt at growth through sharing. Until something is done on this front, we will not move fast enough toward better instructional programs.

An example of a year-long in-service program (a co-operative Research Project sponsored by USDE) was conducted (1964-1965) in the Williamsport, Pennsylvania schools. (23) The goals of the project were: (1) to help first-grade teachers become conversant with research and other professional materials related to beginning reading instruction; and (2) to provide a climate in which teachers could work co-operatively in sharing ideas, teaching techniques, and instructional materials.

Teachers participated in a two-week pre-school seminar and in 25 two-hour seminar sessions held during the first thirty weeks of the school year. The content of the two-week seminar focused on discussion of research relating to reading readiness; children's knowledge of letter names and success in first-grade reading; sex differences in beginning reading; new approaches in reading instruction; and the importance of on-going diagnosis.

In the twenty-five two-hour meetings held throughout the school year, teachers discussed common classroom problems, demonstrated successful teaching techniques, and reported on professional materials read. Each week throughout the course of the project, teachers handed in an evaluation form on which they responded to the following items:

1. List any modifications of teaching procedures, new techniques used, or change of emphasis in instruction.
2. List any concepts or beliefs about the teaching of reading which you have developed, modified, or extended.
3. Professional materials read during the past week.
4. Evaluation of teaching the past week (note any strong points, weaknesses, omissions, insights, etc.).

In response to the above items the 14 teachers listed 86 changes in teaching procedures, 97 modifications of concepts relating to reading instruction, and the reading of 271 professional books and journal articles. The changes most frequently cited by teachers were:

1. Teacher awareness of sex differences in learning to read and teacher efforts to devise motivating experiences for boys.
2. Incorporating children's creative writing with reading instruction.
3. More teacher emphasis on on-going diagnosis.
4. Increased emphasis on pupil-reading of trade books in addition to basal materials.
5. Teacher writing of experience stories for individual pupils.
6. Recognition by teachers of the need for wide reading of professional literature related to reading instruction.

During the course of the in-service project each teacher: (1) observed three half days in the classrooms of three other teachers; (2) served as hostess in her own classroom to the entire group for one or more of the two-hour evening sessions. Rotating the meeting place provided each teacher with an opportunity to point out and discuss bulletin-board displays, children's art work, special interest corners, group and individual projects completed and underway, experience stories written for (and by) individual pupils and other teaching techniques of interest to the group.

GROWTH THROUGH CLASSROOM EXPERIMENTATION

One often hears the statement that we have more research data in education than we use. This is undoubtedly true and applies to fields other than education, such as medicine, community planning, use of natural resources, and sanitary engineering. There is always a lag between discovery and maximum application of knowledge. Nevertheless, educational research is absolutely essential for the improvement of education. The nature of the reading process and the numerous ways in which instruction interacts with the learner make continuous research in reading mandatory.

The classroom is the logical arena in which to test the efficiency of teaching techniques and procedures. Teachers should be doing and reporting more research and trying new approaches. It is not being advocated that teachers take on another chore in *addition to* teaching, but rather that teaching can be structured so that it is essentially research. We should be wary of slogans such as "all reading teachers are researchers." This is not true and will never be true. But many effective teachers could improve their teaching and at the same time make a contribution to methodology if they would organize their instruction and carefully check results over an extended period of time.

Much of the literature on reading which purports to be research fails to be of maximum usefulness to others because of weaknesses in the design of the study or because of the manner in which the data are reported. Some of these weaknesses are listed here.

1. Procedures are stated so vaguely that they cannot be followed or repeated in further study.
2. Important variables are not controlled.
3. The experimenter attempts to support a premise rather than to discover facts.
4. Generalizations are sometimes drawn which are not actually supported by the reported data.
5. Research deals with too small a fragment of a total problem.
6. Differences found between groups taught by different methods may not be tested for significance.

While classroom teachers are in a position to make valuable contributions in methodology, they must guard against poorly conceived studies which result primarily in subjective expressions of opinions. Dolch (10) lists a number of variables which are sometimes not well controlled in classroom studies which involve comparing teaching procedures. These include securing teachers of equal ability who work equally hard, class size, pupil ability, amount of instructional time used, and the misuse of class averages which might cover up data on individual pupils. Once a teacher or a school is ready to do research on a problem, it might be well to run a pilot study. This is likely to identify methodological problems and suggest factors which need to be better controlled. Perhaps at this point the help of a consultant might prove profitable. This is one facet of consultant in-service co-operation which has received little emphasis in the past.

CONCLUSION

A sound and effective reading program depends on many different factors. Chief among these would be *teaching, methodology, materials* and enlightened *administration*. Since these and other factors constantly interact, one might call the results of this interaction the *teaching-learning climate*.

If the climate for learning is less than optimum, one or more of the above factors is likely to be at fault. For example, in recent years teachers and educators have tended to place much faith in the efficacy of materials per se. These were often viewed as panaceas and described as breakthroughs in reading instruction. With the passing of time, it became apparent that instructional programs never rise above the level of instruction found in them. A school system cannot "adopt" a superior reading program — such a program must be built. Improved instructional programs emerge only as a result of significant changes in teacher behavior.

The chief concern in improving teaching should focus on what happens to children as they participate in the program. The chief criterion of excellent reading instruction is evidence that a very large percentage of all children receiving instruction learn to read at a level commensurate with their ability. This implies that every child sees reading as a meaning-making process; and that while learning this process, he comes to enjoy reading. When this occurs, the reader develops a respect for reading as the most highly prized skill he can develop for both school learning and personal development.

YOUR POINT OF VIEW?

What is your opinion relative to the following statements and what is the basis for your position?

1. One example of waste in American education is that little if any provision is made for teachers in a school or school district to meet together as professionals and share ideas and classroom procedures. Thus, the professional growth of all teachers is adversely affected.
2. Teacher-sharing mentioned in point one was referred to by a critic of the idea as a "pooling of ignorance." How would you answer this?
3. In recent years a large array of new materials for the teaching of reading has become available.
   a. The reading teacher has a responsibility to become familiar with new materials and instructional approaches.
   b. The increase in materials for teaching reading has not resulted in any appreciable increase in creative teaching.
   c. The teaching of reading tends to be dominated by materials.
4. Assume a benevolent genie offered to give us a definitive answer to one question relative to reading instruction practice. He stipulates that reading teachers must *agree on the number one priority* of the question to be solved. Hypothesis: "It would be years before we would be able to profit from this offer."
5. "The question we should seek an answer to is ______________________ ____."
6. There should be a number of scholarships available to selected classroom teachers to do needed research in their classrooms. Some of the main objectives of the training would be to help teachers isolate problems, design studies, select statistical treatment of data, and help in reporting their research.
7. Many elementary teachers are relatively unfamiliar with the recent professional literature and research in the field of reading instruction.

BIBLIOGRAPHY

1. Adams, Mary Lourita, "Teachers' Instructional Needs in Teaching Reading," *Reading Teacher*, 17 (January 1964), 260-64.

2. Austin, Mary C., et al., *The Torch Lighters: Tomorrow's, Teachers of Reading*. Cambridge: Harvard University Press, 1961.

3. Belts, Emmett Albert, "Updating Reading Instruction," *Education*, 83 (September 1962), 3-10.

4. Brown, Bob Burton, "Acquisition versus Inquiry," *Elementary School Journal*, 64 (October 1963), 11-17.

5. Calitri, Charles J., "A Structure for Teaching the Language Arts," *Harvard Educational Review*, 35 (Fall 1965), 481-91.

6. Cleary, Florence Damon, *Blueprints for Better Reading*. Bronx, N. Y.: H. W. Wilson Co., 1957.

7. Curtis, Russell W., "Communication: Key to Instructional Improvement," *Education*, LXXX (October 1959), 91-93.

8. Damien, Sister M., "A Classroom "TV" Motivates Reading," *Catholic School Journal*, 65 (November 1965), 50.

9. Dechant, Emerald, "Some Unanswered Questions in the Psychology of Reading," *Eighth Yearbook of the National Reading Conference*. Fort Worth, Texas Christian University Press, 1959, pp. 99-112.

10. Dolch, E. W., "School Research In Reading," *Elementary English*, XXXIII (February 1956), 76-80.

11. Douglas, William O., "Are We Afraid of Ideas?" *Elementary English* XXXXIII (February 1966), 103-08.

12. Eisner, Elliot W., "Instruction, Teaching and Learning an Attempt at Differentiation," *Elementary School Journal*, 65 (December 1964), 115-19.

13. Ellinger, Bernice D., "The Genesis of Creativity," *Reading Teacher*, 19 (April 1966), 493-97.

14. Fattu, Nicholas A., "Research on Teacher Evaluation," *The National Elementary Principal*, XLIII (November 1963), 19-27.

15. Fjeldsted, Lillian W., "Broadening Reading Interest through Creative Expression," *Elementary English*, XXXV (October 1958), 391-94.

16. Gagliardo, Ruth, "Parent and Teacher — Partners in Reading," *Education*, LXXVII (February 1957), 366-69.

17. Gallagher, James J., "Expressive Thought by Gifted Children in the Classroom," *Elementary English*, XXXXII (May 1965), 559-68.

18. Gallen, Albert A., "Co-operative Development of a Summer Workshop in Reading," *Elementary School Journal,* LVII (March 1957), 320-24.

19. Gates, Arthur I., "Improvements in Reading Possible in the Near Future," *Reading Teacher,* XII (December 1958), 83-88.

20. Gjerde, Walemar, and Richard Lattin, "Classroom Use of Educational Recordings," *Education,* LXXVII (January 1957), 270-75.

21. Glock, Marvin D., "Some Psychological Aspects of Teaching Reading," *Education,* LXXVIII (May 1958), 529-33.

22. Guilford, J. P., "Frontiers in Thinking that Teachers Should Know About," *Reading Teacher,* XIII (February 1960), 176-82.

23. Heilman, Arthur W., "Effects of an Intensive In-Service Program on Teacher's Classroom Behavior and Pupils Reading Achievement," USOE Cooperative Research Project No. 2709 (Note: This study summarizd in *Reading Teacher,* 19 May 1966).

24. Jackson, J., "A Reading-Center Approach Within the Classroom," *Journal of Educational Psychology,* XLVII (April 1956), 213-22.

25. Jan-Tausch, James, "The Team Approach to In-Service Education," *Reading Teacher,* 19 (March 1966), 418-23.

26. Karlin, Robert, "Research in Reading," *Elementary English,* XXXVII (March 1960), 177-83.

27. Kasdon, Lawrence M., "In-Service Education in a New Key," *Reading Teacher,* 19 (March 1966), 415-17.

28. Kranyik, Robert D., and Bartlett A. Wagner, "Creativity and the Elementary-School Teacher," *Elementary School Journal,* 66 (October 1965), 2-9.

29. Levin, Harry, "Reading Research: What, Why, and for Whom?" *Elementary English,* XXXXIII (February 1966), 138-47.

30. McCullough, C. M., "What Does Research Reveal About Practices in Teaching Reading?" *English Journal* XLVI (November 1957), 475-90.

31. McFadden, Dorothy L., "How to Run a Book Fair," *Elementary English,* XXXV (March 1958), 168-75.

32. National Society for the Study of Education, *In-Service Education* Fifty-Seventh Yearbook Part I. Chicago: University of Chicago Press, 1947.

33. Niles, Olive S., "Systemwide In-Service Programs in Reading," *Reading Teacher,* 19 (March 1966), 424-28.

34. O'Leary, Helen F., "Vocabulary Presentation and Enrichment," *Elementary English,* XXXXI (October 1964), 613-15.

35. Papillon, Alfred L., "Trimming Curricular Deadwood from the Elementary School," *Catholic Educational Review,* LVIII (January 1960), 12-15.

36. Petersen, Dorothy G., "The Teacher's Professional Reading," *Elementary School Journal,* 63 (October 1962), 1-5.

37. Powell, William R., "Classroom Libraries: Their Frequency of Use," *Elementary English,* XLIII (April 1966), 395-97.

38. Sister Josephina, "The Role of Supervision in Improving Reading," *Elementary School Journal,* 65 (April 1965), 375-81.

39. Strickland, Ruth G., "Creating a Challenging Classroom Environment," *Reading Teacher,* 15 (December 1961), 193-97.

40. Taba, Hilda, "Learning By Discovery: Psychological and Educational Rationale," "*Elementary School Journal,* 63 (March 1963), 308-16.

41. Zaeske, Arnold, "Teacher Education in Reading," *Education,* LXXVIII (February 1958), 360-62.

42. Zirbes, Laura, *Spurs To Creative Teaching.* New York: G. P. Putnam's Sons, 1960.

Index